Pearson New International Edition

Performance Management

Herman Aguinis
Third Edition

Pearson Education Limited
Edinburgh Gate
Harlow
Essex CM20 2JE
England and Associated Companies throughout the world

Visit us on the World Wide Web at: www.pearsoned.co.uk

© Pearson Education Limited 2014

PEARSON

ISBN 10: 1-292-02407-0
ISBN 13: 978-1-292-02407-3

British Library Cataloguing-in-Publication Data
A catalogue record for this book is available from the British Library

Printed in the United States of America

Table of Contents

Performance Management and Reward Systems in Context

*A manager is responsible for the application
and performance of knowledge.*

—PETER F. DRUCKER

LEARNING OBJECTIVES

By the end of this chapter, you will be able to do the following:

- Explain the concept of performance management (PM).
- Distinguish performance management from performance appraisal.
- Explain the many advantages and make a business case for implementing a well-designed performance management system.
- Recognize the multiple negative consequences that can arise from the poor design and implementation of a performance management system. These negative consequences affect all the parties involved: employees, supervisors, and the organization as a whole.
- Understand the concept of a reward system and its relationship to a performance management system.
- Distinguish among the various types of employee rewards, including compensation, benefits, and relational returns.
- Describe the multiple purposes of a performance management system including strategic, administrative, informational, developmental, organizational maintenance, and documentational purposes.
- Describe and explain the key features of an ideal performance management system.

- Create a presentation providing persuasive arguments in support of the reasons that an organization should implement a performance management system, including the purposes that performance management systems serve and the dangers of a poorly implemented system.
- Note the relationships and links between a performance management system and other human resources functions, including recruitment and selection, training and development, workforce planning, and compensation.
- Describe and explain contextual and cultural factors that affect the implementation of performance management systems around the world.

1 DEFINITION OF PERFORMANCE MANAGEMENT

Consider the following scenario:

> Sally is a sales manager at a large pharmaceutical company. The fiscal year will end in one week. She is overwhelmed with end-of-the-year tasks, including reviewing the budget she is likely to be allocated for the following year, responding to customers' phone calls, and supervising a group of 10 salespeople. It's a very hectic time, probably the most hectic time of the year. She receives a phone call from the human resources (HR) department: "Sally, we have not received your performance reviews for your 10 employees; they are due by the end of the fiscal year." Sally thinks, "Oh, those perform- ance reviews. . . .What a waste of my time!" From Sally's point of view, there is no value in filling out those seemingly meaningless forms. She does not see her subordinates in action because they are in the field visiting customers most of the time. All that she knows about their performance is based on sales figures, which depend more on the products offered and geographic territory covered than the individual effort and motivation of each sales- person. And, nothing happens in terms of rewards, regardless of her ratings. These are lean times in her organization, and salary adjustments are based on seniority rather than on merit. She has less than three days to turn in her forms. What will she do? She decides to follow the path of least resistance: to please her employees and give everyone the maximum possible rating. In this way, Sally believes the employees will be happy with their ratings and she will not have to deal with complaints or follow-up meetings. Sally fills out the forms in less than 20 minutes and gets back to her "real job."

There is something very wrong with this picture, which unfortunately happens all too frequently in many organizations. Although Sally's HR department calls this process "performance management," it is not.

Performance management is a *continuous process of identifying, measuring, and devel- oping the performance of individuals and teams and aligning performance with the strategic goals of the organization.* Let's consider each of the definition's two main components:

1. **Continuous process.** Performance management is ongoing. It involves a neverending process of setting goals and objectives, observing performance, and giving and receiving ongoing coaching and feedback.[1]

2. *Alignment with strategic goals.* Performance management requires that managers ensure that employees' activities and outputs are congruent with the organization's goals and, consequently, help the organization gain a competitive advantage. Performance management therefore creates a direct link between employee performance and organizational goals and makes the employees' contribution to the organization explicit.

Note that many organizations have what is labeled a "performance management" system. However, we must distinguish between performance management and performance appraisal. A system that involves employee evaluations once a year without an ongoing effort to provide feedback and coaching so that performance can be improved is not a true performance management system. Instead, this is only a performance appraisal system. Performance appraisal is the systematic description of an employee's strengths and weaknesses. Thus, performance appraisal is an important component of performance management, but it is just a part of a bigger whole because performance management is much more than just performance measurement.[2]

As an illustration, consider how Merrill Lynch has transitioned from a performance appraisal system to a performance management system. Merrill Lynch is one of the world's leading financial management and advisory companies, with offices in 37 countries and private client assets of approximately US$ 1.6 trillion (http://ml.com/). As an investment bank, it is a leading global underwriter of debt and equity securities and strategic adviser to corporations, governments, institutions, and individuals worldwide. Recently, Merrill Lynch started the transition from giving employees one performance appraisal per year to focusing on one of the important principles of performance management: the conversation between managers and employees in which feedback is exchanged and coaching is given if needed. In January, employees and managers set employee objectives. Mid-year reviews assess what progress has been made toward the goals and how personal development plans are faring. Finally, the end-of-the-year review incorporates feedback from several sources, evaluates progress toward objectives, and identifies areas that need improvement. Managers also get extensive training on how to set objectives and conduct reviews. In addition, there is a Web site that managers can access with information on all aspects of the performance management system. In sharp contrast to its old performance appraisal system, Merrill Lynch's goal for its newly implemented performance management program is worded as follows: "This is what is expected of you, this is how we're going to help you in your development, and this is how you'll be judged relative to compensation."[3]

As a second example, consider the performance management system for managers at Germany-based Siemens, which provides mobile phones, computer networks, and wireless technology and employs 475,000 people in 190 countries (www.siemens.com). At Siemens, the performance management system is based on three pillars: setting clear and measurable goals, implementing concrete actions, and imposing rigorous consequences. The performance management at Siemens has helped change people's mind-set, and the organization is now truly performance oriented. Every manager understands that performance is a critical aspect of working at Siemens, and this guiding philosophy is communicated in many ways throughout the organization.[4]

Performance management systems that do not make explicit the employee contribution to the organizational goals are not true performance management systems. Making an explicit link between an employee's performance objectives and the organizational goals also serves the purpose of establishing a shared understanding about what is to be achieved and how it is to be achieved. This is painfully clear in Sally's case described earlier: from her point of view, the performance review forms did not provide any useful information regarding the contribution of each of her subordinates to the organization. Sally's case is unfortunately more common than we would like. A survey conducted by the consulting firm Watson Wyatt showed that only 3 in 10 employees believe their companies' performance review systems actually helped them improve their performance.[5]

Well-designed and implemented performance management systems make substantial contributions to the organization. This is why a recent survey of almost 1,000 HR management professionals in Australia revealed that 96% of Australian companies currently implement some type of performance management system.[6] Similarly, results of a survey of 278 organizations, about two-thirds of which are multinational corporations, from 15 different countries, indicated that about 91% of organizations implement a formal performance management system.[7] Moreover, organizations with formal and systematic performance management systems are 51% more likely to perform better than the other organizations in the sample regarding financial outcomes, and 41% more likely to perform better than the other organizations in the sample regarding other outcomes including customer satisfaction, employee retention, and other important metrics. Based on these results, it is not surprising that senior executives of companies listed in the *Sunday Times* list of best employers in the United Kingdom believe that performance management is one of the top two most important HR management priorities in their organizations.[8] Let's describe these performance management contributions in detail.

2 THE PERFORMANCE MANAGEMENT CONTRIBUTION

There are many advantages associated with the implementation of a performance management system.[9] A performance management system can make the following important contributions:[10]

1. *Motivation to perform is increased.* Receiving feedback about one's performance increases the motivation for future performance. Knowledge about how one is doing and recognition about one's past successes provide the fuel for future accomplishments.

2. *Self-esteem is increased.* Receiving feedback about one's performance fulfills a basic human need to be recognized and valued at work. This, in turn, is likely to increase employees' self-esteem.

3. *Managers gain insight about subordinates.* Direct supervisors and other managers in charge of the appraisal gain new insights into the person being appraised. The importance of knowing your employees is highlighted by the fact that the Management Standards Centre, the government-recognized organization in the United Kingdom for setting standards for the management and leadership areas, has recognized that developing productive relationships with colleagues is a key competency for managers (http://www.management-standards.org, Unit D2). Gaining new insights into a person's performance and personality will help

4

the manager build a better relationship with that person. Also, supervisors gain a better understanding of each individual's contribution to the organization. This can be useful for direct supervisors as well as for supervisors once removed.

4. *The definitions of job and criteria are clarified.* The job of the person being appraised may be clarified and defined more clearly. In other words, employees gain a better understanding of the behaviors and results required of their specific position. Employees also gain a better understanding of what it takes to be a successful performer (i.e., what are the specific criteria that define job success).

5. *Self-insight and development are enhanced.* The participants in the system are likely to develop a better understanding of themselves and of the kind of development activities that are of value to them as they progress through the organization. Participants in the system also gain a better understanding of their particular strengths and weaknesses that can help them better define future career paths.

6. *Administrative actions are more fair and appropriate.* Performance management systems provide valid information about performance that can be used for administrative actions such as merit increases, promotions, and transfers as well as terminations. In general, a performance management system helps ensure that rewards are distributed on a fair and credible basis. In turn, such decisions based on a sound performance management system lead to improved interpersonal relationships and enhanced supervisor–subordinate trust.[11] For example, a good performance management system can help mitigate explicit or implicit emphasis on age as a basis for decisions. This is particularly important given the aging working population in the United States, Europe, and many other countries around the world.[12]

7. *Organizational goals are made clear.* The goals of the unit and the organization are made clear, and the employee understands the link between what she does and organizational success. This is a contribution to the communication of what the unit and the organization are all about and how organizational goals cascade down to the unit and the individual employee. Performance management systems can help improve employee acceptance of these wider goals (i.e., organizational and unit levels).

8. *Employees become more competent.* An obvious contribution is that employee performance is improved. In addition, there is a solid foundation for helping employees become more successful by establishing developmental plans.

9. *Employee misconduct is minimized.*[13] Employee misconduct is an increasingly pervasive phenomenon that has received widespread media coverage. Such misconduct includes accounting irregularities, churning customer accounts, abusing overtime policies, giving inappropriate gifts to clients and potential clients hoping to secure their business, and using company resources for personal use. Although some individuals are more likely to engage in misconduct compared to others based on individual differences in personality and other attributes, having a good performance management in place provides the appropriate context so that misconduct is clearly defined and labeled as such and identified early on before it leads to sometimes irreversible negative consequences.

10. *There is better protection from lawsuits.* Data collected through performance management systems can help document compliance with regulations (e.g., equal treatment of all employees regardless of sex or ethnic background). When performance management systems are not in place, arbitrary performance

evaluations are more likely, resulting in an increased exposure to litigation for the organization.

11. ***There is better and more timely differentiation between good and poor performers.*** Performance management systems allow for a quicker identification of good and poor performers. Also, they force supervisors to face up to and address performance problems on a timely basis (i.e., before the problem becomes so entrenched that it cannot be easily remedied).

12. ***Supervisors' views of performance are communicated more clearly.*** Performance management systems allow managers to communicate to their subordinates their judgments regarding performance. Thus, there is greater accountability in how managers discuss performance expectations and provide feedback. Both assessing and monitoring the performance of others are listed as key competencies for managers by the Management Standards Centre (www.management-standards.org, Units B3, B4, and B7). When managers possess these competencies, subordinates receive useful information about how their performance is seen by their supervisor.

13. ***Organizational change is facilitated.*** Performance management systems can be a useful tool to drive organizational change. For example, assume an organization decides to change its culture to give top priority to product quality and customer service. Once this new organizational direction is established, performance management is used to align the organizational culture with the goals and objectives of the organization to make change possible. Employees are provided training in the necessary skills and are rewarded for improved performance so that they have both the knowledge and motivation to improve product quality and customer service. This is precisely what IBM did in the 1980s when it wanted to switch focus to customer satisfaction: the performance evaluation of every member in the organization was based, to some extent, on customer satisfaction ratings regardless of function (i.e., accounting, programming, manufacturing, etc.).[14] For IBM as well as numerous other organizations, performance management provides tools and motivation for individuals to change, which, in turn, helps drive organizational change. In short, performance management systems are likely to produce changes in the culture of the organization and, therefore, the consequences of such cultural changes should be considered carefully before implementing the system.[15] As noted by Randy Pennington, president of Pennington Performance Group, "The truth is that the culture change is driven by a change in performance. An organization's culture cannot be installed. It can be guided and influenced by policies, practices, skills, and procedures that are implemented and reinforced. The only way to change the culture is to change the way individuals perform on a daily basis."[16]

14. ***Motivation, commitment, and intentions to stay in the organization are enhanced.*** When employees are satisfied with their organization's performance management system, they are more likely to be motivated to perform well, to be committed to their organization, and not try to leave the organization.[17] For example, satisfaction with the performance management system is likely to make employees feel that the organization has a great deal of personal meaning for them. In terms of turnover intentions, satisfaction with the performance management system leads employees to report that they will probably not look for a new job in the next year and that they don't often think about quitting

their present job. As an illustration of this point, results of a study including 93 professors at a university in South Africa suggested that the implementation of a good performance management system would be useful in preventing them from leaving their university jobs.[18]

15. *Voice behavior is encouraged.* A well-implemented performance management system allows employees to engage in voice behavior that can lead to improved organizational processes. Voice behavior involves making suggestions for changes and improvements that are innovative, challenge the status quo, are intended to be constructive, and are offered even when others disagree.[19] For example, the performance review meeting can lead to a conversation during which the employee provides suggestions on how to reduce cost or speed up specific process.

16. *Employee engagement is enhanced.* A good performance management system leads to enhanced employee engagement. Employees who are engaged feel involved, committed, passionate, and empowered. Moreover, these attitudes and feelings result in behaviors that are innovative and, overall, demonstrate good organizational citizenship and take action in support of the organization. Employee engagement is an important predictor of organizational performance and success and, consequently, engagement is an important contribution of good performance management systems.[20]

Table 1 lists the 16 contributions made by performance management systems. Recall Sally's situation earlier in the chapter. Which of the contributions included in Table 1 result from the system implemented at Sally's organization? For example, are Sally's employees more motivated to perform as a consequence of implementing their "performance management" system? Is their self-esteem increased? What about Sally's

TABLE 1 Contributions of Performance Management Systems
Motivation to perform is increased.
Self-esteem is increased.
Managers gain insight about subordinates.
The definitions of job and criteria are clarified.
Self-insight and development are enhanced.
Administrative actions are more fair and appropriate.
Organizational goals are made clear.
Employees become more competent.
Employee misconduct is minimized.
There is better protection from lawsuits.
There is better and more timely differentiation between good and poor performers.
Supervisors' views of performance are communicated more clearly.
Organizational change is facilitated.
Motivation, commitment, and intentions to stay in the organization are enhanced.
Voice behavior is encouraged.
Employee engagement is enhanced.

BOX 1

What CEOs Say About the Contribution of Performance Management Systems

A study conducted by Development Dimensions International (DDI), a global human resources consulting firm specializing in leadership and selection, found that performance management systems are a key tool that organizations use to translate business strategy into business results. Specifically, performance management systems influence "financial performance, productivity, product or service quality, customer satisfaction, and employee job satisfaction." In addition, 79% of the CEOs surveyed say that the performance management system implemented in their organizations drives the "cultural strategies that maximize human assets."[21]

---

insight and understanding of her employees' contributions to the organization? Is Sally's organization now better protected in the face of potential litigation? Unfortunately, the system implemented at Sally's organization is not a true performance management system but simply an administrative nuisance. Consequently, many, if not most, of the potential contributions of the performance management system are not realized. In fact, poorly implemented systems, as in the case of Sally's organization, not only do not make positive contributions but also can be very dangerous and lead to several negative outcomes.

3 DISADVANTAGES/DANGERS OF POORLY IMPLEMENTED PM SYSTEMS

What happens when performance management systems do not work as intended, as in the case of Sally's organization? What are some of the negative consequences associated with low-quality and poorly implemented systems? Consider the following list:

1. *Increased turnover.* If the process is not seen as fair, employees may become upset and leave the organization. They can leave physically (i.e., quit) or withdraw psychologically (i.e., minimize their effort until they are able to find a job elsewhere).
2. *Use of misleading information.* If a standardized system is not in place, there are multiple opportunities for fabricating information about an employee's performance.
3. *Lowered self-esteem.* Self-esteem may be lowered if feedback is provided in an inappropriate and inaccurate way. This, in turn, can create employee resentment.
4. *Wasted time and money.* Performance management systems cost money and quite a bit of time. These resources are wasted when systems are poorly designed and implemented.
5. *Damaged relationships.* As a consequence of a deficient system, the relationship among the individuals involved may be damaged, often permanently.
6. *Decreased motivation to perform.* Motivation may be lowered for many reasons, including the feeling that superior performance is not translated into meaningful tangible (e.g., pay increase) or intangible (e.g., personal recognition) rewards.

7. ***Employee burnout and job dissatisfaction.*** When the performance assessment instrument is not seen as valid and the system is not perceived as fair, employees are likely to feel increased levels of job burnout and job dissatisfaction. As a consequence, employees are likely to become increasingly irritated.[22]

8. ***Increased risk of litigation.*** Expensive lawsuits may be filed by individuals who feel they have been appraised unfairly.

9. ***Unjustified demands on managers' and employees' resources.*** Poorly implemented systems do not provide the benefits provided by well-implemented systems, yet they take up managers' and employees' time. Such systems will be resisted because of competing obligations and allocation of resources (e.g., time). What is sometimes worse, managers may simply choose to avoid the system altogether, and employees may feel increased levels of overload.[23]

10. ***Varying and unfair standards and ratings.*** Both standards and individual ratings may vary across and within units and be unfair.

11. ***Emerging biases.*** Personal values, biases, and relationships are likely to replace organizational standards.

12. ***Unclear ratings system.*** Because of poor communication, employees may not know how their ratings are generated and how the ratings are translated into rewards.

Table 2 summarizes the list of disadvantages and negative consequences resulting from the careless design and implementation of a performance management system. Once again, consider Sally's organization. What are some of the consequences of the system implemented by her company? Let's consider each of the consequences listed in Table 2. For example, is it likely that the performance information used is false and misleading? How about the risk of litigation? How about the time and money invested in collecting, compiling, and reporting the data? Unfortunately, an analysis of Sally's situation, taken with the positive and negative consequences listed in Tables 1 and 2, leads to the conclusion that this particular system is more likely to do harm than good. Now think about

TABLE 2	Disadvantages/Dangers of Poorly Implemented Performance Management Systems
Increased turnover	
Use of false or misleading information	
Lowered self-esteem	
Wasted time and money	
Damaged relationships	
Decreased motivation to perform	
Employee job burnout and job dissatisfaction	
Increased risk of litigation	
Unjustified demands on managers' and employees' resources	
Varying and unfair standards and ratings	
Emerging biases	
Unclear ratings system	

BOX 2

What Happens When Performance Management Is Implemented Poorly?

One example of a poorly implemented performance management system resulted in a $1.2 million lawsuit. A female employee was promoted several times and succeeded in the construction industry until she started working under the supervision of a new manager. She stated in her lawsuit that once she was promoted and reported to the new manager, the boss ignored her and did not give her the same support or opportunities for training that her male colleagues received. After eight months of receiving no feedback from her manager, she was called into his office, where the manager told her that she was failing, resulting in a demotion and a $20,000 reduction in her annual salary. When she won her sex-discrimination lawsuit, a jury awarded her $1.2 million in emotional distress and economic damages.[24]

---

the system implemented at your current organization or at the organization you have worked for most recently. Take a look at Tables 1 and 2. Where does the system fit best? Is the system more closely aligned with some of the positive consequences listed in Table 1 or more closely aligned with some of the negative consequences listed in Table 2?

One of the purposes of a performance management system is to make decisions about employees' compensation (e.g., pay raises). For many employees, this is perhaps one of the most meaningful consequences of a performance management system. We will now discuss some basic features of reward systems and the extent to which the allocation of various types of rewards is dependent on the performance management system.

4 DEFINITION OF REWARD SYSTEMS

An employee's compensation, usually referred to as *tangible returns*, includes cash compensation (i.e., base pay, cost-of-living and merit pay, short-term incentives, and long-term incentives) and benefits (i.e., income protection, work/life focus, tuition reimbursement, and allowances). However, employees also receive intangible returns, also referred to as *relational returns*, which include recognition and status, employment security, challenging work, and learning opportunities. A reward system is the set of mechanisms for distributing both tangible and intangible returns as part of an employment relationship.

It should be noted that not all types of returns are directly related to performance management systems. This is the case because not all types of returns are allocated based on performance. For example, some allocations are based on seniority as opposed to performance. The various types of returns are defined next.[25]

4.1 Base Pay

Base pay is given to employees in exchange for work performed. The base pay, which usually includes a range of values, focuses on the position and duties performed rather than an individual's contribution. Thus, the base pay is usually the same for all employees performing similar duties and ignores differences across employees. However, differences within the base pay range may exist based on such variables as experience and differential performance. In some countries (e.g., United States), there is a difference between wage and salary. Salary is base cash compensation received by employees who are exempt from regulations of the Fair Labor Standards Act and, in most cases, cannot receive overtime pay. Employees in most professional and managerial jobs (also called salaried employees) are exempt employees. On the other hand, nonexempt employees receive their pay calculated on an hourly wage.

4.2 Cost-of-Living Adjustments and Contingent Pay

Cost-of-living adjustments (COLA) imply the same percentage increase for all employees regardless of their individual performance. Cost-of-living adjustments are given to combat the effects of inflation in an attempt to preserve the employees' buying power. For example, in 2003 in the United States, organizations that implemented a COLA used a 2.1% pay increase. In 2001, this same percentage was only 1.4%. Year-by-year COLA percentages can be obtained from such agencies as the Social Security Administration in the United States (http://www.ssa.gov/OACT/COLA/colaseries.html).

Contingent pay, sometimes referred to as *merit pay*, is given as an addition to the base pay based on past performance. In a nutshell, contingent pay means that the amount of additional compensation depends on an employee's level of performance. So, for example, the top 20% of employees in the performance score distribution may receive a 10% annual increase, whereas employees in the middle 70% of the distribution may receive a 4% increase, and employees in the bottom 10% may receive no increase at all.

4.3 Short-Term Incentives

Similar to contingent pay, short-term incentives are allocated based on past performance. However, incentives are not added to the base pay and are only temporary pay adjustments based on the review period (e.g., quarterly or annual). Incentives are one-time payments and are sometimes referred to as *variable pay*.

A second difference between incentives and contingent pay is that incentives are known in advance. For example, a salesperson in a pharmaceutical company knows that if she meets her sales quota, she will receive a $3,000 bonus at the end of the quarter. She also knows that if she exceeds her sales quota by 10%, her bonus will be $6,000. By contrast, in the case of contingent pay, in most cases, the specific value of the reward is not known in advance.

4.4 Long-Term Incentives

Whereas short-term incentives usually involve an attempt to motivate performance in the short term (i.e., quarter, year) and involve cash bonuses or specific prizes (e.g., two extra days off), long-term incentives attempt to influence future performance over a longer period of time. Typically, they involve stock ownership or options to buy stocks at a preestablished and profitable price. The rationale for long-term incentives is that employees will be personally invested in the organization's success, and this investment is expected to translate into a sustained high level of performance.

Both short-term and long-term incentives are quite popular. Take, for example, the public sector in the United States. A survey administered in late 1998 to 25 state and 400

> ### BOX 3
>
> ### Short-Term Incentives for Physicians
>
> Short-term incentives are being used in a test pilot program in Colorado Springs, Colorado. Eight health-care providers and three insurance companies have teamed up with the nonprofit Colorado Business Group on Health to pay physicians up to $100 in cash per patient for providing diabetes care that results in positive outcomes for patients. Doctors in the program receive the additional pay as an incentive without an increase to base salary. The program requires doctors to work closely with patients and focus on preventative medicine, including education, goal-setting, and follow-up meetings. Physical indicators, such as blood pressure, blood sugar, and cholesterol, are measured against goals to determine whether successful outcomes are being achieved. The goals of the program are to provide better disease control for the patient and to cut down on expensive future treatments, such as emergency room visits and inpatient stays in the hospital. Additional savings are expected through reduced medical claims and health insurance premiums paid by employers. In summary, the health providers and insurers are utilizing short-term incentives as part of the performance management systems with the goal of motivating physicians to focus on treatments that will enhance the overall health and well-being of the patient in an ongoing manner.[27]

local governments employing more than six people showed that all but one of the state governments and 242 (i.e., 85%) of the local governments used some type of incentive.[26]

Some organizations are taking this idea to what may be called "big pay for big performance." Consider the case of a Denver, Colorado, energy company, Delta Petroleum, which gave four top executives 1.5 million shares the day the stock closed at $21.76, for a total value of $32.6 million.[28] However, there is a catch: Delta stock will have to reach $40 per share for the executives to be able to sell theirs. If this value is not reached, the executives' shares cannot be cashed in. Moreover, the executives will be able to sell only one-sixth of their shares when the price reaches $40. They will be able to sell another one-sixth if and when the stock price reaches $50, and another sixth if and when it reaches $60. And there is yet another restriction: time. The first batch of stock that vests at $40 must reach that value within 13 months of the time the executives received the options. If the value of $40 is not reached within this time frame, the second and third batches of stock cannot be cashed in and they simply disappear.

4.5 Income Protection

Income protection programs serve as a backup to employees' salaries in the event that an employee is sick, disabled, or no longer able to work. Some countries mandate income protection programs by law. For example, Canadian organizations pay into a fund that provides income protection in the case of a disability. Take, for instance, the University of Alberta, which offers a monthly income of 70% of salary to employees who become severely disabled. In the United States, employers pay 50% of an employee's total contribution to Social Security so that income is protected for family members in case of an employee's death or a disability that prevents the employee from doing substantial work for one year and for an employee when he or she reaches retirement age. For example, a 40-year-old employee earning an annual salary of

$90,000 and expected to continue to earn that salary until retirement age would receive about $1,400 a month if he retired at age 62, about $2,000 a month if he retired at age 67, and about $2,500 if he retired at age 70.

Other types of benefits under the income protection rubric include medical insurance, pension plans, and savings plans. These are optional benefits provided by organizations, but they are becoming increasingly important and often guide an applicant's decision to accept a job offer. In fact, a recent survey including both employees in general and HR professionals in particular showed that health care/medical insurance is the most important benefit, followed by paid time off and retirement benefits.[29]

4.6 Work/Life Focus

Benefits related to work/life focus include programs that help employees achieve a better balance between work and nonwork activities. These include time away from work (e.g., vacation time), services to meet specific needs (e.g., counseling, financial planning, on-site fitness program), and flexible work schedules (e.g., telecommuting, nonpaid time off). For example, Sun Microsystems actively promotes an equal balance between work and home life and closes its Broomfield, Colorado, campus from late December through early January every year. This benefit (i.e., vacation time for all employees in addition to individual yearly vacation time) is part of Sun's culture. Sun believes in a work hard–play hard attitude, as is evidenced by CEO Scott McNealy's motto: "Kick butt and have fun."[30]

4.7 Allowances

Benefits in some countries and organizations include allowances covering housing and transportation. These kinds of allowances are typical for expatriate personnel and are popular for high-level managers throughout the world. In South Africa, for example, it is common for a transportation allowance to include one of the following choices:[31]

- The employer provides a car and the employee has the right to use it both privately and for business.
- The employer provides a car allowance, more correctly referred to as a *travel allowance*, which means reimbursing the employee for the business use of the employee's personal car.

Other allowances can include smart phones and their monthly charges, club and gym fees, discount loans, and mortgage subsidies.[32] Although these allowances are clearly a benefit for employees, some of them directly or indirectly also produce a benefit for the employer. For example, smart phones means that employees are reachable via phone, text, and e-mail 24/7. Similarly, if employees take advantage of a gym fee allowance, they are likely to stay healthier which in turn may lead to less health-related expenses for the organization.

4.8 Relational Returns

Relational returns are intangible in nature. They include recognition and status, employment security, challenging work, opportunities to learn, and opportunities to form personal relationships at work (including friendships and romances).[33] For example, Sun Microsystems allows employees to enroll in SunU, which is Sun's own online education tool. SunU encapsulates a mix of traditional

TABLE 3	Returns and Their Degree of Dependency on the Performance Management System

Return	Degree of Dependency
Cost-of-living adjustment	Low
Income protection	Low
Work/life focus	Moderate
Allowances	Moderate
Relational returns	Moderate
Base pay	Moderate
Contingent pay	High
Short-term incentives	High
Long-term incentives	High

classroom courses with online classes that can be accessed anywhere in the world at any time.[34] Sun offers its employees enormous scope for development and career progression, and there is a commitment to ensuring that all employees are given the opportunity to develop professionally. The new knowledge and skills acquired by employees can help them not only to further their careers within Sun but also to take this knowledge with them if they seek employment elsewhere. Thus, some types of relational returns can be long-lasting.

Table 3 includes a list of the various returns, together with their degree of dependency on the performance management system. As an example of the low end of the dependency continuum, cost-of-living adjustment has a low degree of dependency on the performance management system, meaning that the system has no impact on this type of return. In other words, all employees receive this type of return regardless of past performance. On the other end, short-term incentives have a high degree of dependency, meaning that the performance management system dictates who receives these incentives and who does not. Long-term incentives (e.g., profit sharing and stock options) also have a high degree of dependency; although this type of incentive is not specifically tied to individual performance, it does depend on performance measured at the team, unit, or even organizational levels. Between the high and low end, we find some returns with a moderate degree of dependency on the performance management system such as base pay, a type of return that may or may not be influenced by the system.

Think about the performance management system of your current employer, the system used by your most recent employer, or the system in place at an organization where someone you know is employed at present. Based on Table 3, try to think about the various types of tangible and intangible returns allocated in this organization. To what extent is each of these returns dependent on the organization's performance management system?

5 AIMS AND ROLE OF PM SYSTEMS

The information collected by a performance management system is most frequently used for salary administration, performance feedback, and the identification of employee strengths and weaknesses. In general, however, performance management systems can serve the following six purposes: strategic, administrative, informational, developmental, organizational maintenance, and documentational purposes.[35] Let's consider each of these purposes in turn.

5.1 Strategic Purpose

The first purpose of performance management systems is to help top management achieve strategic business objectives. By linking the organization's goals with individual goals, the performance management system reinforces behaviors consistent with the attainment of organizational goals. Moreover, even if for some reason individual goals are not achieved, linking individual goals with organizational goals serves as a way to communicate what are the most crucial business strategic initiatives.

A second strategic purpose of performance management systems is that they play an important role in the *onboarding* process.[36] Onboarding refers to the processes that lead new employees to transition from being organizational outsiders to organizational insiders. Performance management serves as a catalyst for onboarding because it allows new

---

BOX 4

How Sears Uses Performance Management to Focus on Strategic Business Priorities

New leadership at Sears is utilizing performance management practices and principles to align human resources with business strategy. Headquartered in Hoffman Estates, Illinois, Sears Holdings Corporation is the third largest broad-line retailer in the United States, with approximately $55 billion in annual revenues and with approximately 3,900 retail stores in the United States and Canada. Sears Holdings is the leading home appliance retailer as well as a leader in tools, lawn and garden products, home electronics, and automotive repair and maintenance. The company is the nation's largest provider of home services, with more than 13 million service calls made annually. Following the merger with Kmart Corp. and Sears, Roebuck & Co., Aylwin B. Lewis was promoted to chief executive and tasked with a strategic culture change initiative in hopes of reinvigorating the struggling retail company. A strategic objective is to move from an inward focus to a customer service approach. A second key objective is to bring about an entrepreneurial spirit where store managers strive for financial literacy and are challenged to identify opportunities for greater profits. Several aspects of the performance management system are being utilized to achieve these strategic objectives. For example, employee duties and objectives are being revised so that employees will spend less time in back rooms and more time interacting with customers to facilitate purchases and understand customer needs. In addition, leadership communication with employees and face-to-face interaction are being encouraged. Lewis spends three days per week in stores with employees and frequently quizzes managers on their knowledge, such as asking about profit margins for a given department. The greatest compliment employees receive is to be referred to as "commercial" or someone who can identify opportunities for profits. All Sears headquarters employees are also required to spend a day working in a store, which many had never done before. Executive management has identified 500 employees who are considered potential leaders and given training and development opportunities specifically aimed at cultural and strategic changes. In sum, the performance management system at Sears is used as a strategic tool to change Sears' culture because senior management views encouraging key desired behaviors as critical to the company's success in the marketplace.[37]

employees to understand the types of behaviors and results that are valued and rewarded, which, in turn, lead to an understanding of the organization's culture and its values.

5.2 Administrative Purpose

A second function of performance management systems is to furnish valid and useful information for making administrative decisions about employees. Such administrative decisions include salary adjustments, promotions, employee retention or termination, recognition of superior individual performance, identification of poor performers, layoffs, and merit increases. Therefore, the implementation of reward systems based on information provided by the performance management system falls within the administrative purpose. For example, the government in Turkey mandates performance management systems in all public organizations in that country with the aim to prevent favoritism, corruption, and bribery and to emphasize the importance of impartiality and merit in administrative decisions.[38]

5.3 Informational Purpose

Performance management systems serve as an important communication device. First, they inform employees about how they are doing and provide them with information on specific areas that may need improvement. Second, related to the strategic purpose, they provide information regarding the organization's and the supervisor's expectations and what aspects of work the supervisor believes are most important.

5.4 Developmental Purpose

As noted earlier, feedback is an important component of a well-implemented performance management system. This feedback can be used in a developmental manner. Managers can use feedback to coach employees and improve performance on an ongoing basis. This feedback allows for the identification of strengths and weaknesses as well as the causes for performance deficiencies (which could be due to individual, group, or contextual factors). Of course, feedback is useful only to the extent that remedial action is taken and concrete steps are implemented to remedy any deficiencies. Feedback is useful only when employees are willing to receive it. Organizations should strive to create a "feedback culture" that reflects support for feedback, including feedback that is nonthreatening and is focused on behaviors and coaching to help interpret the feedback provided.[39]

Another aspect of the developmental purpose is that employees receive information about themselves that can help them individualize their career paths. Thus, the developmental purpose refers to both short-term and long-term aspects of development.

5.5 Organizational Maintenance Purpose

A fifth purpose of performance management systems is to provide information to be used in workforce planning. Workforce planning comprises a set of systems that allows organizations to anticipate and respond to needs emerging within and outside the organization, to determine priorities, and to allocate human resources where they can do the most good.[40] An important component of any workforce planning effort is the talent inventory, which is information on current resources (e.g., skills, abilities, promotional potential, and assignment histories of current employees). Performance management systems are the primary means through which accurate talent inventories can be assembled.

Other organizational maintenance purposes served by performance management systems include assessing future training needs, evaluating performance achievements at the organizational level, and evaluating the effectiveness of HR interventions (e.g., whether employees perform at higher levels after participating in a training program). These activities cannot be conducted effectively in the absence of a good performance management system.

5.6 Documentational Purpose

Finally, performance management systems allow organizations to collect useful information that can be used for several documentation purposes. First, performance data can be used to validate newly proposed selection instruments. For example, a newly developed test of computer literacy can be administered to all administrative personnel. Scores on the test can then be paired with scores collected through the performance management system. If scores on the test and on the performance measure are correlated, then the test can be used with future applicants for the administrative positions. Second, performance management systems allow for the documentation of important administrative decisions. This information can be especially useful in the case of litigation.

Several companies implement performance management systems that allow them to accomplish the multiple objectives described earlier. For an example of one such company, consider the case of SELCO Credit Union (http://selco.org/selco/about.asp) in Eugene, Oregon, a not-for-profit consumer cooperative that was established in 1936.[41] SELCO's eight branches serve nearly 80,000 members. SELCO offers many of the same services offered by other banks, including personal checking and savings accounts, loans, and credit cards. Being members of the credit union, however, allows individual members a say in how the credit union is run, something a traditional bank does not permit. Recently, SELCO scrapped an old performance appraisal system and replaced it with a new multipurpose and more effective performance management system. First, the timing of the new system is now aligned with the business cycle instead of the employee's date of hire to ensure that business needs are aligned with individual goals. This alignment serves both strategic and informational purposes. Second, managers are given a pool of money that they can work with to award bonuses and raises as needed, which is more effective than the complex set of matrices that had been in place to calculate bonuses. This improved the way in which the system is used for allocating rewards and therefore serves an administrative purpose. Third, managers are required to sit down and have regular conversations with their employees about their performance and make note of any problems that arise. This gives the employees a clear sense of areas in which they need improvement and provides documentation if disciplinary action is needed. This component serves both informational and documentational purposes. Finally, the time that was previously spent filling out complicated

TABLE 4	Purposes Served by a Performance Management System

Strategic: To help top management achieve strategic business objectives

Administrative: To furnish valid and useful information for making administrative decisions about employees

Informational: To inform employees about how they are doing and about the organization's and the supervisor's expectations

Developmental: To allow managers to provide coaching to their employees

Organizational maintenance: To provide information to be used in workplace planning and allocation of human resources

Documentational: To collect useful information that can be used for various purposes (e.g., test development, administrative decisions)

matrices and forms is now spent talking with the employees about how they can improve their performance, allowing for progress on an ongoing basis. This serves a developmental purpose.

Although multiple purposes are possible, a survey of industrial and organizational psychologists working in HR departments in more than 100 different organizations reported that the two most frequent purposes are administrative (i.e., salary decisions) and developmental (i.e., to identify employees' weaknesses and strengths). Overall, in the organizations that participated in this study, performance management served at least two of the purposes mentioned earlier.[42] These purposes place conflicting demands on the raters because they must be both judges (i.e., make salary decisions) and coaches (i.e., provide useful feedback for performance improvement) at the same time.

Now, think about the performance management system implemented in your organization or the last organization for which you worked. Table 4 summarizes the various purposes served by a performance management system. Which of these purposes are being served by the system you are considering?

6 CHARACTERISTICS OF AN IDEAL PM SYSTEM

So far, we have defined performance management, described the advantages of implementing good performance management systems, discussed some of the dangers of not doing a good job with the design and implementation of the system, and described the various purposes achieved by a good system. But what does a good system look like? The following characteristics are likely to allow a performance management system to be successful. Practical constraints may not allow for the implementation of all these features. The reality is that performance management systems are seldom implemented in an ideal way.[43] For example, there may not be sufficient funds to deliver training to all people involved, supervisors may have biases in how they provide performance ratings, or people may be just too busy to pay attention to a new organizational initiative that requires their time and attention. Also, there may be organizational or even country-level constraints that prevent the implementation of a good performance management system. For example, consider the case of Ghana, which is a country that espouses collectivist values over individual performance, and it is a society that is male-dominated and dominated by political and administrative leaders, where these socio-cultural norms have a clear influence on organizational decision making and practices.[44] These institutional constraints that are so pervasive in Ghana and so many other emerging market countries must be taken into consideration in terms of what type of performance management system will be possible to implement as well as the effectiveness of such a system. However, regardless of the societal, institutional, and practical constraints, we should strive to place a check mark next to each of these characteristics: the more features that are checked, the more likely it will be that the system will live up to its promise.

- *Strategic congruence.* The system should be congruent with the unit and organization's strategy. In other words, individual goals must be aligned with unit and organizational goals.
- *Context congruence.* The system should be congruent with the organization's culture as well as the broader cultural context of the region or country. The importance of context in implementing highly effective performance management systems is emphasized throughout the book. However, for now, consider the example of an organization that has a culture in which communication is not fluid and hierarchies are rigid. In such organizations, a 360-degree feedback system in which individuals receive comments on their performance from their subordinates, peers, and superiors would be resisted and likely not very effective. Regarding broader cultural issues, consider that performance management research published in scholarly journals has been conducted in about 40 countries around the world.[45] Taken together, this body of work suggests that culture plays an important role in the effectiveness of a performance management system. For example, in countries such as Japan, there is an emphasis on the measurement of both behaviors (i.e., how people do the work) and results (i.e., the results of people's work), whereas in the United States results are typically preferred over behaviors. Thus, implementing a results-only system in Japan is not likely to be effective. As a second illustration, a study including 97 multinational corporations suggested that they have adapted their performance management systems in their subsidiaries in Bulgaria and Romania.[46] Specifically, although performance is measured similarly around the world (see standardization criterion below), the interpersonal aspects of the system are adapted and customized to the local culture. For example, performance management systems in the subsidiaries are more likely to differ from those in the headquarters as differences in power distance (i.e., degree to which a society accepts unequal distribution of power) increase between countries.
- *Thoroughness.* The system should be thorough regarding four dimensions. First, all employees should be evaluated (including managers). Second, all major job responsibilities should be evaluated (including behaviors and results). Third, the evaluation should include performance spanning the entire review period, not just the few weeks or months before the review. Finally, feedback should be given on positive performance aspects as well as those that are in need of improvement.
- *Practicality.* Systems that are too expensive, time consuming, and convoluted will obviously not be effective. Good, easy-to-use systems (e.g., performance data are entered via user-friendly software) are available for managers to help

them make decisions. Finally, the benefits of using the system (e.g., increased performance and job satisfaction) must be seen as outweighing the costs (e.g., time, effort, expense).

- *Meaningfulness.* The system must be meaningful in several ways. First, the standards and evaluations conducted for each job function must be considered important and relevant. Second, performance assessment must emphasize only those functions that are under the control of the employee. For example, there is no point in letting an employee know she needs to increase the speed of service delivery when the supplier does not get the product to her on time. Third, evaluations must take place at regular intervals and at appropriate moments. Because one formal evaluation per year is usually not sufficient, informal quarterly reviews are recommended. Fourth, the system should provide for the continuing skill development of evaluators. Finally, the results should be used for important administrative decisions. People will not pay attention to a system that has no consequences in terms of outcomes that they value. For example, a recent study compared performance management systems in the former East versus former West Germany. Results showed that in former West German companies, there was a stronger link between the performance management system and administrative decisions such as promotions. This relationship was weaker in former East German companies, and this difference is probably due to the socialist political system in the former German Democratic Republic, which has had a long-lasting effect that is still observed today.[47]

- *Specificity.* A good system should be specific: it should provide detailed and concrete guidance to employees about what is expected of them and how they can meet these expectations.

- *Identification of effective and ineffective performance.* The performance management system should provide information that allows for the identification of effective and ineffective performance. That is, the system should allow for distinguishing between effective and ineffective behaviors and results, thereby also allowing for the identification of employees displaying various levels of performance effectiveness. In terms of decision making, a system that classifies or ranks all levels of performance and all employees similarly is useless.

- *Reliability.* A good system should include measures of performance that are consistent and free of error. For example, if two supervisors provided ratings of the same employee and performance dimensions, ratings should be similar.

- *Validity.* The measures of performance should also be valid. In this context, validity refers to the fact that the measures include all relevant performance facets and do not include irrelevant performance facets. In other words, measures are relevant (i.e., include all critical performance facets), not deficient (i.e., do not leave any important aspects out), and are not contaminated (i.e., do not include factors outside of the control of the employee or factors unrelated to performance). In short, measures include what is important and do not assess what is not important and outside of the control of the employee. For example, the *gondolieri* in the city of Venice (Italy) have had a performance management system for about 1,000 years. Among other relevant performance dimensions, older versions of the performance management system required *gondolieri* to demonstrate their level of rowing skills and their ability to transport people and goods safely. These are clearly relevant dimensions. However, the system was contaminated because it included the following requirement: "Every brother shall be obliged to confess twice a year, or at least once and if after a warning, he remains impenitent, he shall be expelled . . . [from the *gondolieri* guild]."[48]

- *Acceptability and fairness.* A good system is acceptable and is perceived as fair by all participants. Perceptions of fairness are subjective and the only way to know if a system is seen as fair is to ask the participants about the system. Such perceptions include four distinct components. First, we can ask about *distributive justice*, which includes perceptions of the performance evaluation received relative to the work performed, and perceptions of the rewards received relative to the evaluation received, particularly when the system is implemented across countries. For example, differences in perceptions may be found in comparing employees from more individualistic (e.g., United States) to more collectivistic (e.g., Korea) cultures.[49] If a discrepancy is perceived between work and evaluation or between evaluation and rewards, then the system is likely to be seen as unfair.[50] Second, we can ask about *procedural justice*, which includes perceptions of the procedures used to determine the ratings as well as the procedures used to link ratings with rewards. Third, we can assess perceptions regarding *interpersonal justice*, which refers to the quality of the design and implementation of the performance management system. For example, what are employees' perceptions regarding how they are treated by their supervisors during the performance review meeting? Do they feel that supervisors are empathic and helpful? Finally, *informational justice* refers to fairness perceptions about performance expectations and goals, feedback received, and the information given to justify administrative decisions. For example, are explanations perceived to be honest, sincere, and logical? Because a good system is inherently discriminatory, some employees will receive ratings that are lower than those received by other employees. However, we should strive to develop systems that are regarded as fair from the distributive, procedural, interpersonal, and informational perspectives because each type of justice perception leads to different outcomes.[51] For example, a perception that the system is not fair from a distributive point of view is likely to lead to a poor relationship between employee and supervisor and lowered satisfaction of the employee with the supervisor. On the other hand, a perception that the system is unfair from a procedural point of view is likely to lead to decreased employee commitment toward the organization and increased intentions to leave.[52] One way to improve all four justice dimensions is to set clear rules that are applied consistently by all supervisors.

- *Inclusiveness.* Good systems include input from multiple sources on an ongoing basis. First, the evaluation process must represent the concerns of all the people who will be affected by the outcome. Consequently, employees must participate in the process of creating the system by providing input regarding what behaviors or results will be measured and how. This is particularly important in today's diverse and global organizations including individuals from different cultural backgrounds, which may lead to different views regarding what is performance and how it should be measured.[53] Second, input about employee performance should be gathered from the employees themselves before the appraisal meeting.[54] In short, all participants must be given a voice in the process of designing and implementing the system. Such inclusive systems are likely to lead to more successful systems including less employee resistance, improved performance, and fewer legal challenges.[55]

- **Openness.** Good systems have no secrets. First, performance is evaluated frequently and performance feedback is provided on an ongoing basis. Therefore, employees are continually informed of the quality of their performance. Second, the appraisal meeting consists of a two-way communication process during which information is exchanged, not delivered from the supervisor to the employee without his or her input. Third, standards should be clear and communicated on an ongoing basis. Finally, communications are factual, open, and honest.
- **Correctability.** The process of assigning ratings should minimize subjective aspects; however, it is virtually impossible to create a system that is completely objective because human judgment is an important component of the evaluation process. When employees perceive an error has been made, there should be a mechanism through which this error can be corrected. Establishing an appeals process, through which employees can challenge what may be unjust decisions, is an important aspect of a good performance management system.
- **Standardization.** As noted earlier, good systems are standardized. This means that performance is evaluated consistently across people and time. To achieve this goal, the ongoing training of the individuals in charge of appraisals, usually managers, is a must.
- **Ethicality.** Good systems comply with ethical standards. This means that the supervisor suppresses her personal self-interest in providing evaluations. In addition, the supervisor evaluates only performance dimensions for which she has sufficient information, and the privacy of the employee is respected.[56]

Table 5 lists the characteristics of an ideal performance management system. Think about the performance management system implemented in your organization or the last organization for which you worked. Which of the features listed in Table 5 included in the system you are considering? How far is your system from the ideal?

TABLE 5	Characteristics of an Ideal Performance Management System
Strategic congruence	
Context congruence	
Thoroughness	
Practicality	
Meaningfulness	
Specificity	
Identification of effective and ineffective performance	
Reliability	
Validity	
Acceptability and fairness	
Inclusiveness	
Openness	
Correctability	
Standardization	
Ethicality	

BOX 5

Good Performance Management Implementation Pays Off

Implementing a performance management system that includes the characteristics just described will pay off. A study conducted for Mercer, a global diversified consulting company, revealed that the 1,200 workers surveyed stated that they could improve their productivity by an average of 26% if they were not held back by a lack of "direction, support, training, and equipment." Successfully implementing a performance management system can give workers the direction and support that they need to improve their productivity.[57]

---

7 INTEGRATION WITH OTHER HUMAN RESOURCES AND DEVELOPMENT ACTIVITIES

Performance management systems serve as important "feeders" to other human resources and development activities. For example, consider the relationship between performance management and *training*. Performance management provides information on developmental needs for employees. In the absence of a good performance management system, it is not clear that organizations will use their training resources in the most efficient way (i.e., to train those who most need it in the most critical areas). One organization that is able to link its performance management system to training initiatives is Kimberly-Clark.[58] Kimberly-Clark's global performance management system includes about 57,000 employees across 36 countries (http://www.kimberly-clark.com/ourcompany/overview.aspx). This system makes a clear link between performance and training, allows employees to understand areas that need to be improved, and directs them to appropriate opportunities to enable improvements in performance. For example, in Peru, Kimberly-Clark has partnered with the National Service of Occupational Training in Industry (Senati), a local technical institute, to provide training on manufacturing skills. Kimberly-Clark reached a similar agreement in Malaysia with the University College of Tun Hussein Onn. Similarly, there is a training partner in Korea. The beneficial link between performance management and training became evidenced recently in the Korean operations, where the newspaper *Dong-A Ilbo* named Yuhan-Kimberly one of "the 30 most respected companies in Korea."

Unfortunately, despite the successful Kimberly-Clark example, most organizations do not use performance management systems to determine training content and waste an opportunity to use the performance management system as the needs assessment phase of their training efforts.[59] Specifically, a recent survey including 218 HR leaders at companies with at least 2,500 employees revealed that there is tight integration between performance management and learning/development activities in only 15.3% of the organizations surveyed.[60]

Performance management also provides key information for *workforce planning*. Specifically, an organization's talent inventory is based on information collected through the performance management system. Development plans provide information on what skills will be acquired in the near future. This information is also used in making *recruitment and hiring* decisions. Knowledge of an organization's current and future talent is important when deciding what types of skills need to be acquired externally and what types of skills can be found within the organization.

Finally, there is an obvious relationship between performance management and compensation systems. Compensation and reward decisions are likely to be arbitrary in the absence of a good performance management system.

In short, performance management is a key component of talent management in organizations. It allows for assessing the current talent and making predictions about future needs both at the individual and organizational levels. Implementing a successful performance management system is a requirement for the successful implementation of other HR functions, including training, workforce planning, recruitment and selection, and compensation.

8 PERFORMANCE MANAGEMENT AROUND THE WORLD

Performance management is a global phenomenon and organizations all over the world are implementing various types of performance management systems. We will discuss examples of how systems are implemented in different countries. As a preview and to highlight the increasing importance of performance management globally, consider the following results from recent research relating to 10 specific countries:[61]

- *Performance management in Mexico.* Performance management has become increasingly popular since the 1970s. For the most part, systems in Mexico are similar to those implemented in the United States. For example, the measurement of results is quite pervasive. However, more research is needed for us to gain a better understanding of what types of systems would work best in Mexico.

- *Performance management in the United Kingdom.* Performance management in the United Kingdom has been affected by several factors, including an emphasis on cost effectiveness and the developmental purpose of performance management. Performance management is gaining increased stature and significance given the more recent emphasis on talent management and total rewards management. As noted earlier, performance management provides critical information regarding the identification of top performers, which helps talent management, and critical information to be used in administrative decisions, including the allocation of rewards. Performance management in the United Kingdom is an established organizational practice and is clearly influenced by broader societal issues such as socioeconomic, political, and legal trends.

- *Performance management in France.* Performance management in France faces unique contextual issues such as legal requirements to invest in employee training and development and the need to emphasize individual accountability. Once again, performance management systems are not implemented in a vacuum, and it is important to consider the broader environment when designing and implementing a system.

- *Performance management in Germany.* Performance management in Germany has been affected by the established practice of long-term employment relationships. Thus, performance management systems emphasize long-term goals and usually do not have a short-term focus. In spite of this unique feature, systems share some similarities with France given their membership in the European Union, which provides a common legal framework for many labor-related issues.

- *Performance management in Turkey.* Performance management in Turkey is evolving rapidly given its official candidacy for European Union membership. Negotiations began in 2005, and it is likely that Turkey will become a European Union member by around 2015. Turkey's unique contextual issues involve being a democratic and secular state—yet ruled by a single-party government. Performance management is a fairly novel issue in Turkey, but almost 80% of firms in Turkey are using some type of system. Because personal relationships play an important role in Turkish culture, an important challenge is the implementation of systems that ensure valid, reliable, and fair performance measurement.

- *Performance management in India.* The India economy has been on "overdrive" since the early 1990s and there is intense international business activity, including a significant increase in foreign direct investment going into India as well as India firms going abroad. The intense international business activity is leading to a change in traditional values, at least in work environment, from more collectivistic to more individualistic and short-term. Nevertheless, the traditional paternalistic values do not seem to be changing, and they pose a challenge for the implementation of performance management systems in which the supervisor serves as a coach instead of as a "boss."

- *Performance management in China.* From the founding of the socialist state in 1949 until the 1980s, performance management systems in China emphasized mostly attendance and skills. However, since the 1980s, the view of performance management has expanded to consider broader sets of behaviors as well as the relationship between performance management and other organizational systems (e.g., compensation). Important issues to consider for successful implementation of performance management systems in China include respect for age and seniority and the emphasis on social harmony.

- *Performance management in South Korea.* Work relationships in South Korea are hierarchical in nature and emphasize the importance of groups over individuals. More recently, the establishment of a democratic government in 1987 and the Asian financial crisis of 1997 affected organizational practices substantially. Specifically, the financial crisis led many organizations to adopt what in Korean is called *Yunbongje* (i.e., merit-based systems). The current challenge is how to reconcile a merit-based approach with more traditional cultural values.

- *Performance management in Japan.* Although Japanese firms relied on lifetime employment and seniority as key organizational practices, more recently firms also consider the importance of new knowledge acquisition. For example, competency modeling has become increasingly popular. In general performance management systems in Japan tend to emphasize behaviors to the detriment of results.

- *Performance management in Australia.* The Australian economy has made an important shift from manufacturing to service, and there are important demographic changes in the workforce including an increased presence of women and members of ethnic minority groups. The legal framework in Australia is similar to that in the United States and the United Kingdom. So, much like the United States and the United Kingdom, performance management systems tend to include documentation of performance, considerations regarding equal opportunity, and due process issues.

This brief overview provides us with some information regarding performance management systems around the world. Although there is a common challenge to align individual and organizational goals and enhance the performance of individuals and groups, the way these goals are achieved is influenced by both organizational and societal contextual issues. Thus, these issues should not be ignored when implementing performance management systems.

Summary Points

- Performance management is a continuous process of identifying, measuring, and developing the performance of individuals and teams and aligning performance with the strategic goals of the organization.

- Although many organizations have systems labeled "performance management," they usually are only performance *appraisal* systems. Performance appraisal emphasizes the assessment of an employee's strengths and weaknesses and does not include strategic business considerations. Also, performance appraisal systems usually do not include extensive and ongoing feedback that an employee can use to improve her performance in the future. Finally, performance appraisal is a once-a-year event that is often driven by the HR department, whereas performance management is a year-round way of managing business that is driven by managers.

- Implementing a well-designed performance management system has many advantages. From the perspective of employees, a good system increases motivation and self-esteem, helps improve performance, clarifies job tasks and duties, provides self-insight and development opportunities, and clarifies supervisors' expectations. From the perspective of managers, good systems allow them to gain insight into employees' activities and goals, allow for more fair and appropriate administrative actions, allow them to communicate organizational goals more clearly, let them differentiate good and poor performers, help drive organizational change, encourage voice behavior, and improve employee engagement. Finally, from the perspective of the HR function, a good system provides protection from litigation and can also help minimize employee misconduct which can have so many negative consequences for the organization.

- Poorly designed and implemented performance management systems can have disastrous consequences for all involved. For example, employees may quit, those who stay may be less motivated, and relationships (e.g., supervisor–subordinate) can suffer irreparable damage. Also, poorly designed systems can be biased, resulting in costly lawsuits and wasted time and resources. In the end, low-quality or poorly implemented systems can be a source of enormous frustration and cynicism for all involved.

- Reward systems include all mechanisms for determining and distributing tangible and intangible returns as part of an employment relationship. Tangible returns, collectively referred to as *compensation*, include both cash and benefits. Intangible returns, also referred to as *relational returns*, include recognition and status, employment security, challenging work, and learning opportunities. Not all types of returns are directly related to performance management systems because not all types of returns are allocated based on past performance.

- Performance management systems serve multiple purposes. First, they serve a strategic purpose because they help link employee activities with the organization's mission and goals, they identify results and behaviors needed to carry out strategy, and they maximize the extent to which employees exhibit the desired behaviors and produce the desired results. Second, they serve an administrative purpose in that they produce information used by the reward system and other HR decision making (e.g., promotions, termination, disciplinary actions). Third, they serve an informational purpose because they enable employees to learn about their performance in relation to the organization's expectations. Fourth, they serve a developmental purpose in that performance feedback allows individuals to learn about their strengths and weaknesses, to identify training needs, and to make better decisions regarding job assignments. Fifth, performance management systems serve an organizational maintenance purpose because they provide useful information for workforce planning and for evaluating the effectiveness of other HR systems (e.g., comparing performance before and after an expensive training program to determine whether training made a difference). Finally,

performance management systems also serve a documentational purpose; for example, they support HR decisions and help meet legal requirements.

- Ideal performance management systems are rare. Such ideal systems are
  - congruent with strategy (i.e., there is a clear link among individual, unit, and organizational goals)
  - congruent with context (i.e., the system is consistent with norms based on the culture of the organization and the region and country in which the organization is located)
  - thorough (i.e., they include all relevant performance dimensions)
  - practical (i.e., they do not require excessive time and resources)
  - meaningful (i.e., they have important consequences)
  - specific (i.e., they provide a concrete employee improvement agenda)
  - able to identify effective and ineffective performance (i.e., they help distinguish employees at different performance levels)
  - reliable (i.e., the measurement of performance is consistent)
  - valid (i.e., the measures of performance are not contaminated or deficient)
  - fair (i.e., people participating in the system believe the processes and outcomes are just)
  - inclusive (i.e., they include input from multiple sources on an ongoing basis)
  - open (i.e., they are transparent and there are no secrets)
  - correctable (i.e., they include mechanisms so that errors can be corrected)
  - standardized (i.e., performance is evaluated consistently across people and time)
  - ethical (i.e., they comply with ethical standards)

- Many trade-offs take place in the real-world implementation of performance management systems; however, the closer the system is to the ideal characteristics, the greater the return will be for the employees, supervisors, and the organization as a whole.

- A performance management system is the key factor used in determining whether an organization can manage its human resources and talent effectively. Performance management provides information on who should be trained and in what areas, which employees should be rewarded, and what type of skills are lacking at the organization or unit level. Therefore, performance management also provides information on the type of employees that should be hired. When implemented well, performance management systems provide critical information that allows organizations to make sound decisions regarding their people resources.

- Given the globalized and hyper-competitive nature of business in the twenty-first century, there is a common worldwide challenge to align individual and organizational goals and enhance the performance of individuals and groups. However, the way these goals are achieved is influenced by both organizational and societal contextual issues. A performance management system in China may not be the same as a performance management system in Mexico or France. Although the system's main objectives may be the same, the way the system is implemented and deployed must take contextual considerations into account.

As should be evident by now, implementing an ideal performance management system requires a substantial amount of work; however, this does not start when the system is put into place. The process starts much earlier because unless specific conditions are present before the system is implemented, the system will not achieve its multiple purposes.

CASE STUDY 1

Reality Check: Ideal versus Actual Performance Management System

The table here summarizes the key characteristics of an ideal performance management system as discussed in this chapter. Think about a performance management system you know. This could be the one implemented at your current (or most recent) job. If you don't have information about such a system, talk to a friend or acquaintance who is currently working, and gather information about the system used in his or her organization. Use the Y/N column in the table to indicate whether each of the features is present (Y: yes) or not (N: no) in the system you are considering. In some cases, some elements may be present to a matter of degree and may require that you include some additional information in the Comments column.

Next, prepare a brief report addressing the following issues:

1. How many of the 14 characteristics of an ideal system are present in the system you are evaluating?
2. Identify two characteristics that are not present at all, or barely present, in your system. Discuss the implications that the lack of these characteristics has on the effectiveness of the system.
3. Identify one characteristic that is clearly present in your system. Discuss the implications of the presence of this characteristic on the effectiveness of the system.
4. Identify the characteristic in your system that is furthest from the ideal. What can be done to produce a better alignment between your system and the ideal? Who should be responsible for doing what so that your system becomes "ideal" regarding this characteristic? ∎

Characteristics	Y/N	Definition	Comments
Strategic congruence		Individual goals are aligned with unit and organizational goals.	
Context congruence		The system is congruent with norms based on the organization's culture.	
		The system is congruent with norms based on the culture of the region and country where the organization is located.	
Thoroughness		All employees are evaluated.	
		Evaluations include performance spanning the entire review period.	
		All major job responsibilities are evaluated.	
		Feedback is provided on both positive and negative performance.	
Practicality		It is readily available for use.	
		It is easy to use.	
		It is acceptable to those who use it for decisions.	
		Benefits of the system outweigh the costs.	
		Standards and evaluations for each job function are important and relevant.	
		Only the functions that are under the control of the employee are measured.	
Meaningfulness		Evaluations take place at regular intervals and at appropriate moments.	
		System provides for continuing skill development of evaluators.	
		Results are used for important administrative decisions.	
Specificity		Detailed guidance is provided to employees about what is expected of them and how they can meet these expectations.	
Identification of effective and ineffective performance		The system distinguishes between effective and ineffective behaviors and results, thereby also identifying employees displaying various levels of performance effectiveness.	
Reliability		Measures of performance are consistent.	
		Measures of performance are free of error.	
Validity		Measures include all critical performance facets.	
		Measures do not leave out any important performance facets.	
		Measures do not include factors outside employee control.	

Characteristics	Y/N	Definition	Comments
Acceptability and fairness		Employees perceive the performance evaluation and rewards received relative to the work performed as fair (distributive justice). Employees perceive the procedures used to determine the ratings and subsequent rewards as fair (procedural justice). Employees perceive the way they are treated in the course of designing and implementing the system as fair (interpersonal justice). Employees perceive the information and explanations they receive as part of the performance management system as fair (informational justice).	
Inclusiveness		Employee input about their performance is gathered from the employees before the appraisal meeting. Employees participate in the process of creating the system by providing input on how performance should be measured.	
Openness		Performance is evaluated frequently and feedback is provided on an ongoing basis. Appraisal meeting is a two-way communication process and not one-way communication delivered from the supervisor to the employee. Standards are clear and communicated on an ongoing basis. Communications are factual, open, and honest.	
Correctability		There is an appeals process, through which employees can challenge unjust or incorrect decisions.	
Standardization		Performance is evaluated consistently across people and time.	
Ethicality		Supervisors suppress their personal self-interest in providing evaluations. Supervisors evaluate performance dimensions only for which they have sufficient information. Employee privacy is respected.	

CASE STUDY 2

Performance Management at Network Solutions, Inc.

Network Solutions, Inc.,[*] is a worldwide leader in hardware, software, and services essential to computer networking. Until recently, Network Solutions, Inc., used more than 50 different systems to measure performance within the company, many employees did not receive a review, fewer than 5% of all employees received the lowest category of rating, and there was no recognition program in place to reward high achievers. Overall, it was recognized that performance problems were not being addressed, and tough pressure from competitors was increasing the costs of managing human performance ineffectively. In addition, quality initiatives were driving change in several areas of the business, and Network Solutions decided that these initiatives should also apply to "people quality." Finally, Network Solutions wanted to improve its ability to meet its organizational goals and realized that one way of doing this would be to ensure that they were linked to each employee's goals.

Given this situation, in 2001, Network Solutions' CEO announced that he wanted to implement a forced distribution performance management system in which a set percentage of employees were classified in each of several categories (e.g., a rating of 1 to the top 20% of performers; a rating of 2 to the middle 70% of performers; and a rating of 3 to the bottom 10% of performers). A global cross-divisional HR team was put in place to design and implement the new system. The first task for the design team was to build a business case of the new system by showing that if organizational strategy was carried down to team contributions and team contributions were translated into individual goals, then business goals would be met. Initially the program was rolled out as a year-round people management system that would raise the bar on performance management at Network Solutions by aligning individual performance objectives with organizational goals by focusing on the development of all employees. The desired outcomes of the new system included raising the performance level of all employees, identifying and retaining top talent, and identifying low performers and improving their performance. Network Solutions also wanted the performance expectations for all employees to be clear.

Before implementing the program, the design team received the support of senior leadership by communicating that the performance management system was the future of Network Solutions and by encouraging all senior leaders to ensure that those reporting directly to them understood the process and accepted it. In addition, they encouraged senior leaders to use the system with all of their direct subordinates and to demand and utilize output from the new system. Next, the design team encouraged the senior leaders to stop the development and use of any other performance management system and explained the need for standardization of performance management across all divisions. Finally, the team asked senior leaders to promote the new program by involving employees in training of talent management and by assessing any needs in their divisions that would not be addressed by the new system. The Network Solutions global performance management cycle consisted of the following process:

1. Goal cascading and team building
2. Performance planning
3. Development planning
4. Ongoing discussions and updates between managers and employees
5. Annual performance summary

Training resources were made available on Network Solutions' intranet for managers and individual contributors, including access to all necessary forms. In addition to the training available on the intranet, 1- to 2-hour conference calls took place before each phase of the program was begun.

Today, part of the training associated with the performance management system revolves around the idea that the development planning phase of the system is the joint year-round responsibility of managers and employees. Managers are responsible for scheduling meetings, guiding employees on preparing for meetings, and finalizing all development plans. Individual contributors are responsible for documenting the developmental plans. Both managers and employees are responsible for preparing for the meeting, filling out the development planning preparation forms, and attending the meeting.

With forced distribution systems, there is a set number of employees that have to fall into set rating classifications. As noted, in the Network Solutions system employees are given a rating of 1, 2, or 3. Individual ratings are determined by

---

[*] This case study is based, in part, on actual information. Network Solutions, Inc., is a pseudonym which is being used to protect the identity of the actual company in question.

the execution of annual objectives and job requirements as well as by a comparison rating of others at a similar level at Network Solutions. Employees receiving a 3, the lowest rating, have a specified time period to improve their performance. If their performance does improve, then they are released from the plan, but they are not eligible for stock options or salary increases. If performance does not improve, they can take a severance package and leave the company or they can start on a performance improvement plan, which has more rigorous expectations and time lines than did the original action plan. If performance does not improve after the second period, they are terminated without a severance package. Individuals with a rating of 2 receive average to high salary increases, stock options, and bonuses. Individuals receiving the highest rating of 1 receive the highest salary increases, stock options, and bonuses. These individuals are also treated as "high potential" employees and given extra development opportunities by their managers. The company also makes significant efforts to retain all individuals who receive a rating of 1.

Looking to the future, Network Solutions plans to continue reinforcing the needed cultural change to support forced distribution ratings. HR Centers of Expertise of Network Solutions continue to educate employees about the system to ensure that they understand that Network Solutions still rewards good performance; they are just measuring it in a different way

than in the past. There is also a plan to monitor for and correct any unproductive practices and implement correcting policies and practices. To do this, Network Solutions plans on continued checks with all stakeholders to ensure that the performance management system is serving its intended purpose.

Consider Network Solutions' performance management system in light of what we discussed as an ideal system. Then answer the following questions:

1. Overall, what is the overlap between Network Solutions' system and an ideal system?
2. What are the features of the system implemented at Network Solutions that correspond to the features described in the chapter as ideal characteristics? Which of the ideal characteristics are missing? For which of the ideal characteristics do we need additional information to evaluate whether they are part of the system at Network Solutions?
3. Based on the description of the system at Network Solutions, what do you anticipate will be some advantages and positive outcomes resulting from the implementation of the system?
4. Based on the description of the system at Network Solutions, what do you anticipate will be some disadvantages and negative outcomes resulting from the implementation of the system? ▣

Distinguishing Performance Management Systems from Performance Appraisal Systems

What are the differences between a performance appraisal system and a performance management system? How are the two systems related to each other? After answering these questions, consider the following 11 criticisms. Which of the following criticisms pertain to performance appraisal systems but not to performance management systems? Which criticisms pertain to both performance appraisal and performance management systems? Use Xs on the table below to denote answers. Then, provide an explanation for categorizing the 11 criticisms in the way you did.

Criticism 1: "[There can be] inconsistency between comments and scores on an employee's evaluation."

Criticism 2: "The annual performance review is a bad management tool. To start with, it is not timely. If your subordinate is deficient in some ways, you wait 11

months to say something about it. How does that help next week's performance?"

Criticism 3: "Never make the evaluation a hit-and-run. It should take the form of a dialogue between the supervisor and subordinate, not an isolated event but rather a part of performance/career management more generally."

Criticism 4: "A number of years ago, the U.S. Equal Employment Opportunity Commission (EEOC) created a 'Like Me' task force. Its general conclusion—there was a human tendency to favor employees who are like the managers making the employment assessment."

Criticism 5: "Few managers jump with glee at appraisal time. When they triage workplace demands, many times appraisals end up at the bottom. As a result, late appraisals are often the norm and not the exception."

Criticism 6: "Because performance is ultimately measured on a nonstop, continuous basis, managers may become overwhelmed with cognitive load, paperwork, and generally more work to do."

Criticism 7: "What's left is the more important strategic role of raising the reputational and intellectual capital of the company—but HR is, it turns out, uniquely unsuited for that."

Criticism 8: "Goal-setting, when done wrong, gives the employee the wrong goals—those, for instance, which are not aligned with the organization's strategic orientation."

Criticism 9: "Often an employee with substandard performance is evaluated as meeting expectations or even better, and the average employee receives an above-average evaluation."

Criticism 10: "[The process does not involve helping or making employees] set goals for the future."

Criticism 11: "Coaching can be tricky. When done wrong, it can be devastating. For example, a coach's feedback can have detrimental effects if it focuses on the employee as a whole as opposed to specific work behaviors at work." ▪

Criticisms	Pertains to performance appraisal systems only	Pertains to performance management systems only	Pertains to both performance appraisal and management systems
1			
2			
3			
4			
5			
6			
7			
8			
9			
10			
11			

Source: Some of these criticisms were derived from the following sources: (a) Ryan, Liz. (2009, June 30). CEOs should skip performance reviews in 2009. *Bloomberg Businessweek*. Available online at http://www.businessweek.com/managing/content/jun2009/ca20090630_736385.htm. Retrieval date: March 3, 2011; (b) Segal, Jonathan, A. (2011, January 14). The dirty dozen performance appraisal errors. *Bloomberg Businessweek*. Available online at http://www.businessweek.com/managing/content/jan2011/ca20110114_156455.htm. Retrieval date: March 3, 2011; and (c) Hammonds, Keith H. (2005, August 1). Why we hate HR. *Fast Company*. Available online at from http://www.fastcompany.com/magazine/97/open_hr.html?page=0%2C0. Retrieval date: March 3, 2011.

Endnotes

1. DeNisi, A. S., & Kluger, A. N. (2000). Feedback effectiveness: Can 360-degree appraisals be improved? *Academy of Management Executive, 14*, 129–139.
2. Halachmi, A. (2005). Performance measurement is only one way of managing performance. *International Journal of Productivity and Performance Management, 54*, 502–516.
3. Fandray, D. (2001, May). Managing performance the Merrill Lynch way. *Workforce Online*. Available online at http://www.workforce.com/archive/feature/22/28/68/223512.php. Retrieval date: August 25, 2011.
4. Bisoux, T. (2004). Man, one business. *BizEd, 3*(4), 18–25.
5. Holland, K. (2006, September 10). Performance reviews: Many need improvement. *The New*

York Times, Section 3, Column 1, Money and Business/Financial Desk, 3.

6. Nankervis, A. R., & Compton, R. (2006). Performance management: Theory in practice? *Asia Pacific Journal of Human Resources, 44,* 83–101.

7. Cascio, W. F. (2006). Global performance management systems. In I. Bjorkman & G. Stahl (Eds.), *Handbook of research in international human resources management* (pp. 176–196). London, UK: Edward Elgar Ltd.

8. Maxwell, G., & Farquharson, L. (2008). Senior managers' perceptions of the practice of human resource management. *Employee Relations, 30,* 304–322.

9. Aguinis, H., Joo, H., & Gottfredson, R. K. (in press). Why we hate performance management—and why we should love it. *Business Horizons.*

10. Thomas, S. L., & Bretz, R. D. (1994). Research and practice in performance appraisal: Evaluating employee performance in America's largest companies. *SAM Advanced Management Journal, 59*(2), 28–34.

11. Keeping, L. M., & Levy, P. E. (2000). Performance appraisal reactions: Measurement, modeling, and method bias. *Journal of Applied Psychology, 85,* 708–723.

12. Hedge, J. W., Borman, W. C., & Lammlein, S. E. (2006). Training, performance management, and career management. In *The aging workforce: Realities, myths, and implications for organizations* (pp. 137–154). Washington, DC: American Psychological Association.

13. Werbel, J., & Balkin, D. B. (2010). Are human resource practices linked to employee misconduct? A rational choice perspective. *Human Resource Management Review, 20,* 317–326.

14. Peters, T. (1987). *The new masters of excellence.* Niles, IL: Nightingale Conant Corp.

15. Bititci, U. S., Memdibil, K., Nudurupati, S., Turner, T., & Garengo, P. (2004). The interplay between performance measurement, organizational culture and management styles. *Measuring Business Excellence, 8,* 28–41.

16. Pennington, R. G. (2003). Change performance to change the culture. *Industrial and Commercial Training, 35,* 251.

17. Kuvaas, B. (2006). Performance appraisal satisfaction and employee outcomes: Mediating and moderating roles of work motivation. *International Journal of Human Resource Management, 17,* 504–522.

18. Pienaar, C., & Bester, C. (2009). Addressing career obstacles within a changing higher education work environment: Perspectives of academics. *South African Journal of Psychology, 39,* 376–385.

19. Whiting, S. W., Podsakoff, P. M., & Pierce, J. R. (2008). Effects of task performance, helping, voice, and organizational loyalty on performance appraisal ratings. *Journal of Applied Psychology, 93,* 125–139.

20. Mone, E. M., & London, M. (2010). *Employee engagement through effective performance management.* New York: Routledge.

21. Sumlin, R. (2011). *Performance management: Impacts and trends.* DDI white paper. Available online at http:// www.exinfm.com/pdffiles/ pm.pdf. Retrieval date: August 25, 2011.

22. Gabris, G. T., & Ihrke, D. M. (2001). Does performance appraisal contribute to heightened levels of employee burnout? The results of one study. *Public Personnel Management, 30,* 157–172.

23. Brown, M., & Benson, J. (2005). Managing to overload? Work overload and performance appraisal processes. *Group & Organization Management, 30,* 99–124.

24. FMI Corporation. (2000, November 15). *Using performance reviews to improve employee retention: Contractor's business management report,* 2. Denver, CO: FMI Corporation.

25. The following discussion is based in large part on Chapter 1 from G. T. Milcovich and J. M. Newman, *Compensation management.* (7th ed). New York: McGraw-Hill, 2002.

26. Lewin, D. (2002, January). *Incentive compensation in the U.S. public sector: A study of usage, perceptions, and preferences.* Paper presented at the annual meeting of the Industrial Relations Research Association, Atlanta, GA.

27. Kelley, D. Doctors test pay-for-performance program. *The Gazette,* Colorado Springs, CO. http://www.redorbit.com/news/health/483 516/colorado_springs_colo_doctors_test_pay- forperformance_program.

28. Milstead, D. (2007, February 28). Delta Petroleum sets a high bar in execs' performance award. *Rocky Mountain News, Business Section,* 3.

29. Esen, E. (2003). *Job benefits survey.* Alexandria, VA: Society for Human Resource Management.

30. *Why choose Sun?* Available online at http://au.sun.com/employment/student/whysun.html. Retrieval date: August 25, 2011.

31. *Company car or allowance?* Available online at http://www.cartoday.com/content/car_magazine/booklets/ 2005/buyingcar/10.asp. Retrieval date: August 25, 2011.

32. Shields, J. (2007). *Managing employee performance and reward.* New York: Cambridge University Press.

33. Pierce, C. A., Aguinis, H., & Adams, S. K. R. (2000). Effects of a dissolved workplace romance and rater characteristics on responses to a sexual harassment accusation. *Academy of Management Journal, 43,* 869–880.

34. *Why choose Sun?* Available online at http://au.sun.com/employment/student/whysun.html. Retrieval date: August 25, 2011.

35. Cleveland, J. N., & Murphy, R. E. (1989). Multiple uses of performance appraisal: Prevalence and correlates. *Journal of Applied Psychology, 74,* 130–135.

36. Bauer, T. N., & Erdogan. B. (2011). Organizational socialization: The effective onboarding of new employees. In Zedeck, S. (Ed.), *APA handbook of industrial and organizational psychology* (Vol. 3, pp. 51–64). Washington, DC: American Psychological Association.

37. Berner, R. (October 31, 2005). At Sears, a great communicator. *Business Week.* http://www.businessweek.com/magazine/content/05_44/b3957103.htm. Retrieval date: August 25, 2011.

38. Bilgin, K. U. (2007). Performance management for public personnel: Multi-analysis approach toward personnel. *Public Personnel Management, 36,* 93–113.

39. London, M., & Smither, J. W. (2002). Feedback orientation, feedback culture, and the longitudinal performance management process. *Human Resource Management Review, 12,* 81–100.

40. Cascio, W. F., & Aguinis, H. (2005). *Applied psychology in human resources management* (6th ed). Upper Saddle River, NJ: Prentice Hall.

41. Fandray, D. (2001, May). The new thinking in performance appraisals. *Workforce Online.* Available online at http://www.workforce.com/archive/feature/22/28/68/index.php?ht=selco%20selco. Retrieval date: August 25, 2011.

42. Cleveland, J. N., & Murphy, R. E. (1989). Multiple uses of performance appraisal: Prevalence and correlates. *Journal of Applied Psychology, 74,* 130–135.

43. McAdam, R., Hazlett, S., & Casey, C. (2005). Performance management in the UK public sector: Addressing multiple stakeholder complexity. *International Journal of Public Sector Management, 18,* 256–273.

44. Kwaku Ohemeng, F. L. (2009). Constraints in the implementation of performance management systems in developing countries: The Ghanaian case. *International Journal of Cross Cultural Management, 9,* 109–132.

45. Claus, L., & Briscoe, D. (2009). Employee performance management across borders: A review of relevant academic literature. *International Journal of Management Reviews, 11,* 175–196.

46. Claus, L., & Hand, M. L. (2009). Customization decisions regarding performance management systems of multinational companies: An empirical view of Eastern European firms. *International Journal of Cross Cultural Management, 9,* 237–258.

47. Grund, C., & Sliwka, D. (2009). The anatomy of performance appraisals in Germany. *International Journal of Human Resource Management, 20,* 2049–2065.

48. Johnston, J. (2005). Performance measurement uncertainty on the Grand Canal: Ethical and productivity conflicts between social and economic agency? *International Journal of Productivity and Performance Management, 54,* 595–612.

49. Chang, E., & Hahn, J. (2006). Does pay-for-performance enhance perceived distributive justice for collectivistic employees? *Personnel Review, 35,* 397–412.

50. Taylor, M. S., Masterson, S. S., Renard, M. K., & Tracy, K. B. (1998). Managers' reactions to procedurally just performance management systems. *Academy of Management Journal, 41,* 568–579.

51. Thurston, P. W., Jr., & McNall, L. (2010). Justice perceptions of performance appraisal practices. *Journal of Managerial Psychology, 25,* 201–228.

52. Erdogan, B. (2002). Antecedents and consequences of justice perceptions in performance appraisals. *Human Resource Management Review, 12,* 555–578.

53. Taormina, R. J., & Gao, J. H. (2009). Identifying acceptable performance appraisal criteria: An international perspective. *Asia Pacific Journal of Human Resources, 47*, 102–125.

54. Cawley, B. D., Keeping, L. M., & Levy, P. E. (1998). Participation in the performance appraisal process and employee reactions: A meta-analytic review of field investigations. *Journal of Applied Psychology, 83*, 615–633.

55. Elicker, J. D., Levy, P. E., & Hall, R. J. (2006). The role of leader-member exchange in the performance appraisal process. *Journal of Management, 32*, 531–551.

56. Eddy, E. R., Stone, D. L., & Stone-Romero, E. F. (1999). The effects of information management policies on reactions to human resource information systems: An integration of privacy and procedural justice perspectives. *Personnel Psychology, 52*, 335–358.

57. Sumlin, R. (2011). *Performance management: Impacts and trends.* DDI white paper. Available online at http:// www.exinfm.com/pdffiles/ pm.pdf. Retrieval date: August 25, 2011.

58. Ruiz, G. (2006). Kimberly-Clark: Developing talent in developing world markets. *Workforce Management, 85*(7), 34.

59. Kirkpatrick, D. L. (2006). Training and performance appraisal—Are they related? *T+D, 60*(9), 44–45.

60. Ruiz, G. (2006). Performance management underperforms. *Workforce Management, 85*(12), 47–49.

61. Varma, A., Budhwar, P. S., & DeNisi, A. (Eds.). (2008). *Performance management systems: A global perspective.* New York: Routledge.

Performance Management Process

In theory, the Performance Review process can be thought of
as a positive interaction between a "coach" and an employee,
working together to achieve maximum performance.
In reality, it's more like finding a dead squirrel in your
backyard and realizing the best solution is to fling it onto
your neighbor's roof.

—SCOTT ADAMS (*THE DILBERT PRINCIPLE*)

LEARNING OBJECTIVES

By the end of this chapter, you will be able to do the following:

- Understand that performance management is an ongoing process that includes the interrelated components of prerequisites, performance planning, performance execution, performance assessment, performance review, and performance renewal and recontracting.
- Conduct a job analysis to determine the job duties, knowledge, skills, and abilities (KSAs), and working conditions of a particular job.
- Write a job description that incorporates the KSAs of the job and information on the organization and unit mission and strategic goals.
- Understand that the poor implementation of any of the performance management process components has a negative impact on the system as a whole.
- Understand that a dysfunctional or disrupted link between any two of the performance management process components has a negative impact on the system as a whole.
- Understand important prerequisites needed before a performance management system is implemented, including knowledge of the organization's mission and strategic goals and knowledge of the job in question.

- Distinguish results from behaviors, and understand the need to consider both in performance management systems.

- Describe the employee's role in performance execution, and distinguish areas over which the employee has primary responsibility from areas over which the manager has primary responsibility.

- Understand the employee's and the manager's responsibility in the performance assessment phase.

- Understand that the appraisal meeting involves the past, the present, and the future.

- Understand the similarities between performance planning and performance renewal and recontracting.

- Create results- and behavior-oriented performance standards.

Performance management is an ongoing process. Performance management does not take place just once a year. Performance management is a continuous process including several components.[1] These components are closely related to each other, and the poor implementation of any of them has a negative impact on the performance management system as a whole. The components in the performance management process are shown in Figure 1. This chapter provides a brief description of each of these components. Let's start with the prerequisites.

1 PREREQUISITES

There are two important prerequisites that are required before a performance management system is implemented: (1) knowledge of the organization's mission and strategic goals and (2) knowledge of the job in question.[2] Knowledge of the organization's mission and strategic goals is a result of strategic planning (the strategic planning process may take place *after* the mission and vision statements are created; thus, there is a constant interplay between mission and vision and strategic planning). Strategic planning allows an organization to clearly define its purpose or reason for existing, where it wants to be in the future, the goals it wants to achieve, and the strategies it will use to attain these goals. Once the goals for the entire organization have been established, similar goals cascade downward, with departments setting objectives to support the organization's overall mission and objectives. The cascading continues downward until each employee has a set of goals compatible with those of the organization.

Unfortunately, it is often the case that many organizational units are not in tune with the organization's strategic direction. However, there seems to be a trend in the positive direction. For example, a study including public sector organizations in Queensland, Australia, showed a fairly high level of strategic integration of the human resources (HR) function. Specifically, approximately 80% of the organizations that participated in the study were categorized as having achieved the highest level of strategic integration. This level is characterized by a dynamic and multifaceted linkage based on an "integrative relationship between people management and strategic management process."[3] Recall that an important objective of any performance management system is to enhance each employee's contribution to the goals of the organization. If there is a lack

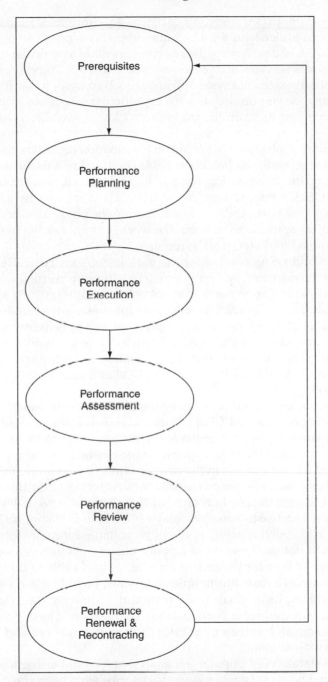

FIGURE 1   **Performance Management Process**

of clarity regarding where the organization wants to go, or if the relationship between the organization's mission and strategies and the unit's mission and strategies is not clear, there will be a lack of clarity regarding what each employee needs to do and achieve to help the organization get there.

The second important prerequisite before a performance management system is implemented is to understand the job in question. This is done through job analysis. Job analysis is a process of determining the key components of a particular job, including activities, tasks, products, services, and processes. A job analysis is a fundamental prerequisite of any performance management system. Without a job analysis, it is difficult to understand what constitutes the required duties for a particular job. If we don't know what an employee is supposed to do on the job, we won't know what needs to be evaluated and how to do so.

As a result of a job analysis, we obtain information regarding the tasks carried out and the knowledge, skills, and abilities (KSAs) required of a particular job. Knowledge includes having the information needed to perform the work, but not necessarily having done it. Skills refer to required attributes that are usually acquired by having done the work in the past. Ability refers to having the physical, emotional, intellectual, and psychological aptitude to perform the work, but neither having done the job nor having been trained to do the work is required.[4]

The tasks and KSAs needed for the various jobs are typically presented in the form of a job description, which summarizes the job duties, needed KSAs, and working conditions for a particular job. As an illustration, see the box "Job Description for Trailer Truck Driver." This job description includes information about what tasks are performed (e.g., operation of a specific type of truck). It also includes information about the needed knowledge (e.g., manifests, bills of lading), skills (e.g., keeping the truck and trailer under control, particularly in difficult weather conditions), and abilities (e.g., physical and spatial abilities needed to turn narrow corners).

Job analysis can be conducted using observation, off-the-shelf questionnaires, or interviews. Data are collected from job incumbents (i.e., those doing the job at present) and their supervisors. Alternatively, if the job is yet to be created, data can be gathered from the individual(s) responsible for creating the new position and those who will supervise individuals in the new position. Observation methods include job analysts watching incumbents do the job, or even trying to do the work themselves, and then producing a description of what they have observed. This method can be subject to biases because job analysts may not be able to distinguish important from unimportant tasks. Such analysis may not be suitable for many jobs. For example, a job analyst could not do the work of a police officer for safety reasons or the work of a software programmer for the lack of knowledge and skills to do the work. Off-the-shelf methods involve distributing questionnaires, including a common list of tasks or KSAs, and asking individuals to fill them out, indicating the extent to which each task or KSA is required for a particular job in question. These generic off-the-shelf tools can be practical, but they might not capture the nuances and idiosyncrasies of jobs out of the mainstream.

Interviews are a very popular job analysis method. During a job analysis interview, the job analyst asks the interviewee to describe what he or she does (or what individuals in the position do) during a typical day at the job from start to finish (i.e., in chronological order). Alternatively, the job analyst can ask the interviewee to describe the major duties involved in the job and then ask him or her to break down these duties into specific tasks. Once a list of tasks has been compiled, all incumbents should have

BOX 1

Job Description for Trailer Truck Driver: Civilian Personnel Management Service, U.S. Department of Defense

Operates gasoline- or diesel-powered truck or truck tractor equipped with two or more driving wheels and with four or more forward speed transmissions, which may include two or more gear ranges. These vehicles are coupled to a trailer or semitrailer by use of a turntable (fifth wheel) or pintle (pivot) hook. Drives over public roads to transport materials, merchandise, or equipment. Performs difficult driving tasks such as backing truck to loading platform, turning narrow corners, negotiating narrow passageways, and keeping truck and trailer under control, particularly on wet or icy highways. May assist in loading and unloading truck. May also handle manifest, bills of lading, expense accounts, and other papers pertinent to the shipment.

an opportunity to review the information and rate each task in terms of frequency and criticality. The frequency and criticality scales may be the following:[5]

Frequency	Criticality
0: not performed	0: not critical
1: every few months to yearly	1: low level of criticality
2: every few weeks to monthly	2: below average level of criticality
3: every few days to weekly	3: average level of criticality
4: every few hours to daily	4: above average level of criticality
5: hourly to many times each hour	5: extremely critical

Rating both frequency and criticality is necessary because some tasks may be performed regularly (e.g., making coffee several times a day) but may not be very critical. The job analyst can then multiply the frequency scores by the criticality scores to obtain an overall score for each task. So, if making coffee receives a frequency score of 4 (i.e., "every few hours to daily") and a criticality score of 0 (i.e., "not critical"), the overall score would be $4 \times 0 = 0$. Considering frequency scores alone would have given us the wrong impression that making coffee is a task that deserved a prominent role in the job description. Overall scores for all tasks can be ranked from highest to lowest to obtain a final list of tasks.

Numerous job analysis questionnaires are available on the Internet. These questionnaires, which can be administered online, with a paper survey or in interview format, can be used for a variety of positions. For example, the state of Delaware uses a job analysis questionnaire available at http://www.delawarepersonnel.com/class/forms/jaq/jaq.shtml or http://www.delawarepersonnel.com/class/forms/jaq/jaq.htm. This questionnaire includes 18 multiple-choice job content questions. Job content information is assessed through three factors: (1) knowledge and skills, (2) problem solving, and (3) accountability and end results. As a second example, the city of

Alexandria, Virginia, uses a job analysis questionnaire available at http://alexandriava.gov/class_comp/job_analysis.html. This instrument does not include multiple-choice questions. Instead, employees answer more general questions about their jobs together with the allocation of the percentage of time employees spend performing each duty. In addition, respondents are encouraged to attach forms, work schedules, reports, memoranda, and other materials that may help explain the responses provided. Conducting a Google search for the phrase "job analysis questionnaire" leads to several other instruments. Be aware that some of these instruments may have been created for specific types of jobs and industries (e.g., service jobs, nonsupervisory jobs). Make sure you check the suitability of the instrument before using it in a different organizational context. Combining items and formats from various instruments already available may be the most effective way to proceed.

An important component of a good job analysis is rater training. In other words, there are several biases that can affect the accuracy of the information provided by individuals regarding KSAs needed for a job.[6] Consider the following biasing factors:

1. *Self-serving bias:* This bias leads people to report that their own behaviors and personality traits are more needed for successful job performance compared to behaviors and personality traits of others. This is because people tend to attribute success to themselves and failure to external causes (i.e., factors outside of their control).
2. *Social projection and false consensus bias:* Social projection bias leads people to believe that others behave similarly to themselves and, hence, lead people to think about themselves when reporting KSAs for their job instead of people in general. False consensus bias is similar in that it leads people to believe that others share the same beliefs and attitudes as themselves.

Taken together, self-serving, social projection, and false consensus biases affect job analysis ratings because they lead people to believe that their own KSAs are those driving success on their jobs. So, these lead to an exaggerated view regarding the KSAs needed—and this exaggeration is based on precisely the KSAs that job incumbents have.

How do we address these biases? A recent experimental study involving two independent samples of 96 administrative support assistants and 95 supervisors working for a large city government implemented a successful Web-based training program that succeeded in mitigating these biases.[7] Specifically, across the five job characteristics rated in that study, individuals who did not participate in the Web-based training program were 62% (administrative support assistants) and 68% (supervisors) more likely to provide a higher rating than if the same individual provided the job analysis ratings after participating in the training program. The Web-based training program, which takes about 15 minutes to administer, provides a common frame of reference for all raters and includes the following five steps:

1. provide raters with a definition of each rating dimension
2. define the scale anchors
3. describe what behaviors were indicative of each dimension
4. allow raters to practice their rating skills, and
5. provide feedback on the practice

The information obtained from a job analysis is used for writing a job description. Writing a job description may seem like a daunting task; however, it does not have to be difficult. Generic job descriptions can be obtained from the Occupational Informational Network (O*NET) (http://online.onetcenter.org/find/). O*NET is a comprehensive database of worker attributes and job characteristics that provides a common language for defining and describing occupations. The descriptions available via O*NET can serve as a foundation for a job description. O*NET descriptions can be easily adapted and changed to accommodate specific local characteristics. For example, see O*NET's generic description for truck drivers in the box "Summary Report for Tractor-Trailer Truck Drivers" (from O*NET). First, the summary description can be checked for accuracy and relevance by supervisors. Then, the list of KSAs provided by O*NET can be readily rated by incumbents (and additional KSAs may be added if needed).

O*NET can also be a very useful resource for small businesses because, for most of them, conducting a job analysis may not be feasible simply because there are not sufficient numbers of people from whom to collect data. In addition, O*NET can be used when organizations expand and new positions are created. One thing needs to be clear, however: jobs change. Thus, job descriptions must be checked for accuracy and updated as needed.

Job descriptions are a key prerequisite for any performance management system because they provide the criteria (i.e., yardsticks) that will be used in measuring performance. Such criteria may concern behaviors (i.e., how to perform) or results (i.e., what outcomes should result from performance). In our truck driver example, a behavioral criterion could involve the skill "equipment maintenance." For example, a supervisor may rate the extent to which the employee "performs routine maintenance on equipment and determines when and what kind of maintenance is needed." Regarding results, these criteria usually fall into one of the following categories: (1) quality, (2) quantity, (3) cost-effectiveness, and (4) timeliness.[8] In the truck driver example, results-oriented criteria can include number of accidents (i.e., quality) and amount of load transported over a specific period of time (i.e., quantity).

Some organizations are becoming aware of the importance of considering prerequisites before implementing a performance management system. Take the case of Deaconess Hospital in Oklahoma City, Oklahoma, which includes a workforce of 650 physicians and a total of 1,400 employees (http://www.deaconessokc.org/). Deaconess Hospital has been able to effectively integrate employees' job descriptions within their performance management system. The need for this integration was reinforced by results from an employee survey revealing that employees did not know what they were being evaluated on. Therefore, with the input of employees, the hospital updated each of the 260 job descriptions. At present, each employee's job description is part of the performance review form. The new forms incorporate task performance standards as well as behaviors specific to individual jobs. For example, a nurse may be evaluated on "how well he or she safely, timely, and respectfully administers patient medication and on his or her planning and organization skills." In addition, Deaconess Hospital has been able to link each employee's performance to the strategy and goals of the organization. Specifically, all employees are rated on the following core behaviors considered to be of top strategic importance for this particular organization: (1) adaptability, (2) building customer loyalty, (3) building trust, and (4) contributing to team success.[9]

Performance Management Process

BOX 2

Summary Report for Tractor-Trailer Truck Drivers (from O*NET)

Description

Drive a tractor-trailer combination or a truck with a capacity of at least 26,000 gross vehicle weight (GVW) to transport and deliver goods, livestock, or materials in liquid, loose, or packaged form. May be required to unload truck. May require use of automated routing equipment. Requires commercial driver's license.

Tasks

- Follow appropriate safety procedures when transporting dangerous goods.
- Check vehicles before driving them to ensure that mechanical, safety, and emergency equipment is in good working order.
- Maintain logs of working hours and of vehicle service and repair status, following applicable state and federal regulations.
- Obtain receipts or signatures when loads are delivered, and collect payment for services when required.
- Check all load-related documentation to ensure that it is complete and accurate.
- Maneuver trucks into loading or unloading positions, following signals from loading crew as needed; check that vehicle position is correct and any special loading equipment is properly positioned.
- Drive trucks with capacities greater than 3 tons, including tractor-trailer combinations, in order to transport and deliver products, livestock, or other materials.
- Secure cargo for transport, using ropes, blocks, chain, binders, and/or covers.
- Read bills of lading to determine assignment details.
- Report vehicle defects, accidents, traffic violations, or damage to the vehicles.

Knowledge

- Transportation—Knowledge of principles and methods for moving people or goods by air, rail, sea, or road, including the relative costs and benefits.
- Public Safety and Security—Knowledge of relevant equipment, policies, procedures, and strategies to promote effective local, state, or national security operations for the protection of people, data, property, and institutions.
- English Language—Knowledge of the structure and content of the English language including the meaning and spelling of words, rules of composition, and grammar.
- Law and Government—Knowledge of laws, legal codes, court procedures, precedents, government regulations, executive orders, agency rules, and the democratic political process.
- Mathematics—Knowledge of arithmetic, algebra, geometry, calculus, statistics, and their applications.

Skills

- Equipment Maintenance—Performing routine maintenance on equipment and determining when and what kind of maintenance is needed.
- Active Listening—Giving full attention to what other people are saying, taking time to understand the points being made, asking questions as appropriate, and not interrupting at inappropriate times.

(continued)

44

Box 2 (*Continued*)

- Time Management—Managing one's own time and the time of others.
- Coordination—Adjusting actions in relation to others' actions.
- Judgment and Decision Making—Considering the relative costs and benefits of potential actions to choose the most appropriate one.
- Reading Comprehension—Understanding written sentences and paragraphs in work-related documents.
- Troubleshooting—Determining causes of operating errors and deciding what to do about it.
- Speaking—Talking to others to convey information effectively.
- Mathematics—Using mathematics to solve problems.
- Critical Thinking—Using logic and reasoning to identify the strengths and weaknesses of alternative solutions, conclusions, or approaches to problems.

Abilities

- Far Vision—The ability to see details at a distance.
- Reaction Time—The ability to quickly respond (with the hand, finger, or foot) to a signal (sound, light, picture) when it appears.
- Static Strength—The ability to exert maximum muscle force to lift, push, pull, or carry objects.
- Response Orientation—The ability to choose quickly between two or more movements in response to two or more different signals (lights, sounds, pictures). It includes the speed with which the correct response is started with the hand, foot, or other body part.
- Spatial Orientation—The ability to know your location in relation to the environment or to know where other objects are in relation to you.
- Near Vision—The ability to see details at close range (within a few feet of the observer).
- Depth Perception—The ability to judge which of several objects is closer or farther away from you, or to judge the distance between you and an object.
- Extent Flexibility—The ability to bend, stretch, twist, or reach with your body, arms, and/or legs.
- Multilimb Coordination—The ability to coordinate two or more limbs (e.g., two arms, two legs, or one leg and one arm) while sitting, standing, or lying down. It does not involve performing the activities while the whole body is in motion.
- Manual Dexterity—The ability to quickly move your hand, your hand together with your arm, or your two hands to grasp, manipulate, or assemble objects.

In summary, there are two important prerequisites that must exist before the implementation of a successful performance management system. First, there is a need to have good knowledge of the organization's mission and strategic goals. This knowledge, combined with knowledge regarding the mission and strategic goals of their unit, allows employees to make contributions that will have a positive impact on the unit and on the organization as a whole. Second, there is a need to have good knowledge of the job in question: what tasks need to be done, how they should be done, and what KSAs are needed. Such knowledge is obtained through a job analysis. If we have good information regarding a job, then it is easier to establish criteria for job success.

2 PERFORMANCE PLANNING

Employees should have a thorough knowledge of the performance management system. In fact, at the beginning of each performance cycle, the supervisor and the employee meet to discuss and agree upon what needs to be done and how it should be done. This performance planning discussion includes a consideration of both results and behaviors as well as a development plan.

2.1 Results

Results refer to what needs to be done or the outcomes an employee must produce. A consideration of results needs to include the *key accountabilities*, or broad areas of a job for which the employee is responsible for producing results. This information is typically obtained from the job description. A discussion of results also includes specific *objectives* that the employee will achieve as part of each accountability. Objectives are statements of important and measurable outcomes. Finally, discussing results also means discussing *performance standards*. A performance standard is a yardstick used to evaluate how well employees have achieved each objective. Performance standards provide information about acceptable and unacceptable performance (e.g., quality, quantity, cost, and time).

Consider the job of university professors. Two key accountabilities are (1) teaching (preparation and delivery of instructional materials to students) and (2) research (creation and dissemination of new knowledge). An objective for teaching could be "to obtain a student evaluation of teaching performance of 3 on a 4-point scale." An objective for research could be "to publish two articles in scholarly refereed journals per year." Performance standards could be "to obtain a student evaluation of teaching performance of at least 2 on a 4-point scale" and "to publish at least one article in scholarly referred journals per year." Thus, the objective is the desired level of performance, whereas the standard is usually a minimum acceptable level of performance.

2.2 Behaviors

Although it is important to measure results, an exclusive emphasis on results can give a skewed or incomplete picture of employee performance. For example, for some jobs it may be difficult to establish precise objectives and standards. For other jobs, employees may have control over how they do their jobs but not over the results of their behaviors. For example, the sales figures of a salesperson could be affected more by the assigned sales territory than by the salesperson's ability and performance. Behaviors, or how a job is done, thus constitute an important component of the planning phase. This is probably why results from a survey indicated that, in addition to sales figures, salespeople would like to be appraised on such behavioral criteria as communications skills and product knowledge.[10]

A consideration of behaviors includes discussing *competencies*, which are measurable clusters of KSAs that are critical in determining how results will be achieved. Examples of competencies are customer service, written or oral communication, creative thinking, and dependability. Returning to the example of the professor, assume that teaching is done online and numerous technology-related problems exist, so that

---

BOX 3

Performance Planning at Discover

At Discover (http://www.discoverfinancial.com/data/corporate/), steps are being taken to ensure that performance planning and employee development support the organization's business goals. Discover Financial Services is a business unit of Morgan Stanley, and operates the Discover® Card brands. The business offers a variety of cards including the Discover Classic Card, the Discover Gold Card, the Discover Platinum Card, the Miles Card from Discover Card, and an array of affinity cards. Additional services include Discover CDs and Money Market Accounts, auto insurance, and home loans. Discover is headquartered in Riverwoods, Illinois, and employs approximately 14,000 people. Discover has initiated an approach that addresses the development needs of specific business units by assigning human resources professionals to attend business meetings regularly to gain an understanding of what knowledge, skills, and abilities are required. The company asks managers to go through the same curriculum with classroom and online learning opportunities. These managers form discussion groups to discuss what they've learned and how it applies to the challenges of their specific role. In addition, part of the strategy includes meeting with employees to agree upon metrics in the performance planning stage, creating an action plan, and following up with evaluations and ratings to determine to what degree the learning experience was successful. In summary, Discover utilizes the various stages of the performance management process to ensure that employee development is a focus that matches the mission of providing a workplace that supports high performance.[11]

---

the resulting teaching evaluations are deficient (i.e., lower than the standard of 2). This is an example of a situation in which behaviors should be given more importance than results. In this situation, the evaluation could include competencies such as online communication skills (e.g., in the chat room).

2.3 Development Plan

An important step before the review cycle begins is for the supervisor and employee to agree on a development plan. At a minimum, this plan should include identifying areas that need improvement and setting goals to be achieved in each area. Development plans usually include both results and behaviors.

In summary, performance planning includes the consideration of results and behaviors and the development plan. A discussion of results needs to include key accountabilities (i.e., broad areas for which an employee is responsible), specific objectives for each key accountability (i.e., goals to be reached), and performance standards (i.e., what constitutes acceptable and unacceptable levels of performance). A discussion of behaviors needs to include competencies (i.e., clusters of KSAs). Finally, the development plan includes a description of areas that need improving and goals to be achieved in each area.

Once the prerequisites are met and the planning phase has been completed, we are ready to begin the implementation of the performance management system. This includes performance execution, assessment, review, and renewal and recontracting.

3 PERFORMANCE EXECUTION

Once the review cycle begins, the employee strives to produce the results and display the behaviors agreed upon earlier as well as to work on developmental needs. The employee has primary responsibility and ownership of this process. Employee participation does not begin at the performance execution stage, however. As noted earlier, employees need to have active input in the development of job descriptions, performance standards, and the creation of the rating form. In addition, at later stages, employees are active participants in the evaluation process in that they provide a self-assessment and the performance review interview is a two-way communication process. At the performance execution stage, the following factors must be present:[12]

1. *Commitment to goal achievement.* The employee must be committed to the goals that were set. One way to enhance commitment is to allow the employee to be an active participant in the process of setting the goals.

2. *Ongoing performance feedback and coaching.* The employee should not wait until the review cycle is over to solicit performance feedback. Also, the employee should not wait until a serious problem develops to ask for coaching. The employee needs to take a proactive role in soliciting performance feedback and coaching from her supervisor.[13]

3. *Communication with supervisor.* Supervisors are busy with multiple obligations. The burden is on the employee to communicate openly and regularly with the supervisor.

4. *Collecting and sharing performance data.* The employee should provide the supervisor with regular updates on progress toward goal achievement, in terms of both behaviors and results.

5. *Preparing for performance reviews.* The employee should not wait until the end of the review cycle approaches to prepare for the review. On the contrary, the employee should engage in an ongoing and realistic self-appraisal so that immediate corrective action can be taken if necessary. The usefulness of the self-appraisal process can be enhanced by gathering informal performance information from peers and customers (both internal and external).

Although the employee has primary responsibilities for performance execution, the supervisor also needs to do his or her share of the work. In fact, monitoring the performance of colleagues has been identified as a key competency by the Management Standards Centre (www.management-standards.com, Unit B5). Supervisors have primary responsibility over the following issues:[14]

1. *Observation and documentation.* Supervisors must observe and document performance on a daily basis. It is important to keep track of examples of both good and poor performance.

2. *Updates.* As the organization's goals may change, it is important to update and revise initial objectives, standards, and key accountabilities (in the case of results) and competency areas (in the case of behaviors).

3. *Feedback.* Feedback on progression toward goals and coaching to improve performance should be provided on a regular basis certainly before the review cycle is over.

TABLE 1	Performance Execution Stage: Areas for Which Employees and Managers Have Primary Responsibility

Employees	Managers
Commitment to goal achievement	Observation and documentation
Ongoing performance feedback and coaching	Updates
Communication with supervisor	Feedback
Collecting and sharing performance data	Resources
Preparing for performance reviews	Reinforcement

4. *Resources.* Supervisors should provide employees with resources and opportunities to participate in developmental activities. Thus, they should encourage (and sponsor) participation in training, classes, and special assignments. Overall, supervisors have a responsibility to ensure that the employee has the necessary supplies and funding to perform the job properly.

5. *Reinforcement.* Supervisors must let employees know that their outstanding performance is noticed by reinforcing effective behaviors and progress toward goals. Also, supervisors should provide feedback regarding negative performance and how to remedy the observed problem. Observation and communication are not sufficient. Performance problems must be diagnosed early, and appropriate steps must be taken as soon as the problem is discovered.

The summary list included in Table 1 makes it clear that both the employee and the manager are responsible for performance execution. As an example of this shared responsibility in an actual organization, consider the case of Lockheed Martin Corporation. Lockheed Martin Corporation, an advanced technology company, was formed in March 1995 with the merger of two of the world's premier technology companies: Lockheed Corporation and Martin Marietta Corporation. Lockheed Martin has approximately 140,000 employees worldwide. They are engaged in the research, design, development, manufacture, and integration of advanced technology systems, products, and services (www.lockheedmartin.com). Lockheed Martin's performance management system includes the active participation of both employees and their supervisors. Specifically, employees write their own performance management objectives based on organization and unit objectives. Then, managers approve the objectives and are encouraged to give ongoing feedback about the progress toward meeting the objectives. The actual performance appraisal form is an electronic, one-page computer screen. The program was designed to "involve employees in setting their own goals, to make those goals clear and to provide regular feedback on their progress toward achieving those goals."[15]

4 PERFORMANCE ASSESSMENT

In the assessment phase, both the employee and the manager are responsible for evaluating the extent to which the desired behaviors have been displayed, and whether the desired results have been achieved. Although many sources can be used to collect performance information (e.g., peers, subordinates), in most cases the direct supervisor provides the information. This also includes an evaluation of the extent to which the goals stated in the development plan have been achieved.

It is important that both the employee and the manager take ownership of the assessment process. The manager fills out her appraisal form, and the employee should also fill out his form. The fact that both parties are involved in the assessment provides good information to be used in the review phase. When both the employee and the supervisor are active participants in the evaluation process, there is a greater likelihood that the information will be used productively in the future. Specifically, the inclusion of self-ratings helps emphasize possible discrepancies between self-views and the views that important others (i.e., supervisors) have of our behavior. It is the discrepancy between these two views that is most likely to trigger development efforts, particularly when feedback from the supervisor is more negative than are employee self-evaluations.[16]

The inclusion of self-appraisals is also beneficial regarding important additional factors. Self-appraisals can reduce an employee's defensiveness during an appraisal meeting and increase the employee's satisfaction with the performance management system as well as enhance perceptions of accuracy and fairness and therefore acceptance of the system.[17] This point is addressed in more detail in later chapters.

In sum, both the employee and the supervisor must evaluate employee performance. Employee involvement in the process increases employee ownership and commitment to the system. In addition, it provides important information to be discussed during the performance review, which is discussed next.

5 PERFORMANCE REVIEW

The performance review stage involves the meeting between the employee and the manager to review their assessments. This meeting is usually called the *appraisal meeting* or *discussion*. The appraisal meeting is important because it provides a formal setting in which the employee receives feedback on his or her performance. In spite of its importance in performance management, the appraisal meeting is often regarded as the "Achilles' heel of the entire process."[18] This is because many managers are uncomfortable providing performance feedback, particularly when performance is deficient.[19] This high level of discomfort, which often translates into anxiety and the avoidance of the appraisal interview, can be mitigated through training those responsible for providing feedback. Providing feedback in an effective manner is extremely important because it leads not only to performance improvement but also to employee satisfaction with the system. For example, a study involving more than 200 teachers in Malaysia, including individuals with distinct Chinese, Malay, and Indian cultural backgrounds, found that when they received effective feedback, they reported greater satisfaction with the system even when they received low performance ratings.[20] At this point, however, let's emphasize that people are apprehensive about both receiving *and* giving performance information, and this apprehension reinforces the importance of a formal performance review as part of any performance management system.[21] For example, Jack Welch, former CEO of GE, has addressed this issue in many of his public appearances since he retired.[22] At an appearance in front of an audience of about 2,000 managers, he asked them if their organizations had integrity. As was expected, a vast majority of managers, about 95%, raised their hands. Then, he asked the same audience if their organization's leaders provide subordinates with honest and straightforward performance feedback. Only

---

BOX 4

Performance Assessment at ENSR

ENSR (http://www.ensr.aecom.com) is a full-service global provider of environmental and energy development services to industry and government. ENSR's 2,000 professionals provide clients with consulting, engineering, remediation, and related services from more than 70 worldwide locations, including 45 in the United States. ENSR has created and utilizes a scorecard with six categories that are directly linked to its five-year vision: health and safety, employee engagement, client loyalty, cost management, profitability, and revenue growth. This information is used in the company's evaluation of current performance for individuals and groups with a scorecard that shows current performance against "average" internal performance and "top 25 percent performance." Managers are expected to utilize the scorecard in discussions about performance and to discuss the relationship between the metrics and the directives and initiatives from senior management. The scorecard is a tool used to motivate employees to achieve top performance and to provide a clear link between each individual and team activity to the strategic objectives of the organization. In summary, ENSR utilizes a balanced scorecard tool to assist managers in assessing and reviewing performance and ensuring a close link to the objectives of the organization.[23]

---

about 5% of the people raised their hands. Avoiding giving negative feedback is very dangerous because it conveys the message that mediocrity is acceptable and damages the morale of the top performers who are about four times as productive as the poor performers.

In most cases, the appraisal meeting is regarded as a review of the past, that is, what was done (i.e., results) and how it was done (i.e., behaviors). For example, a survey including more than 150 organizations in Scotland showed that performance management systems in more than 80% of organizations emphasize the past.[24] The appraisal meeting should also include a discussion of the employee's developmental progress as well as plans for the future. The conversation should include a discussion of goals and development plans that the employee will be expected to achieve over the period before the next review session. In addition, a good appraisal meeting includes information on what new compensation, if any, the employee may be receiving as a result of his performance. In short, the appraisal discussion focuses on the past (what has been done and how), the present (what compensation is received or denied as a result), and the future (goals to be attained before the upcoming review session).

As noted earlier, the discussion about past performance can be challenging, particularly when performance levels have not reached acceptable levels. Following is a script reflecting what the first few seconds of the appraisal meeting can be like.[25]

> Good afternoon, Lucy, please have seat. As you know, we take performance very seriously, and we scheduled our meeting today to talk about the work you have done over the past year. Because we believe in the importance of talking about performance issues, I blocked an hour of my time during which I won't take any phone calls and I also won't be texting or emailing with anyone. I want to be able to focus 100% on our conversation because talking

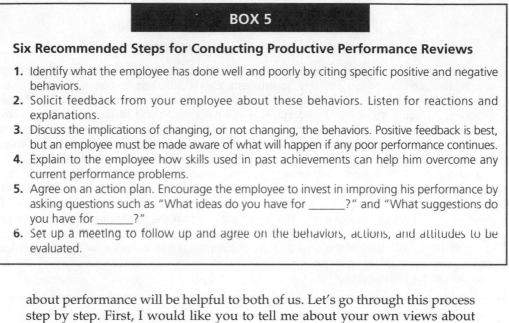

about performance will be helpful to both of us. Let's go through this process step by step. First, I would like you to tell me about your own views about your performance during the past year. Specifically, please share with me the things you believe you did particularly well and areas in which you think you may have been able to do better. As a second step, I will tell you about the performance evaluation I prepared. As a third step, we will talk about the issues on which you and I agree. As a fourth step, we can talk about issues for which we may have different perspectives. I will explain the reasoning behind my views and I want to hear the reasoning behind yours. In terms of my evaluation of your work, I want to first make sure we agree on the specific goals and objectives of your job. Then, we will talk about the results you achieved this year and the section on the evaluation form about job skills and competencies. After we talk about that, I will tell you what my overall rating is and why I believe this is an appropriate score. Ok, let's go ahead and start. Please tell me about how things went this past year.

Consider the centrality of the performance review stage in the performance management process by reading the box "Six Recommended Steps for Conducting Productive Performance Reviews."[26]

6 PERFORMANCE RENEWAL AND RECONTRACTING

The final stage in the performance process is renewal and recontracting. Essentially, this is identical to the performance planning component. The main difference is that the renewal and recontracting stage uses the insights and information gained from the other phases. For example, some of the goals may have been set unrealistically high given an unexpected economic downturn. This would lead to setting less ambitious goals for the upcoming review period.

The performance management process includes a cycle which starts with prerequisites and ends with performance renewal and recontracting. The cycle is not over after the renewal and recontracting stage. In fact, the process starts all over again: there needs to be a discussion of prerequisites, including the organization's mission and strategic goals and the job's KSAs. Because markets change, customers' preferences and needs change, and products change, there is a need to continuously monitor the prerequisites so that performance planning and all the subsequent stages are consistent with the organization's strategic objectives. Recall that, in the end, one of the main goals of any performance management system is to promote the achievement of organization-wide goals. Obviously, if managers and employees are not aware of these strategic goals, it is unlikely that the performance management system will be instrumental in accomplishing the strategic goals.

Summary Points

- Performance management is an ongoing process. It never ends. Once established in an organization, it becomes part of an organization's culture. The performance management process includes six closely related components: (1) prerequisites, (2) performance planning, (3) performance execution, (4) performance assessment, (5) performance review, and (6) performance renewal and recontracting.

- Job analysis can be conducted using interviews, observation, or off-the-shelf questionnaires. It is important to train individuals to fill out job analysis instruments so as to minimize biases (i.e., self-serving bias, social projection, and false consensus) in the resulting ratings. Once a list of tasks has been compiled, all incumbents should have an opportunity to review the information and rate each task in terms of its frequency and criticality.

- Each of the six components of the performance management process plays an important role. If any of these components is implemented poorly, then the entire performance management system suffers. For example, the lack of knowledge of the organization's mission and strategic goals and the job in question (i.e., prerequisites) will not allow performance planning (i.e., performance road map) to be aligned with organizational goals, which in turn will lead to poor performance execution. In short, a performance management system is only as good as its weakest component.

- The links between the various components must be clearly established. For example, performance planning needs to be closely related to performance execution. Performance planning is a futile exercise if execution does not follow from it. The same applies to all the arrows linking the various components, as shown in Figure 1.

- The first component of the performance management process involves two prerequisites. First, there is a need to have good knowledge of the organization's mission and strategic goals. This knowledge, combined with knowledge regarding the mission and strategic goals of one's unit, allows employees to make contributions that will have a positive impact on their units and on the organization as a whole. Second, there is a need to have good knowledge of the job in question. A job analysis allows for the determination of the key components of a particular job: what tasks need to be done, how they should be done, and what KSAs are needed. If we have good information regarding a job, then it is easier to establish criteria for job success.

- The second component of the performance management process involves performance planning. Performance planning includes the consideration of results and behavior as well as a development plan. A discussion of results needs to include key accountabilities (i.e., broad areas for which an employee is responsible), specific objectives for each key accountability (i.e., goals to be reached), and performance standards (i.e., what are acceptable and unacceptable levels of performance). A discussion of behaviors needs to include competencies (i.e., clusters of KSAs). Finally, the development plan includes a description of areas that need improvement and goals to be achieved in each area.

- The third component involves performance execution. Both the employee and the manager are responsible for performance execution. For example, the employee needs to be committed to goal achievement and should take a proactive role in seeking feedback from his or her supervisor. The burden is on the employee to communicate openly and regularly with the supervisor. Also, the employee has a responsibility to be prepared for the performance review by conducting regular and realistic self-appraisals. On the other hand, the supervisor also has important responsibilities. These include observing and documenting performance, updating the employee on any changes in the

goals of the organization, and providing resources and reinforcement so that the employee can succeed and continue to be motivated.

- The fourth component involves performance assessment. Both the employee and the supervisor must evaluate employee performance. Involvement of the employee in the process increases his or her ownership and commitment to the system. In addition, it provides important information to be discussed during the performance review. In the absence of self-appraisals, it is often not clear to supervisors if employees have a real understanding of what is expected of them.

- The fifth component involves performance review when the employee and manager meet to discuss employee performance. This meeting is usually called the appraisal meeting. This meeting typically emphasizes the past: what the employee has done and how it was done. An effective appraisal meeting also focuses on the present and the future. The present involves the changes in compensation that may result from the results obtained. The future involves a discussion of goals and development plans that the employee will be expected to achieve during the period before the next review session.

- The final component involves performance renewal and recontracting. Although this component is identical to the performance planning stage, this component uses information gathered during the review period to make adjustments as needed. For example, some new key accountabilities and competencies may be included. Conversely, some goals may have to be adjusted either upward or downward.

CASE STUDY 1

Job Analysis Exercise

Please conduct a job analysis for the position "graduate student enrolled in a master's program in the general field of business." This job analysis may benefit from interviewing incumbents (i.e., other students) as well as supervisors (i.e., faculty). In addition, of course, you can rely on your own knowledge of the "job." By the end of your job analysis, follow the O*NET format to create a summary description for the position as well as a list of tasks, knowledge, skills, and abilities needed for successful performance. Use the box "Summary Report for Tractor-Trailer Truck Drivers (from O*NET)" as a template.

Your job description should include four lists—one for tasks, one for knowledge, one for skills, and one for abilities. For each of the four lists, rate the corresponding elements in terms of frequency and criticality. Use the scales provided below to rate each element. Then, multiply the frequency and criticality scores for each of the elements in each list to obtain its overall score. Then, arrange the list of elements in order of importance from high to low.

Have one or more people (who are knowledgeable about the position "graduate student enrolled in a master's program

Frequency and Criticality Scales

Frequency	Criticality
0: not performed	0: not critical
1: every few months to yearly	1: low level of criticality
2: every few weeks to monthly	2: below average level of criticality
3: every few days to weekly	3: average level of criticality
4: every few hours to daily	4: above average level of criticality
5: hourly to many times each hour	5: extremely critical

in the general field of business) do the same rating task with the same job description. Then, answer the following questions.

1. Are there any disagreements between or among the resulting orderings? If so, why do you think that is the case?
2. What can be done to mitigate any observed disagreement between or among the resulting orderings? After discussing some possible techniques to reducing disagreement, if there were indeed any disagreements, apply some of those techniques until 100% agreement is reached.

3. Recall that tasks listed in a job description can largely be divided into behaviors (i.e. how to perform) and results (i.e. what outcomes should result from performance). In the job description you created, which of the tasks are behaviors and which tasks are outcomes? Are there more behaviors or more outcomes? Or, is there a strong balance between the two types of tasks? Whether there is such an imbalance or balance, do you think the observed (im)balance is justified? Explain. ■

CASE STUDY 2

Disrupted Links in the Performance Management Process at "Omega, Inc."

Omega, Inc., is a small manufacturing company whose sales success or failure rests in the hands of sales representatives employed by franchised dealers operating independently.

Omega faces a challenging situation because it does not have control over the people working for the independent dealerships. It is the performance of these individuals that dictates

Omega's sales success. To make things more complicated, until recently there was no clear understanding of the role of the sales representatives and there were no formal sales processes in place. Sales representatives varied greatly in terms of their level of skill and knowledge; most put out little effort beyond taking orders, and they did not feel motivated to make additional sales. Finally, franchises varied greatly regarding their management strategies and follow-up with Omega.

Recently, understanding the need to improve the performance of sales representatives, Omega agreed to partially fund and support a training program for them. The network of franchise owners in turn agreed to work together to implement a performance management system. As a first step in creating the performance management system, the franchise owners conducted a job analysis of the role of the sale representatives, wrote a job description, and distributed it to all sales representatives. The franchise owners also adopted a franchise-wide mission statement based primarily on the need to provide high-quality customer service. This mission statement was posted in all franchise offices, and each franchise owner spoke with his employees about the contribution made by individual sales on achieving their mission. As a second step, the managers set performance goals (i.e., sales quotas) for each employee. Then, all sales representatives attended extensive training sessions. The employees received feedback based on their performance in the training course and then were reminded once again of their sales quotas.

Back on the job, managers gave feedback to their employees regarding their standing in relation to their sales quotas. Since the employees had no way of monitoring their own progress toward their quotas, the performance feedback consisted of little more than a reiteration of monthly sales goals. There was no performance appraisal form in place, so

discussions were not documented. This lack of feedback continued, and although sales quotas were being met for the first few months, franchise owners received complaints from customers about the low quality of customer service they were receiving. Subsequently, sales began to decline. Furthermore, many orders were often incorrect, forcing customers to return items to Omega.

While the new performance management process was an improvement over no performance management (at least initially), the franchise owners were still far from having a system that included a smooth transition between each of the components of the performance management process. Based on Omega's situation, please answer the following questions.

1. Consider each of the links of the performance management process as shown in Figure 1:
   a. prerequisites → performance planning
   b. performance planning → performance execution
   c. performance execution → performance assessment
   d. performance assessment → performance review
   e. performance review → performance renewal and recontracting
   f. performance renewal and recontracting → prerequisites

   Discuss whether each of the links is present, and in what form, in the performance management system described.
2. Given your answers to question 1, what can be done to fix each of the disrupted links in the process?

Source: This case study is loosely based on J. Swinney and B. Couch, Sales Performance Improvement Getting Results Through a Franchise Sales Organization. International Society for Performance Improvement Case Studies (2003). Available online at http://www.ispi.org/services/gotResults/2003/GotResults_Swinney.pdf. Retrieval date: March 6, 2007.

CASE STUDY 3

Performance Management at the University of Ghana

The University of Ghana in Legon, Ghana, was established in 1948 as an affiliate college of the University of London called University College of the Gold Coast. In 1961, the university was reorganized by an act of Parliament into what it is today: the independent, degree-granting University of Ghana (http://www.ug.edu.gh/).

The Balme Library is the main library in the University of Ghana library system. Situated on the main Legon campus, it coordinates a large number of libraries attached to the university's various schools, institutes, faculties, departments, and halls of residence, most of which are autonomous. The

library was started as the College Library in 1948 and was then situated in Achimota College, which was about 8 kilometers from the present Legon campus. In 1959, the College Library moved into its brand-new buildings at the Legon campus and was named after the University College of the Gold Coast's first principal, David Mowbrary Balme.

As in the case of many other modern university libraries worldwide that face resources challenges and the need to serve an increasingly diverse customer base, the Balme Library has implemented numerous initiatives. One such initiative is a performance management system. However, several of the components of the performance management process at the Balme Library are in need of improvement. First, there is no evidence that a systematic job analysis was conducted for any of the jobs at the library. Second, the forms that the employees are rated on contain vague items such as "general behavior." The forms include no specific definition of what "general behavior" is or examples explaining to employees (or managers) what would lead to a high or a low rating in this category. In addition, all library employees are rated on the same form, regardless of their job responsibilities. Third, there is no evidence that managers have worked with employees in setting mutually agreed-upon goals. Fourth, there is no formal or informal discussion of results and needed follow-up steps after the subordinates and managers complete their form. Not surprisingly, an employee survey revealed that more than 60% of the employees have never discussed their performance with their managers. Finally, employees are often rated by different people. For example, sometimes the head of the library rates

an employee, even though he may not be in direct contact with that employee.

Based on the above description, please answer the following questions.

1. Please identify one component in the performance management process at the Balme Library that has not been implemented effectively (there are several; choose only one).
2. Describe how the poor implementation of the specific component you have chosen has a negative impact on the flow of the performance management process as a whole.
3. Discuss what should be done to improve the implementation of the component you have chosen in question 1.

Source: This case study is loosely based on Martey, A. K. (2002). "Appraising the performance of library staff in a Ghanaian Academic Library." *Library Management, 23,* 403–416. ∎

End notes

1. The general framework and labels for these components are based on Grote, D. (1996). The performance management system. In *The complete guide to performance appraisal.* New York: American Management Association.
2. Aguinis, H. (2009). An expanded view of performance management. In J. W. Smither and M. London (Eds.), *Performance management: Putting research into practice* (pp. 1–43). San Francisco, CA: Wiley.
3. Teo, S. (2000). Evidence of strategic HRM linkages in eleven Australian corporatized public sector organizations. *Public Personnel Management, 29,* 557–574.
4. Clifford, J. P. (1994). Job analysis: Why do it, and how should it be done? *Public Personnel Management, 23,* 321–340.
5. Rodriguez, D., Patel, R., Bright, A., Gregory, D., & Gowing, M. K. (2002). Developing competency models to promote integrated human-resource practices. *Human Resource Management, 41,* 309–324.
6. Aguinis, H., Mazurkiewicz, M. D., & Heggestad, E. D. (2009). Using web-based frame-of-reference training to decrease biases in personality-based job analysis: An experimental field study. *Personnel Psychology, 62,* 405–438.
7. Aguinis, H., Mazurkiewicz, M. D., & Heggestad, E. D. (2009). Using web-based frame-of-reference training to decrease biases in personality-based job analysis: An experimental field study. *Personnel Psychology, 62,* 405–438.
8. Banner, D. K., & Graber, J. M. (1985). Critical issues in performance appraisal. *Journal of Management Development, 4,* 27–35.
9. Erickson, P. B. (2002, March 24). Performance feedback boosts employee morale, experts in Oklahoma City say. *The Daily Oklahoman,* OK-Worker-Reviews section.
10. Pettijohn, L. S., Parker, R. S., Pettijohn, C. E., & Kent, J. L. (2001). Performance appraisals: Usage, criteria and observations. *Journal of Management Development, 20,* 754–781.
11. Whitney, K. (2005, August). Discover: It pays to develop leaders. *Chief Learning Officer,* 48.
12. Grote, D. (1996). *The complete guide to performance appraisal* (pp. 22–24). New York: American Management Association.
13. VandeWalle, D., Ganesan, S., Challagalla, G. N., & Brown, S. P. (2000). An integrated model of feedback-seeking behavior: Disposition, context, and cognition. *Journal of Applied Psychology, 85,* 996–1003.

14. Grote, D. (1996). *The complete guide to performance appraisal* (pp. 27–32). New York: American Management Association.

15. The best appraisals of workers can be simple; objectivity, feedback are important features. (2003, December 14). *The Baltimore Sun*, p. D6.

16. Brutus, S., London, M., & Martineau, J. (1999). The impact of 360-degree feedback on planning for career development. *Journal of Management Development, 18,* 676–693.

17. Shore, T. H., Adams, J. S., & Tashchian, A. (1998). Effects of self-appraisal information, appraisal purpose, and feedback target on performance appraisal ratings. *Journal of Business and Psychology, 12,* 283–298.

18. Kikoski, J. F. (1999). Effective communication in the performance appraisal interview: Face-to-face communication for public managers in the culturally diverse workplace. *Public Personnel Management, 28,* 301–322.

19. Ghorpade, J., & Chen, M. M. (1995). Creating quality-driven performance appraisal systems. *Academy of Management Executive, 9,* 32–39.

20. Rahman, S. A. (2006). Attitudes of Malaysian teachers toward a performance-appraisal system. *Journal of Applied Social Psychology, 36,* 3031–3042.

21. London, M. (2003). *Job feedback: Giving, seeking, and using feedback for performance improvement* (2nd ed.) Mahwah, NJ: Lawrence Erlbaum.

22. Rogers, B. (2006). High performance is more than a dream—it's a culture. *T+D, 60*(1), 12.

23. LaChance, S. (2006). Applying the balanced scorecard. *Strategic HR Review, 5*(2), 5.

24. Soltani, E. (2003). Towards a TQM-driven HR performance evaluation: An empirical study. *Employee Relations, 25,* 347–370.

25. This material is based on Grote, D. (1998). Painless performance appraisals focus on results, behaviors. *HR Magazine, 43*(11), 52–56.

26. Grossman, J. H., & Parkinson, J. R. (2002). *Becoming a successful manager: How to make a smooth transition from managing yourself to managing others* (pp. 142–145). Chicago: McGraw-Hill Professional.

Performance Management and Strategic Planning

> *Strategy is a style of thinking, a conscious and deliberate process, an intensive implementation system, the science of insuring future success.*
>
> —PETE JOHNSON

LEARNING OBJECTIVES

By the end of this chapter, you will be able to do the following:

- Define strategic planning and its overall goal.
- Describe the various specific purposes of a strategic plan.
- Explain why the usefulness of a performance management system relies to a large degree on its relationship with the organization's and the unit's strategic plans.
- Understand how to create an organization's strategic plan, including an environmental analysis resulting in a mission statement, vision statement, goals, and strategies.
- Conduct an environmental analysis that includes a consideration of both internal (strengths and weaknesses) and external (opportunities and threats) trends.
- Understand how a gap analysis resulting from a consideration of internal and external trends dictates an organization's mission.
- Define the concept of a mission statement and describe the necessary components of a good mission statement.
- Define the concept of a vision statement and understand its relationship to the mission statement.

From Chapter 3 of *Performance Management*, Third Edition. Herman Aguinis. Copyright © 2013 by Pearson Education, Inc. All rights reserved.

- Describe the basic components of a good vision statement.

- Create organizational- and unit-level mission and vision statements.

- Understand the relationship between mission and vision statements, goals, and strategies.

- Understand the relationship between an organization's vision, mission, goals, and strategies and the vision, mission, goals, and strategies of each of its divisions or units.

- Understand the relationship between a unit's vision, mission, goals, and strategies and individual job descriptions.

- Explain why job descriptions must be linked to the organization's and the unit's strategic plans.

- Understand how a strategic plan determines various choices regarding performance management system design.

- Explain why a consideration of strategic issues is a building block for creating support for a performance management system.

Good performance management systems encourage employees to make tangible and important contributions toward the organization's strategic objectives. When these contributions to the top organizational and unit priorities are made clear, performance management systems are likely to receive crucial top management support. Without this support, it is unlikely that a performance management system will be successful. How, then, are these strategic organizational objectives identified? How does an organization know what the "target" should be, what it is trying to accomplish, and how to do it? These questions are answered by considering an organization's strategic plan.

1 DEFINITION AND PURPOSES OF STRATEGIC PLANNING

Strategic planning is a process that involves describing the organization's destination, assessing barriers that stand in the way of that destination, and selecting approaches for moving forward. The main goal of strategic planning is to allocate resources in a way that provides organizations with a competitive advantage.[1] Overall, a strategic plan serves as a blueprint that defines how the organization will allocate its resources in pursuit of its goals.

Strategic planning serves the following purposes: First and foremost, strategic planning allows organizations to define their identities. In other words, it provides organizations with a clearer sense of who they are and what their purposes are. Second, strategic planning helps organizations prepare for the future because it clarifies the desired destination. Knowing where the organization wants to go is a key first step in planning how to get there. Third, strategic planning allows organizations to analyze their environment, and doing so enhances their ability to adapt to environmental changes and even anticipate future changes. Although knowledge of the environment does not guarantee that an organization will be more likely to change and adapt, knowledge is the first step toward possible adaptation. Fourth, strategic planning provides organizations with focus and allows them to allocate resources to what matters most.

TABLE 1	Strategic Plan: Purposes
Helps define the organization's identity	
Helps organizations prepare the future	
Enhances ability to adapt to environmental changes	
Provides focus and allows better allocation of resources	
Produces an organizational culture of cooperation	
Allows for the consideration of new options and opportunities	
Provides employees with information to direct daily activities	

In turn, the improved allocation of resources is likely to stimulate growth and improve profitability. Fifth, strategic planning can produce a culture of cooperation within the organization given that a common set of goals is created. Such a culture of cooperation can gain organizations a key competitive advantage. Sixth, strategic planning can be a good corporate eye-opener because it generates new options and opportunities to be considered. New opportunities to be considered may include expanding to new markets or offering new products. Finally, strategic planning can be a powerful tool to guide employees' daily activities because it identifies the behaviors and results that really matter. A strategic plan provides critical information to be used in the performance management system. To summarize, Table 1 lists key purposes of a strategic plan.

2 PROCESS OF LINKING PERFORMANCE MANAGEMENT TO THE STRATEGIC PLAN

The mere presence of a strategic plan does not guarantee that this information will be used effectively as part of the performance management system. In fact, countless organizations spend thousands of hours creating strategic plans that lead to no tangible actions. Many organizations spend too much time and effort crafting their mission and vision statements without undertaking any concrete follow-up actions. The process then ends up being a huge waste of time and a source of frustration and long-lasting cynicism. For example, consider a recent study including more than 350 individuals in firms in India in the following eight sectors: textiles, staple fiber, chemicals, cement, insulators, aluminum, mining, and services. Examples of companies included in this study are Grasim Cement, Jayashree Textiles, Birla NGK Insulators, Essel Mining Industries, and INDAL (Indian Aluminum Industries). Results indicated that although there was a good strategic planning process in place in most firms, there was no clear relationship between firm-level and individual-level goals.[2] Thus, to ensure that strategy cascades down the organization and leads to concrete actions, a conscious effort must be made to link the strategic plan with individual performance.

Figure 1 provides a useful framework for understanding the relationship among an organization's strategic plan, a unit's strategic plan, job descriptions, and individual and team performance. The organization's strategic plan includes a mission statement and a vision statement as well as goals and strategies that will allow for the fulfillment of the mission and vision. The strategies are created with the participation of managers at all

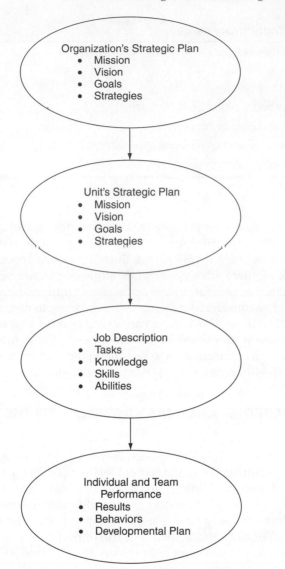

FIGURE 1 Link Among Organization and Unit Strategic Plans, Job Descriptions, and Individual and Team Performance

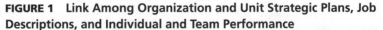

levels. The higher the level of involvement, the more likely it is that managers will see the resulting strategies favorably.[3] As soon as the organizational strategies have been defined, senior management proceeds to meet with department or unit managers, who in turn solicit input from all people within their units to create unit-level mission and vision statements, goals, and strategies. A critical issue is to ensure that each unit's or department's mission and vision statements, goals, and strategies are consistent with those at the organizational level. Job descriptions are then revised to make sure they are consistent with unit and organizational priorities. Finally, the performance management system includes results, behaviors, and developmental plans consistent with the organizational- and department-level priorities as well as the individual job descriptions.

Does the process of aligning organizational, unit, and individual priorities actually work in practice? Is this doable? The answer to these questions is "yes" and the benefits of doing so are widely documented. Performance management systems have a critical role in translating strategy into action.[4] In fact, a recent study including 338 organizations in 42 countries found that performance management is the third most important factor affecting the success of a strategic plan. This is particularly true for larger organizations and for organizations that operate in rapidly changing environments.

As a concrete example, consider the case of Key Bank USA, a financial services company with assets of $92 billion that provides investment management, retail and commercial banking, consumer finance, and investment banking products and services. Key Bank of Utah successfully developed a performance management system that is aligned with the strategic plan of the organization.[5] To do this, the bank first involved managers at all hierarchical levels to develop an organization mission statement. Next, it developed goals and strategies that would help achieve Key Bank's mission. The mission statement, goals, and strategies at the organizational level served as the foundation for developing the strategies for individual departments and units. To develop these, senior managers met with each department manager to discuss the organization's goals and strategies and to explain the importance of having similar items in place in each department. Subsequently, each of the departmental managers met with his or her employees to develop the department's mission statement and goals. One important premise in this exercise was that each department's mission statement and objectives had to be aligned with the corporate mission statement, goals, and strategies. After organizational and departmental goals and strategies were aligned, managers and employees reviewed individual job descriptions. Each job description was tailored so that individual job responsibilities were clear and contributed to meeting the department's and the organization's objectives. Involving employees in this process helped them to gain a clear understanding of how their performance affected the department and, in turn, the organization.

Finally, based on the key responsibilities identified, the performance management system included behaviors, results, and developmental plans. For example, each employee record included information on various responsibilities, standards expected, goals to be reached, and actions to be taken to improve performance in the future. A summary of the entire process implemented at Key Bank of Utah is shown in Figure 2.

What happened after Key Bank of Utah implemented this system? In general terms, Key Bank was able to enjoy several positive consequences of aligning corporate, departmental, and individual goals. After the implementation of its new performance management system, Key Bank found several meaningful benefits, including the following:

- Managers knew that employees were focused on meeting important goals.
- Employees had more decision-making power.
- Lower-level managers had a better understanding of higher-level managers' decisions.
- Communication increased and improved (among managers, between managers and employees, etc.).

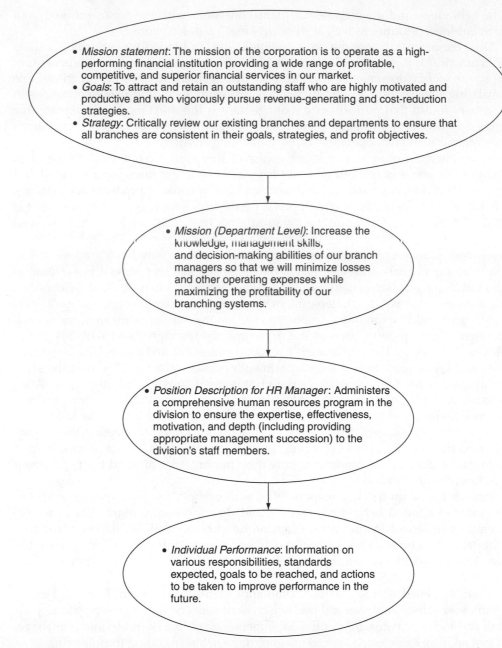

FIGURE 2   Summary of Alignment of Performance Management and Strategic Plan at Key Bank of Utah

In sum, to be most useful, organizations' performance management systems must rely on their strategic plans. The behaviors, results, and developmental plans of all employees must be aligned with the vision, mission, goals, and strategies of the organization and unit. Organizations can expect greater returns from implementing a performance management system when such alignment is in place.

2.1 Strategic Planning

The development of an organization's strategic plan requires a careful analysis of the organization's competitive situation, the organization's current position and destination, the development of the organization's strategic goals, the design of a plan of action and implementation, and the allocation of resources (human, organizational, physical) that will increase the likelihood of achieving the stated goals.[6]

There are several steps that must be considered in the creation of a successful strategic plan. These include (1) the conduct of an environmental analysis (i.e., the identification of the internal and external parameters of the environment in which the organization operates); (2) the creation of an organizational mission (i.e., statement of what the organization is all about); (3) the creation of an organizational vision (i.e., statement of where the organization intends to be in the long term, say, about 10 years); (4) setting goals (i.e., what the organization intends to do in the short term, say, one to three years); and (5) the creation of strategies that will allow the organization to fulfill its mission and vision and achieve its goals (i.e., descriptions of game plans or how-to procedures to reach the stated objectives). After each of these issues has been defined, organizational strategies are created so that the mission and vision are fulfilled and the stated goals are met.

The strategic planning process is not linear, however. For example, there may first be a rough draft of the organization's mission and vision and *then* the conduct of an environmental analysis may follow to help define the mission and vision more clearly. In other words, the mission and vision may be drafted first and the environmental analysis may follow second. The important point is that there is a constant interplay among these issues: the vision and mission affect the type of environmental analysis to be conducted, and the results of an environmental analysis are used to revise the mission and vision. By necessity, we need to discuss them one by one; however, keep in mind that they affect and inform each other on an ongoing basis. Let's begin with a discussion of environmental analysis.

2.1.1 ENVIRONMENTAL ANALYSIS The first step in conducting a strategic plan is to step back to take in the "big picture." This is accomplished through what is called an environmental analysis. An environmental analysis identifies external and internal parameters with the purpose of understanding broad issues related to the industry where the organization operates so that decisions can be made against the backdrop of a broader context.[7]

An examination of the *external environment* includes a consideration of opportunities and threats. Opportunities are characteristics of the environment that can help the organization succeed. Examples of such opportunities might be markets not currently being served, untapped labor pools, and new technological advances. On the other hand, threats are characteristics of the external environment that can prevent the organization from being successful. Examples of such threats range from economic recession to the innovative products of competitors. For example, consider the case of Frontier, which is currently the second largest jet carrier at Denver International Airport with an average of 250 daily departures and arrivals. Frontier is an affordable-fare airline which provides service to 60 cities, 50 in the United States, 8 in Mexico, and 2 in Canada. Frontier commenced operations in July 1994 given two key opportunities in the external environment. First, a major competing airline engaged in a dramatic downsizing of its Denver operations, leading to service gaps in various major markets that Frontier filled. Second, the city of Denver replaced the heavily congested Stapleton Airport with the much larger Denver International Airport.[8] In February 2004, United Airlines, the largest carrier operating out of Denver International Airport, made changes in the environment that may have had a direct impact on Frontier's strategic plan: United Airlines launched its own low-fare affiliate. The new affiliate, Ted, is going toe-to-toe with Frontier. Peter McDonald, vice president for operations for United Airlines, reported that Ted's cost per available seat mile is in the ballpark of Frontier's 8.3 cents.[9] So, what had been an opportunity for Frontier may no longer remain one, given the launching of Ted.

The following is a nonexhaustive list of external factors that should be considered in any environmental analysis:

- *Economic.* For example, is there an economic recession on the horizon? Or, is the current economic recession likely to end in the near future? How would these economic trends affect our business?
- *Political/legal.* For example, how will political changes in domestic or international markets we are planning on entering affect our entry strategy?
- *Social.* For example, what is the impact of an aging workforce on our organization?
- *Technological.* For example, what technological changes are anticipated in our industry and how will these changes affect how we do business?
- *Competitors.* For example, how do the strategies and products of our competitors affect our own strategies and products? Can we anticipate our competitors' next move?
- *Customers.* For example, what do our customers want now, and what will they want in the next five years or so? Can we anticipate such needs?
- *Suppliers.* For example, what is the relationship with our suppliers now and is it likely to change, and in what way, in the near future?

Although an examination of external trends is important for all types of organizations, this issue is particularly important for multinational organizations because they are concerned with both domestic and international trends. In fact, monitoring the external environment is so important in the strategic planning of multinational organizations that a survey of U.S. multinational corporations showed that 89% of departments responsible for the assessment of the external environment report directly to a member of the board of directors.[10]

An examination of the *internal environment* includes a consideration of strengths and weaknesses. Strengths are internal characteristics that the organization can use to its advantage. For example, what are the organization's assets and the staff's key skills? At Frontier, several key executives from other airlines were recruited, an important strength that was considered before launching the airline in 1994. These executives created a senior management team with long-term experience in the Denver market.

Weaknesses are internal characteristics that are likely to hinder the success of the organization. These could include an obsolete organizational structure that does not allow for effective organization across units and creates the misalignment of organizational-, unit-, and individual-level goals.

The following is a nonexhaustive list of internal issues that should be considered in any environmental analysis:

- *Organizational structure.* For example, is the current structure conducive to fast and effective communication?
- *Organizational culture.* Organizational culture includes the unwritten norms and values espoused by the members of the organization. For example, is the current organizational culture likely to encourage or hinder innovation and entrepreneurial behaviors on the part of middle-level managers?
- *Politics.* For example, are the various units competing for resources in such a way that any type of cross-unit collaboration is virtually impossible? Or, are units likely to be open and collaborative in cross-unit projects?
- *Processes.* For example, are the supply chains working properly? Can customers reach us when they need to and receive a satisfying response when they do?
- *Size.* For example, is the organization too small or too large? Are we growing too fast? Will we be able to manage growth (or downsizing) effectively?

Table 2 includes a summary list of internal and external trends to be considered in conducting an environmental analysis. Think about your current employer (or last employer, if you are not currently employed). Take a look at Table 2. Where does your organization stand in regard to each of these important internal and external issues? Regarding the external issues, what are some of the opportunities and threats? Regarding the internal issues, what are some of the strengths and weaknesses?

After external and internal issues have been considered, information is collected regarding opportunities, threats, strengths, and weaknesses. This information is used to conduct a *gap analysis*, which analyzes the external environment in relation to the internal environment. The pairing of external opportunities and threats with internal strengths and weaknesses leads to the following situations (ranked from most to least competitive):

1. *Opportunity + Strength = Leverage.* The best combination of external and internal factors occurs when there is an opportunity in the environment and a matching strength within the organization to take advantage of that opportunity. These are

TABLE 2	Trends to Consider in Conducting an Environmental Analysis
Internal	**External**
Organizational structure	Economic
Organizational culture	Political/legal
Politics	Social
Processes	Technological
Size	Competitors
	Customers
	Suppliers

obvious directions that the organization should pursue. Consider the case of IBM, the world's largest information technology company as well as the world's largest business and technology services provider (US\$ 36 billion). In the past few years, IBM has concluded that the PC-driven client-server computing model no longer applies and that network-based computing is taking over. This realization shifted the focus to servers, databases, and software for transaction management. Furthermore, IBM recognized the upsurge of network-connected devices including personal digital assistants (PDAs), cell phones, and video game systems. To take advantage of this external opportunity, IBM now focuses its resources on supporting network systems, developing software for the network-connected devices, and manufacturing specialized components. IBM has also improved its server technology and revamped its storage systems. IBM built up its software capabilities through internal development and outside acquisitions. In short, IBM developed a leverage factor by identifying internal strengths that matched external opportunities, which in turn leads to a successful business model.

2. *Opportunity + Weakness = Constraint.* In a constraint situation, the external opportunity is present; however, the internal situation is not conducive to taking advantage of the external opportunity. At IBM, this situation could have taken place if IBM did not have the internal capabilities to develop software for the network-connected devices and specialized components. The external opportunity would still be there but, absent the internal capabilities, it would not turn into an advantageous business scenario.

3. *Threat + Strength = Vulnerability.* In this situation, there is an external threat, but this threat can be contained because of the presence of internal strengths. If this had been the case at IBM, the company would not have been able to take advantage of a new situation; nevertheless, existing strengths would have allowed IBM to continue to operate in other areas.

4. *Threat + Weakness = Problem.* In the worst scenario, there is an external threat and an accompanying internal weakness. For example, in the 1980s, IBM refused to adapt to the demands of the emerging microcomputer market (i.e., today's PCs). IBM did not have the internal capability to address customers' needs for PCs and instead continued to focus on its internal strength: the mainframe computer. IBM's poor performance in the early 1990s was a direct consequence of this problem situation: the external threat (increasing demand for PCs and dwindling demand for mainframe computers) was met with an internal weakness (the lack of ability to shift internal focus from the mainframe to the PC).

Consider the organization you are currently working for, or the organization for which you have worked most recently. Try to identify one leverage and one problem based on an analysis of opportunities, threats, strengths, and weaknesses. What was the situation like? What were the results?

In sum, the process of creating a strategic plan begins with an environmental analysis, which considers internal as well as external trends. Internal trends can be classified as either strengths or weaknesses, and external trends can be classified as either opportunities or threats. A gap analysis consists of pairing strengths and weaknesses with opportunities and threats and determining whether the situation is advantageous (i.e., leverage), disadvantageous (i.e., problem), or somewhere in between (i.e., constraint and vulnerability).

2.1.2 MISSION After the environmental analysis has been completed and the gap analysis reveals an organization's leverage, constraints, vulnerabilities, and problems, the members of the organization must determine who they are and what they do. This information will then be incorporated into the organization's mission statement. The mission statement summarizes the organization's most important reason for its existence. Mission statements provide information on the purpose of the organization and its scope. Good mission statements provide answers to the following questions:

- Why does the organization exist?
- What is the scope of the organization's activities?
- Who are the customers served?
- What are the products or services offered?

Consider the mission statement for the Coca-Cola Company:
Everything we do is inspired by our enduring mission:

- To Refresh the World ... in body, mind, and spirit.
- To Inspire Moments of Optimism ... through our brands and our actions.
- To Create Value and Make a Difference ... everywhere we engage.[11]

Presumably, this mission statement was preceded by an environmental analysis examining internal and external trends. We do not have information on this. What we do know is that this mission statement provides some information regarding the four questions noted earlier. Based on this mission statement, we have information about why the company exists (i.e., "to refresh the world") and the scope of the organization's activities (i.e., "to create value and make a difference"). The mission statement does not, however, include information about who are the customers served and what are the products and services offered. Also, there is no information about specific products (e.g., Sprite, Minute Maid, Powerade, Dasani).

More specific and detailed information is needed if Coca-Cola's mission statement is to be used by its various units to create their own mission statements. More detailed information is also needed if both the organization and unit mission statements will be used as input for individual job descriptions and for managing individual and team performance. In general, thorough mission statements include the following components:

- Basic product or service to be offered (does what?)
- Primary markets or customer groups to be served (to whom?)
- Unique benefits and advantages of products or services (with what benefits?)
- Technology to be used in production or delivery
- Fundamental concern for survival through growth and profitability

Mission statements also typically include information about the organization's values and beliefs, including:

- Managerial philosophy of the organization
- Public image sought by the organization
- Self-concept of business adopted by employees and stockholders

In sum, a mission statement defines why the organization exists, the scope of its activities, the customers served, and the products and services offered. Mission statements also include specific information, such as the technology used in production or delivery, and the unique benefits or advantages of the organization's products and services. Finally, a mission statement can include a statement of values and beliefs, such as the organization's managerial philosophy.

2.1.3 VISION An organization's vision is a statement of future aspirations. In other words, the vision statement includes a description of what the organization would like to become in the future (about 10 years in the future). Vision statements are typically written after the mission statement is completed because the organization needs to know what it is and what its purpose is before they can figure out who they will be in the future. Note, however, that mission and vision statements are often combined and, therefore, in many cases it is difficult to differentiate one from the other. In such cases, the vision statement usually includes two components: a core ideology, which is referred to as the mission, and an envisioned future, which is what is referred to as the vision per se. The core ideology contains the core purpose and core values of an organization, and the envisioned future specifies long-term objectives and a picture of what the organization aspires to.

Spectrum Brands (formerly Rayovac Corporation) provides an example of combining mission and vision into one statement. Spectrum Brands is a global consumer products company and a leading supplier of batteries, kitchen appliances, shaving and grooming products, personal care products, pet supplies, and home and garden products. Originally founded in 1906 as the French Battery Company in Madison, Wisconsin, and renamed Rayovac Company during the 1930s, the company changed its name to Spectrum Brands in 2005 to reflect its diverse portfolio and position as a publicly-held company which employs 10,000 individuals worldwide. Spectrum Brands' combined mission and vision statement is the following:

Spectrum Brands is a rapidly growing, global, diversified, market-driven consumer products company.

We will continue to grow our company through a combination of strategic acquisitions and organic growth.

We will strengthen our brands and generate growth through emphasis on brand strategy/marketing and innovative product technology, design and packaging.

We will leverage IT infrastructure, distribution channels, purchasing power and operational structure globally to continue to drive efficiencies and reduce costs.

We will profitably expand distribution in all served markets.[12]

This statement includes components of a mission statement (i.e., "a rapidly growing, global, diversified, market-driven consumer products company") as well as components of a vision statement (e.g., "will strengthen our brands and generate growth through emphasis on brand strategy/marketing and innovative product technology, design and packaging"). This statement combines the present (i.e., who the company is, what it does) with the future (i.e., aspirations).

Other organizations make a more explicit differentiation between the mission and vision statements. Consider the vision statement for Greif, a global company headquartered in Delaware, Ohio, with approximately 16,000 employees providing industrial packaging products and services in more than 55 countries in Africa, Asia, Australia, Europe, the Middle East, North America, and South America.[13] Greif reported US$ 3.5 billion in net sales for the fiscal year that ended October 31, 2010. Greif's vision statement is the following:

Vision Statement

One Company   Though we encourage and embrace our diversity of language, location, business and origin, we are one company: Greif.

One Mission   We provide the packaging that gives ultimate value to our customers.

One Vision   We will be the best packaging company in the world, working in true partnership with our customers, our suppliers, and among ourselves.

Our Core Values

Our people are our past, present, and future   We will honor The Greif Way, building upon our rich history as a special place to work. We will operate within a culture of integrity, character, and respect. We will maintain a safe working environment. We will attract and cultivate a responsible, competent, efficient, and empowered workforce. We will provide opportunities to excel. We will communicate. We will listen.

Our customers are our reason for being   We will keep our promises to our customers. We will be synonymous with quality and service. We will solve their packaging challenges. We will prove the value of our relationship by being the best at what we do.

Our products are our livelihood   We will be a low-cost manufacturer and the high-value supplier in our business segments. We will innovate, using our ingenuity and creativity to provide better solutions. We will maintain our focus on where we can be the best and apply our expertise to do it better.

Our shareholders are our support   We will conduct our business ethically and with transparency. We will establish rigorous financial goals that will drive our business decisions and measure our progress. We will strive to attain a superior rate of return and maintain trust with our investors.

Our stage is the world. Our communities and the environment are our backdrop   We will be a conscientious global citizen, a responsive community neighbor, and a responsible steward of the earth's natural resources.

Greif's vision statement is clearly future oriented. It provides direction and focus. In addition, it includes several features that are required of useful vision statements. First, it focuses attention on what is most important and thus eliminates unproductive activities. Second, it provides a context from which to evaluate new external opportunities and threats. For example, the vision statement indicates that new opportunities for profitable growth in the industrial packaging and services business should be pursued. In addition, good vision statements have the following characteristics, not all of which are present in Greif's vision statement:

- *Brief.*   A vision statement should be brief so that employees can remember it.
- *Verifiable.*   A good vision statement should be able to stand the reality test. For example, how can we verify if Greif indeed becomes "one of the most desirable

companies to work for in our industries, focusing on establishing a work atmosphere in which our employees can excel"?

- **Bound by a timeline.** A good vision statement specifies a timeline for the fulfillment of various aspirations.
- **Current.** Outdated vision statements are not useful. Vision statements should be updated on an ongoing basis, ideally as soon as the old vision is fulfilled.
- **Focused.** A good vision statement is not a laundry list of aspirations, but rather focuses on just a few (perhaps not more than three or four) aspects of an organization's performance that are important to future success.
- **Understandable.** Vision statements need to be written in a clear and straightforward manner so that they are understood by all employees.
- **Inspiring.** Good vision statements make employees feel good about their organization's direction and motivate them to help achieve the vision.
- **A stretch.** Consider Microsoft's vision statement of "putting a computer on every desk and in every home," which was the vision when CEO Bill Gates started the MS-DOS operating system in the 1980s. This vision statement was such a stretch that it was considered ludicrous at a time when the mainframe computer still reigned supreme and the first minicomputer models (now PCs) were being made and sold. But that vision is now a reality. Microsoft has come up with a new vision: "putting a computer in every car and every pocket."[14]

In sum, a vision statement includes a description of future aspirations. Whereas the mission statement emphasizes the present, the vision statement emphasizes the future. Table 3 includes a list of the features that should be present in a good vision statement. Think about your current employer (or last employer, if you are not currently employed). Take a look at Table 3. How many of these features are reflected in your organization's vision statement?

2.1.4 GOALS After an organization has analyzed its external opportunities and threats as well as internal strengths and weaknesses and has defined its mission and vision, it can realistically establish goals that will further its mission. The purpose of setting such goals is to formalize statements about what the organization hopes to achieve in the medium- to long-range period (i.e., within the next three years or so). Goals provide more specific information regarding how the mission will be implemented. Goals can

TABLE 3	Characteristics of Good Vision Statements
	Brief
	Verifiable
	Bound by a timeline
	Current
	Focused
	Understandable
	Inspiring
	A stretch

also be a source of motivation and provide employees with a more tangible target for which to strive. Goals also provide a good basis for making decisions by keeping desired outcomes in mind. And, finally, goals provide the basis for performance measurement because they allow for a comparison of what needs to be achieved versus what each unit, group, and individual is achieving.

Consider the case of Harley-Davidson, Inc., the motorcycle manufacturer. In January 2004, Jeffrey L. Bleustein, chairman and chief executive officer, said that the expectation was to continue to grow the business. Specifically, he said that the new goal was to satisfy a yearly demand of 400,000 Harley-Davidson motorcycles in 2007. Moreover, he also said that he was confident that Harley-Davidson, Inc., would be able to deliver an earnings growth rate in the mid-teens for the foreseeable future.[15]

These goals provide a clear direction for Harley-Davidson. In fact, they provide useful information to guide unit-level goals as well as individual and team performance. The entire organization has a clear sense of focus because all members know that there is a goal to deliver 400,000 motorcycles in 2007.

2.1.5 STRATEGIES   At this point, we know what the organization is all about (mission), what it wants to be in the future (vision), and some intermediate steps to follow to get there (goals). What remains is a discussion of how to fulfill the mission and vision and how to achieve the stated goals. This is done by creating strategies, which are descriptions of game plans or how-to procedures to reach the stated objectives. The strategies could address issues of growth, survival, turnaround, stability, innovation, and leadership, among others.

BOX 1

Linking Performance Management to the Company's Vision at Loop Customer Management

At Loop Customer Management (http://www.loop.co.uk) a new direction and a new company vision statement included the alignment with an effective performance management system. Loop Customer Management is part of the United Kingdom-based Kelda Group. The company provides clients with managed customer services, contact centers, and collection services. In 2001 the company moved from being part of a utility company to becoming an outsourced provider of services. With this change, a new vision was created which centered around the phrase "great customer experiences through great people." The company then sought to create a performance management system that would align the staff skills and behaviors to this new vision. Based on the need to focus on customer service as primary to success, Loop sought to define, measure, and reward the best service behaviors. The process meant identifying the specific behaviors that create a quality customer interaction and incorporating those behaviors into performance appraisals and reward systems. Creating behavioral statements allowed employees to have a clear understanding of how their work linked directly to the company's vision. In summary, Loop Customer Management provides an example of how a performance management system can align with a vision statement to bring about organizational change and execution of a business strategy.[16]

The human resources (HR) function plays a critical role in creating and implementing the strategies that will allow the organization to realize its mission and vision. Specifically, the HR function can make the following contributions:

- *Communicate knowledge of strategic plan.* The HR function can be a good conduit to communicate the various components of the strategic plan (e.g., mission, vision, and goals) to all the employees.
- *Outline knowledge, skills, and abilities (KSAs) needed for strategy implementation.* The HR function, through job analyses and the resulting job descriptions, serves as a repository of knowledge regarding what KSAs are needed for a successful implementation of the strategic plan. Thus, the HR function is in a unique situation to provide information about whether the current workforce has the KSAs needed to support the strategic plan and, if not, to offer suggestions about what types of employees should be hired and what types of plans should be put in place to develop the needed KSAs internally.
- *Propose reward systems.* The HR function can provide useful information on what type of reward system should be implemented to motivate employees to support the strategic plan.

2.2 Developing Strategic Plans at the Unit Level

As shown in Figure 1, the organization's strategic plan has a direct impact on the units' strategic plans. The case of Key Bank of Utah described earlier illustrates how the branch administration division had a mission statement that was aligned with the overall organizational mission statement. Similarly, the vision statement, goals, and strategies of the various units need to be congruent with the overall organizational vision, goals, and strategies. Consider the case of Microsoft Corporation's mission statement:[17]

> *Our Mission* At Microsoft, we work to help people and businesses throughout the world realize their full potential.
>
> *Our Values* As a company, and as individuals, we value:
>
> - Integrity, honesty, openness, personal excellence, constructive self-criticism, continual self-improvement, and mutual respect.
> - We are committed to our customers and partners and have a passion for technology.
> - We take on big challenges, and pride ourselves on seeing them through. We hold ourselves accountable to our customers, shareholders, partners, and employees by honoring our commitments, providing results, and striving for the highest quality.

Now, consider the mission statement of one of Microsoft's units, Training and Education:

> With the charter to enable Microsoft engineering workgroups to realize their full potential for innovation and performance through world-class learning strategies, Microsoft Training and Education (MSTE) provides performance support strategies to support the overall corporation's software engineering efforts. Our efforts include the design, development, and delivery of learning

programs, on-line information, and resources for Microsoft employees. MSTE's integrated suite of technical offerings supports our goal of having a significant impact on Microsoft's business. We promote best practices, cross-group communication, Microsoft expertise and Industry expertise.

As you can see, the mission of the training and education unit is consistent with the overall mission in that the *realization of full potential* plays a central role. Of course, MSTE's mission is more focused on issues specifically relevant to the training and education function. Nevertheless, the link between the two mission statements is readily apparent.

The congruence between the mission of the organization and its various units is important regardless of the type of industry and the size of the organization. High-performing organizations have a clear alignment in the mission and vision of the overall and unit-level mission and vision statements. Consider the case of Norfolk State University (NSU, http://www.nsu.edu/), located in Norfolk, Virginia. NSU, with a current enrollment of about 6,000 students, is the seventh-largest historically African American university in the United States, and it serves many students who are the first in their families to attend college. It offers more than 50 academic programs, including 16 master's, and 2 doctoral degree programs. NSU has five main schools: School of Business, School of Education, School of Liberal Arts, School of Social Work, and School of Science and Technology. The university's mission statement is the following:

> To provide an affordable, high-quality education for an ethnically and culturally diverse student population, equipping them with the capability to become productive citizens who continuously contribute to a global and rapidly changing society.[18]

The mission statement for the School of Business indicates that its goal is to prepare students for careers in all types of organizations and this is achieved in a learning environment that fosters academic achievement, professional growth, and a recognition of diversity, technology, globalization, and ethics in the workplace and society.[19]

Note that both mission statements are aligned and refer to similar issues including the (1) delivery of a high-quality education and academic achievement to a (2) diverse student body with the goal of (3) educating productive citizens who will contribute to a (4) global society.

In sum, the organization's strategic plan including the mission, vision, goals, and strategies cascades down to all organizational levels. Thus, each division or unit also creates its own strategic plan, which should be consistent with the organization's overall plan.

2.2.1 CONSENSUS ABOUT STRATEGIES AND GOALS ACROSS ORGANIZATIONAL UNITS

Strategic consensus occurs when the various organizational units agree on a common set of strategic priorities. Although it may seem that the greater the consensus across units, the better firm performance, this is not always the case because we must differentiate between consensus regarding strategies and consensus regarding goals. In the early development of strategic management as a field, the dominant approach was for a firm to focus first on goals, and then create strategies on how to compete. This process has been described as "formal," "normative," or "grand strategy." A more recent way of thinking about consensus within the context of strategic planning has been influenced by the industrial organization perspective from economics. This perspective argues that a firm must first agree on a strategy (e.g., low cost or differentiation), and then subsequently decide on goals. These two alternative sequences, strategies → goals versus goals → strategies, were contrasted against each other in a study involving the heads of purchasing and manufacturing of more than 100 manufacturing companies in Spain. Results suggested that the strategies → goals sequence was superior in terms of predicting firm performance. In sum, it is beneficial for the cascading of strategic planning to first have units agree on common strategies before they agree on what goals will be set to reach those strategic priorities.[20]

2.3 Job Descriptions

Continuing with the sequence of components shown in Figure 1, job descriptions also need to be congruent with the organization and unit mission, vision, goals, and strategies.

After the strategic plan is completed, some rewriting of the existing job descriptions may be in order. Recall the job description for Trailer Truck Driver as used by the Civilian Personnel Management Service (U.S. Department of Defense) (see the accompanying box).

This description provides information about the various tasks performed together with a description of some of the KSAs required for the position. But what is the link with the organization and unit strategic plans? How do the specific tasks make a contribution to the strategic priorities of the transportation division and the organization as a whole? This description includes only cursory and indirect information regarding these issues. For example, one can assume that the proficient handling of bills of lading, expense accounts, and other papers pertinent to the shipment contributes toward a smooth shipping operation and, therefore, makes a contribution to the transportation division. However, this link is not sufficiently clear.

On the other hand, consider a job announcement describing the position of Performance Solutions Group Manager in Microsoft's training and education unit (see the accompanying box).

This job description makes the link between the individual position and MSTE quite clear. First, the description includes MSTE's mission statement so that individuals become aware of how their specific roles fit within the overall mission of the department. Second, the job description includes language to the effect that the work must lead to an "industry leading" product, which is consistent not only with MSTE's mission but also with Microsoft's overall mission. Third, in the needed qualifications section, there is a clear overlap between those needed for this specific position and those mentioned in MSTE's as well as in Microsoft's overall mission. In short, the person working as Performance Solutions Group Manager has a clear sense not only of her position but also of how behaviors and expected results are consistent with expectations about MSTE and Microsoft in general.

In sum, the tasks and KSAs included in individual job descriptions must be congruent with the organization's and unit's strategic plans. In other words, job descriptions should include activities that, if executed well, will help execute the mission and vision. Job descriptions that are detached from strategic priorities will lead to performance evaluations focused on behaviors and results that are not central to an organization's success.

2.4 Individual and Team Performance

Finally, the performance management system needs to motivate employees to display the behaviors and produce the results required to support the organization's and the unit's mission, vision, and goals. Developmental plans need to be aligned with unit and organizational priorities as well. Well-designed performance management systems define a clear path from organizational mission, vision, and goals to individual and team performance. This is critical because organizational success is a direct function of the alignment between collective and individual objectives.

In addition to serving as a necessary guide for individual and team performance, knowledge of organization- and unit-level mission and vision provides information about how to design the performance management system. Specifically, there are many choices in how the system is designed. For example, the system might place more emphasis on behaviors (i.e., processes) than on results (i.e., outcomes), or the system might emphasize more short-term criteria (i.e., quarterly goals) than long-term criteria (triennial). Some of these choices are presented in Table 4.

Knowledge of the organization and unit vision and mission allows the HR function to make informed decisions about design choices. More detailed information on each of the factors guiding each of these design choices is provided in subsequent chapters. For now, as one illustration, assume an organization is producing a mature product in a fairly stable industry. In this situation, an emphasis on behaviors rather than results may be preferred because the relationship between processes and outcomes is well known, and the top priority is that employees display reliable and consistent behaviors in making the product. Regardless of the type of criteria used, be it behaviors or results, these must be observable (i.e., the person rating the criteria needs to have the ability to observe what is rated) and verifiable (i.e., there needs to be evidence to confirm the criteria rated). As a second example, consider the actual case of Dell computers. Dell is one of the top players in the personal computer industry through its mode of online direct selling. Dell's main strategic business strategy is to be a low-cost leader in an industry that deals with a product that is increasingly regarded as a commodity. However, in addition to a low-cost strategy, Dell has a customer relationship business strategy of maintaining customer service at a high level, while reducing

---

BOX 2

Job Description for Trailer Truck Driver: Civilian Personnel Management Service, U.S. Department of Defense

Operates gasoline or diesel powered truck or truck tractor equipped with two or more driving wheels and with four or more forward speed transmissions, which may include two or more gear ranges. These vehicles are coupled to a trailer or semi-trailer by use of a turntable (fifth wheel) or pintle (pivot) hook. Drives over public roads to transport materials, merchandise, or equipment. Performs difficult driving tasks such as backing truck to loading platform, turning narrow corners, negotiating narrow passageways, and keeping truck and trailer under control, particularly on wet or icy highways. May assist in loading and unloading truck. May also handle manifest, bills of lading, expense accounts, and other papers pertinent to the shipment.

BOX 3

Job Description for Performance Solutions Group Manager at Microsoft

The Performance Solutions Group Manager is accountable for developing and delivering on a portal strategy that touches over 20,000 employees worldwide and involves a complex data delivery system. Additionally, the person is responsible for defining the cutting-edge tool suite used by the team to develop and maintain the portal, the content housed by the group, and all e-learning solutions. Key initiatives include redesigning the Engineering Excellence Guide within the next 6 months and evolving it over the next 18 months to 3 years to become the industry leading performance support site. Key challenges include maintaining and managing the cutting-edge tool suite used by the team and driving a clear vision for an industry leading portal and content delivery plan.

Qualifications for this position are a minimum of five years of senior management experience, preferably in knowledge management, e-learning, or Web-based product development roles; ability to think strategically and exercise sound business judgment on behalf of Microsoft; excellent leadership, communication, interpersonal, and organizational skills; firsthand experience delivering/shipping Web-based learning and content management solutions; proven record of successful team management; and ability to work well independently and under pressure, while being flexible and adaptable to rapid change. Knowledge of performance support and training procedures, standards, and processes is preferred.

With the charter to enable Microsoft engineering workgroups to realize their full potential for innovation and performance through world-class learning strategies, Microsoft Training and Education (MSTE) provides performance support strategies to support the overall corporation's software engineering efforts. Our efforts include the design, development, and delivery of learning programs, online information, and resources for Microsoft employees. MSTE's integrated suite of technical offerings supports our goal of having a significant impact on Microsoft's business. We promote best practices, cross-group communication, Microsoft expertise and Industry expertise.

---

costs. Dell's performance management system provides a strong link between individual goals and organizational performance by including a results component (i.e., cost) and a behavioral component (i.e., customer service).[21] At Dell, both low cost and high levels of customer service (for both internal and external customers) are important dimensions of the performance management system. Also, the system is strongly linked not only to the strategic objectives (i.e., low cost and high levels of customer service) but

TABLE 4	Some Choices in Performance Management System Design

Criteria: Behavioral criteria vs. results criteria

Participation: Low employee participation vs. high employee participation

Temporal dimension: Short-term criteria vs. long-term criteria

Level of criteria: Individual criteria vs. team/group criteria

System orientation: Developmental orientation vs. administrative orientation

Rewards: Pay for performance (i.e., merit-based) vs. pay for tenure/position

also to the organization's "winning culture" (i.e., achievement of personal and business objectives through its focus on interaction between managers and team members).

In summary, the criteria measured in the performance management system are behaviors or results (or both) that must be relevant to the unit and the organization. Performance criteria need to make a contribution to the strategic priorities. It is unlikely that a performance management system will make an important contribution to the organization's bottom line if (1) there is no clear sense of direction about where the organization and unit are going, or (2) there is a clear sense of direction but this information is not reflected in the job descriptions and the actual behaviors and results measured.

3 BUILDING SUPPORT

Given the many competing projects and the usual scarcity of resources, some organizations may be reluctant to implement a performance management system. Primarily, the reason is a lack of any perceived value added to a system that requires many resources (particularly time from supervisors) and that seems to produce little tangible payoffs. The need to align organization and unit priorities with the performance management system is one of the key factors contributing to obtaining the much-needed top management support for the system.

Top management is likely to ask, "Why is performance management important?" One answer to this question is that performance management is the primary tool that will allow top management to carry out its vision. The performance management system, when aligned with organization and unit priorities, is a critical tool to (1) allow all employees to understand where the organization stands and where it needs to go and (2) provide tools to employees (e.g., motivation, developmental resources) so that their behaviors and results will help the organization get there. Fundamentally, the implementation of any performance management system requires that the "What's in it for me?" question be answered convincingly. In the case of top management, the answer to the "What's in it for me?" question is that performance management can serve as a primary tool to realize its vision.

Building support for the system does not stop with top management, however. All participants in the system need to understand the role they play and receive a clear answer to the "What's in it for me?" question. Communication about the system is key. This includes a clear description of the system's mechanics (e.g., when the performance planning meetings will take place, how to handle disagreements between supervisor and employees) and the system's consequences (e.g., relationship between performance evaluation and rewards). Not involving people in the process of system design and implementation can create resistance, and the performance management system may result in more harm than good.

Consider the role that good communication played in the launching of a revamped performance management system at Bankers Life and Casualty (http://www.bankerslife.com), an insurance company specializing in insurance for seniors and headquartered in Chicago. In November 2000, Edward M. Berube was appointed as its new president and CEO. Berube understood that Bankers Life and Casualty was facing important challenges, including new customer demands, the impact of the Internet, outsourcing, and increased competition. So, Bankers Life and

Casualty engaged in a very aggressive marketing campaign, which included retaining actor Dick Van Dyke as its company spokesperson. In spite of these efforts, however, internal focus groups revealed that while employees understood the organization's strategic plan, they did not understand what role each person was supposed to play in helping the organization execute its strategy. In other words, employees did not have a clear understanding of how each person could help achieve the organization's strategic goals, including focusing on the following three key areas: (1) distribution scope, scale, and productivity; (2) home office productivity and unit costs; and (3) product revenue and profitability.

Bankers Life and Casualty realized that a better link between strategy and individual and team performance could be established by improving its performance management process. The HR department, therefore, proceeded to overhaul the performance management system so that the three areas of strategic importance just outlined would be part of everyone's performance evaluation and improvement efforts. The design and implementation of the new system was a *joint venture* between the HR and the communications departments. First, the HR and communications team spoke candidly with the CEO about his expectations. The CEO responded with overwhelming support, stating that the performance management system would be implemented for every employee on preestablished dates, and that he would hold his team accountable for making this happen. Then, to implement the performance management system, each unit met with its VP. During these meetings, each VP discussed how his or her unit's goals were linked to the corporate goals. Next, HR and communications led discussions surrounding goal setting, giving feedback, and writing developmental plans. Managers were then given the opportunity to share any feedback, concerns, or questions that they had about the program. During this forum, managers exchanged success stories and offered advice to one another. These success stories were then shared with the CEO. The CEO then shared these stories with those who reported directly to him to strengthen the visibility of his support for the program.

In short, the performance management system at Bankers Life and Casualty helped all employees understand their contributions to the organization's strategic plan. This was a key issue that motivated the CEO to give unqualified support to the system. This support gave a clear message to the rest of the organization that the performance management system was an important initiative. The support of the CEO and other top executives, combined with a high degree of participation from all employees and their ability to voice concerns and provide feedback regarding the system, was a critical factor in the success of the performance management system at Bankers Life and Casualty.

Summary Points

- Strategic planning involves defining the organization's present and future identity. The overall purpose of a strategic plan is to serve as a blueprint that allows organizations to allocate resources in a way that provides the organization with a competitive advantage.

- Strategic planning serves several purposes, including defining an organization's identity, preparing for the future, analyzing the environment, providing focus, creating a culture of cooperation, generating new options, and serving as a guide for the daily activities of all organizational members.

- Performance management systems must rely on the strategic plan to be useful. The behaviors, results, and developmental plans of all employees must be aligned with the vision, mission, goals, and strategies of the organization and unit.
- The process of creating a strategic plan begins with an environmental analysis, which considers internal (e.g., organizational structure, processes) as well as external (e.g., economic, technological) trends. Internal trends can be classified as either strengths or weaknesses, and external trends can be classified as either opportunities or threats. A gap analysis consists of pairing strengths and weaknesses with opportunities and threats and determining whether the situation is advantageous (i.e., leverage), disadvantageous (i.e., problem), or somewhere in between (i.e., constraint and vulnerability).
- The second step in creating a strategic plan is to write a mission statement based on the results of the gap analysis. A mission statement defines why the organization exists, the scope of its activities, the customers served, and the products and services offered. Mission statements also include information about what technology is used in production or delivery, and the unique benefits or advantages of the organization's products and services. Finally, a mission statement can include a statement of values and beliefs, such as the organization's managerial philosophy.
- The third component of a strategic plan is the vision statement, which includes a description of future aspirations. Whereas the mission statement emphasizes the present, the vision statement emphasizes the future. In many cases, however, the mission and vision statements are combined into one statement. For vision statements to be most useful they must be brief, verifiable, bound by a timeline, current, focused, understandable, inspiring, and a stretch.
- After the mission and vision statements are created, the next step in the strategic planning process is to generate specific goals that will help fulfill the mission and vision. Goals provide more specific information regarding how the mission and vision will be implemented. Typically, goals span a five-year period.
- The final step in the strategic planning process is to identify strategies that will help achieve the stated goals. These strategies are game plans and usually address issues surrounding growth, survival, turnaround, stability, innovation, and leadership. The HR department plays an important role in identifying strategies because its members have knowledge of the organization's mission and vision as well as the organization's internal capabilities, or what is called an organization's human capital.
- The organization's strategic plan, including the mission, vision, goals, and strategies, cascades down to all organizational levels. Thus, each division or unit also creates its own strategic plan, which should be consistent with the organization's overall plan. The most effective sequence for doing so is for the units to first agree on common strategies and then specify unit-level goals.
- The tasks and KSAs included in individual job descriptions must be congruent with the organization's and unit's strategic plans. In other words, job descriptions should include activities that, if executed well, will in turn help execute the mission and vision. Job descriptions that are detached from

strategic priorities will lead to performance evaluations focused on behaviors and results that are not central to an organization's success.

- The various choices in designing the performance management system are directly affected by an organization's strategic plan. Different missions and visions lead to different types of systems, for example, emphasizing behaviors (e.g., processes) as opposed to results (e.g., outcomes).
- Top management must be aware that the performance management system

is a primary tool to execute an organization's strategic plan. This awareness will lead to top management's support for the system. In addition, all organizational members need to be able to answer the "What's in it for me?" question regarding the system. Implementing the performance management system will require considerable effort on the part of all those involved. Those doing the evaluation and those being evaluated should know how the system will benefit them directly.

CASE STUDY 1

Evaluating Vision and Mission Statements at PepsiCo

Consider the mission and vision statements for PepsiCo (http://www.pepsico.com/Company.html) and then answer the questions included below:

PepsiCo's Mission Statement*

Our mission is to be the world's premier consumer products company focused on convenient foods and beverages. We seek to produce financial rewards to investors as we provide opportunities for growth and enrichment to our employees, our business partners and the communities in which we operate. And in everything we do, we strive for honesty, fairness and integrity.

PepsiCo's Vision Statement

"PepsiCo's responsibility is to continually improve all aspects of the world in which we operate—environment, social, economic—creating a better tomorrow than today." Our vision is put into action through programs and a focus on environmental stewardship, activities to benefit society, and a commitment to build

shareholder value by making PepsiCo a truly sustainable company.

1. The table below summarizes the key characteristics of ideal mission and vision statements. Use the Y/N columns in the table to indicate whether each of the features is present, or not, in the mission and vision statements of PepsiCo.

2. How do the mission and vision statements relate to the eight characteristics of an ideal mission statement and the eight characteristics of an ideal vision statement? What are the gaps?

3. How useful are the mission and vision statements of PepsiCo in terms of linking organizational priorities with individual and team performance? In creating such a linkage, which ideal mission/vision statement characteristics (shown in the table above) seem to be more important than others? What other places might the HR department at PepsiCo look for information regarding how to more effectively cascade firm-level strategy to each individual's goals? ■

	Characteristics	Y/N
Mission statement—Summarizes the organization's most important reason for its existence	Basic product/service to be offered (does what)	
	Primary markets or customer groups to be served (to whom)	
	Unique benefits, features, and advantages of products/services (with what benefits)	
	Technology to be used in production or delivery	
	Fundamental concern for survival through growth and profitability	
	Managerial philosophy of the firm	
	Public image sought by organization	
	Self-concept of business adopted by employees and stockholders	
	Brief—so that employees can remember it	
	Verifiable—able to stand the reality test	
	Bound by a timeline—specifies a timeline for fulfillment of the various aspirations	
	Current—updated on an ongoing basis	
Vision—Statement of future aspirations	Focused—lists a few (3–4) aspects of organization's performance that are important to future success	
	Understandable—written in a clear and straightforward manner so that they are understood by all employees	
	Inspiring—makes employees feel good about their organization's direction and motivates them to help achieve the vision	
	Stretch—goal not easily attained	

*PepsiCo. (2011) Our Mission and Vision. Retrieved March 3, 2011 from: http://www.pepsico.com/Company/Our-Mission-and-Vision.html 2011, PepsiCo, Inc. Used with permission.

CASE STUDY 2

Dilbert's Mission Statement Generator

Please visit Dilbert's Web page and play the "mission statement generator" game (http://www.dilbert.com/comics/dilbert/games/career/bin/ms.cgi). Generate two different mission statements and provide a critique of the resulting statements based on whether they comply with the characteristics of an ideal statement. Because generated statements will vary, please also provide a critique of the following statement: "We strive to continually administrate timely opportunities and enthusiastically utilize enterprise-wide technology while promoting personal employee growth." In addition, answer the following questions:

1. What are the dangers of having a flawed mission statement?

2. How does a flawed statement affect the development of a unit's mission statement and subsequent individual job descriptions and goals? ■

CASE STUDY 3

Linking Individual with Unit and Organizational Priorities

Obtain a copy of the job description for your current or most recent job. If this is not feasible, obtain a copy of a job description of someone you know. Then, obtain a copy of the mission statements for the organization and unit in question.

Revise the job description so that it is aligned with the unit and organizational strategic priorities. Revisions may include adding tasks and KSAs important in the mission statement that are not already included in the job description. ■

CASE STUDY 4

Linking Performance Management to Strategy at Procter & Gamble

Consider the following description of a firm-wide strategy pursued by Procter & Gamble:*

Procter & Gamble (P&G), the world's largest consumer products company, follows a fairly unique strategy: P&G appeals to the heart and cares about human needs. In other words, P&G attempts to touch and improve the lives of its consumers all over the world. As an example, take the razor-and-blade innovation pioneered by Gillette's Himalaya team, which focuses on India but is a global group based partly in Boston, USA. The team received information about how men in India shave: about half of them use barbershops and barbers usually break double-sided blades in two and used them repeatedly, which crates unsanitary conditions. With the strategic goal of improving the lives of its customers, the team created a razor-and-blade innovation that simplified the essential features of the shaving done in barbershops. The products were a success in terms of improving both the human condition and profitability. As a second example, consider a situation in P&G Brazil, where P&G feared a shutdown due to decreased business volume. Low-income consumers were the fastest growing segment of the population, but P&G's global premium products were too expensive for this market segment. Local P&G teams decided to live with families, scrutinized every

P&G process in an attempt to reduce costs, and ended up creating an innovative products line they dubbed "basico" (for "essential" in Portuguese). The team members felt that they were doing good for the world, not just making money for the corporation. Demand immediately outpaced supply when the first "basico" products were launched, which included women's hygiene, diapers, and greener laundry detergent. The company quickly captured market share through small neighborhood shops and premium products were lifted. The business in Brazil became a profitable global growth model, and not just for emerging countries. As a consequence, "Tide Basic" was recently introduced in the United States.

In sum, P&G's strategy inspires employees to add their hearts to their heads and aims at finding creative solutions when purpose-inspired opportunities and commercial considerations seem to collide.

Imagine you are an HR executive at P&G. Given the company's strategic orientation toward purpose and values, what would you do to help align a new performance management system with the strategic plan? How would you explain this relationship? What would you say and do to garner company-wide support for your performance management system? ■

*The description is adapted from the following source: Kanter, R. M. (2009, September 15) Inside Procter & Gamble's New Values-Based Strategy. *Bloomberg Businessweek.* Retrieved March 3, 2011 from: http://www.businessweek.com/managing/content/sep2009/ca20090915_398234.htm

End Notes

1. Addams, H. L., & Embley, K. (1988). Performance management systems: From strategic planning to employee productivity. *Personnel, 65,* 55–60.

2. Rao, A. S. (2007). Effectiveness of performance management systems: An empirical study in Indian companies. *International Journal of Human Resource Management, 18,* 1812 1840.

3. Collier, N., Fishwick, F., & Floyd, S. W. (2004). Managerial involvement and perceptions of strategy process. *Long Range Planning, 37,* 67–83.

4. Tapinos, E., Dyson, R. G., & Meadows, M. (2005). The impact of performance measurement in strategic planning. *International Journal of Productivity and Performance Management, 54,* 370–384.

5. Adapted from Addams and Embley (1988), op. cit.

6. Adapted from C. D. Fisher, L. F. Schoenfeldt, & J. B. Shaw. *Human Resource Management*, 5th ed. (Boston: Houghton Mifflin, 2003).

7. The discussion regarding environmental analysis is adapted from W. Drohan, "Principles of Strategic Planning," *Association Management 49* (1997): 85–87.

8. Company profile. Available online at http://www.frontierairlines.com/frontier/who-we-are/company-info/fact-sheet.do. Retrieval date: May 1, 2011.

9. Low-cost Ted may help United fly out of bankruptcy (2004, February 13). *USA Today.* Available online at http://www.usatoday.com/travel/news/2004-02-13-ted-wrap_x.htm. Retrieval date: May 1, 2011.

10. Kennedy, C. R., Jr. (1984). The external environment-strategic planning interface: U.S. multinational corporate practices in the 1980s. *Journal of International Business Studies, 15,* 99–108.

11. Collins, J. C., & Porras, J. I. (1996, September–October). Building your company's vision. *Harvard Business Review, 74,* 65–77.

12. Mission statement. Available online at http://www.spectrumbrands.com/AboutUs/Mission.aspx. Retrieval date: May 1, 2011.

13. Company profile. Available online at http://www.greif.com/about-greif/vision-statement.asp. Retrieval date: May 1, 2011. Greif, Inc.

14. Bill Gates. Available online at http://www.microsoft.com/billgates/speeches/industry&tech/iayf2005.asp. Retrieval date: May 1, 2011.

15. Harley-Davidson reports record fourth quarter and 18th consecutive record year. Available online at http://www.harley-davidson.com/CO/NEW/en/PressRelease_Date.asp?locale=en_US&bmLocale=en_US&id_in=552&dspmm=1&dspyy=2004. Retrieval date: May 1, 2011.

16. Wilson, N. (2004). Rewarding values at Loop Customer Management. *Strategic HR Review, 3*(January–February), 12–13.

17. Microsoft Corporation. Our mission. Available online at http://www.microsoft.com/about/en/us/default.aspx. Retrieval date: July 29, 2011.

18. Mission statement of NSU. Available online at http://www.nsu.edu/about/. Retrieval date: May 1, 2011.

19. The School of Business mission statement. Available online at http://www.nsu.edu/business/. Retrieval date: May 1, 2011.

20. González-Benito, J., Aguinis, H., Boyd, B. K., and Suarez-González, I. (in press). Coming to consensus on strategic consensus: A mediated moderation model of consensus and performance. *Journal of Management.*

21. Building people capability. Available online at http://www1.ap.dell.com/content/topics/topic.aspx/global/hybrid/careers/content/8012aa1f-fa50-4634-ac65-fa149b26228f?c=au&l=en&s=corp. Retrieval date: May 1, 2011.

Defining Performance and Choosing a Measurement Approach

*How you measure the performance of your managers
directly affects the way they act.*

—GUSTAVE FLAUBERT

LEARNING OBJECTIVES

By the end of this chapter, you will be able to do the following:

- Define what performance is and what it is not.

- Understand the evaluative and multidimensional nature of performance.

- Identify the various factors that determine performance, including declarative knowledge, procedural knowledge, and motivation.

- Gather information about a performance problem and understand which of the three main determinants of performance need to be addressed to solve the problem.

- Design a performance management system that includes both task and contextual performance dimensions.

- Understand that performance should be placed within a context: a performer in a specific situation engaging in behaviors leading to specific results.

- Adopt a behavior approach to measuring performance, which basically focuses on how the job is done and ignores the performer's traits and results produced.

- Adopt a results approach to measuring performance, which basically focuses on the outcomes of work and ignores the performer's traits as well as the manner in which the work is done.

- Adopt a trait approach to measuring performance, which basically focuses on the performer and ignores the situation, his or her behaviors, and the results produced.
- Understand the situations under which a behavior, results, or trait approach to measuring performance may be most appropriate.

In this chapter we address operational concerns, such as the determinants of performance and how to measure performance. Let's begin by defining performance.

1 DEFINING PERFORMANCE

Performance management systems usually include measures of both behaviors (what an employee does) and results (the outcomes of an employee's behavior). The definition of performance does not include the results of an employee's behaviors but only the behaviors themselves. Performance is about behavior or what employees do, not about what employees produce or the outcomes of their work.

Also, there are two additional characteristics of the behaviors we label "performance."[1] First, they are *evaluative.* This means that such behaviors can be judged as negative, neutral, or positive for individual and organizational effectiveness. In other words, the value of these behaviors can vary based on whether they make a contribution toward the accomplishment of individual, unit, and organizational goals. Second, performance is *multidimensional.*[2] This means that there are many different kinds of behaviors that have the capacity to advance (or hinder) organizational goals.

As an example, consider a set of behaviors that can be grouped under the general label "contribution to effectiveness of others in the work unit." This set of behaviors can be defined as follows:

Works with others within and outside the unit in a manner that improves their effectiveness; shares information and resources; develops effective working relationships; builds consensus; and constructively manages conflict.

Contribution to the effectiveness of others in the work unit could be assessed by using a scale including anchors demonstrating various levels of competence. For example, anchors could be words and phrases such as "outstanding," "significantly exceeds standards," "fully meets standards," "does not fully meet standards," and "unacceptable." This illustrates the evaluative nature of performance because this set of behaviors is judged as positive, neutral, or negative. In addition, this example illustrates the multidimensional nature of performance because there are several behaviors that, combined, affect the overall perceived contribution that an employee makes to the effectiveness of others in the work unit. In other words, we would be missing important information if we only considered, for example, "shares information and resources" and did not consider the additional behaviors listed earlier.

Because not all behaviors are observable or measurable, performance management systems often include measures of results or consequences that we infer are the direct result of employees' behaviors. Take the case of a salesperson whose job consists of visiting clients to offer them new products or services. The salesperson's supervisor is back in the home office and does not have an opportunity to observe the salesperson's behaviors first-hand. In this case sales volume may be used as a proxy for a behavioral measure. In other words, the supervisor makes the assumption that if the salesperson is able to produce high sales figures, then she is probably engaging in the right behaviors.

2 DETERMINANTS OF PERFORMANCE

What factors cause an employee to perform at a certain level? Why do certain individuals perform better than others? A combination of three factors allows some people to perform at higher levels than others: (1) *declarative knowledge*, (2) *procedural knowledge*, and (3) *motivation*.[3] Declarative knowledge is information about facts and things, including information regarding a given task's requirements, labels, principles, and goals. Procedural knowledge is a combination of knowing what to do and how to do it and includes cognitive, physical, perceptual, motor, and interpersonal skills. Finally, motivation involves three types of choice behaviors:

1. Choice to expend effort (e.g., "I will go to work today")
2. Choice of level of effort (e.g., "I will put in my best effort at work" versus "I will not try very hard")
3. Choice to persist in the expenditure of that level of effort (e.g., "I will give up after a little while" versus "I will persist no matter what")

Table 1 summarizes the components of declarative knowledge, procedural knowledge, and motivation. All three determinants of performance must be present for performance to reach high levels. In other words, the three determinants have a multiplicative relationship such that

$$\text{Performance} = \text{Declarative Knowledge} \times \text{Procedural Knowledge} \times \text{Motivation}$$

If any of the determinants has a value of 0, then performance also has a value of 0. For example, consider the case of Jane, a salesclerk who works in a national clothing retail chain. Jane has excellent declarative knowledge regarding the merchandise. Specifically, she knows all of the brands, prices, sizing charts, and sales promotions. We would consider her declarative knowledge to be very high. Jane is also intelligent and physically able to conduct all of the necessary tasks. We would consider Jane's procedural knowledge also to be very high. Jane does not, however, show motivation to perform. When customers enter the store, she does not approach them; instead, she sits behind the cash

TABLE 1	Factors Determining Performance	
Declarative Knowledge	*Procedural Knowledge*	*Motivation*
Facts	Cognitive skill	Choice to perform
Principles	Psychomotor skill	Level of effort
Goals	Physical skill	Persistence of effort
	Interpersonal skill	

register and talks on the phone. When her manager is in the store, she shows a high level of effort, but her coworkers complain that, as soon as the manager leaves, Jane stops working. Her overall performance, therefore, is likely to be poor because, although she has the declarative and procedural knowledge necessary to do the job, she is not motivated to apply them to her job when her supervisor is not watching her.

We can think of a handful of individuals who have achieved the top level of performance in their fields. Think about Tiger Woods as a golf player, Bill Gates as Microsoft's founder and businessman, Bobby Fischer as a chess player, Thomas Edison as an inventor, and Socrates as a philosopher. How did they achieve such excellence? What made these individuals' performance so extraordinary? How were they able to improve their performance constantly even when others would believe they had reached a plateau? What these individuals have in common is that they devoted large number of hours to *deliberate practice*.[4] Deliberate practice is different from regular practice and from simply working many hours a week. Professor K. Anders Ericsson of Florida State University gives the following example: "Simply hitting a bucket of balls is not deliberate practice, which is why most golfers don't get better. Hitting an eight-iron 300 times with a goal of leaving the ball within 20 feet of the pin 80% of the time, continually observing results and making appropriate adjustments, and doing that for hours every day—that's deliberate practice." Top performers in all fields engage in deliberate practice consistently, daily, including weekends. The famous pianist Vladimir Horowitz was quoted as saying: "If I don't practice for a day, I know it; if I don't practice for two days, my wife knows it; if I don't practice for three days, the world knows it." Deliberate practice involves the following five steps:

1. Approach performance with the goal of getting better and better.
2. As you are performing, focus on what is happening and why you are doing things the way you do.
3. Once your task is finished, seek performance feedback from expert sources, and the more sources the better.
4. Build mental models of your job, your situation, and your organization.
5. Repeat steps 1–4 continually and on an ongoing basis.

2.1 Implications for Addressing Performance Problems

The fact that performance is affected by the combined effect of three different factors has implications for addressing performance problems. In order to address performance problems properly, managers must find information that will allow them to understand whether the source of the problem is declarative knowledge, procedural knowledge, motivation, or some combination of these three factors. If an employee lacks motivation but the manager believes the source of the problem is declarative knowledge, the manager may send the employee to a company-sponsored training program so he can acquire the knowledge that is presumably lacking. This would obviously be a waste of time and resources for the individual, manager, and organization in Jane's case because it is lack of motivation, and not lack of declarative knowledge, that is causing her poor performance. This is why performance management systems need not only to measure performance but also to provide information about the source of any performance deficiencies.

2.2 Factors Influencing Determinants of Performance

The factors that determine performance are affected by the employee (i.e., abilities and previous experience), human resources (HR) practices, and the work environment. For example, some companies offer more opportunities for training than do others. At the top of the list in terms of annual training investment are IBM ($1 billion), Accenture ($717 million), and Ford Motor ($500 million).[5] In these companies, declarative knowledge is not likely to be a big problem because, when lack of knowledge is identified, employees have multiple opportunities to fill in the gap. However, performance problems may be related more to procedural knowledge and motivation. In terms of procedural knowledge, employees may actually have the knowledge to perform certain tasks but may not have the skill to do them because of lack of opportunity for practice. In terms of motivation, downsizing interventions may have caused a "survivor syndrome," which includes retained employees' feelings of frustration, resentment, and even anger. These feelings are likely to have strong negative effects on motivation, and employees may expend minimal energy on their jobs.

Thus, there are three individual characteristics that determine performance: procedural knowledge, declarative knowledge, and motivation. In addition, HR practices and the work environment can affect performance. When addressing performance problems, managers first need to identify which of these factors is hampering performance and then help the employee improve his or her performance.

3 PERFORMANCE DIMENSIONS

As noted earlier, performance is multidimensional, meaning that we need to consider many different types of behaviors to understand performance. Although we can identify many specific behaviors, two types of behaviors or performance facets stand out: task performance and contextual performance.[6] Some authors also use the labels "prosocial behaviors" and "organizational citizenship behaviors" in referring to contextual performance.[7]

Contextual and task performance must be considered separately because they do not necessarily occur in tandem. An employee can be highly proficient at her task, but be an underperformer regarding contextual performance.[8] Task performance is defined as

- activities that transform raw materials into the goods and services that are produced by the organization
- activities that help with the transformation process by replenishing the supply of raw materials, distributing its finished products, or providing important planning, coordination, supervising, or staff functions that enable the organization to function effectively and efficiently.[9]

Contextual performance is defined as those behaviors that contribute to the organization's effectiveness by providing a good environment in which task performance can occur. Contextual performance includes behaviors such as the following:

- persisting with enthusiasm and exerting extra effort as necessary to complete one's own task activities successfully (e.g., being punctual and rarely absent, expending extra effort on the job)
- volunteering to carry out task activities that are not formally part of the job (e.g., suggesting organizational improvements, making constructive suggestions)

- helping and cooperating with others (e.g., assisting and helping coworkers and customers)
- following organizational rules and procedures (e.g., following orders and regulations, showing respect for authority, complying with organizational values and policies)
- endorsing, supporting, and defending organizational objectives (e.g., organizational loyalty, representing the organization favorably to outsiders)

Both task and contextual performance are important dimensions to take into account in performance management systems. Imagine what would happen to an organization in which all employees are outstanding regarding task performance but do not perform well regarding contextual performance. What if a colleague whose cubicle is next to yours needs to take a bathroom break and asks you to answer the phone if it rings because an important client will call at any moment? What if we said, "That is not MY job?"

Many organizations now realize that there is a need to focus on both task and contextual performance because organizations cannot function properly without a minimum dose of positive contextual behaviors on the part of all employees. Consider the case of TRW Automotive Inc., one of the world's 10 largest automotive suppliers and one of the top financial performers in the industry (http://www.trw.com). TRW had 2006 sales of $13.1 billion and employed approximately 63,800 people. With increasing market pressures and sluggish growth, TRW wanted to become more performance driven, experiment in new markets, and offer greater value to its shareholders. To do so, the senior management team developed what they labeled the "TRW behaviors." These behaviors are communicated throughout the company and have a prominent role in the performance management process. The majority of the TRW behaviors actually focus on *contextual performance.* Specifically, the TRW behaviors emphasize many of the elements of contextual performance, including teamwork and trust.

Table 2 summarizes the main differences between task and contextual performance. First, task performance varies across jobs. For example, the tasks performed by an HR manager are different from those performed by a line manager. The tasks performed by a senior HR manager (i.e., more strategic in nature) differ from those performed by an entry-level HR analyst (i.e., more operational in nature). On the other hand, contextual performance is fairly similar across functional and hierarchical levels. All employees, regardless of job title, function, and responsibilities, are equally responsible for, for example, volunteering to carry out task activities that are not formally part of the job. Second, task performance is likely to be role prescribed, meaning

TABLE 2 Main Differences Between Task and Contextual Performance

Task Performance	Contextual Performance
Varies across jobs	Fairly similar across jobs
Likely to be role prescribed	Not likely to be role prescribed
Antecedents: abilities and skills	Antecedent: personality

that task performance is usually included in one's job description. On the other hand, contextual performance behaviors are usually not role prescribed and, instead, are typically expected without making them explicit. Finally, task performance is mainly influenced by abilities and skills (e.g., cognitive, physical), whereas contextual performance is mainly influenced by personality (e.g., conscientiousness).[10]

There are numerous pressing reasons why both task and contextual performance dimensions should be included in a performance management system. First, global competition is raising the levels of effort required of employees. Thus, whereas it may have sufficed in the past to have a workforce that was competent regarding task performance, today's globalized world and accompanying competitive forces make it imperative that the workforce also engage in positive contextual performance. It is difficult to compete if an organization employs a workforce that does not engage in contextual behaviors. Second, related to the issue of global competition is the need to offer outstanding customer service. Contextual performance behaviors can make a profound impact on customer satisfaction. Imagine what a big difference it makes, from a customer perspective, when an employee puts in extra effort to satisfy a customer's needs. Third, many organizations are forming employees into teams. Although some teams may not be permanent because they are created to complete specific short-term tasks, the reality of today's world of work is that teams are here to stay. Interpersonal cooperation is a key determinant of team effectiveness. Thus, contextual performance becomes particularly relevant for teamwork. Fourth, including both task and contextual performance in the performance management system provides an additional benefit: Employees being rated are more satisfied with the system and believe the system is fairer if contextual performance is measured in addition to task performance.[11] It seems that employees are aware that contextual performance is important in affecting organizational effectiveness and, therefore, believe that these types of behaviors should be included in a performance management system in addition to the more traditional task performance. Finally, when supervisors evaluate performance, it is difficult for them to ignore the contextual performance dimension, even though the evaluation form they are using may not include any specific questions about contextual performance.[12] Consequently, since contextual performance has an impact on ratings of overall performance even when only task performance is measured, it makes sense to include contextual performance more explicitly.[13] Measuring contextual performance explicitly is also important because, unless carefully defined, it can be more subjective and subject to bias compared to measuring task performance.

Finally, there is an additional type of behavior that is another facet of contextual performance, but it is different from traditional ways of thinking about it: *voice behavior*.[14] Voice behavior is a type of behavior that emphasizes expression of constructive challenge with the goal to improve rather than merely criticize, it challenges the status quo in a positive way, and it is about making innovative suggestions for change and recommending modifications to standard procedures even when others, including an employee's supervisor, disagree. Consider an employee who has just been hired into your organization. This new colleague was recruited from a competitor, which is known to implement top-notch performance management practices. This employee, having the benefit of an outsider perspective, can point to processes that could be improved. For example, the new colleague may suggest that more feedback be given to the members of the team regarding their performance. This employee may even send an e-mail message to all members of her team and to her supervisor including suggestions for improvement based on proven practices directly observed elsewhere. Some of these suggestions may not be applicable in the new organizational environment due to different equipment, processes, products, and clients. However, others, if implemented, may produce immediate and highly beneficial results. Although such type of behavior can be included as part of the broader category of contextual behavior, it is different in that it is not conformist in nature. In fact, voice behavior can be seen as a threat by the new employee's supervisor who is used to "doing things the same way we've done them before." Such supervisors may perceive the suggestions for changes and improvements as a threat to the status quo. Moreover, more senior organizational members may also feel personally threatened by the knowledge, energy, and innovative ideas of the new employee. These reactions to voice behavior can be a sign that the wrong people are occupying leadership positions in the organization and a sign of imminent organizational decline.[15] On the other hand, healthier organizational environments that are more adaptive and promote innovation and improvements are more receptive to voice behavior and even reward it. For example, a recent study found that, although voice behavior was not explicitly included as part of a performance management system, raters gave higher performance scores to employees who engaged in voice behavior in spite of similarities regarding task and contextual performance ratings.[16]

It is important to understand contextual factors and how they affect how different organizations choose to define and measure performance. For example, consider the important role that cultural differences can play in this regard.[17] Organizations in the United States are likely to value behaviors that are individualistic in nature and that demonstrate individual achievement, self-reliance, competition, and disengaged emotional styles. In such organizations, individuals from ethnic minority groups who align themselves with more collectivistic values may receive lower performance ratings compared to members of the majority group and may be seen as helpless, dependent, and lacking sufficient commitment to their work and organizations. This is another important reason for including both task and contextual performance in the system so that all organizational members are given an opportunity to demonstrate their value-added to the organization regardless of different behaviors, styles, and cultural values and norms.

In short, performance includes both a task and a contextual dimension. Both should be considered because both dimensions contribute to organizational success. In the case of both task and contextual performance, each behavior should be defined clearly so that employees understand what is expected of them. Organizations that include both task and contextual dimensions are likely to be more successful, as in the case of O_2 Ireland, Ireland's second largest mobile phone operator. Headquartered in Dublin, O_2 Ireland employs more than 1,750 people. In 2000, O_2 Ireland implemented a performance management system in its 320-seat customer care center in Limerick. O_2's performance management system includes task-related facets centered in hard metrics regarding productivity as well as contextual-related facets such as involvement in staff socialization and contribution to team development. The targets set for each employee are also aligned with company objectives. O_2 concluded that this focus on both task and contextual performance has led to higher levels of customer service and employee satisfaction.

4 APPROACHES TO MEASURING PERFORMANCE

Before we discuss how to measure performance, we must remember that employees do not perform in a vacuum. Figure 1 shows that employees work in an organizational context, engaging in certain behaviors that produce certain results. The same employee may behave differently (and produce different results) if placed in a different situation (e.g., working with a different supervisor or using better or worse equipment).

Given the model shown in Figure 1, there are three approaches that can be used to measure performance: the *behavior, results, and trait* approaches.[18]

4.1 Behavior Approach

The behavior approach emphasizes what employees do on the job and does not consider employees' traits or the outcomes resulting from their behaviors. This is basically a process-oriented approach that emphasizes *how* an employee does the job.

The behavior approach is most appropriate under the following circumstances:

- *The link between behaviors and results is not obvious.* Sometimes the relationship between behaviors and the desired outcomes is not clear. In some cases, the desired result may not be achieved in spite of the fact that the right behaviors are in place. For example, a salesperson may not be able to close a deal because of a downturn in the economy. In other cases, results may be achieved in spite of the absence of the correct behaviors. For example, a pilot may not check all the items in the preflight checklist but the flight may nevertheless be successful (i.e., take off and land safely and on time). When the link between behaviors and results is not always obvious, it is beneficial to focus on behaviors as opposed to outcomes.

- *Outcomes occur in the distant future.* When the desired results will not be seen for months, or even years, the measurement of behaviors is beneficial. Take the case of NASA's Mars Exploration Rover Mission program. NASA launched the exploration rover Spirit on June 10, 2003, which landed on Mars on January 3, 2004, after traveling 487 million kilometers (302.6 million miles). Its twin, the exploration rover Opportunity, was launched on July 7, 2003, and landed on the opposite side of Mars on January 24, 2004. From launching to landing, this mission took about six months to complete. In this circumstance, it is certainly appropriate to assess the performance of the engineers involved in the mission by measuring their behaviors in short intervals during this six-month period rather than waiting until the final result (i.e., successful or unsuccessful landing) is observed.

- *Poor results are due to causes beyond the performer's control.* When the results of an employee's performance are beyond the employee's control, it makes sense to

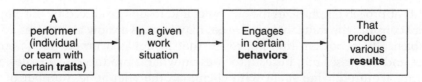

FIGURE 1 Job Performance in Context *Source:* Adapted from Grote, D. (1996). *The complete guide to performance appraisal* (Fig. 3-1, p. 37). New York: American Management Association.

BOX 1

Task and Contextual Performance at Sprint Nextel

Sprint Nextel (http://www.sprint.com) is a provider of local, wireless, long-distance voice, and voice-over IP services. The company is headquartered in Reston, Virginia. At Sprint Nextel, all employees are evaluated, and development plans are created through the use of five core competencies or "dimensions." These dimensions include act with integrity, focus on the customer, deliver results, build relationships, and demonstrate leadership. The dimensions are used not only for business strategy and objectives but also as a template for what successful performance looks like at the company. These dimensions include the consideration of both task and contextual performance, and employees in the evaluation and development process are asked to write behavioral examples of how they have performed on each dimension. For example, the delivering results dimension clearly links to performing specific tasks of one's job. Each employee has certain tasks to complete on a regular basis to keep the business moving. On the other hand, the company is concerned about how the work gets done and contributing to a good work environment that allows greater effectiveness. This is apparent through the dimensions that look at how employees develop relationships with others and act with integrity in their day-to-day functioning. In summary, Sprint Nextel has recognized the importance of considering both task and contextual components of a job in its performance management system. Employees are evaluated not only on results but also on how they are achieved through working with others.[19]

---

emphasize the measurement of behaviors. For example, consider a situation involving two assembly-line workers, one of them working the day shift and the other the night shift. When the assembly line gets stuck because of technical problems, the employee working during the day receives immediate technical assistance, so the assembly line is back in motion in less than five minutes. By contrast, the employee working the night shift has very little technical support and, therefore, when the assembly line breaks down, it takes about 45 minutes for it to be up and running again. If we measured results, we would conclude that the performance of the day-shift employee is far superior to that of the night-shift employee, but this would be an incorrect conclusion. Both employees may be equally competent and do the job equally well. The results produced by these employees are uneven because they depend on the amount and quality of technical assistance they receive when the assembly line is stuck.

Next, let's discuss the results approach to measuring performance.

4.2 Results Approach

The results approach emphasizes the outcomes and results produced by the employees. It does not consider the traits that employees may possess or how employees do the job. This is basically a bottom-line approach that is not concerned about employee behaviors and processes but, instead, focuses on what is produced (e.g., sales, number of accounts acquired, time spent with clients on the telephone, number of errors). Defining and measuring results usually takes less time than defining and measuring behaviors needed to achieve these results. Also, the results approach is usually seen as

---

BOX 2

**Implementing a Behavior Approach to Measuring Performance
at Dollar General**

At Dollar General (http://www.dollargeneral.com), a behavior approach is utilized to measure performance. Tennessee-based Dollar General has 8,000 stores operating in the United States with more than 64,000 employees. The company sells consumable basics such as paper products, cleaning supplies, health and beauty products, foods and snacks, housewares, toys, and basic apparel. As part of the performance management system, Dollar General has identified behaviors that serve as indicators to underlying competencies. These behaviors are reviewed and utilized to encourage certain outcomes and provide feedback and rewards to staff members. For example, the company management sought to improve attendance among employees. In order to encourage employees to arrive to work on time, a system was developed to group employees into teams who earn points. A wall chart was created displaying a racetrack, and each team was given a car that would be moved forward by the number of points earned each day. After a certain number of laps around the track, employees on the teams with the most points would be given a choice about how to celebrate. The program was successful within the first two weeks and increased attendance significantly. In summary, Dollar General's performance management system includes the use of a behavior approach to measuring performance.[20]

---

more cost-effective because results can be less expensive to track than behaviors. Overall, data resulting from a results approach seem to be objective and are intuitively very appealing.

The results approach is most appropriate under the following circumstances:

- *Workers are skilled in the needed behaviors.* An emphasis on results is appropriate when workers have the necessary knowledge and skills to do the work. In such situations, workers know what specific behaviors are needed to achieve the desired results and they are also sufficiently skilled to know what to do to correct any process-related problems when the desired results are not obtained. Consider the example of a professional basketball player. A free throw is an unhindered shot made from the foul line and is given to one team to penalize the other team for committing a foul. Free throw shooting can make the difference between winning and losing in a close basketball game. Professional players know that there is really no secret to becoming a great free throw shooter: just hours and hours of dedicated practice besides actual basketball play. In assessing the performance of professional basketball players, the free throw shooting percentage is a key results-oriented performance indicator because most players have the skills to do it well. It's just a matter of assessing whether they do it or not.

- *Behaviors and results are obviously related.* In some situations, certain results can be obtained only if a worker engages in certain specific behaviors. This is the case of jobs involving repetitive tasks such as assembly-line work or newspaper delivery. Take the case of a person delivering newspapers. Performance can be measured adopting a results approach: whether the newspaper is delivered to every customer within a particular time frame. For the employee to obtain this result, she needs to pick up the papers at a specific time and use the most effective delivery route. If these behaviors are not present, the paper will not be delivered on time.

- *Results show consistent improvement over time.* When results improve consistently over time, it is an indication that workers are aware of the behaviors needed to complete the job successfully. In these situations, it is appropriate to adopt a results approach to assessing performance.
- *There are many ways to do the job right.* When there are different ways in which one can do the tasks required for a job, a results approach is appropriate. An emphasis on results can be beneficial because it could encourage employees to achieve the desired outcomes in creative and innovative ways.

Table 3 summarizes the conditions under which a behavior or a results approach may be best suited for assessing performance. However, these approaches are not mutually exclusive. In fact, measuring *both* behavior and results is the approach adopted by many organizations. Consider the case of The Limited, Inc., a retailer head-quartered in Columbus, Ohio.[21] The Limited, Inc. now operates 3,500 retail stores and seven retail brands including Victoria's Secret, Express, The Limited, Bath & Body Works, C. O. Bigelow, The White Barn Candle Co., and Henri Bendel. The Limited aims to foster an entrepreneurial culture for its managers; therefore, managers who thrive in the company have a history of delivering impressive business results. The Limited decided to design a new performance management system that is now used uniformly by all The Limited companies. With the involvement of outside consultants and employees, The Limited developed a performance management system wherein managers are measured on business results including total sales, market share, and expense/sale growth ratio as well as leadership competencies that are tailored to The Limited. A few of these competencies include developing fashion sense, financial acumen, and entrepreneurial drive. Overall, The Limited has been pleased with the new system because it helps align individual goals with business strategy and results. Raters like the new system because behavioral anchors help define the competencies, which make ratings more straightforward. Finally, employees comment that they appreciate the new focus on *how* results are achieved, as opposed to focusing only on *what* is achieved (i.e., sales).

TABLE 3 Behavior Approach Versus Results Approach

Adopting a behavior approach to measuring performance is most appropriate when
- The link between behaviors and results is not obvious
- Outcomes occur in the distant future
- Poor results are due to causes beyond the performer's control

Adopting a results approach to measuring performance is most appropriate when
- Workers are skilled in the needed behaviors
- Behaviors and results are obviously related
- Results show consistent improvement over time
- There are many ways to do the job right

BOX 3

Implementing a Results Approach to Measuring Performance at HomeLoanCenter.com

Companies frequently utilize rewards and incentives as a part of performance management systems. At HomeLoanCenter.com, there are many bonus and reward opportunities that emphasize outcomes, or a results approach to measuring performance. HomeLoanCenter.com is a company based in Irvine (California) that provides home mortgage loans directly to consumers over the Internet and employs over 600 people. Some of the criteria used to evaluate performance based on outcomes include closing the most loans in a given time period, bringing in the most revenue, and providing the most referrals. Rewards include getting the use of a Mercedes or Hummer and a special parking place to the top loan agent of the month as an acknowledgment of his or her success. Other awards include using the company's suite at the Staples Center in Los Angeles for sporting events or concerts or winning trips to Mexico on CEO Anthony Hsieh's 60-foot private yacht. In summary, HomeLoanCenter.com utilizes a performance management system focusing on outcomes or results in order to motivate employees and bring about business results. The company looks at what is produced at work rather than at behaviors or how the job gets done.[22]

4.3 Trait Approach

The trait approach emphasizes the individual performer and ignores the specific situation, behaviors, and results. If one adopts the trait approach, raters evaluate relatively stable traits. These can include abilities, such as cognitive abilities (which are not easily trainable) or personality (which is not likely to change over time). For example, performance measurement may consist of assessing an employee's intelligence and conscientiousness at the end of each review period. This approach is justified based on the positive relationship found between abilities (such as intelligence) and personality traits (such as conscientiousness) and desirable work-related behaviors.[23],[24] Several vendors provide tools to assess relatively stable traits such as these, sometimes with the capability of administering them online. Vendors who describe their products online include ddi.com, www.appliedpsych.com, www.previsor.com, www.kenexa.com, www.personneldecisions.com, and www.vangent-hcm.com.

What are some of the challenges of implementing a system that emphasizes the measurement of traits only? First, traits are not under the control of individuals. In most cases, they are fairly stable over one's life span. They are not likely to change even if an individual is willing to exert substantial effort to do so. Consequently, employees may feel that a system based on traits is not fair because the development of these traits is usually beyond their control.[25] Second, the fact that an individual possesses a certain trait (e.g., intelligence) does not mean that this trait will necessarily lead to desired results and behaviors. As noted in Figure 1, individuals are embedded in specific situations. If the equipment is faulty and coworkers are uncooperative, even a very intelligent and conscientious employee is not likely to engage in behaviors conducive to supporting the organization's goals.

In spite of these challenges, there are situations in which a trait-oriented approach can be fruitful. For example, as part of its business strategy, an organization may anticipate drastic structural changes that will lead to the reorganization of most functions and the resulting reallocation of employees. In such a circumstance, it may be useful to assess the traits possessed by the various individuals so that fair and appropriate decisions are made regarding the allocation of human resources across the newly created organizational units. This is, of course, a fairly unique circumstance. In most organizations, performance is not measured using the trait approach. This is why two more popular approaches to measuring performance are based on behaviors and results, as we discussed earlier.

Summary Points

- Performance is about behavior or what employees do, not about what employees produce or the outcomes of their work. Performance management systems typically include the measurement of both behaviors (how the work is done) and the results (the outcomes of one's work). Performance is evaluative (i.e., we judge it based on whether it helps advance or hinder organizational goals) and multidimensional (i.e., many behaviors are needed to describe an employee's performance).

- Performance is determined by a combination of declarative knowledge (i.e., information), procedural knowledge (i.e., know-how), and motivation (i.e., willingness to perform). Thus, Performance = Declarative Knowledge × Procedural Knowledge × Motivation. If any of the three determinants of performance has a very small value (e.g., very little procedural knowledge), then performance will also have a low level. All three determinants of performance must be present for performance to reach satisfactory (and better) levels.

- There are two important facets of performance: task and contextual. Task performance refers to the specific activities required by one's job. Contextual performance refers to the activities required to be a good "organizational citizen" (e.g., helping coworkers, supporting company initiatives). In addition, voice behavior is another important facet of contextual performance (i.e., raising constructive challenges with the goal to improve rather than merely criticize, challenge the status quo in a positive way, and make innovative suggestions for change when others, including an employee's supervisor, disagree). Both task and contextual performance are needed for organizational success, and both should be included in a performance management system.

- Employees do not perform in a vacuum. Employees work in a specific situation, engaging in specific behaviors that produce certain results. An emphasis on behaviors leads to a behavior-based approach to assessing performance. An emphasis on results leads to a results-based approach to assessing performance. An emphasis on the employee leads to a trait-based approach to assessing performance. The relative emphasis given to each of these approaches to measuring performance should be influenced by the organization's business strategy. For example, an organization emphasizing research and development as its main strategy would be concerned about results that are not easily observable in the short term. Thus, an emphasis on behaviors would be consistent with such a business strategy.

- A behavior approach emphasizes what employees do (i.e., how work is done). This approach is most appropriate when (1) the link between behaviors and results is not obvious, (2) outcomes occur in the distant future, and/or (3) poor results are due to causes beyond the employee's control. A behavior approach may not be the best choice if most of these conditions are not present. In most situations, however, the inclusion of at least some behavior based measures is beneficial.

- A results approach emphasizes the outcomes and results produced by employees. This is basically a bottom-line approach that is not concerned with how the work is done as long as certain specific results are obtained. This approach is most appropriate when (1) workers are skilled in the needed behaviors, (2) behaviors and results are obviously related, (3) results show consistent improvement over time, and/or (4) there are many ways to do the job right. An emphasis on results can be beneficial because it could encourage employees to achieve the desired outcomes in creative and innovative ways. On the other hand, measuring only results is typically not welcomed by employees even in types of jobs for which the expected result is very clear (e.g., sales jobs).

- A traits approach emphasizes individual traits that remain fairly stable throughout an individual's life span (e.g., cognitive abilities or personality). This approach may be most appropriate when an organization anticipates undertaking drastic structural changes. A major disadvantage of this approach is that traits are not under the control of individuals, and even when individuals possess a specific positive trait (e.g., high intelligence), this does not necessarily mean that the employee will engage in productive behaviors that lead to desired results.

CASE STUDY 1

Diagnosing the Causes of Poor Performance

Heather works in the training department of a large information technology (IT) organization. She is in charge of designing and delivering interpersonal skills training, including communication skills, networking, and new manager training classes. Heather has excellent knowledge of how to design a training class. She incorporates behavioral modeling and practice into all of her classes. She has also conducted research on what good communication consists of, how to network, and what new managers need to know to be successful. However, individuals who attend Heather's training classes often give her low ratings, stating that she has a hard time answering specific questions in classes and that she does not seem approachable after the classes when individuals want to ask questions.

1. You are Heather's manager. In your opinion, what is causing Heather's poor performance? Is it due to a deficiency in declarative knowledge or procedural knowledge?
2. What can be done to remedy the performance problem? ▪

CASE STUDY 2

Differentiating Task from Contextual Performance

Consider the following adaptation of a job description for the position of a district business manager for a sales organization in Bristol-Myers Squibb (BMS) (www.bms.com). BMS produces pharmaceuticals, infant formulas and nutritional products, ostomy and advanced wound care products, cardiovascular imaging supplies, and over-the-counter products. Some of its brands include Enfamil, Cardiolite, and Plavix. Its stated mission is to "extend and enhance human life by providing the highest-quality pharmaceutical and related health care products." In addition, all employees live by the BMS pledge: "We pledge—to our patients and customers, to our employees and partners, to our shareholders and neighbors, and to the world we serve—to act on our belief that the priceless ingredient of every product is the honor and integrity of its maker."

DBM JOB RESPONSIBILITIES

The following are the core performance objectives for the district business manager (DBM) position: Create the environment to build an innovative culture, create and articulate a vision, drive

innovation by embracing diversity and change, set the example, and thereby shape the culture. Develop and communicate the business plan, understand and explain BMS strategies, translate national plan to business plans for districts and territories, set goals and expectations of performance, set priorities, and allocate resources. Execute and implement the business plan, maximize rank order lists of medical education professional-relationships, achieve optimum coverage frequency of highest potential physicians, take accountability, and achieve results. Build relationships focused on customer retention, develop relationships (i.e., networks), influence others (i.e., internal and external), and develop self and others. Strong skills are acquired in the following areas: written and oral communication, negotiation, strategic analysis, leadership, team building, and coaching.

1. Based on the DBM job description, extract a list of task and contextual performance behaviors. Refer to Table 2 for a review of the differences between task and contextual performance. ■

CASE STUDY 3

Choosing a Performance Measurement Approach at Paychex, Inc.

The following job description is for an account executive at Paychex, Inc. (www.paychex.com). Paychex, Inc., is a leading national provider of payroll, human resources, and benefits outsourcing solutions for small- to medium-sized businesses. Paychex is headquartered in Rochester, New York, but the company has more than 100 offices and serves hundreds of thousands of clients nationwide. Because account executives often make sales calls individually, their managers do not always directly observe their performance. Furthermore, managers are also responsible for sales in their markets and for staying up-to-date on payroll laws. However, account executives are responsible for training new account executives and networking in the industries in which they sell products. For example, if an account manager is responsible for retail

companies, then that account executive is expected to attend retail trade shows and professional meetings to identify potential clients and to stay current with the issues facing the retail industry.

ACCOUNT EXECUTIVE JOB RESPONSIBILITIES

- Performing client needs analysis to ensure that the major market services product can meet a client's requirements and expectations.
- Establishing clients on the host processing system.
- Acting as primary contact for the client during the conversion process.
- Supporting clients during the first few payrolls.

- Completing the required documentation to turn the client over to customer service for ongoing support.
- Scheduling and making client calls and, when necessary, supporting sales representatives in presales efforts.
- Keeping abreast of the major market services system and software changes, major changes and trends in the PC industry, and changes in wage and tax law.

1. Based on the above description, assess whether Paychex should use a behavior approach, a results approach, or a combination of both to measure performance.
2. Using the accompanying table as a guide, place check marks next to the descriptions that apply to the job of account executive. Explain why you chose the approach you did. ■

Behavior approach to measuring performance is most appropriate when

the link between behaviors and results is not obvious

outcomes occur in the distant future

poor results are due to causes beyond the performer's control

---

Results approach to measuring performance is most appropriate when

workers are skilled in the necessary behaviors

behaviors and results are obviously related

results show consistent improvement over time

there are many ways to do the job right

CASE STUDY 4

Deliberate Practice Makes Perfect

Ricardo is an associate financial analyst in a large financial consulting firm. He works in the emerging markets division developing low-cost products for the Southeast Asia region. He was selected for this position because of his wide range of skills, relevant experience, and analytical abilities.

During his time at the firm, he has worked on a variety of projects and has become well respected among his peers. He is satisfied with his job and with his progress so far, but he strives to work on more challenging projects, wants to make a greater impact, and seeks a leadership-centered role. Ricardo has a strong drive and eventually hopes to get a position at the highest levels of the organization.

In recent years, the firm has remained stable but has struggled with growth. The recent economic downturn changed the financial landscape and is requiring new and innovative solutions to common issues such as reducing and calculating risk. As a result, the firm decided to launch a company-wide competition for the best risk assessment model in order to motivate all of its employees to work on solving this issue. After several rounds of assessment and interviews, the top two finalists will be invited to present their ideas to the CEO who will make the final decision regarding the winner of the competition. The winning team will receive a substantial cash prize alongside significant prestige.

Ricardo sees this as the perfect chance to impress his colleagues and supervisors and to establish himself as a top performer. This competition presents the ideal circumstances for him to not only prove himself but also really shine. He and his team are incredibly excited about this opportunity and have been working tirelessly on this project. Ricardo's strong math and finance background help him come up with a comprehensive and complex algorithm that seems to be surprisingly effective in predicting risk. Each member contributes to different aspects of the project and together they create a strong proposal that they believe is worthy of winning the competition.

Ricardo emerges as leader of the group due to his detailed knowledge and understanding of its proposed model. He is excellent at motivating and guiding his small team, but he gets very nervous in formal situations and speaking in public, which questions his ability to influence people. He knows that part of the selection process will involve presenting his team's idea to different departments and important stakeholders and that he will be expected to take the lead during these presentations. He also knows that the key to passing through each round of the selection process will be to get people on board with their idea and convincing them of its potential.

You are Ricardo's manager, and he comes to you for advice and guidance about the current situation. You believe that he is one of the brightest employees in the company and that he has the potential to become the most successful as well. However, he will need to overcome his fear of public speaking and develop his presentation skills in order to win this competition and reach his goals. Ricardo is committed to improvement and to becoming a top performer, and he understands that this will require a considerable amount of time and dedication. However, he hasn't heard of the concept of deliberate practice and is unsure of how to get the most value out of the time he dedicates to improving his performance.

1. Based on the concept of deliberate practice, list the five steps that lead to excellence.
2. Provide Ricardo with specific recommendations on how he can "deliberately practice" his presentation skills. ■

End Notes

1. Motowidlo, S. J., Borman, W. C., & Schmit, M. J. (1997). A theory of individual differences in task and contextual performance. *Human Performance, 10,* 71–83.

2. Murphy, K. R., & Shiarella, A. H. (1997). Implications of the multidimensional nature of job performance for the validity of selection tests: Multivariate frameworks for studying test validity. *Personnel Psychology, 50,* 823–854.

3. McCloy, R. A., Campbell, J. P., & Cudeck, R. (1994). A confirmatory test of a model of performance determinants. *Journal of Applied Psychology, 79,* 493–505.

4. Colvin, G. (2006). What it takes to be great. *Fortune, 154,* 88–96.

5. Edward Jones, A. G. Edwards lauded for training efforts (2002, February 20). *St. Louis Business Journal.* Available online at http://stlouis.bizjournals.com/stlouis/stories/2002/02/18/daily31.html. Retrieval date: May 1, 2011.

6. Borman, W. C., Penner, L. A., Allen, T. D., & Motowidlo, S. (2001). Personality predictors of citizenship performance. *International Journal of Selection and Assessment, 9,* 52–69.

7. Borman, W. C. (2004). The concept of organizational citizenship. *Current Directions in Psychological Science, 13,* 238–241.

8. Borman, W. C., Hanson, M., & Hedge, J. (1997). Personnel selection. *Annual Review of Psychology, 48,* 299–337.

9. Cascio, W. F., & Aguinis, H. (2001). The Federal Uniform Guidelines on Employee Selection Procedures (1978): An update on selected issues. *Review of Public Personnel Administration, 21,* 200–218.

10. Arvey, R. D., & Murphy, K. R. (1998). Performance evaluation in work settings. *Annual Review of Psychology, 49,* 141–168.

11. Febles, M. (2005). *The role of task and contextual performance in appraisal fairness and satisfaction.* Unpublished doctoral dissertation, California School of Organizational Studies, Alliant International University, San Diego, CA.

12. Van Scotter, J. R., Motowidlo, S. J., & Cross, T. C. (2000). Effects of task performance and contextual performance on systemic rewards. *Journal of Applied Psychology, 85,* 526–535.

13. Bolino, M. C., Varela, J. A., Bande, B., & Turnley, W. H. (2006). The impact of impression-management tactics on supervisor ratings of organizational citizenship behavior. *Journal of Organizational Behavior, 27,* 281–297.

14. Van Dyne, L., & LePine, J. A. (1998). Helping and voice extra-role behaviors: Evidence of construct and predictive validity. *Academy of Management Journal, 41*, 108–119.

15. Bedeian, A. G., & Armenakis, A. A. (1998). The cesspool syndrome: How dreck floats to the top of declining organizations. *Academy of Management Executive, 12*, 58–63.

16. Whiting, S. W., Podsakoff, P. M., & Pierce, J. R. (2008). Effects of task performance, helping, voice, and organizational loyalty on performance appraisal ratings. *Journal of Applied Psychology, 93*, 125–139.

17. Stone, D. L., Stone-Romero, E. F., & Lukaszewski, K. M. (2007). The impact of cultural values on the acceptance and effectiveness of human resource management policies and practices. *Human Resource Management Review, 17*, 152–165.

18. The discussion of each of these approaches is based on D. Grote. *The Complete Guide to Performance Appraisal* (New York: American Management Association, 1996), chap. 3.

19. Ellis, K. (2004). Individual development plans: The building blocks of development. *Training, 41*, 20–25.

20. Daniels, A. (2005, October). Daniels' scientific method. *Workforce Management, 84*, 44–45.

21. Heneman, R. L., & Thomas, A. L. (1997). The Limited, Inc.: Using strategic performance management to drive brand leadership. *Compensation and Benefits Review, 29*, 33–40.

22. Chang, J. (2004). Trophy value. *Sales and Marketing Management, 156*, 24–30.

23. Viswesvaran, C., & Ones, D. S. (2000). Perspectives on models of job performance. *International Journal of Selection and Assessment, 8*, 216–226.

24. Schmidt, F. L. (2002). The role of general cognitive ability and job performance: Why there cannot be a debate. *Human Performance, 15*, 187–210.

25. Smither, J. W., & Walker, A. G. (2004). Are the characteristics of narrative comments related to improvement in multirater feedback ratings over time? *Journal of Applied Psychology, 89*, 575–581.

Measuring Results and Behaviors

Measuring Results and Behaviors

The reason most people never reach their goals is that they don't define them, or ever seriously consider them as believable or achievable. Winners can tell you where they are going, what they plan to do along the way, and who will be sharing the adventure with them.

—DENIS WAITLEY

LEARNING OBJECTIVES

By the end of this chapter, you will be able to do the following:

- Adopt a results approach to measuring performance, including the development of accountabilities, objectives, and standards.

- Determine accountabilities and their relative importance.

- Identify objectives that are specific and clear, challenging, agreed upon, significant, prioritized, bound by time, achievable, fully communicated, flexible, and limited in number.

- Identify performance standards that are related to the position, concrete, specific, measurable, practical to measure, meaningful, realistic and achievable, and reviewed regularly.

- Adopt a behavior approach to measuring performance, including the identification and assessment of competencies.

- Develop competencies that are defined clearly, provide a description of specific behavioral indicators that can be observed when someone demonstrates a competency effectively, provide a description of specific behaviors that are likely to occur when someone doesn't demonstrate a competency effectively (what a competency is not), and include suggestions for developing them further.

- Develop comparative performance measurement systems such as simple rank order, alternation rank order, paired comparisons, relative percentile, and forced distribution (being aware of the relative advantages and disadvantages of each).
- Develop absolute performance measurement systems such as essays, behavior checklists, critical incidents, and graphic rating scales, and understand their advantages and disadvantages.

In this chapter, we provide a detailed description of how to measure performance, adopting the two most common approaches: results and behavior.

1 MEASURING RESULTS

If one adopts a results approach to measure performance, one needs to ask the following key questions:

- What are the different areas in which this individual is expected to focus efforts (key accountabilities)?
- Within each area, what are the expected objectives?
- How do we know how well the results have been achieved (performance standards)?[1]

As a reminder, key accountabilities are broad areas of a job for which the employee is responsible for producing results. A discussion of results also includes specific objectives that the employee will achieve as part of each accountability. Objectives are statements of important and measurable outcomes. Finally, discussing results also means discussing performance standards. A performance standard is a yardstick used to evaluate how well employees have achieved each objective. Performance standards provide information on acceptable and unacceptable performance, for example, regarding quality, quantity, cost, and time. Organizations that implement a management by objectives (MBO) philosophy are likely to implement components of performance management systems, including objectives and standards. For example, the contract for the chief of police of the city of Flevoland in the Netherlands includes a direct link between objectives of the police department and his personal income.[2] Similarly, the police department of the city of Utrecht (also in the Netherlands) has specific performance objectives including that 150 suspects of public violence and 1,050 minors suspected of any crime should be brought before the public prosecutor annually. Similar objectives have been set by police departments in England and Wales. Setting these objectives has not always led to the intended results because, in many cases, police officers resort to gaming strategies to achieve the objectives, often at the expense of providing a high-level quality of service to their local communities.[3] Nevertheless, overall, an emphasis on objectives and standards is likely to allow employees to translate organizational goals into individual goals, which is a key goal of MBO philosophies.[4]

1.1 Determining Accountabilities

The first step in determining accountabilities is to collect information about the job. The primary source is, of course, the job description that has resulted from the job analysis and a consideration of unit- and organization-level strategic priorities. The job description provides information on the tasks performed. Tasks included in the job description can be grouped into clusters of tasks based on their degree of relatedness. Each of these clusters or accountabilities is a broad area of the job for which the employee is responsible for producing results.

After the accountabilities have been identified, we need to determine their relative degree of importance. To understand this issue, we need to ask the following questions:

- What percentage of the employee's time is spent performing each accountability?
- If the accountability were performed inadequately, would there be a significant impact on the work unit's mission?
- Is there a significant consequence of error? Could inadequate performance of the accountability contribute to the injury or death of the employee or others, serious property damage, or loss of time and money?

Although determining accountabilities may at first seem like a daunting task, it is not that difficult. Let's discuss an example based on a real job in a real organization to illustrate how it is done. Consider the position of Training Specialist/Consultant—Leadership & Team Development for Target Corporation, a growth company focused exclusively on general merchandise retailing (www.target.com). The job description is the following:

Identifies the training and development needs of Target Corporation's work force (in collaboration with partners), with primary emphasis on exempt team members. Designs and delivers training and development workshops and programs and maintains an ongoing evaluation of the effectiveness of those programs. Assumes leadership and strategic responsibility for assigned processes. May supervise the non-exempt staff.

Based on the job description and additional information found on Target's Web page regarding the company's strategic priorities, a list of the accountabilities, consequences of performing them inadequately, consequences of making errors, and percentage of time spent in each are shown in the following:

- *Process leadership.* Leads the strategy and direction of assigned processes. Coordinates related projects and directs or manages resources. This is extremely important to the functioning of Target leadership and the ability of executives to meet strategic business goals. If this position is managed improperly, then it will lead to a loss of time and money in training costs and leadership ineffectiveness. (40% of time)
- *Supervision of nonexempt staff.* Supervises nonexempt staff working in the unit. This is relatively important to the functioning of the work unit. If nonexempt staff members are supervised improperly, then the development of the employees and the ability to meet business targets will be compromised. (10% of time)
- *Coaching.* Conducts one-on-one executive coaching with managers and executives. This is extremely important to the development of internal leaders. If managers and executives are not coached to improve their performance, there is a loss of time and money associated with their poor performance as well as the cost of replacing them if necessary. (20% of time)
- *Team-building consultation.* Assists company leaders in designing and delivering their own team-building sessions and other interventions. This is relatively important to the successfulness of teams at Target. Mismanagement of this

function will result in teams not meeting their full potential and wasting time and resources on conducting the team sessions. (10% of time)

- *Assessment instrument feedback.* Delivers feedback based on scores obtained on assessment instruments of skills, ability, personality, and other individual characteristics. This is relatively important to the development of leaders. If assessment is incorrect, it could derail leader development. (10% of time)
- *Product improvement.* Continuously seeks and implements opportunities to use technology to increase the effectiveness of leadership and team development programs. This is important to the effectiveness of training delivery and could result in significant gains in efficiencies of the systems if carried out effectively. (10% of time)

1.2 Determining Objectives

After the accountabilities have been identified, the next step in measuring results is to determine specific objectives. Objectives are statements of an important and measurable outcome that, when accomplished, will help ensure success for the accountability. The purpose of establishing objectives is to identify a limited number of highly important results that, when achieved, will have a dramatic impact on the overall success of the organization. After objectives are set, employees should receive feedback on their progress toward attaining the objective. Rewards should be allocated to those employees who have reached their objectives.

Objectives are clearly important because they help employees guide their efforts. To serve a useful function, objectives must have the following characteristics[5]:

1. *Specific and clear.* Objectives must be easy to understand. In addition, they must be verifiable and measurable, for example, a directive: "Cut travel cost by 20%."
2. *Challenging.* Objectives need to be challenging (but not impossible to achieve). They must be a stretch, but employees should feel that the objective is reachable.
3. *Agreed upon.* To be most effective, objectives need to result from an agreement between the manager and the employee. Employees need an opportunity to participate in setting objectives. Participation in the process increases objective aspirations and acceptance, and it decreases objective resistance.
4. *Significant.* Objectives must be important to the organization. Employees must believe that if the objective is achieved, it will make a critical impact on the overall success of the organization. In addition, achieving the objective should give the employee the feeling of congruence between the employee's performance and the goals of the organization. This, in turn, is likely to enhance feelings of value to the organization.
5. *Prioritized.* Not all objectives are created equal; therefore, objectives should be prioritized and tackled one by one.
6. *Bound by time.* Good objectives have deadlines and mileposts. Objectives lacking a time dimension are likely to be neglected.
7. *Achievable.* Good objectives are doable; that is, employees should have sufficient skills and training to achieve them. If they don't, then the organization should make resources available so that the necessary skills are learned and equipment is made available to achieve the goals.
8. *Fully communicated.* In addition to the manager and employee in question, the other organizational members who may be affected by the objectives need to be aware of them.

9. *Flexible.* Good objectives are not immutable. They can and likely will change based on changes in the work or business environments.

10. *Limited in number.* Too many objectives may become impossible to achieve, but too few may not make a sufficient contribution to the organization. Objectives must be limited in number. Between 5 and 10 objectives per review period is a manageable number, but this can change based on the position and organization in question.

Several organizations set goals following these guidelines. For example, Microsoft Corporation has a long history of using individual goals in its performance management system. The goals at Microsoft are described by the acronym SMART: specific, measurable, achievable, results-based, and time-specific.[6]

Table 1 summarizes the characteristics of good objectives. Using this list as our guide, let's return to the position Training Specialist/Consultant—Leadership & Team Development at Target Corporation.

Examples of objectives (one or two per accountability) are the following:

- *Process leadership.* Develop leadership development processes and training programs within budget and time commitments. Meet budget targets and improve executive leaders' "leadership readiness" scores across organization by 20% in the coming fiscal year.
- *Supervision of nonexempt staff.* Receive acceptable managerial effectiveness rating scores from your nonexempt staff in the coming fiscal year.
- *Coaching.* Improve the managerial effectiveness scores of executive coaching clients in the coming fiscal year.
- *Team-building consultation.* Deliver necessary team-training sessions throughout the year within budget and with an acceptable satisfaction rating (as measured by the follow-up survey that is sent to every team) for team-training sessions in the coming fiscal year.
- *Assessment instrument feedback.* Deliver assessment feedback with an acceptable approval rating from your coaching clients in the coming fiscal year.
- *Product improvement.* Improve satisfaction with training delivery in the coming fiscal year by receiving acceptable scores while staying on budget.

Do these objectives comply with each of the 10 characteristics of good objectives listed in Table 1?

TABLE 1	Characteristics of Good Objectives
	Specific and clear
	Challenging
	Agreed upon
	Significant
	Prioritized
	Bound by time
	Achievable
	Fully communicated
	Flexible
	Limited in number

1.3 Determining Performance Standards

After accountabilities and objectives have been determined, the next step is to define performance standards. These are yardsticks designed to help people understand to what extent the objective has been achieved. The standards provide raters with information about what to look for to determine the level of performance that has been achieved. Standards can refer to various aspects of a specific objective, including quality, quantity, and time. Each of these aspects can be considered a criterion to be used in judging the extent to which an objective has been achieved.

- Quality: how well the objective has been achieved? This can include usefulness, responsiveness, effect obtained (e.g., problem resolution), acceptance rate, error rate, and feedback from users or customers (e.g., customer complaints, returns).
- Quantity: how much has been produced, how many, how often, and at what cost?
- Time: due dates, adherence to schedule, cycle times, deadlines (how quickly?) (e.g., timetables, progress reports)?

Standards must include an action, the desired result, a due date, and some type of quality or quantity indicator. For example, a standard might be the following: *Reduce overtime from 150 hours/month to 50 hours/month by December 1, 2012, at a cost not to exceed $12,000.* The action is *reduce*, the due date is *December 1, 2012*, and the indicators are the *reduction in hours from 150 to 50* and *at a cost not to exceed $12,000*.

Standards usually describe fully satisfactory performance. As soon as a standard has been created, one can create standards that describe minimum performance and outstanding performance. For example, the minimum standard could be the following: *Reduce overtime from 150 hours/month to 75 hours/month by December 1, 2012, at a cost not to exceed $12,000.* The standard suggesting outstanding performance could be the following: *Reduce overtime from 150 hours/month to 40 hours/month by October 1, 2012, at a cost not to exceed $12,000.*

In writing standards, consider the following characteristics that often determine whether one has a useful standard:

1. *Related to the position.*   Good standards are based on the job's key elements and tasks, not on individual traits or person-to-person comparisons.
2. *Concrete, specific, and measurable.*   Good standards are observable and verifiable. They allow us to distinguish between different performance levels. A good standard allows supervisors to measure the employee's actual performance to determine if it is below expectations, fully satisfactory, or above expectations. Standards are specific and concrete so that there should be no dispute over whether and how well they were met.
3. *Practical to measure.*   Good standards provide necessary information about performance in the most efficient way possible. Good standards are created by taking into account the cost, accuracy, and availability of the needed data.
4. *Meaningful.*   Good standards are about what is important and relevant to the purpose of the job, to the achievement of the organization's mission and objectives, and to the user or recipient of the product or service.

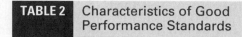

TABLE 2	Characteristics of Good Performance Standards

Related to the position
Concrete, specific, and measurable
Practical to measure
Meaningful
Realistic and achievable
Reviewed regularly

5. *Realistic and achievable.* Standards are possible to accomplish, but they require a stretch. There should be no apparent barriers to achieving the standard. Employees should be able to reach the standards within the specified time frame.
6. *Reviewed regularly.* Information should be available on a regular basis to determine whether the employee has reached the standard, and if not, remedial action should be taken.[7]

Table 2 lists the characteristics described here that are typical of good standards. Using this list as a guide, let's once again return to the position of Training Specialist/Consultant—Leadership & Team Development at Target Corporation.

Examples of standards (one per objective for each accountability) are the following:

- *Process leadership.* Increase the executive leaders' "leadership readiness" scores across organization by 20% by December 31, 2012, at a cost not to exceed $70,000.
- *Supervision of nonexempt staff.* Receive managerial effectiveness rating scores of 80% approval from the nonexempt staff in December 2012.
- *Coaching.* Improve the managerial effectiveness scores of executive coaching clients by 5% in December 2012.
- *Team-building consultation.* Design and deliver 95% of scheduled team-building sessions with a cost not to exceed $30,000 for an 85% satisfaction rating with team-training sessions by December 2012.
- *Assessment instrument feedback.* Deliver assessment feedback with an 85% approval rating from the coaching clients in December 2012.
- *Product improvement.* Improve satisfaction scores with training delivery by 5% by December 31, 2012, at a cost not to exceed $30,000.

2 MEASURING BEHAVIORS

A behavior approach to measuring performance includes the assessment of competencies. Competencies are measurable clusters of knowledge, skills, and abilities (KSAs) that are critical in determining how results will be achieved.[8] Examples of competencies are customer service, written or oral communication, creative thinking, and dependability.

We can consider two types of competencies: first, differentiating competencies, which are those that allow us to distinguish between average and superior performers; and, second, threshold competencies, which are those that everyone needs to display to do the job to a minimally adequate standard. For example, for the position Information

Technology (IT) Project Manager, a differentiating competency is process management. Process management is defined as the "ability to manage project activities." For the same position, a threshold competency is change management.[10] The change management competency includes knowledge of behavioral sciences, operational and relational skills, and sensitivity to motivators. Therefore, in order for an information technology project manager to be truly effective, she has to possess process management and change management competencies.

As noted earlier, competencies should be defined in behavioral terms. Take the case of a professor teaching an online course. An important competency could be "communication." This competency is defined as the set of behaviors that enables a professor to convey information so that students are able to receive it and understand it. For example, one such behavior might be whether the professor is conveying information during preassigned times and dates. That is, if the professor is not present at the chat room at the prespecified dates and times, no communication is possible.

To understand the extent to which an employee possesses a competency, we measure indicators. Each indicator is an observable behavior that gives us information regarding the competency in question. In other words, we don't measure the competency directly, but we measure indicators that tell us whether the competency is present or not.

Figure 1 shows the relationship between a competency and its indicators. A competency can have several indicators. Figure 1 shows a competency with five

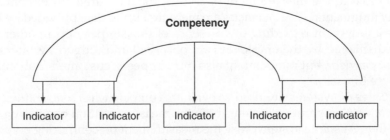

FIGURE 1   Competency and Indicators

indicators. An indicator is a behavior that, if displayed, suggests that the competency is present. In the example of the competency communication for a professor teaching an online course, one indicator is whether the professor shows up at the chat room at the preestablished dates and times. Another behavioral indicator of the competency communication could be whether the responses provided by the professor address the questions asked by the students or whether the answers are only tangential to the questions asked. As another example, consider the two competencies that define good leadership: consideration and initiation structure.[11] Consideration is the degree to which the leader looks after the well-being of his or her followers. Initiating structure is the degree to which the leader lays out task responsibilities. Five indicators whose presence would indicate the existence of the consideration competency are the following:

- Supports subordinates' projects
- Asks about the well-being of employees' lives outside of work
- Encourages subordinates to reach their established goals
- Gets to know employees personally
- Shows respect for employees' work and home lives

In describing a competency, the following components must be present:

1. Definition of competency
2. Description of specific behavioral indicators that can be observed when someone demonstrates a competency effectively
3. Description of specific behaviors that are likely to occur when someone doesn't demonstrate a competency effectively (what a competency is not)
4. List of suggestions for developing the competency in question[12]

Using the competency consideration, let's discuss the four essential elements in describing a competency. We defined consideration: it is the degree to which a leader shows concern and respect for followers, looks out for their welfare, and expresses appreciation and support. Next, we listed five indicators or behaviors that can be observed when a leader is exhibiting consideration leadership. Leaders who do not show consideration may speak with subordinates only regarding task assignments, repeatedly keep employees late with no consideration of home lives, take no interest in an employee's career goals, and assign tasks based only on current expertise. Finally, how do leaders develop the consideration competency? One suggestion would be to ask employees, on a regular basis, how their lives outside of work are going. This may lead to knowledge about an employee's family and interests outside of work.

In contrast to the measurement of results, the measurement of competencies is intrinsically judgmental. Competencies are measured using data provided by individuals who make a judgment regarding the presence of the competency. In other words, the behaviors displayed by the employees are observed and judged by raters (typically, the direct supervisor, but raters might also include peers, customers, subordinates, and the employee himself).

Two types of systems are used to evaluate competencies: *comparative systems* and *absolute systems*. Comparative systems base the measurement on comparing employees with one other. Absolute systems base the measurement on comparing employees with a prespecified performance standard.

TABLE 3	Comparative and Absolute Behavioral Measurement Systems
Comparative	*Absolute*
Simple rank order	Essays
Alternation rank order	Behavior checklists
Paired comparisons	Critical incidents
Relative percentile	Graphic rating scales
Forced distribution	

Table 3 lists the various types of comparative and absolute systems that could be used. Let's discuss how to implement each of these systems and point out some advantages and disadvantages of each.[13]

2.1 Comparative Systems

Comparative systems of measuring behaviors imply that employees are compared to one other. If a *simple rank order* system is used, employees are simply ranked from best performer to worst performer. Alternatively, in an *alternation rank order* procedure, the supervisor initially lists all employees. Then, the supervisor selects the best performer (#1), then the worst performer (#n), then the second best (#2), then the second worst (#n − 1), and so forth, alternating from the top to the bottom of the list until all employees have been ranked.

Paired comparisons is another comparative system. In contrast to the simple and alternation rank order procedures, explicit comparisons are made between all pairs of employees to be evaluated.[14] In other words, supervisors systematically compare the performance of each employee against the performance of all other employees. The number of pairs of employees to be compared is computed by the following equation:

$$\frac{n(n-1)}{2}$$

where n is the number of employees to be evaluated. If a supervisor needs to evaluate the performance of 8 employees, she would have to make $[8(8-1)]/2 = 28$ comparisons. The supervisor's job is to choose the better of each pair, and each individual's rank is determined by counting the number of times he or she was rated as better.

Another type of comparison method is the *relative percentile method*.[15] This type of measurement system asks raters to consider all ratees at the same time and to estimate the relative performance of each by using a 100-point scale. The 50-point mark on this scale (i.e., 50th percentile) suggests the location of an average employee—about 50% of employees are better performers and about 50% of employees are worse performers than this individual. Relative percentile methods may include one such scale for each competency and also include one scale on which raters evaluate the overall performance of all employees. Figure 2 includes an example of a relative percentile method scale to measure the competency "communication." In this illustration, the rater has placed employee DS at roughly the 95th percentile, meaning that DS's performance regarding communication is

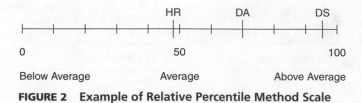

FIGURE 2 Example of Relative Percentile Method Scale

higher than 95% of other employees. On the other hand, HR has been placed around the 48th percentile, meaning that about 52% of employees are performing better than him.

A fifth comparison method is called *forced distribution*. In this type of system, employees are apportioned according to an approximately normal distribution. For example, 20% of employees must be classified as exceeding expectations, 70% must be classified as meeting expectations, and 10% must be classified as not meeting expectations. General Electric (GE) is one organization that has adopted a forced distribution system. Former GE CEO Jack Welch labeled GE's forced distribution system the "vitality curve." In his view, forced ranking enables managers to manage low-achieving performers better. GE's success in implementing a forced ranking system is cited as the model by many of the 20% of U.S. companies that have adopted it in recent years. At GE, each year 10% of managers are assigned the "C" grade, and if they don't improve they are asked to leave the company.[16]

What are some of the advantages of using comparative measurement methods? First, these types of measurement procedures are usually easy to explain. Second, decisions resulting from these types of systems are fairly straightforward: it is easy to see which employees are where in the distributions. Third, they tend to control several

---

BOX 2

Using a Forced Distribution System at Yahoo!

Yahoo! Inc. is one of the most trafficked Internet destinations worldwide. Yahoo! provides online products and services, offering a full range of tools and marketing solutions for businesses to connect with Internet users around the world. Yahoo! is headquartered in Sunnyvale, California. The performance management system at Yahoo! has utilized a forced distribution system in the past for assessing and reviewing employee performance. In this system, all departments are required to compare employees to one another and assign "top," "middle," and "bottom" performers based on a predetermined percentage that must fall in each category. Such systems are known for "weeding" out the bottom performers. Yahoo! has now removed the labeling of employee performance in an attempt to have a better dialogue between employees and managers and less focus on explaining the decision about which performance grade they were assigned in the evaluations. This change has also meant comparing employee performance to a predetermined standard and not directly to peers. The company has kept some of the comparisons because managers are asked to rank order the staff members to determine compensation increases and bonuses. Although the employees are not assigned a rank number, managers are generally expected to explain how the increases in pay compare to others in the work group. In summary, companies have developed many different methods for assessing and reviewing employees. Yahoo! gives an example of how one company has worked to find the most effective methods with important consideration to business objectives and the culture of the organization.[17]

biases and errors made by those rating performance better than do those in absolute systems. Such errors include leniency (i.e., giving high scores to most employees), severity (i.e., giving low scores to most employees), and central tendency (i.e., not giving any above-expectations or below-expectations ratings).

On the other hand, there are also disadvantages associated with the use of comparative systems, which may explain why only about 4% of all published research on performance appraisal has used them as opposed to the use of absolute systems.[18] First, employees usually are compared only in terms of a single overall category. Employees are not compared based on individual behaviors or even individual competencies, but instead are compared based on an overall assessment of performance. As a consequence, the resulting rankings are not sufficiently specific so that employees can receive useful feedback, and also these rankings may be subject to legal challenge. Second, because the resulting data are based on rankings and not on actual scores, there is no information about the relative distance between employees. All we know is that employee A received a higher score than employee B, but we do not know if this difference is, for example, similar to the difference between employee B and employee C. Some of these disadvantages were experienced recently by Microsoft and were noticed by Lisa E. Brummel, the senior vice president in charge of human resources.[19] She noted that, by using a forced distribution system, "people were beginning to feel like their placement in one of the buckets was a larger part of the evaluation than the work the person actually did." Similarly, a posting in June 2005 on an anonymous Microsoft employee's blog called MiniMicrosoft read as follows: "I LOVE this company, but I hate the Curve."

Finally, there are specific issues that should be considered in the implementation of a forced distribution method. This method assumes that performance scores are normally distributed, with some employees performing very highly, some poorly, and the majority

---

BOX 3

The Evolution of the Forced Distribution System at GE

General Electric (http://www.ge.com) is one of the most frequently cited companies to have utilized a comparative rating system with a forced distribution. GE, based in Fairfield, Connecticut, provides a wide array of products and services globally to customers in the areas of financial services, media entertainment, health care, and energy technologies, and products such as appliances and plastics. In recent years, the rigid system of requiring managers to place employees into three groups (top 20%, middle 70%, and bottom 10%) has been revised to allow managers more flexibility. While the normal distribution curve is still referenced as a guideline, the reference to the 20/70/10 split has been removed, and work groups are now able to have more "A players" or "no bottom 10's." The company did not view the forced distribution system of the past as a match for fostering a more innovative culture in which taking risks and failure are part of the business climate. As a result, the company has begun evaluating employees relative to certain traits, including one's ability to act in an innovative manner or have an external business focus. In summary, GE's performance management system and revisions to the system provide an example of how decisions about the measurement of performance need to consider the ramifications and resulting behaviors that are encouraged or discouraged. The consideration of culture and overall business strategy is also crucial in determining how to measure performance.[20]

somewhere in between. This assumption, however, may not hold true for all units within an organization. Some units may have a high-performing culture and systems in place so that the majority of members perform at a very high level. Conversely, other units may have a majority of members who perform at a below-expectations level. In fact, in some professions such as researchers in universities, athletes in a variety of sports, actors and entertainers in a variety of industries, and politicians, job performance is rarely normally distributed.[21] The pattern is such that a small minority of individuals account for the majority of results such as number of publications, goals, and how many times individuals are re-elected into office. Another disadvantage of implementing a forced distribution system is that such a system may discourage employees from engaging in contextual performance behaviors. After all, some employees may think, "The better my colleague does, the smaller the chance that I will be rated at the top of the distribution, so why should I help her do her job?" Obviously, this can undermine teamwork and the goals of the organization; it is important to consider what the culture of the organization is before implementing this type of system. If there is a culture with an unhealthy level of compet itiveness, then a forced distribution may produce an effect opposite to what is intended and create performance problems. Finally, a forced distribution system is very difficult to implement in an organization that is not experiencing any growth. This is especially true for an organization that is experiencing cutbacks. If it is the same group or, even worse, a smaller group being evaluated one year later, people who had been in the middle position are by default moved to the bottom, even if their performance has not changed. This is because the employees who were rated at the bottom previously are no longer with the organization. It is not easy for employees to understand why, given the same level of performance, they are now placed in the C instead of the B category. University of Southern California professor Ed Lawler gives a great example of a forced distribution system using a salamander as a comparison: the salamander's tail grows back when you chop it off, but this doesn't happen in companies. In companies, if a forced distribution system is used and a prespecified percentage of employees are let go every year because someone has to be placed in the C category, at some point you will be cutting into the "bone" of the organization. Computer simulations have confirmed that the benefits of implementing a forced distribution system in terms of performance improvement are most noticeable in the first several years of program implementation.[22]

2.2 Absolute Systems

In absolute systems, supervisors provide evaluations of an employee's performance without making direct reference to other employees. In the simplest absolute system, a supervisor writes an *essay* describing each employee's strengths and weaknesses and makes suggestions for improvement. One advantage of the essay system is that supervisors have the potential to provide detailed feedback to employees regarding their performance. On the other hand, essays are almost totally unstructured so that some supervisors may choose to be more detailed than others. Some supervisors may be better at writing essays than others. Because of this variability, comparisons across individuals, groups, or units are virtually impossible because essays written by different supervisors, and even by the same supervisor regarding different employees, may address different aspects of an employee's performance. Finally, essays do not provide any quantitative information, making it difficult to use them in some personnel decisions (e.g., allocation of rewards).

A second type of absolute system involves a *behavior checklist*, which consists of a form listing behavioral statements that are indicators of the various competencies to be measured. The supervisor's task is to indicate ("check") statements that describe the employee being rated. When this type of measurement system is in place, supervisors are not so much evaluators as they are "reporters" of employee behavior. Because it is likely that all behaviors rated are present to some extent, behavior checklists usually include a description of the behavior in question (e.g., "the employee arrives at work on time") followed by several response categories such as "always," "very often," "fairly often," "occasionally," and "never." The rater simply checks the response category she feels best describes the employee. Each response category is weighted—for example, from 5 ("always") to 1 ("never") if the statement describes desirable behavior such as arriving at work on time. Then, an overall score for each employee is computed by adding the weights of the responses that were checked for each item. Figure 3 includes an example of an item from a form using a behavior checklist measurement approach.

How do we select response categories for behavior checklist scales? Often, this is a quite arbitrary decision, and equal intervals between scale points are simply assumed. For example, in Figure 3, we would assume that the distance between "never" and "sometimes" is the same as the distance between "fairly often" and "always" (i.e., 1 point in each case). Great care must be taken in how the anchors are selected. Table 4 includes anchors that can be used for scales involving frequency and amount.[23]

Table 4 includes anchors to be used in both seven-point and five-point scales. For most systems, a five-point scale should be sufficient to capture an employee's performance on the behavior being rated. One advantage of using five-point scales is that they are less complex than seven-point scales. Also, five-point scales are superior to three-point scales because they are more likely to motivate performance improvement

The employee arrives at work on time.

1	2	3	4	5
Never	Sometimes	Often	Fairly Often	Always

FIGURE 3   Example of Behavior Checklist Item

TABLE 4   Anchors for Checklists of Frequency and Amount

Anchors for Checklists of Frequency

Seven-Point Scale	Five-Point Scale
Always	Always
Constantly	Very often
Often	Fairly often
Fairly often	Occasionally
Sometimes	Never
Once in a while	
Never	

(continued)

Anchors for Checklists of Amount	
Seven-Point Scale	**Five-Point Scale**
All	All
An extraordinary amount of	An extreme amount of
A great amount of	Quite a bit of
Quite a bit of	Some
A moderate amount of	None
Somewhat	
None	

because employees believe it is more doable to move up one level on a five-point scale than it is on a three-point scale.[24]

Table 5 includes anchors that can be used in scales involving agreement and evaluation.[25] This table includes 13 anchors that can be chosen if one uses a scale of evaluation and 13 anchors that can be used if a scale of agreement is used.

Table 5 also includes ratings that can be used to choose anchors for a scale of evaluation or agreement. In creating scales, we must choose anchors that are approximately equally spaced based on the ratings included in Table 5. So, if we were to create a five-point scale of evaluation using the information provided in this table, one possible set of anchors might be the following:

1. Terrible
2. Unsatisfactory
3. Decent
4. Good
5. Excellent

TABLE 5	Anchors to Be Used in Checklists of Evaluation and Agreement

Anchors for Checklists of Evaluation	
Terrible	1.6
Bad	3.3
Inferior	3.6
Poor	3.8
Unsatisfactory	3.9
Mediocre	5.3
Passable	5.5
Decent	6.0
Fair	6.1
Average	6.4
Satisfactory	6.9
Good	7.5
Excellent	9.6

Anchors for Checklists of Agreement	
Slightly	2.5
A little	2.7
Mildly	4.1
Somewhat	4.4
In part	4.7
Halfway	4.8
Tend to	5.3
Inclined to	5.4
Moderately	5.4
Generally	6.8
Pretty much	7.0
On the whole	7.4
Very much	9.1

In this set of anchors, the distance between all pairs of adjacent anchors ranges from 1.5 to 2.3 points. Note, however, that the use of the anchor "terrible" has a very negative connotation such that we may want to use a less negative anchor such as "bad" or "inferior." In this case, we would be choosing an anchor that is closer to the next one ("unsatisfactory") than we may wish, but using the new anchor may lead to less defensive and overall negative reactions on the part of employees who receive this rating.

In summary, behavior checklists are easy to use and to understand.[26] On the other hand, detailed and useful feedback is difficult to extract from the numerical rating provided. Overall, however, the practical advantages of checklists probably account for their current widespread popularity.

Every job includes some critical behaviors that make a crucial difference between doing a job effectively and doing it ineffectively. The *critical incidents* measurement approach involves gathering reports of situations in which employees exhibited behaviors that were especially effective or ineffective in accomplishing their jobs.[27] The recorded critical incidents provide a starting point for assessing performance. For example, consider the following incident as recorded by a high school principal regarding the performance of Tom Jones, the head of the disability services office:

> A sophomore with learning disabilities was experiencing difficulty in writing. Her parents wanted a laptop computer for her. Tom Jones ordered a computer and it was delivered to the student's teacher. No training was provided to the child, her teacher, or her parents. The laptop was never used.

This recorded incident is actually the synthesis of a series of incidents:

1. A problem was detected (a student with a special need was identified).
2. Corrective action was taken (the computer was ordered).
3. Corrective action was initially positive (the computer was delivered).
4. Corrective action was subsequently deficient (the computer was not used because of the lack of training).

When critical incidents are collected, this measurement method allows supervisors to focus on actual job behavior rather than on vaguely defined traits. On the other hand, collecting critical incidents is very time consuming. As is the case with essays, it is difficult to attach a score quantifying the impact of the incident (either positive or negative). A revised version of the critical incidents technique involves summarizing critical incidents and giving them to supervisors in the form of scales (e.g., behavior checklist). One example following up on the critical incident involving Tom Jones might be the following:

Addresses learning needs of special-needs students efficiently

Strongly Agree	*Agree*	*Undecided*	*Disagree*	*Strongly Disagree*

A second variation of the critical incidents technique is the approach adopted in the performance management system implemented by the city of Irving, Texas.[28] First, the city identified core competencies and classified them as core values, skill group competencies, or performance essentials. Then, the team in charge of implementing the system wrote dozens of examples of different levels of performance on each competency from ineffective to highly effective. In other words, this team was in charge of compiling critical incidents illustrating various performance levels for each competency. Then, managers used this list by simply circling the behavior that best described each of the employees in the work unit.

As an example, consider the competency Adaptability/Flexibility. For this competency, critical incidents were used to illustrate various performance levels:

Completely Ineffective	*Somewhat Ineffective*	*Effective*	*Highly Effective*	*Exceptional*
Able to focus on only one task at a time	Easily distracted from work assignments/ activities	Handles a variety of work assignments/ activities with few difficulties	Handles a variety of work assignments/ activities concurrently	Easily juggles a large number of assignments and activities
Avoids or attempts to undermine changes	Complains about necessary changes	Accepts reasons for change	Understands and responds to reasons for change	Encourages and instructs others about the benefits of change
Refuses to adopt changes policies	Makes only those changes with which they agree	Adapts to changing circumstances and attitudes of others	Adapts to changes and develops job aids to assist others	Welcomes change and looks for new opportunities it provides
Considers only own opinion when seeking solution	Occasionally listens to others but supports own solutions	Listens to others and seeks solutions acceptable to all	Ensures that everyone's thoughts and opinions are considered in reaching a solution	Actively seeks input in addition to recognized sources and facilitates implementation of solution

A third variation of the critical incidents technique is the use of behaviorally anchored rating scales (BARS), which are described next as one of several types of graphic rating scales.

The *graphic rating scale* is the most popular tool used to measure performance. The aim of graphic rating scales is to ensure that the response categories (ratings of behavior) are clearly defined, that interpretation of the rating by an outside party is clear, and that the supervisor and the employee understand the rating. An example of a graphic rating scale used to rate the performance of a project manager is the following:

Project management awareness is the knowledge of project management planning, updating status, working within budget, and delivering project on time and within budget. Rate _____'s project management awareness using the following scale:

1	2	3	4	5
Unaware or not interested	Needs additional training	Aware of responsibilities	Excellent knowledge and performance of skills	Superior performance of skill; ability to train others

BARS use graphic rating scales that use critical incidents as anchors.[29] BARS improve on the graphic rating scales by first having a group of employees identify all of the important dimensions of a job. Then, another group of employees generates critical incidents illustrating low, average, and high skills of performance for each dimension. A third group of employees and supervisors takes each dimension and the accompanying definitions and a randomized list of critical incidents. They must match the critical incidents with the correct dimensions. Finally, a group of judges assigns a scale value to each incident. Consider the following BARS for measuring job knowledge:

Job Knowledge: The amount of job-related knowledge and skills that an employee possesses.

Consider the following BARS which assess one of 10 performance dimensions identified as important for auditors:[30]

5	*Exceptional*: Employee consistently displays high level of job knowledge in all areas of his or her job. Other employees go to this person for training.
4	*Advanced*: Shows high levels of job knowledge in most areas of his or her job. Consistently completes all normal tasks. Employee continues searching for more job knowledge, and may seek guidance in some areas.
3	*Competent*: Employee shows an average level of job knowledge in all areas of the job. May need assistance completing difficult tasks.
2	*Improvement Needed*: Does not consistently meet deadlines or complete tasks required for this job. Does not attempt to acquire new skills or knowledge to improve performance.
1	*Major Improvement Needed*: Typically performs tasks incorrectly or not at all. Employee has no appreciation for improving his or her performance.

Knowledge of Accounting and Auditing Standards/Theory: Technical foundation, application of knowledge on the job, ability to identify problem areas and weigh theory vs. practice.

---

3 *High-Point Performance*: Displays very strong technical foundation, able to proficiently apply knowledge on the job, willingly researches areas, able to identify problems, can weigh theory vs. practice considerations.

2 *Midpoint Performance*: Can resolve normal accounting issues, has adequate technical foundation and skills, application requires some refinement, has some problems in weighing theory vs. practice, can identify major problem areas.

1 *Low-Point Performance*: Displays weak accounting knowledge and/or technical ability to apply knowledge to situations/issues on an engagement, has difficulty in identifying problems and/or weighing factors of theory vs. practice.

For graphic rating scales to be most useful and accurate, they must include the following features:

- The meaning of each response category is clear.
- The individual who is interpreting the ratings (e.g., a human resources manager) can tell clearly what response was intended.
- The performance dimension being rated is defined clearly for the rater.

Compare the two examples of BARS shown earlier. Which is better regarding each of these three features? How can these BARS be revised and improved?

In summary, several types of methods are available for assessing performance. These methods differ in terms of practicality (i.e., some take more time and effort to be developed than others), usefulness for administrative purposes (i.e., some are less useful than others because they do not provide a clear quantification of performance), and usefulness for users (i.e., some are less useful than others in terms of the feedback they produce that allows employees to improve performance in the future). Practicality and usefulness are key considerations in choosing one type of measurement procedure over another.

Summary Points

- The first step in measuring performance by adopting a results approach is to identify accountabilities. Accountabilities are the various areas in which an individual is expected to focus.
- After all key accountabilities have been identified, the second step in the results

approach is to set objectives for each. Objectives should be (1) specific and clear, (2) challenging, (3) agreed upon, (4) significant, (5) prioritized, (6) bound by time, (7) achievable, (8) fully communicated, (9) flexible, and (10) limited in number.

- Finally, the third step in the results approach involves determining performance standards. These yardsticks are designed to help people understand to what extent the objective has been achieved. In creating standards, we must consider the dimensions of quality, quantity, and time. Good standards are (1) related to the position; (2) concrete, specific, and measurable; (3) practical to measure; (4) meaningful; (5) realistic and achievable; and (6) reviewed regularly.

- The first step in measuring performance adopting a behavior approach involves identifying competencies. Competencies are measurable clusters of KSAs that are critical in determining how results will be achieved. Examples of competencies are customer service, written or oral communication, creative thinking, and dependability.

- The second step in the behavior approach involves identifying indicators that will allow us to understand the extent to which each individual possesses the competency in question. These indicators are behavioral manifestations of the underlying (unobservable) competency.

- In describing a competency, one must first clearly define it, then describe behavioral indicators showing the presence of the competency, describe behavioral indicators showing the absence of the competency, and list suggestions for developing the competency.

- After the indicators have been identified, the third step in the behavior approach includes choosing an appropriate measurement system, either comparative or absolute.

- Comparative systems base the measurement on comparing employees with one another and include simple rank order, alternation rank order, paired comparisons, relative percentile, and forced distribution. Comparative systems are easy to explain, and the resulting data are easy to interpret, thereby facilitating administrative decisions. On the other hand, employees are usually compared to one another in terms of one overall single category instead of in terms of specific behaviors or competencies. This produces less useful feedback that employees can use for their future improvement.

- Absolute systems include evaluations of employees' performance without making direct reference to other employees. Such systems include essays, behavior checklists, critical incidents, and graphic rating scales. Essays are difficult to quantify but produce useful and often detailed feedback. Behavior checklists are easy to use and understand, but the scale points used are often arbitrary, and we cannot assume that a one-point difference has the same meaning along the entire scale (i.e., the difference between an employee who scores 5 and an employee who scores 4 may not have the same meaning as the difference between an employee who scores 3 and one who scores 2). Critical incidents allow supervisors to focus on actual job behavior rather than on vaguely defined traits, but gathering critical incident data may be quite time consuming. Graphic rating scales are arguably the measurement method most frequently used to assess performance. For this type of measurement to be most useful, the meaning of each response category should be clear, the individual interpreting the ratings (e.g., the human resources manager) should be able to tell clearly what response was intended, and the performance dimension being rated should be defined clearly for the rater.

CASE STUDY 1

Accountabilities, Objectives, and Standards

Below is an actual job description for a sourcing and procurement internship position that was available at Disney Consumer Products/Studios. Based on the information in the job description, create accountabilities, objectives, and standards for this position.

TITLE

Graduate Associate, Sourcing, & Procurement (Disney Consumer Products/Studios)

THE POSITION

- Provide analytical support for sourcing projects impacting business units, specifically targeting Disney Consumer Products & Studios.
- Benchmark current pricing models and develop new approaches to pricing/buying various products and services that yield creative and business advantage.
- Support the continuing efforts to increase the percentage of spend influenced, specifically as it relates to business units where we have had only a minor impact.
- Assist in the development of spend profiles, key stakeholder lists, savings opportunities where existing contracts are leveraged, savings opportunities in commodity areas that have not been sourced.
- Assist in developing overall Sourcing & Procurement strategy for partnering with business units, specifically targeting Disney Consumer Products & Studios.

THE COMPANY

The Walt Disney Company is a diversified, international family entertainment and media company with 2003 annual revenues of $27.1 billion. Its operations include theme parks and resorts, filmed entertainment, including motion pictures and television shows, home video and DVD products, records, broadcast and cable networks, Internet and direct marketing, consumer products, radio and television stations, theatrical productions, publishing activities, and professional sports enterprises.

THE IDEAL CANDIDATE

- Ability to conceptualize issues and problems and develop hypotheses around appropriate responses.
- Intellectual curiosity and professional commitment to excellence.
- Superior analytical skills defined by an ability to identify and rearticulate critical aspects of a business situation from a large data pool (both qualitative and quantitative).
- Superior Microsoft Excel modeling skills.
- Strong written and verbal communication skills with the ability to build relationships.
- Ability to work independently.
- Demonstrated ability to manage multiple tasks, meanwhile retaining focus on project deliverables and strategic priorities.

THE OPPORTUNITY

This will be an opportunity for an MBA intern to utilize project management skills he or she has learned in the classroom. The intern will be faced with difficult and/or skeptical clients and will learn how to work with them. They will have an opportunity to execute portions of the sourcing methodology and work in teams. This will also be an opportunity for those individuals who have not experienced working in Corporate America, and for those that have had some experience, to further their learnings. The intern will gain experience from working in the Media and Entertainment industry. Through these various experiences, we hope the intern will find value in the internship we are offering. ■

CASE STUDY 2

Evaluating Objectives and Standards

Using the results from Case Study 1, use the accompanying checklist to evaluate each objective and standard you produced. For each objective and standard, use the first column in the checklist, and place a check mark next to each of the ideal characteristics if the characteristic is present. Then, use the Comments column to provide a description of why or why each objective and standard meets or does not meet the ideal. Finally, review your tables, and provide an overall assessment of the quality of the objectives and standards you created. ■

Objectives must have the following characteristics:	*Comments*
Specific and clear	
Challenging	
Agreed upon	
Significant	
Prioritized	
Bound by time	
Achievable	
Fully communicated	
Flexible	
Limited in number	

Performance standards must have the following characteristics:	*Comments*
Related to the position	
Concrete, specific, and measurable	
Practical to measure	
Meaningful	
Realistic and achievable	
Reviewed regularly	

Measuring Competencies at the Department of Transportation

The Department of Transportation (DOT) of a large midwestern state uses core competencies to measure performance in its organization. Two of its core competencies on which all employees are measured are "organizational knowledge" and "learning and strategic systems thinking." Organizational knowledge is defined as follows: "Understands the DOT's culture. Accurately explains the DOT's organizational structure, major products/services, and how various parts of the organization contribute to one other. Gets work done through formal channels and informal networks. Understands and can explain the origin and reasoning behind key policies, practices, and procedures. Understands, accepts, and communicates political realities and implications." Learning and strategic systems thinking is defined as follows: "Accepts responsibility for continued improvement/learning. Appreciates and can explain

the mission of each individual work unit and the importance of the time between them to make the entire operation whole. Acquires new skills and competencies and can explain how they benefit the DOT. Regularly takes all transportation forms (i.e., bicycle, light rail, highway, etc.) into account planning and problem solving. Seeks information and ideas from multiple sources. Freely and intentionally shares ideas with others."

Using the accompanying table as a guide, evaluate each of these two competencies, and place a check mark next to each of the components of a good competency description if the component is present.

Next, using the organizational knowledge and learning and strategic systems thinking competencies, create a five-point graphic rating scale for each indicator using anchors of frequency, amount, agreement, or evaluation. ■

In describing a competency, the following components must be present:

Definition

Description of specific behavioral indicators that can be observed when someone demonstrates a competency effectively

Description of specific behaviors that are likely to occur when someone does not demonstrate a competency effectively (what a competency is not)

List of suggestions for developing the competency in question

---

Source: Adapted from D. GROTE, "Public sector organizations: Today's innovative leaders in performance management," *Public Personnel Management, 29* (Spring 2000), 1–20.

CASE STUDY 4

Creating BARS-Based Graphic Rating Scales for Evaluating Business Student Performance in Team Projects

In many universities, students are required to conduct team projects. A description of these "job" duties is the following:

> Work with team members to deliver project outcomes on time and according to specifications. Complete all individual assignments to the highest quality, completing necessary background research, making any mathematical analysis, and preparing final documents. Foster a good working environment.

Please do the following:

1. Generate a list of competencies for the position described.
2. Identify a list of critical behavioral indicators for each competency.
3. Generate critical incidents (high, average, and poor performance) for each behavioral indicator.
4. Create graphic rating scales using BARS to measure each competency. ■

End Notes

1. The following discussion of accountabilities, objectives, and standards is based on D. Grote. *The complete guide to performance appraisal* (New York: AMACOM, 1996), chap. 4.
2. Hoogenboezem, J. A., & Hoogenboezem, D. B. (2005). Coping with targets: Performance measurement in the Netherlands police. *International Journal of Productivity and Performance Management, 54,* 568–578.
3. Loveday, B. (2006). Policing performance: The impact of performance measures and targets on police forces in England and Wales. *International Journal of Police Science & Management, 8,* 282–293.
4. Daley, D. M. (1991). Great expectations, or a tale of two systems: Employee attitudes toward graphic rating scales and MBO-based performance appraisal. *Public Administration Quarterly, 15,* 188–209.
5. Adapted from D. Grote, *The complete guide to performance appraisal* (New York: AMACOM, 1996), 91–94.
6. Shaw, K. N. (2004). Changing the goal-setting process at Microsoft. *Academy of Management Executive, 18,* 139–142.
7. Adapted from D. L. Kirkpatrick, *How to improve performance through appraisal and coaching* (New York: AMACOM, 1982), 35–36.

8. Levenson, A. R., Van Der Stede, W. A., & Cohen, S. G. (2006). Measuring the relationship between managerial competencies and performance. *Journal of Management, 32,* 360–380.

9. Chughtai, J. (2006). Identifying future leaders at Xerox Capital Services. *Strategic HR Review.* Available online at www.allbusiness .com/periodicals/article/892962-1.html. Retrieval date: May 1, 2011.

10. Kendra, K. A., & Taplin, L. J. (2004). Change agent competencies for information technology project managers. *Consulting Psychology Journal: Practice & Research, 56,* 20–34.

11. Judge, T. A., Piccolo, R. F., & Illies, R. I. (2004). The forgotten ones? The validity of consideration and initiating structure in leadership research. *Journal of Applied Psychology, 89,* 36–51.

12. Grote, D. (1996). *The complete guide to performance appraisal* (p. 118). New York: AMACOM.

13. The material that follows on comparative and absolute systems is based primarily on W. F. Cascio and H. Aguinis, *Applied psychology in human resources management* (7th ed.). Upper Saddle River, NJ: Prentice Hall, 2011.

14. Siegel, L. (1982). Paired comparison evaluations of managerial effectiveness by peers and supervisors. *Personnel Psychology, 37,* 703–710.

15. Goffin, R. D., Jelley, R. B., Powell, D. M., & Johnston, N. G. (2009). Taking advantage of social comparisons in performance appraisal: The relative percentile method. *Human Resource Management, 48,* 251–268.

16. Davis, P., & Rogers, B. (2003). Managing the "C" performer: An alternative to forced ranking of appraisals. Available online at http://www.workinfo.com/free/Downloads/150.htm. Retrieval date: May 1, 2011.

17. McGregor, J. (2006, January). The struggle to measure performance. *Business Week.* Available online at http://www.businessweek.com/magazine/content/06_02/b3966060.htm. Retrieval date: May 1, 2011.

18. Goffin, R. D., Jelley, R. B., Powell, D. M., & Johnston, N. G. (2009). Taking advantage of social comparisons in performance appraisal: The relative percentile method. *Human Resource Management, 48,* 251–268.

19. Holland, K. (2006, September 10). Performance reviews: Many need improvement. *The New York Times, Section 3-Money and Business/Financial Desk,* 3.

20. McGregor, J. (2006, January). The struggle to measure performance. *Business Week.* Available online at http://www.businessweek.com/magazine/content/06_02/b3966060.htm. Retrieval date: May 1, 2011.

21. O'Boyle, E., Jr., & Aguinis, H. (in press). The best and the rest: Revisiting the norm of normality of individual performance. *Personnel Psychology.*

22. Scullen, S. E., Bergey, P. K., & Aiman-Smith, L. (2005). Forced distribution rating systems and the improvement of workforce potential: A baseline simulation. *Personnel Psychology, 58,* 1–32.

23. This table is based on Bass, B. M., Cascio, W. F., & O'Connor, E. J. (1974). Magnitude estimations of expressions of frequency and amount. *Journal of Applied Psychology, 59,* 313–320.

24. Bartol, K. M., Durham, C. C., & Poon, J. M. L. (2001). Influence of performance evaluation rating segmentation on motivation and fairness perceptions. *Journal of Applied Psychology, 86,* 1106–1119.

25. This table is based on Spector, P. (1976). Choosing response categories for summated rating scales. *Journal of Applied Psychology, 61,* 374–375.

26. Hennessy, J., Mabey, B., & Warr, P. (1998). Assessment centre observation procedures: An experimental comparison of traditional, checklist and coding methods. *International Journal of Selection and Assessment, 6,* 222–231.

27. Pulakos, E. D., Arad, S., Donovan, M. A., & Plamondon, K. E. (2000). Adaptability in the workplace: Development of a taxonomy of adaptive performance. *Journal of Applied Psychology, 85,* 612–624.

28. Grote, D. (2000, Spring). Public sector organizations: Today's innovative leaders in performance management. *Public Personnel Management, 29,* 1–20.

29. Cocanougher, A. B., & Ivancevich, J. M. (1978). "BARS" performance rating for sales force personnel. *Journal of Marketing, 42,* 87–95.

30. Harrell, A., & Wright, A. (1990). Empirical evidence on the validity and reliability of behaviorally anchored rating scales for auditors. *Auditing, 9,* 134–149.

Gathering Performance Information

From Chapter 6 of *Performance Management*, Third Edition. Herman Aguinis. Copyright © 2013 by Pearson Education, Inc. All rights reserved.

Gathering Performance Information

Unless a reviewer has the courage to give you unqualified praise, I say ignore the bastard.

—JOHN STEINBECK

LEARNING OBJECTIVES

By the end of this chapter, you will be able to do the following:

- Understand why each of several basic components is included in the appraisal form.
- Design effective appraisal forms.
- Compute an overall employee performance score based on information found on the appraisal form.
- Select an appropriate time period to document performance as part of a performance review.
- Determine how many formal meetings are needed between the subordinate and the supervisor to discuss performance issues.
- Understand advantages and disadvantages of using supervisors, peers, subordinates, self, and customers as sources of performance information.
- Know how to deal with potential disagreements involved with different sources evaluating the performance of the same employee.
- Understand the psychological mechanisms leading to the inflation and deflation of performance ratings.
- Understand that the implementation of training programs can address intentional and unintentional rating distortion.

The performance management process includes several stages: prerequisites, performance planning, performance execution, performance assessment, performance review, and performance renewal and recontracting. An important component of the performance assessment stage is the use of appraisal forms. These forms are instruments used to document and evaluate performance. This chapter provides a comprehensive description of the use of appraisal forms and their content. In addition, this chapter describes other issues related to the administration of appraisal forms, such as how often the supervisor and subordinate should meet to discuss performance issues and how to choose the source(s) of performance data (e.g., supervisors, self, subordinates, peers, or customers). The chapter concludes with a discussion of reasons why raters are likely, either intentionally or unintentionally, to distort performance ratings and what can be done to improve the accuracy of ratings.

1 APPRAISAL FORMS

At the core of any performance management system is the assessment of performance. Information on performance is collected by using forms, which can be filled out on paper or electronically. One advantage of filling out forms electronically is that the information is stored and can easily be shared, for example, between the manager filling out the form and the human resources (HR) department. Also, having the data available in electronic form can help in subsequent analyses, for example, in making comparisons of the relative average performance levels of various units within the organization. Finally, using electronic forms is beneficial because, as change take place in the organization or job in question, forms need to be revised and updated,[1] and electronic forms are usually easier to modify than paper forms.

Regardless of whether they are electronic or paper, appraisal forms usually include a combination of the following components[2]:

- *Basic employee information.* This section of the form includes basic employee information such as job title, division, department and other work group information, employee number, and pay grade or salary classification. In addition, forms usually include the dates of the evaluation period, the number of months and years the rater has supervised or worked with the employee, an employee's starting date with the company and starting date in the current job, the reason for the appraisal, current salary and position in range, and the date of the next scheduled evaluation.
- *Accountabilities, objectives, and standards.* If the organization adopts a results approach, this section of the form would include the name and description of each accountability, objectives agreed upon by manager and employee, and the extent to which the objectives have been achieved. In many instances, the objectives are weighted in terms of importance, which facilitates the calculation of an overall performance score. Finally, this section can also include a subsection describing conditions under which performance was achieved, which may help explain why the employee achieved the (high or low) performance level described. For example, a supervisor may have the opportunity to describe specific circumstances

surrounding performance during the review period, including a tough economy, the introduction of a new line of products, and so forth.

- *Competencies and indicators.* If the organization adopts a behavior approach, this section of the form includes a definition of the various competencies to be assessed, together with their behavioral indicators.
- *Major achievements and contributions.* Some forms include a section in which a rater is asked to list the two or three major accomplishments of the individual being rated during the review period. These could refer to results, behaviors, or both.
- *Developmental achievements.* This section of the form includes information about the extent to which the developmental goals set for the review period have been achieved. This can include a summary of activities, such as workshops attended and courses taken as well as results, such as new skills learned. Evidence of having learned new skills can be documented, for example, by obtaining a professional certification. Although some organizations include developmental achievements in the appraisal form, others choose to include them in a separate form. Sun Microsystems is an example of an organization that separates these forms. Some organizations do not include development content as part of the appraisal form because it is often difficult for employees to focus constructively on development if they have received a less-than-ideal performance review.
- *Developmental needs, plans, and goals.* This section of the form is future oriented and includes information about specific goals and timetables in terms of employee development. As noted before, some organizations choose to create a separate development form and do not include this information as part of the performance appraisal form.
- *Stakeholder input.* Some forms include sections to be filled out by other stakeholders, such as customers with whom the employee interacts. Overall, stakeholders are defined as people who have firsthand knowledge of and are affected by the employee's performance. In most cases, input from other stakeholders is collected from them by using forms separate from the main appraisal because not all sources of performance information are in the position to rate the same performance dimensions. For example, an employee may be rated on the competency "teamwork" by peers and on the competency "reliability" by a customer. A more detailed discussion of the use of various sources of performance information is offered later in this chapter.
- *Employee comments.* This section includes reactions and comments provided by the employee being rated. In addition to allowing formal employee input, which improves the perceived fairness of the system, the inclusion of this section helps with legal issues because it documents that the employee has had an opportunity to participate in the evaluation process.
- *Signatures.* The final section of most forms includes a section in which the employee being rated, the rater, and the rater's supervisor provide their signatures to show they have seen and discussed the content of the form. The HR department may also provide approval of the content of the form.

Table 1 summarizes the major components of appraisal forms. Let's consider some examples to see which of these components are present in each.

TABLE 1	Major Components of Appraisal Forms

Basic employee information

Accountabilities, objectives, and standards

Competencies and indicators

Major achievements and contributions

Developmental achievements (could be included in a separate form)

Developmental needs, plans, and goals (could be included in a separate form)

Stakeholder input

Employee comments

Signatures

First, consider the form included in Figure 1. This is a generic form that can be used for almost any position in a company. Let's evaluate this form in relation to the components listed in Table 1. First, the form asks for the employee's basic information. Second, while the form asks the manager to list the expected versus the actual accountabilities, it does not include objectives or standards. Third, the form includes five competencies, but it does not include a definition of those competencies nor does it list the indicators to look for to determine whether the employee has mastered the

---

Performance Review Form

Employee Name: _____

Title:

Manager: _____

Date of Appraisal Meeting: _____

Employee Performance Reviews improve employee performance and development by encouraging communication, establishing performance expectations, identifying developmental needs, and setting goals to improve performance. Performance reviews also provide an ongoing record of employee performance, which is helpful for both the supervisor and employee.

Use the form below to list examples of outstanding performance or achievements as well as areas of performance that need improvement. Please provide open comments on your employee's performance. Complete each section and list examples of performance where applicable.

1. Job description/key responsibilities/required tasks:

_____

_____

_____

_____

2. Note expected accomplishments vs. actual accomplishments:

_____

_____

_____

_____

FIGURE 1   Basic Performance Review Form

3. List the areas where the employee developed in ways enabling him or her to take on additional responsibilities or be eligible for high-profile assignments:

_____
_____
_____
_____

4. Areas of development for upcoming quarter (i.e., communication skills, teamwork, project management skills, budgeting experience, etc.):

_____
_____
_____
_____

5. Goals for upcoming quarter (Please list S.M.A.R.T. goals):

_____
_____
_____
_____

Please circle the number below that best describes the employee's performance in the following areas:

Areas of concentration	Did not meet expectations	Achieved most expectations	Achieved expectations	Achieved expectations and exceeded on a few	Significantly exceeded expectations
Teamwork	1	2	3	4	5
Leadership	1	2	3	4	5
Business acumen	1	2	3	4	5
Customer service	1	2	3	4	5
Project management	1	2	3	4	5

Average Performance Score	

Employee Use Only:

Please provide comments and examples of behaviors to describe your performance in the past quarter.

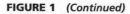
_____
_____
_____
_____

_____   _____   _____   _____
Manager Signature   Date   Employee Signature   Date

FIGURE 1 *(Continued)*

relevant competencies. The form does include space to list major achievements, developmental needs, and employee comments. The form does not solicit information from all relevant stakeholders. In short, the following table summarizes the components that are present:

Major Components of Appraisal Forms: Evaluation of Form in Figure 1	
X	Basic employee information
	Accountabilities, objectives, and standards
	Competencies and indicators
X	Major achievements and contributions
X	Developmental achievements
X	Developmental needs, plans, and goals
	Stakeholder input
X	Employee comments
X	Signatures

As a second example, consider the form included in Figure 2. Similar to the form in Figure 1, this form has a section for basic employee information, developmental areas, goals, and employee comments. This form does not include a list of the employee's accountabilities, objectives, and standards. The competencies needed for the position are listed, but the behavioral indicators to look for to evaluate the presence of the competency

---

Employee Performance Appraisal

Employee Name: _____

Department: _____

Date of Hire: _____

Date of Performance Review: _____

Ratings: Please rate the employee on the following factors:

	Did not meet expectations	Achieved most expectations	Achieved expectations	Achieved expectations and exceeded on a few	Significantly exceeded expectations
Flexibility	1	2	3	4	5
Teamwork	1	2	3	4	5
Oral communication	1	2	3	4	5
Written communication	1	2	3	4	5
Initiative	1	2	3	4	5
Decision making	1	2	3	4	5
Job knowledge	1	2	3	4	5
Quality work	1	2	3	4	5
Productivity	1	2	3	4	5
				Total Points:	

FIGURE 2   Employee Performance Appraisal Form

Level of Performance	Description of Performance	Increase
Unsatisfactory (0–15 pts)	Did not meet the responsibilities associated with position. Place on personal improvement performance plan.	NA
Needs improvement (16–31 pts)	Met main responsibilities, but did not fulfill all responsibilities. Inconsistent level of performance across tasks.	1–2%
Fulfills responsibilities (32–37 pts)	Fulfilled all key responsibilities. Consistently performed to established work standards.	3–4%
Exceeds responsibilities (38–48 pts)	Fulfilled key responsibilities, and took on more and completed additional responsibilities. Consistently a high performer.	4–5%
Far exceeds responsibilities (49–55 pts)	Far exceeded the job responsibilities in all areas and took charge of major projects. Consistent high performer and expert at position.	5–6%

Note: Percentage increases listed are to be used as a guideline.

Employee strengths/areas of expertise:

_____
_____
_____
_____

Developmental areas:

_____
_____
_____
_____

Goals for upcoming year in relation to job responsibilities and developmental areas:

_____
_____
_____
_____

Employee comments (optional):

_____
_____
_____
_____

Employee:_____   Date:_____

Reviewer:_____   Date:_____

FIGURE 2 *(Continued)*

**Major Components of Appraisal Forms:
Evaluation of Form in Figure 2**

X   Basic employee information

Accountabilities, objectives, and standards

Competencies and indicators

Major achievements and contributions

Developmental achievements

X   Developmental needs, plans, and goals

Stakeholder input

X   Employee comments

X   Signatures

---

are not. Furthermore, unlike the form in Figure 1, the employee's developmental and major achievements are not acknowledged. Again, stakeholders are not asked for their input. In short, the following components are present:

This analysis shows that although the forms included in Figures 1 and 2 seem to be quite complete and thorough, they are not. Thus, before implementing appraisal forms, make sure that all their necessary components are present.

2 CHARACTERISTICS OF APPRAISAL FORMS

We should be aware that there is no such thing as a universally correct appraisal form. In some cases, a form may emphasize competencies and ignore results. This would be the case if the system adopted a behavior approach as opposed to a results approach to measuring performance. In others, the form may emphasize developmental issues and minimize or even completely ignore both behaviors and results. In such cases, the form would be used for developmental purposes only and not for administrative purposes. One size does not fit all, and different components are appropriate based on the purposes of the appraisal.

In spite of the large variability in terms of format and components, there are certain desirable features that make appraisal forms particularly effective:

- *Simplicity.* Forms must be easy to understand, easy to administer, quick to complete, clear, and concise. If forms are too long, convoluted, and complicated, it is likely that the performance assessment process will not be effective.
- *Relevancy.* Good forms include information related directly to the tasks and responsibilities of the job; otherwise, they will be regarded as an administrative burden and not as a tool for performance improvement.
- *Descriptiveness.* Good forms require that the raters provide evidence of performance regardless of the performance level. The form should be sufficiently descriptive that an outside party (e.g., supervisor's supervisor or HR department) has a clear understanding of the performance information conveyed.

TABLE 2	Desirable Features of All Appraisal Forms
	Simplicity
	Relevancy
	Descriptiveness
	Adaptability
	Comprehensiveness
	Definitional clarity
	Communication
	Time orientation

- *Adaptability.* Good forms allow managers in different functions and departments to adapt them to their particular needs and situations. This feature encourages widespread use of the form.
- *Comprehensiveness.* Good forms include all the major areas of performance for a particular position for the entire review period.
- *Definitional clarity.* Desirable competencies and results are clearly defined for all raters so that everyone evaluates the same attributes. This feature enhances consistency of ratings across raters and levels of the organization.
- *Communication.* The meaning of each of the components of the form must be successfully communicated to all people participating in the evaluation process. This enhances acceptance of the system and motivation to participate in it both as raters and as ratees.
- *Time orientation.* Good forms help clarify expectations about performance. They address not only the past but also the future.[3]

Table 2 includes a summary of the features that are desirable in all forms regardless of specific content and format. Let's consider the two illustrative forms discussed earlier to see how they fare in relation to these desirable features. First, consider the form shown in Figure 1. It is simple because it is easy to understand and clear. The fact that it includes an essay format implies that it would take a little more time to complete, but the number of essays is kept to a minimum. The form is also relevant, but only if the supervisor enters the correct job description and actual accountabilities. This form can be extremely descriptive owing to its narrative nature. The form encourages the manager to give examples of relevant behavior. Next, the form is also adaptable, perhaps too adaptable; it would be hard to compare performance across employees because the manager can adapt the form to each employee. This form is comprehensive, but again only if the manager lists all of the expected accountabilities. This form does not have definitional clarity. Because the competencies listed are not clearly defined, ratings are likely to be inconsistent across raters. Next, this form can be communicated across the organization. Manager acceptance may be hard to gain, however, because of the amount of detail required by the essay answers. Finally, the form is time oriented. It asks for past and future performance expectations and goals. In short, the following table summarizes which of the desirable characteristics are present in this form:

Desirable Features of All Appraisal Forms: Evaluation of Form in Figure 1	
X	Simplicity
X	Relevancy
X	Descriptiveness
X	Adaptability
X	Comprehensiveness
	Definitional clarity
X	Communication
X	Time orientation

Next, let's evaluate the form shown in Figure 2 in relation to the desirable features listed in Table 2. First, it is simple because it is easy to administer, quick to complete, clear, and concise. This form is easier to administer than the form shown in Figure 1 because this form does not include an essay format. On the other hand, it scores low on the relevance dimension because it does not enumerate and specify the employee's tasks and responsibilities of the job. Third, this form is not descriptive. Although the different levels of performance are described, the actual expectations of the individual employees are not clear. Fourth, the form is only somewhat adaptable. The beginning ratings regarding the competencies are exact, but the second half of the form can be adapted to each employee. This form is not comprehensive because it does not include all the major components that indicate performance for a particular position for the entire review period. This form does not provide definitional clarity because the competencies that are listed are not defined and there is no mention of the employee's key responsibilities. All of the levels of performance are explained well, but they are not tailored to each individual employee. Next, the form could not be communicated throughout the organization. Since the competencies are not defined, it would be hard to explain the process to all stakeholders. Finally, the form makes no mention of time, so it does not focus on past or future expectations. The table below summarizes this analysis:

Desirable Features of All Appraisal Forms: Evaluation of Form in Figure 2	
X	Simplicity
	Relevancy
	Descriptiveness
X	Adaptability
	Comprehensiveness
	Definitional clarity
	Communication
	Time orientation

Many organizations use forms very similar to those presented in Figures 1 and 2. A careful analysis of these forms against the desired features indicates that the forms, particularly the one shown in Figure 2, could be improved substantially. An important point to consider regarding these and other forms is that they should include the critical components discussed here because such forms help organizations implement a performance-focused culture. An exclusive emphasis on the appraisal form should be avoided; it is just one component of the performance management system.

3 DETERMINING OVERALL RATING

After the form has been completed, there is usually a need to compute an overall performance score. This is particularly necessary for making administrative decisions such as the allocation of rewards. Computing overall performance scores is also useful in determining whether employees, and groups of employees, are improving their performance over time.

Two main strategies are used to obtain an overall performance score for each employee: judgmental and mechanical. The judgmental procedure consists of considering every aspect of performance and then arriving at a defensible summary. This basically holistic procedure relies on the ability of the rater to arrive at a fair and accurate overall score. The mechanical procedure consists of first considering the scores assigned to each section of the appraisal form and then adding them up to obtain an overall score. When adding scores from each section, weights are typically used based on the relative importance of each performance dimension measured.

Consider the performance evaluation form shown in Figure 3, which is used to evaluate the performance of sales associates at a supermarket chain.[4] This form includes the hypothetical ratings obtained by a sales associate on just two competencies and just two key results (the complete form probably includes more than just four performance dimensions). You can see that, in the Competencies section, each competency is weighted according to its value to the organization. Specifically, Follow-Through/Dependability is given a weight of .7 whereas Decision Making/Creative Problem Solving is given a weight of .3. For the competency Follow-Through/Dependability, Anthony Carmello obtained a score of 4 for the first half of the review period and a score of 3 for the second half of the review period; consequently, the scores for this competency are $4 \times .7 = 2.8$ for the first half and $3 \times .7 = 2.1$ for the second half of the review period. Adding up the

				1st	2nd	Wgt	Pts	Pts
Decision Making/Creative Problem Solving Points:				3	2	0.3	.9	.6
4	3	2	1					
Anticipates, recognizes, and confronts problems with extraordinary skill. Perseveres until solution is reached. Extremely innovative and takes risks.	Defines and addresses problems well. Typically reaches useful solutions and decisions are sound. Innovative, with above-average risk taking.	Acknowledges and attempts to solve most problems when presented. Usually comes to conclusions on solving basic issues. Little innovation and sometimes takes risks.	Has difficulty recognizing problems and making decisions. Always needs guidance. No innovation and never takes risks.					
Comments:								
			Total Score for Competencies Section				3.7	2.7

FIGURE 3 Performance Appraisal Form Used by Grocery Retailer

Key Results: Rate each area to the performance demonstrated in the achievement of budgeted numbers.

KR #1: Achieved Budgeted Sales (U.S. dollars)

	Budgeted	Actual	% of achievement (1, 2, 3, 4)	Wgt 0.6
1st half objective	$78,000	$77,000	2	
2nd half objective	$80,000	$83,000	3	Pts

4 = 108%+ 3 = 107–103% 2 = 102–98% 1 – Below 97%				1.2	1.8

Comments:

KR #2: Margin Balance (gain/loss in U.S. dollars)

	Budgeted	Actual	% of achievement (1, 2, 3, 4)	Wgt 0.4
1st half objective	$30,000	$29,000	1	
2nd half objective	$31,000	$34,000	4	Pts

4 = 108%+ 3 = 107–103% 2 = 102–98% 1 = Below 97%				.4	1.6

Comments:

TOTAL SCORE FOR KEY RESULTS:				1.6	3.4

	Comp. Score 1st half	Comp. Score 2nd half	KR Score 1st half	KR Score 2nd half	Subtotal
Circle Rating:	3.7	2.7	1.6	3.4	11.4/4 = 2.85
Excellent	Above average	Average	Unsatisfactory		
3.6–4.0	2.6–3.5	1.6–2.5	1–1.5		

Associate   Date

Store Director   Date

FIGURE 3 *(Continued)*

scores obtained for the first and second half in each competency leads to a total of 3.7 points for the first half and 2.7 for the second half of the review period.

The form also indicates that the key results have different weights. Specifically, KR #1 has a weight of .6 whereas KR #2 has a weight of .4. Consider KR #1. The objective for the first half was to achieve a sales figure of $78,000. The actual sales figure achieved by Carmello was $77,000, representing a 98.71% achievement, which is a score of 2. Multiplying this score times the weight of .6 yields 1.2 points for the first half of the review period. Similarly, for the second half, the goal was $80,000 and Carmello surpassed it by achieving a figure of $83,000, which represents a score of 3 (i.e., 103.75% achievement); therefore, the score for the second half is 3 × .6 = 1.8. Finally, the form shows that the total score for the first half for all key results combined is 1.6, whereas the score for the second half is 3.4. These scores were computed by simply adding the scores obtained in each half.

Finally, the form shows the scores obtained for the competencies and the key results in each of the two halves of the review period. To obtain the overall performance score, we simply take an average of these four numbers: $(3.7 + 2.7 + 1.6 + 3.4)/4 = 2.85$. This puts Carmello in the 2.6–3.5 range, which represents a qualification of "above average."

Now, suppose that we do not follow a mechanical procedure to compute overall performance score, and instead we use a judgmental method. That is, suppose raters have no information on weights. How would James LeBrown, Carmello's supervisor, compute the overall performance score? One possibility is that he might give equal weights to all competencies and would therefore consider that Follow-Through/Dependability is as important as Decision Making/Creative Problem Solving. This would lead to different scores compared to using weights of .7 and .3. As an alternative, the supervisor may have his own ideas about what performance dimensions should be given more weight and decide to ignore how the work is done (i.e., behaviors) and instead assign an overall score based primarily on the key results (i.e., sales and margin balance).

The use of weights allows the supervisor to come to an objective and clear overall performance score for each employee. As this example illustrates, the use of clearly specified weights allows the supervisor to come to a verifiable score for each employee. Thus, the supervisor and the employees can be sure that the overall performance rating is reflective of the employee's performance in each category.

Which strategy is the best: judgmental or mechanical? In most cases, the mechanical method is superior to the judgmental method.[5] A supervisor is more likely to introduce his or her own biases in computing the overall performance score when no clear rules exist regarding the relative importance of the various performance dimensions and there is no direction on how to combine the various performance dimensions in calculating the overall score.[6] As far as the computation of overall scores goes, the mechanical method is superior to the judgmental method.

Finally, you will notice that the form included in Figure 3 includes sections labeled "comments." These open-ended sections are common in most appraisal forms. However, this information is typically not used effectively.[7] Likely, there are two chief reasons that this is the case. First, it is not easy to systematically categorize and analyze such comments. Second, the quality, length, and content of these comments may be more a function of the culture of the organization and the writing skills of the person filling out the form than actual KSAs of the employee being rated. Regarding the first challenge, the increasing sophistication of computer-aided text analysis (CATA) software that allows for an analysis of text (as opposed to numbers) may allow for more and better use of such information. For example, the software package DICTION 5.0 allows for the analysis of text by first creating categories of terms or phrases and then counting the relative frequency of each.[8] So, an organization may wish to classify the comments in terms of, for example, task and contextual performance. Then, a "dictionary" of terms and phrases related to each of these performance dimensions is created and the software automatically counts the number of times that such types of behaviors are mentioned in the comments. The second challenge is more difficult to overcome because if raters are not given any training or general instructions on what two write, comments may range from none at all to very detailed descriptions of what employees have done (i.e., past orientation) and very detailed descriptions of what employees should do (i.e., future orientation). Thus, to overcome this second challenge, it is important to first establish the goals of the information that raters are asked to include in these open-ended sections and then offer raters training on how to do that in a systematic and standardized fashion across ratees. If these two challenges are overcome, then the information included in the open-ended sections can be used to supplement the quantitative information offered on the forms.

4 APPRAISAL PERIOD AND NUMBER OF MEETINGS

How long should the appraisal period be? In other words, what period of time should be included in the appraisal form? Organizations with a performance management system typically conduct an annual review; however, others choose to conduct semiannual or even quarterly formal reviews. Conducting only an annual review might not provide sufficient opportunity for the supervisor and subordinate to discuss performance issues in a formal setting. The recommendation then is to conduct semiannual or quarterly reviews. For example, Colorado-based Hamilton Standard Commercial Aircraft uses a semiannual review system.[9] Twice a year, the company performs a modified 360-degree appraisal, meaning that performance information is collected from several sources. This type of system allows individuals to receive feedback and adjust goals or objectives if necessary in preparation for the more in-depth annual review. An example of a company implementing quarterly reviews is Synygy, Inc., a Philadelphia-based compensation software and services company.[10] Each quarter, employees receive a summary of comments and specific examples from coworkers about how they are performing. Synygy states that the goal of the system is to encourage open communication. Employees are trained to write effective comments to their coworkers to facilitate growth by pointing out positive and negative areas of performance. In areas that need improvement, coworkers are encouraged to suggest ways in which an employee could improve his or her performance.

When is the best time to complete the reviews? Most organizations adopt one of two possibilities. First, the appraisal form could be completed on or around the annual anniversary date. In the case of semiannual reviews, the first review would be six months before the annual anniversary date and the second review would be on or around the anniversary date. The biggest advantage of this choice is that the supervisor does not have to fill out everyone's forms at one time. The disadvantage of this choice is that, because results are not tied to a common cycle for all employees, resulting rewards cannot be tied to the fiscal year.

The second choice is to complete the appraisal forms toward the end of the fiscal year. In the case of a system including semiannual reviews, one review would be completed halfway through the fiscal year and the other one toward the end of the fiscal year. Adopting this approach leads to the completion of the appraisal form for all employees at about the same time, thereby facilitating cross-employee comparisons as well as the distribution of rewards. An additional advantage of following the fiscal year cycle is that individual goal setting can be more easily tied to corporate goal setting because most companies align their goal cycle with their fiscal year. This helps employees synchronize their work and objectives with those of their unit and organization. But what about the additional work imposed on the supervisors who need to evaluate all employees at once during a short period of time? This can be a major problem if the performance management system is not implemented using the best practices described in this book and performance appraisal is a once-a-year event. If there is ongoing communication between the supervisor and the employee about performance issues throughout the year, completing appraisal forms should not uncover any major surprises and filling out the appraisal form should not create a major time burden for the supervisors.

Performance management systems can include six formal meetings between the subordinate and the supervisor[11]:

- System inauguration
- Self-appraisal
- Classical performance review
- Merit/salary review
- Development plan
- Objective setting

Recall that informal performance discussions take place throughout the year. In addition, however, there should be regularly scheduled formal meetings for the specific purpose of discussing the various aspects of performance and the performance management system. The fact that the supervisor allocates time to this activity sends a message that performance management is important.

The first meeting, system inauguration, includes a discussion of how the system works and the identification of the requirements and responsibilities resting primarily on the employee and on the supervisor. This discussion includes the role of self-appraisal and the dates when the employee and supervisor will meet formally to discuss performance issues. This meeting is particularly important for new employees, who should be introduced to the performance management system as soon as they become members of the organization.

The second meeting, the self-appraisal, involves the employee's assessment of herself. This meeting is informational in nature and, at this point, the supervisor does not pass judgment on how the employee regards her own performance. This meeting provides an opportunity for the employee to describe how she sees her own performance during the review period. It is helpful if the employee is given the same form to be filled out later by the supervisor so that she can provide self-ratings using the same dimensions that will be used by the supervisor.

The third meeting, the classical performance review meeting, during which employee performance is discussed, includes both the perspective of the supervisor and that of the employee. Most performance management systems include this type of meeting only. No other formal meetings to discuss performance are usually scheduled. This meeting is mainly past oriented and typically does not focus on what performance should look like in the future.

The fourth meeting, the merit/salary review, discusses what, if any, compensation changes will result from the period's performance. It is useful to separate the discussion of rewards from the discussion of performance so that the employee can focus on performance first and then on rewards. If these meetings are not separated, employees may not be very attentive during the discussion of performance and are likely to feel it is merely the price they must pay to move on to the part of the meeting that really matters: the discussion about rewards. Although these meetings are separate, supervisors should explain clearly the link between the employee's performance, discussed in detail in a previous meeting, and the rewards given. Rewards are not likely to carry their true weight if they are not linked directly to performance.

The fifth meeting, the development plan, discusses the employee's developmental needs and what steps will be taken so that performance will be improved during the following period. This meeting also includes information about what types of resources will be provided to the employee to facilitate the development of any required new skills.

The sixth and final meeting, objective setting, includes setting goals, both behavioral and result oriented, regarding the following review period. At this point, the employee has received very clear feedback about her performance during the past review period, knows what rewards will be allocated (if any), understands developmental needs and goals, and knows about resources available to help in the process of acquiring any required skills.

Although these six meetings are possible, not all six take place separately. For example, the self-appraisal, classical performance review, merit/salary review, developmental plan, and objective setting meetings may all take place during one umbrella meeting. Nonetheless, it is best to separate the various types of information discussed so that the employee and the supervisor will focus on each of the components separately.

Take the case of Johnsonville Foods (www.johnsonville.com), a sausage-making plant in Wisconsin. Johnsonville Foods has a performance management system that includes the following meetings: self-appraisal, classical performance review, merit/salary review, development plan, and objective setting.[12] Team members (i.e., employees) and coaches (i.e., supervisors) write six-month contracts stating their goals for the following six months and how they plan to meet those goals (objective setting). This contract also asks the employee to state developmental goals for the upcoming six months (developmental plan). These goals may include reading a book on leadership or learning a new computer software program. In addition, each month the employee writes up a contract with his goals for the month. That contract is posted on the company electronic bulletin board and sent to three internal customers who evaluate that employee's performance over the month. The next month, employees and their coaches discuss how the goals were met (classical performance review) and how much bonus the employee should receive (merit/salary review), and they set new goals for the upcoming month (objective setting). If the employee does not expect to meet his goals, a meeting is scheduled halfway through the month to discuss options.

In short, Johnsonville Foods includes all the formal meetings that can take place in a performance management system; however, it does not involve six separate meetings. Instead, the company holds only two formally scheduled meetings, but the system allows for the addition of more meetings if the need arises.

BOX 1

Performance Review Meetings at Central Florida Healthcare Federal Credit Union

Central Florida Healthcare Federal Credit Union (http://www.cfhcfcu.org) is a nonprofit organization that provides financial services to those who join on a membership basis. The organization, which employs about 40 people, is based in Orlando, Florida. The credit union utilizes a Web-based system that allows tailoring each position's performance evaluation to specific duties performed. The performance management system also involves quarterly meetings and goal setting which allow both supervisor and employee to track progress. The frequent performance reviews, including self-appraisals, were instituted in order to ensure that all employees receive regular performance feedback from supervisors who might otherwise spend more time focusing on those whose performance is considered substandard. This allows employees and supervisors to focus regularly on progress toward goals. The information systems facilitate the process by allowing both supervisor and employee to keep track of progress electronically. In summary, the Central Florida Healthcare Federal Credit Union utilizes a performance management system that includes frequent performance review meetings, combined with an emphasis on setting goals and tracking progress to ensure all employees and supervisors are focused on performance management.[13]

5 WHO SHOULD PROVIDE PERFORMANCE INFORMATION?

So far, we have assumed that the supervisor is the primary source for performance information. This is the case in most organizations because the supervisor observes employees directly and has good knowledge about performance standards. However, there are also alternative sources of performance information. Let's consider the use of the direct supervisor as a source of performance information, followed by the use of other sources including peers, subordinates, self, and customers.[14]

5.1 Supervisors

An advantage of using supervisors as a source of performance information is that they are usually in the best position to evaluate performance in relation to strategic organizational goals. Also, supervisors are often those making decisions about rewards associated with performance evaluation. In addition, supervisors are able to differentiate among various performance dimensions (e.g., adaptability, coaching, and development) regardless of the level of experience of the employee being rated.[15] In short, supervisors are often the most important source of performance information because they are knowledgeable about strategic issues, understand performance, and are usually in charge of managing employee performance. Moreover, in some cultural contexts, supervisors are seen as the exclusive source due to the pervasiveness of hierarchical organizational structures. For example, a survey of 74 HR directors in Jordan revealed that, in every one of these organizations, the supervisor had almost an exclusive input in terms of providing performance information, 95% of respondents reported that peers had no input, 82% reported that employees had no input, and 90% reported that customers had no input either.[16]

Although supervisors are usually the most important, and sometimes only, source of performance information, other sources should be considered as well. For example, we have already seen that self-appraisals are an important component in the performance review process. In addition to self-appraisals and supervisor appraisals, performance information can be collected from peers, customers, and subordinates (assuming there are any). Alternative sources are usually considered because, for some jobs, such as teaching, law enforcement, or sales, the supervisor may not observe her subordinates' performance on a regular basis. Also, performance evaluations given by the supervisor may be biased because the supervisor may evaluate performance based on whether the ratee is contributing to goals valued by the supervisor as opposed to goals valued by the organization as a whole.[17] For example, a supervisor may provide high performance ratings to employees who help the supervisor advance his or her career aspirations within the company, as opposed to those who engage in behaviors conducive to helping achieve organizational strategic goals.

5.2 Peers

Many organizations use performance evaluations provided by peers. Take, for example, the system implemented at a large international financial services bank.[18] Through acquisitions, the bank has been growing rapidly and has as its strategic goal the consolidation of its offices. Change management is extremely important to the successful implementation of this consolidation. The company is therefore revising how it assesses the competency "teamwork" at the senior and middle management levels, with the belief that successful teamwork is crucial to change management initiatives. Specifically, one-third of the score for this competency is determined by ratings provided by peers. As an additional example, the Australian National University Medical School recently introduced a system in which students rate their peers in terms of personal and professional performance. Students begin to provide anonymous ratings online at the end of their first year in medical school. The system allows students to share their assessment of their peers and provides faculty with early-warning signs to assist students who may not be performing up to personal or professional standards.[19]

Peer evaluations suffer from three problems, however. First, such evaluations may not be readily accepted when employees believe there is friendship bias at work. In other words, if an employee believes that ratings provided by his peers will be lower than those provided for another employee because the other employee has more friends than he does, then performance evaluations will not be taken seriously. It is not likely that the employee will use the feedback received to improve his performance. A second problem with peer evaluations is that peers are less discriminating among performance dimensions than are supervisors. In other words, if one is rated high on one dimension, one is also likely to be rated high on all the other dimensions, even though the performance dimensions rated may not be related to one another and may require very different knowledge, skills, and abilities. Finally, peer evaluations are likely to be affected by what is called *context effects*.[20] For example, consider the situation in which peers evaluate communication behaviors. The salience of such behaviors will be affected by context: these behaviors are much more salient when there is a conflict as compared to routine daily work. The resulting peer evaluations can thus be quite different based on whether the peer providing the rating is thinking about one specific situation versus another one, or communication behaviors across situations in general.

Given these weaknesses of peer evaluations, it would not be wise to use them as the sole source of performance information. Peer evaluations can be part of the system, but information should also be obtained from other sources, including the supervisor.

5.3 Subordinates

Subordinates are a good source of information regarding the performance of their managers.[21] For example, subordinates are in a good position to evaluate leadership competencies, including delegation, organization, and communication. In addition, subordinates may be asked to rate their manager's ability to (1) remove barriers that employees face, (2) shield employees from politics, and (3) raise employees' competence. With this type of system, subordinates may hesitate to provide upward feedback if put on the spot; however, if managers take the time to involve employees in the process by soliciting their input, employees are more likely to give honest feedback.[22]

Many organizations take upward feedback very seriously. Take the case of computer giant Dell, which employs over 78,700 individuals worldwide. In 1984 Michael Dell founded Dell based on the simple concept of selling computer systems directly to customers. In 2004 *Fortune* magazine ranked Dell the number one most admired company in the United States.[23] At Dell, all employees rate their supervisors, including

Michael Dell himself, every six months, using "Tell Dell" surveys. Michael Dell said, "If you are a manager and you're not addressing [employee] issues, you're not going to get compensation. And if you consistently score in the bottom rungs of the surveys, we're going to look at you and say 'Maybe this isn't the right job for you.' "[24]

The intended purpose of the evaluation provided by subordinates has an impact on the accuracy of the information provided. Overall, performance information provided by subordinates is more accurate when the resulting ratings are to be used for developmental purposes rather than administrative purposes. When evaluation data are intended for administrative purposes (i.e., whether the manager should be promoted), subordinates are likely to inflate their ratings.[25] Most likely, this is because subordinates may fear retaliation if they provide low performance scores. Confidentiality is key if subordinates are to be used as a source of performance information.

5.4 Self

As discussed earlier, self-appraisals are an important component of any performance management system. When employees are given the opportunity to participate in the performance management process, their acceptance of the resulting decision is likely to increase, and their defensiveness during the appraisal interview is likely to decrease. An additional advantage associated with self-appraisals is that the employee is in a good position to keep track of activities during the review period, whereas a supervisor may have to keep track of the performance of several employees. On the other hand, self-appraisals should not be used as the sole source of information in making administrative decisions because they are more lenient and biased than are ratings provided by other sources such as a direct supervisor.[26,27] This may explain why the vast majority of Fortune 500 companies do not include self-appraisals as part of their performance management systems.[28] Fortunately, self-ratings tend to be less lenient when they are used for developmental as opposed to administrative purposes. In addition, the following suggestions may improve the quality of self-appraisals:

- *Use comparative as opposed to absolute measurement systems.* For example, instead of asking individuals to rate themselves using a scale ranging from "poor" to "excellent," provide a relative scale that allows them to compare their performance with that of others (e.g., "below average," "average," "above average").
- *Allow employees to practice their self-rating skills.* Provide multiple opportunities for self-appraisal because the skill of self-evaluation may well be one that improves with practice.
- *Assure confidentiality.* Provide reassurance that performance information collected from oneself will not be disseminated and shared with any one other than the direct supervisor and other relevant parties (e.g., members of the same work group).
- *Emphasize the future.* The developmental plan section of the form should receive substantial attention. The employee should indicate his plans for future development and accomplishments.

5.5 Customers

Customers, and other key stakeholders in general, provide yet another source of performance information.[29] Collecting information from customers can be a costly and time-consuming process; however, performance information provided by customers is particularly useful for jobs that require a high degree of interaction with the public or with particular job-related individuals (e.g., purchasing managers, suppliers, sales representatives). Also, performance information can be collected from *internal* customers. For example, line managers may provide information regarding the performance of their HR representative. Although the clients served may not have full knowledge of the organization's strategic direction, they can provide useful information. For example, consider how this is done at Federal Express (http://www.fedex.com/us//). Federal Express revised its performance management system to include measures of customer service.[30] Currently, the company uses a six-item customer-satisfaction survey, which is evaluated by a representative sample of the employee's customers at the end of the year. As a result of adding customer input and customer-developed goals to the performance review process, employees are more focused on meeting customer expectations.

Although Federal Express is now using external customer input in evaluating performance, organizations in other industries have some catching up to do. For example, a recent study examining appraisal forms used to evaluate the performance of account executives in the largest advertising agencies in the United States found that much more emphasis is placed on internal than on external customers.[31] Specifically, external client feedback was measured in only 12% of the agencies studied. About 27% of agencies do not evaluate the contributions that account executives make to client relationships and to growing the client's business. In short, advertising agencies might benefit from assessing the performance of account executives from the perspective not only of internal but also external customers.

5.6 Disagreement Across Sources: Is This a Problem?

If performance information is collected from more than one source, it is likely that there will be some overlap in the dimensions measured.[32] For example, a manager's peers and direct supervisor may rate him on the competency "communication." In addition to the overlapping dimensions across sources, each source is likely to evaluate performance dimensions that are unique to each source. For example, subordinates may evaluate "delegation," but this competency may not be included on the form used by the direct supervisor. Once the competencies and results that need to be measured are identified for a particular position, a decision needs to be made regarding which source of information will be used to assess each dimension. Of course, it is likely that there will be some overlap, and some dimensions will be rated by more than one source. Regardless of the final decision, it is important that employees take an active role in deciding which sources will rate which dimensions. Active participation in the process is likely to enhance acceptance of results and perceptions that the system is fair. Moreover, studies including master of business administration (MBA) students, executive MBA students, and managers in a large Canadian insurance company found that, when given a choice, individuals tend to select raters whom they think are most acquainted with their work as opposed to how much they like them and how much they think the raters like them.[33]

When the same dimension is evaluated across sources, we should not necessarily expect ratings to be similar.[34] Different sources disagreeing about an employee's performance is not necessarily a problem. For example, self-ratings of salespeople do not necessarily agree with the ratings given by their direct supervisor, which may indicate misunderstandings regarding the nature of performance.[35] Also, those rating the same employee may be drawn from different organizational levels, and they probably observe different facets of the employee's performance, even if they are evaluating the same general competency (e.g., "communication" or "sales behavior"). In fact, the behavioral indicators for the same competency may vary across sources. For example, an employee may be able to communicate very well with his superior but not very well with his subordinates. The important issue to take into account is that, for each source, the behaviors and results to be rated must be defined clearly so that biases are minimized. In terms of feedback, however, there is no need to come up with one overall conclusion regarding the employee's performance. On the contrary, it is important that the employee receive information on how her performance was rated by each of the sources used. This is the crux of what are called 360-degree feedback systems. When feedback is broken down by source, the employee can place particular attention and effort on the interactions involving the source that has detected performance deficiencies.

If disagreements are found, a decision must be made regarding the relative importance of the rating provided by each source. For example, is it equally important to please external and internal customers? Is communication an equally important competency regarding subordinates and peers? Answering these questions can lead to assigning differential weights to the scores provided by the different sources in computing the overall performance score used for administrative purposes.

6 A MODEL OF RATER MOTIVATION

Regardless of who rates performance, the rater is likely to be affected by biases that distort the resulting ratings. Performance ratings may be intentionally or unintentionally distorted or inaccurate. When this happens, incorrect decisions may be made, employees are likely to feel they are treated unfairly, and the organization is more prone to litigation. In other words, when performance ratings are distorted, the performance management system not only fails to result in desired outcomes but also may lead to very negative consequences for the organization. To prevent these negative outcomes, we need to understand why raters are likely to provide distorted ratings.

Rating behaviors are influenced by (1) the motivation to provide accurate ratings and (2) the motivation to distort ratings.[36] The motivation to provide accurate ratings is determined by whether the rater expects positive and negative consequences of accurate ratings and by whether the probability of receiving these rewards and punishments will be high if accurate ratings are provided. Similarly, the motivation to distort ratings is determined by whether the rater expects any positive and negative consequences of rating distortion and by the probability of experiencing such consequences if ratings are indeed distorted. Consider a supervisor and his motivation to provide accurate ratings. What will the supervisor gain if ratings are accurate? What will he lose? Will his own performance be rated higher and will he receive any rewards if this happens? Or will the relationship with his or her subordinates suffer? The answers to these questions provide information about whether this supervisor is likely to be motivated to provide accurate ratings. Similarly, are there any positive and negative consequences associated with rating distortion? What is the probability that this will indeed happen? The answers to these questions will determine the supervisor's motivation to distort ratings.

There are motivational barriers that prevent raters from providing accurate performance information. Raters may be motivated to distort performance information and provide inflated or deflated ratings.[37] In fact, supervisors may not even be trying to measure performance accurately and may attempt to use performance ratings for other goals.[38] For example, a supervisor may be motivated to provide inflated ratings to

- *Maximize the merit raise/rewards.* A supervisor may want to produce the highest possible reward for his employees, and he knows this will happen if he provides the highest possible performance ratings.
- *Encourage employees.* A supervisor may believe that employees' motivation will be increased if they receive high performance ratings.
- *Avoid creating a written record.* A supervisor may not want to leave a "paper trail" regarding an employee's poor performance because such documentation may eventually lead to negative consequences for the employee in question. This situation is possible if the supervisor and employee have developed a friendship.
- *Avoid confrontation with employees.* A supervisor may feel uncomfortable providing negative feedback and, in order to avoid a possible confrontation with the employee, may decide to take the path of least resistance and give inflated performance ratings.
- *Promote undesired employees out of unit.* A supervisor may believe that if an employee receives very high ratings she may be promoted out of the unit. The supervisor may regard this as an effective way to get rid of undesirable employees.
- *Make the manager look good to his/her supervisor.* A supervisor may believe that if everyone receives very high performance ratings, the supervisor will be considered an effective unit leader. Moreover, when the performance ratings for the manager himself depend on the performance of his subordinates, managers are likely to inflate their subordinates' ratings.[39]

We can understand each of the reasons for a supervisor's choosing to inflate ratings using a model or rater motivation. For example, looking good in the eyes of one's own supervisor can be regarded as a positive consequence of providing inflated ratings. Avoiding a possible confrontation with an employee can also be regarded as a positive consequence of providing inflated ratings. Thus, given these anticipated positive consequences of rating inflation, the supervisor may choose to provide distorted ratings.

Supervisors may also be motivated to provide ratings that are artificially deflated. Some reasons for this are to

- *Shock an employee.* A supervisor may believe that giving an employee a "shock treatment" and providing deflated performance ratings will jolt the employee, demonstrating that there is a problem.
- *Teach a rebellious employee a lesson.* A supervisor may wish to punish an employee or force an employee to cooperate with the supervisor and believes that the best way to do this is to give deflated performance ratings.

- *Send a message to the employee that he should consider leaving.* A supervisor lacking communication skills may wish to convey the idea that an employee should leave the unit or organization. Providing deflated performance ratings may be seen as a way to communicate this message.
- *Build a strongly documented, written record of poor performance.* A supervisor may wish to get rid of a particular employee and decides that the best way to do this is to create a paper trail of substandard performance.

We can also understand the psychological mechanisms underlying the decision to provide deflated ratings. For example, if shocking employees and building strongly documented records about employees are considered to be positive consequences of rating deflation, it is likely that the supervisor will choose to provide distorted ratings.

Fundamentally, this discussion should allow us to see that the process of evaluating performance can be filled with emotional overtones and hidden agendas that are driven by the goals and motivation of the person providing the rating.[40] If raters are not motivated to provide accurate ratings, they are likely to use the performance management system to achieve political and other goals, such as rewarding allies and punishing enemies or competitors, instead of using it as a tool to improve employee and, ultimately, organizational performance.[41] Thus, it is important to understand the influence of context on the accuracy of performance ratings and be aware that performance measurement does not take place in a vacuum, but in an organizational context with written and unwritten norms.[42]

What can be done to prevent conscious distortion of ratings? Considering a model of rater motivation, we need to provide incentives so that raters will be convinced that they have more to gain by providing accurate ratings than they do by providing inaccurate ratings. For example, if a supervisor is able to see the advantages of a well-implemented performance management system, as opposed to one dominated by office politics, he or she will be motivated to help the system succeed. Also, if a supervisor believes there is accountability in the system and ratings that are overly lenient are likely to be easily discovered, resulting in an embarrassing situation for the supervisor, leniency is also likely to be minimized. Lenient ratings may be minimized when supervisors understand they will have to justify their ratings to their own supervisors.[43] In terms of increasing accountability, specific recommendations include the following[44]:

1. *Have raters justify their ratings.* Ratings are more accurate when raters are told they will have to justify their ratings to someone with authority, such as their own supervisors. However, rating accuracy does not necessarily improve if raters need to justify their ratings to others with less authority such as their own subordinate.
2. *Have the raters justify their ratings in a face-to-face meeting.* Ratings are also more accurate when the rating justifications are offered in a face-to-face meeting compared to justifications offered in writing only.

In a nutshell, a supervisor asks herself, "What's in it for me if I provide accurate ratings versus inflated or deflated ratings?" The performance management system needs to be designed in such a way that the benefits of providing accurate ratings outweigh the benefits of providing inaccurate ratings. This may include assessing the performance of the supervisor in how she is implementing performance management within her unit, and communicating that performance management is a key part of a supervisor's job. Also, supervisors need to have tools available to make their job of providing accurate ratings and feedback easier. This includes training on, for example, how to conduct the appraisal interview so that supervisors are able to provide both positive and negative feedback and are skilled at conveying both positive and, negative news regarding performance.

In addition to conscious and intentional errors in the rating process, raters are likely to make unintended errors. Observing information about performance, storing this information in memory, and then recalling it when it is time to fill out the appraisal form is a complex task. This task becomes more complex with more complex jobs that include several unrelated performance dimensions. Because of the cognitive complexity of the performance evaluation process, raters are likely to make not only intentional but also unintentional errors in evaluating performance. To a large extent, these errors can be minimized by improving the skills of those responsible for providing performance evaluations. These training programs, which target mostly supervisors, are discussed next.

7 PREVENTING RATING DISTORTION THROUGH RATER TRAINING PROGRAMS

Rater training programs have the overall objective of providing raters with tools that will allow them to implement the performance management system effectively and efficiently. These training programs also help prevent rating distortion. Table 3 summarizes the reasons discussed earlier for why raters are likely to inflate or deflate ratings.

How can training programs help mitigate the reasons causing intentional rating distortion listed in Table 3? Remedial programs include content related to information, motivation, and skills. Recall that, in addition to intentional errors, raters are likely to make unintentional errors in rating performance. Training programs, therefore, must address both types of errors and essentially, the goal is to align the goals of the rater with the goals of the performance management system so that raters are partners and active contributors to the process.[45] Specifically, training programs may cover the following topics:

- *Reasons for implementing the performance management system.* This includes an overview of the entire system, its purpose, and benefits for all employees.

TABLE 3	Reasons for Rating Distortion
Rating Inflation	*Rating Deflation*
Maximize the merit raise/rewards	Shock employees
Encourage employees	Teach a rebellious employee a lesson
Avoid creating a written record	Send a message that employee should
Avoid a confrontation with employees	consider leaving
Promote undesired employees out of unit	Build a record of poor performance
Make manager look good to his or her supervisor	

- *How to identify and rank job activities.* This includes information about how to conduct a job analysis and understand the most important accountabilities and competencies.
- *How to observe, record, and measure performance.* This may include observational skills such as how to observe the behaviors that really matter and not be distracted by behaviors not related to the performance dimensions to be measured. It also includes skills needed to fill out the appraisal form.
- *Information on the appraisal form and system mechanics.* This includes a detailed description of the content of the appraisal form and what each section is intended to measure. It also includes information about the number of recommended meetings and the expectations regarding each participant.
- *How to minimize rating errors.* This includes steps that can be taken to minimize unintentional errors caused by the cognitive demands associated with the observation and evaluation of performance.
- *How to conduct an appraisal interview.* This includes listening skills and communication skills and how to provide feedback during the appraisal interview. It also includes skills on how to help the employee create a development plan.
- *How to train, counsel, and coach.* This includes skills that the supervisor needs to help employees improve their performance on an ongoing basis.

For example, consider the training program used by the city of Aurora, Colorado. This program includes many of the issues listed here. First, it addresses general considerations about the performance management system, including the reasons performance management is important. Second, it covers the difference between results and job-oriented (i.e., behavior-based) performance dimensions. Third, the trainer discusses how to weigh properly the various performance dimensions. Fourth, training includes a definition of the different levels of performance along several sample job-oriented dimensions. For example, it includes an explanation of the dimension "problem solving" and examples of unacceptable, acceptable, and exceptional performance. Next, it teaches managers how to develop individual performance objectives and gives examples of good objectives. Finally, it teaches managers different ways to monitor performance and the benefits of doing so. Overall, Aurora's rater training program is fairly thorough and covers many of the subjects discussed here. It does not, however, seem to include steps that can be taken to minimize unintentional errors or the way to conduct the appraisal interview or the way to train, counsel, and coach employees.

In sum, raters are likely to make both intentional and unintentional errors in rating performance. Training programs that address motivational issues, demonstrate how the system works, and provide a clear answer to the "What's in it for me?" question can help minimize intentional errors. In addition, training programs that include information on and skills regarding how to observe and rate performance can help minimize the presence of unintentional errors.

Summary Points

- Appraisal forms are the key instruments used to measure performance. Care and attention are required to ensure that the forms include all the necessary components. Most forms include a combination of the following: (1) basic employee information; (2) accountabilities, objectives, and standards; (3) competencies and indicators; (4) major achievements and contributions; (5) developmental achievements; (6) developmental needs, plans, and goals; (7) stakeholder input; (8) employee comments; and (9) signatures. Note, however, that one size does not fit all, and different components are appropriate based on the purposes of the appraisal.

- Regardless of the specific components included in the appraisal form, there are several characteristics that make appraisal forms particularly effective. These are (1) simplicity, (2) relevancy, (3) descriptiveness, (4) adaptability, (5) comprehensiveness, (6) definitional clarity, (7) communication, and (8) time orientation. Before it is used, each form needs to be evaluated based on the extent to which it complies with each of these characteristics.

- For administrative purposes, it is usually desirable to compute an employee's overall performance score. Two approaches are available: judgmental and mechanical. The judgmental procedure consists of considering every aspect of performance and then arriving at a fair and defensible summary. The mechanical procedure consists of combining the scores assigned to each performance dimension, usually taking into account the relative weight given to each dimension. The mechanical procedure is recommended over the judgmental procedure, which is more prone to biases. Rounding of overall scores can be implemented (upward or downward)

based on the information included in the "comments" section of the appraisal forms. However, for this to happen, there must be a systematic analysis of this text-based information and raters must be provided clear guidelines regarding what to include in these "comments" sections.

- It is recommended that the period for review be six months (i.e., semiannual) or three months (i.e., quarterly). This provides fairly frequent opportunities for a formal discussion about performance issues between the subordinate and the supervisor. It is more convenient if the completion of the appraisal form coincides with the fiscal year so that rewards can be allocated shortly after the employee has received his or her performance review.

- Performance management systems can include up to six separate formal meetings between the supervisor and the subordinate: (1) system inauguration, (2) self appraisal, (3) classical performance review, (4) merit/salary review, (5) development plan, and (6) objective setting. In practice, these meetings are usually condensed into two or so meetings during each review cycle. One point that should be emphasized is that these are *formal* meetings. *Informal* meetings involving a discussion of performance issues should take place on an ongoing basis.

- Several sources can be used to obtain performance information: supervisors, peers, subordinates, self, and customers. Before selecting a source, one needs to be sure that the source has firsthand knowledge of the employee's performance. Using each of these sources has advantages and disadvantages, none of which are foolproof, and not all may be available in all situations. However, it is important that employees take part in the process of selecting which sources will evaluate which performance dimensions. Active participation in the process is likely to enhance acceptance of results and perceptions that the system is fair.

• When multiple sources of performance information are used, there may be disagreements about an employee's performance level, even if these multiple sources are rating the same performance dimension. The people rating the same employee may be drawn from different organizational levels, and they may observe different facets of the employee's performance, even if they are evaluating the same general competency (e.g., "communication"). If an overall score is needed that considers all sources, then a weighting mechanism is needed. For example, a decision needs to be made regarding whether performance information provided by the supervisor has more or less relative importance than that provided by customers. There is no need to summarize the information across the sources for feedback purposes; in fact, it is beneficial for the employee to receive feedback broken down by source so that the employee can place particular attention and effort on the interactions involving any source that has detected performance deficiencies.

• In providing performance information, raters may make intentional errors. These errors may involve inflating or deflating performance scores. For example, a supervisor may want to avoid a confrontation with his or her employees and inflate ratings. A peer may believe that providing accurate ratings may jeopardize the relationship with a colleague and may, consequently, provide inflated ratings. When raters provide performance ratings, they are faced with providing either accurate or inaccurate ratings. They weigh costs and benefits of

choosing one or the other path. If the cost/benefit equation does not favor providing accurate ratings, it is likely that ratings will be distorted. When this happens, incorrect decisions may be made, employees are likely to feel they have been treated unfairly, and the organization is more prone to litigation. In other words, when performance ratings are distorted because raters are not motivated to provide accurate scores, the performance management system not only will fail to achieve desired outcomes but also may lead to very negative consequences for the organization.

• In addition to intentional errors, raters may make unintentional errors in providing performance ratings. This happens because observing information about performance, storing this information in memory, and then recalling it when it is time to fill out the appraisal form is a complex cognitive task.

• Intentional and unintentional distortion in performance ratings can be minimized by providing raters with extensive training. Such training programs include content related to information, motivation, and skills. For example, regarding information, training programs address an overview of the entire performance management system. Regarding motivation, raters are given information about how rating employees accurately will provide them with direct and tangible benefits. Training programs can demonstrate how to conduct an appraisal interview. No performance management system is foolproof, and performance ratings are inherently subjective; however, the implementation of such training programs, together with accountability (i.e., having to justify ratings to superiors in a face-to-face meeting) and rewards associated with accurate ratings, provides raters with the needed motivation and skills to minimize rating errors.

CASE STUDY 1

Evaluating an Appraisal Form Used in Higher Education

Consider the appraisal form shown below, which is a form used by a university in the United States for non-faculty staff members. First, use the table to place check marks next to each component that is present. Second, in the Comments section, please write, (1) for those components that are present, whether any changes or revisions are needed in the form and why and, (2) for those components that are absent, why they should be added and what are the possible negative consequences of not doing so. ■

Major Components of Appraisal Forms	Comments
Basic employee information	
Accountabilities, objectives, and standards	
Competencies and indicators	
Major achievements and contributions	
Developmental achievements	
Developmental needs, plans, and goals	
Stakeholder input	
Employee comments	
Approvals	

UC Berkeley
Performance evaluation and planning form   **Professional**

Employee:_____ Job Title: _____ Department: _____

Control Unit: _____

Evaluation Period: From _____ to _____   Annual _____   Other _____

Appointment: Limited/Contract, end date: _____   Career _____   Probationary period ends: _____

Instructions:

Effective evaluation of job performance is an on-going process. Annually, each manager or supervisor provides a summary of progress toward meeting job expectations and last year's goals. This form is to be used for annual evaluations, and at other times during the year when formal feedback is needed.

These forms have been approved for employees covered by the Personnel Policies for Staff Members (PPSM). For represented employees, departments will want to use forms that have been approved by the respective bargaining units.

Part I—Job Success Factors
These include key responsibilities and basic competencies. Rate each factor based on performance during the period identified above. The factors include key responsibilities specific to this position (Part 1-A), and competencies common to the campus professional job standards (Part 1-B).

(Continued)

(Continued)

Part II—Goals from Last Year or Last Evaluation Period

Rate the progress made on each of the goals established at the beginning of the period. Also include any new goals established during the evaluation period and note any modifications to the original goals.

Part III—Goals for This Coming Year or Evaluation Period

Enter the performance goals for the next period to be evaluated. Individual goals and objectives should align with those of the department and the campus.

Part IV—Professional Development Plan

Enter any actions that will be taken by the employee or manager/supervisor to support the goals indicated in Part III above, or specific job success factors in Part I. The plan may include career growth, job mastery, or actions to correct performance.

Rating Scale*:

Level 5 (E)   **Exceptional**

Performance far exceeded expectations due to exceptionally high quality of work performed in all *essential* areas of responsibility, resulting in an overall quality of work that was superior; and either 1) included the completion of a major goal or project or 2) made an exceptional or unique contribution in support of unit, department, or University objectives. This rating is achievable by any employee though given infrequently.

Level 4 (EE)   **Exceeds expectations**

Performance consistently exceeded expectations in all *essential* areas of responsibility, and the quality of work overall was excellent. Annual goals were met.

Level 3 (ME)   **Meets expectations**

Performance consistently met expectations in all *essential* areas of responsibility, at times possibly exceeding expectations, and the quality of work overall was very good. The most critical annual goals were met.

Level 2 (I)   **Improvement needed**

Performance did not *consistently* meet expectations—performance failed to meet expectations in one or more *essential* areas of responsibility, and/or one or more of the most critical goals were not met. A professional development plan to improve performance must be outlined in Section 4, including timelines, and monitored to measure progress.

Level 1 (U)   **Unsatisfactory**

Performance was consistently below expectations in most *essential* areas of responsibility, and/or reasonable progress toward critical goals was not made. Significant improvement is needed in one or more important areas. In Section 4, a plan to correct performance, including timelines, must be outlined and monitored to measure progress.

*The inclusion of goals is typically a consideration in assessing the overall rating.

Part I. Job Success Factors

Factors	Rating (bold or underline to select)					Comments
A. KEY RESPONSIBILITIES SPECIFIC TO THIS JOB						
Performs key responsibilities as articulated in the job description. • *(may give a global rating OR insert here essential functions as listed in the job description, include them by reference in an attached copy of the job description, or paraphrase from the job description)*	U	I	ME	EE	E	
B. CORE COMPETENCIES						
1. Inclusiveness Shows respect for people and their differences; promotes fairness and equity; engages the talents, experiences, and capabilities of others; fosters a sense of belonging; works to understand the perspectives of others; and creates opportunities for access and success. •	U	I	ME	EE	E	
2. Stewardship Implements a process or takes some action that significantly reduces risk on campus (e.g., making information for decision making more accessible, reliable, consistent, and secure; supporting continuity planning or emergency preparedness; etc.). •	U	I	ME	EE	E	
3. Problem solving/Decision making Problem solving—Identifies problems, involves others in seeking solutions, conducts appropriate analyses, searches for the best solutions, responds quickly to new challenges. Decision making—Makes clear, consistent, transparent decisions; acts with integrity in all decision making; distinguishes relevant from irrelevant information and makes timely decisions. •	U	I	ME	EE	E	
4. Strategic planning and organizing Understands big picture and aligns priorities with broader goals, measures outcomes, uses feedback to change as needed, evaluates alternatives, solutions oriented, seeks alternatives and broad input; can see connections within complex issues. •	U	I	ME	EE	E	
5. Communication Connects with peers, subordinates, and customers; actively listens; clearly and effectively shares information; demonstrates effective oral and written communication skills. •	U	I	ME	EE	E	
6. Quality improvement Strives for efficient, effective, high-quality performance in self and the unit; delivers timely and accurate results; resilient when responding to situations that are not going well; takes initiative to make improvements. •	U	I	ME	EE	E	

(Continued)

CORE COMPETENCIES (*Continued*)						
7. Leadership Accepts responsibility for own work; develops trust and credibility; demonstrates honest and ethical behavior. •	U	I	ME	EE	E	
8. Teamwork Cooperates and collaborates with colleagues as appropriate; works in partnership with others. •	U	I	ME	EE	E	
9. Service focus Values the importance of delivering high-quality, innovative service to internal and external clients; understands the needs of the client; customer service focus. •	U	I	ME	EE	E	
10. Unit- or department-specific competency (optional)	U	I	ME	EE	E	

Part II. Last Period's Goals

Rate the progress made on each of the goals established at the beginning of the period and any new goals. Note any modifications to the original goals.

Goal	Rating					Comments
1.	U	I	ME	EE	E	
2.	U	I	ME	EE	E	
3.	U	I	ME	EE	E	
4.	U	I	ME	EE	E	
5.	U	I	ME	EE	E	

OVERALL RATING (based on Parts I and II) Relative weights of job success factors and performance goals are determined by the manager or supervisor. Higher priority items may be highlighted.	U	I	ME	EE	E	

Part III. Next Period's Goals

Enter the performance goals for the next period to be evaluated. Individual goals and objectives should align with those of the department and the campus.

1.
Measure of success:
2.
Measure of success:
3.
Measure of success:
4.
Measure of success:
5.
Measure of success:

Progress toward meeting these goals will be reviewed at the time of the next evaluation.

Part IV. Professional Development Plan

Signatures:

Employee:_____ Date: _____

My signature indicates that I have received a copy of this evaluation.

____ I would like to include comments from my self-assessment.

Manager/supervisor: Name:_____

Signature: _____ Date: _____

Department manager: Name: _____

Signature: _____ Date: _____

The employee being evaluated is to receive a copy of the completed evaluation form and one copy shall be placed in the personnel file.

Source: Appraisal form has been adapted from those available on UC Berkeley's Human Resource Department website. Human Resources at UC Berkeley. (2011). *Performance appraisal forms.* Available online at http://hrweb.berkeley.edu/files/attachments/Perf_Eval_Form_Professional. doc. Retrieval date: July 22, 2011. Copyright UC Regents. All rights reserved. Reproduced with permission from the University of California, Berkeley.

CASE STUDY 2

Judgmental and Mechanical Methods of Assigning Overall Performance Score at *The Daily Planet*

The form here shows performance ratings obtained by David Kuhn, a hypothetical reporter at a major newspaper in the United States. First, use the judgmental method to come up with his overall performance score. What is Kuhn's overall[*] performance score?

The weights for the various competencies are the following:

Now compute Kuhn's overall performance score using the weights in the table. Is there a difference between the score computed using a subjective rather than the mechanical method? If yes, what are the implications of these differences for the employee being rated, for the supervisor, and for the organization? ■

Competency	Weight
Productivity	.15
Quality of work	.50
Dependability and adherence to company values and policies	.25
Contribution to effectiveness of others/unit	.10

Name: David Kuhn	Job Title: Reporter				
Dept.: International	Supervisor: John DuBoss				
Performance Period:	from Jan 07	to Dec 07			

Job Description: Researches and writes news, features, analyses, human interest stories. Develops and cultivates news sources and contacts. Completes assignments by deadlines, ensuring accuracy by verifying sources. Attends newsworthy events and interviews key sources. Respects confidentiality as appropriate.

	Unacceptable	Does not fully meet standards	Fully meets standards	Significantly exceeds standards	Outstanding
Productivity—Production is high relative to time and resources consumed; develops expected number of stories and covers beat adequately to ensure stories are detected as they break; stories are developed within time frame that enables deadlines to be met; and appropriate reviews are performed as they are refined.	1	②	3	4	5

---

[*] Adapted from Greene, R. J. (2003). Contributing to organizational success through effective performance appraisal. *SHRM Online*. Available online at http://www.shrm.org/Education/hreducation/Documents/09-0294%20 Performance Management_IM%20v4.pdf. Retrieval date: September 7, 2011.

	1	2	3	4	5
Quality of work—Work meets quality standards and established editorial standards; stories are written in clear and appropriate manner, are consistent with editorial policy, and are fair and balanced; research is thorough and encompasses all relevant sources, which are verified to ensure accuracy; works with editors to revise and improve content; develops and maintains network of contacts who can provide early notification of breaking stories.	1	2	3	④	5
Dependability and adherence to company values and policies— Consistently meets deadlines; conforms to attendance policies; adapts to work demands; conforms to established values and policies; adheres to ethical standards of the paper and the profession; respects confidentiality as appropriate; behaves in manner that enhances the image of the paper.	1	2	3	4	⑤
Contribution to effectiveness of others/ unit—Works with others within and outside the unit in a manner that improves their effectiveness; shares information and resources; develops effective working relationships; builds consensus; constructively manages conflict; contributes to the effectiveness of own unit/group and the paper.	1	②	3	4	5

CASE STUDY 3

Minimizing Intentional and Unintentional Rating Errors

Consider the areas typically covered by rater training programs (Section 7). Use the table to identify which of these content areas address intentional errors and which address unintentional errors. Please place a check mark where appropriate. Fill in the Comments section to describe the rationale that guided each of your responses. ■

Intentional Errors	Unintentional Errors	Content Area	Comments
		Reasons for implementing the performance management system. This includes an overview of the entire system, its purpose, and benefits for all employees.	
		How to identify and rank job activities. This includes information on how to conduct a job analysis and understand the most important accountabilities and competencies.	
		How to observe, record, and measure performance. This may include observational skills such as how to observe the behaviors that really matter and not be distracted by behaviors not related to the performance dimensions to be measured. It also includes skills needed to fill out the appraisal form.	
		Information on the appraisal form and system mechanics. This includes a detailed description of the content of the appraisal form and what each section is intended to measure. It also includes information on number of meetings and the expectations regarding each participant.	
		How to minimize rating errors. This includes steps that can be taken to minimize unintentional errors caused by the cognitive demands associated with the observation and evaluation of performance.	
		How to conduct an appraisal interview. This includes listening skills and communication skills and how to provide feedback during the appraisal interview. It also includes skills on how to help the employee create a development plan.	
		How to train, counsel, and coach. This includes skills that the supervisor needs to help employees improve their performance on an ongoing basis.	

CASE STUDY 4

Minimizing Biases in Performance Evaluation at Expert Engineering, Inc.

Under various engineer titles, veteran engineer Demetri worked for Expert Engineering, Inc., for almost 15 years. The firm's performance evaluation history is both unique and long. He has recently been promoted to the position of Principal at the engineering firm. All principals are involved in evaluating engineers because the founders of the firm believed in multiple source evaluation and feedback to prevent favoritism and promote a merit-based culture. At the same time, the firm has a long history of using quality performance appraisal forms and review meetings to better ensure accurate performance evaluations. Several months ago, however, the firm initiated a big hiring initiative of a dozen new engineers, nine of whom turned out to be graduates from Purdue

University, which is the same university from which Demetri graduated. Indeed, Demetri was active in moving forward the hiring initiative. There is tension and discontent among the other principals, who fear that a time of unchecked favoritism, biased performance ratings, and unfair promotion decisions is on the rise.

1. Provide a detailed discussion of the intentional and unintentional rating distortion factors that may come into play in this situation.
2. Evaluate the kinds of training programs that could minimize the factors you have described. What do you recommend and why? ■

End Notes

1. Tannenbaum, S. I. (2006). Applied performance measurement: Practical issues and challenges. In W. Bennett, C. E. Lance, & D. J. Woehr (Eds.), *Performance measurement: Current perspectives and future challenges* (pp. 297–318). Mahwah, NJ: Lawrence Erlbaum.
2. Adapted from Grote, D. (1996). *The complete guide to performance appraisal.* New York: AMACOM.
3. Grote, D. (1996). *The complete guide to performance appraisal.* New York: AMACOM.
4. Adapted from Workforce Research Center (2003, April). "Busch Performance Evaluations," *Workforce Online.* Available online at http://www.workforce.com/archive/article/23/42/03.php. Retrieval date: May 1, 2011.
5. Ganzach, Y., Kluger, A. N., & Klayman, N. (2000). Making decisions from an interview: Expert measurement and mechanical combination. *Personnel Psychology, 53,* 1–20.
6. Kraiger, K., & Aguinis, H. (2001). Training effectiveness: Assessing training needs, motivation, and accomplishments. In M. London (Ed.), *How people evaluate others in organizations* (pp. 203–220). Mahwah, NJ: Lawrence Erlbaum.
7. Brutus, S. (2010). Words versus numbers: A theoretical exploration of giving and receiving narrative comments in performance appraisal. *Human Resource Management Review, 20,* 144–157.
8. Short, J. C., Broberg, J. C., Cogliser, C. C., & Brigham, K. (2010). Construct validation using computer-aided text analysis (CATA): An illustration using entrepreneurial orientation. *Organizational Research Methods, 13,* 320–347.
9. Milliman, J. F., Zawacki, R. A., Schulz, B., Wiggins, S., & Norman, C. A. (1995). Customer service drives 360-degree goal setting. *Personnel Journal, 74,* 136–142.
10. Workforce Research Center. ED: April 29, 2001 The new thinking in performance appraisals: Writing effective co-worker comments. *Workforce Online.* Available online at http://www.workforce.com/archive/feature/22/28/68/223579.php. Retrieval date: May 1, 2011.
11. Adapted from Grote, D. (1996). *The complete guide to performance appraisal.* New York: AMACOM.
12. Talbott, S. P. (1994). Peer review drives compensation at Johnsonville. *Personnel Journal, 73,* 126–132.

13. Courter, E. (2006). Measuring up. *Credit Union Management, 29*(6), 30–33.

14. The discussion of the various sources of performance information is based, in part, on Cascio, W. F., and Aguinis, H. (2005). *Applied psychology in human resources management*, (6th ed.). Upper Saddle River, NJ: Prentice Hall.

15. Greguras, G. J. (2005). Managerial experience and the measurement equivalence of performance ratings. *Journal of Business and Psychology, 19*, 383–397.

16. Abu-Doleh, J., & Weir, D. (2007). Dimensions of performance appraisal systems in Jordanian private and public organizations. *International Journal of Human Resource Management, 18*, 75–84.

17. Hogan, R., & Shelton, D. (1998). A socioanalytic perspective on job performance. *Human Performance, 11*, 129–144.

18. Workforce Research Center. Dear workforce: ED: March 6, 2002. How are peer reviews used for compensation? *Workforce Online.* Available online at http://www.workforce.com/archive/article/22/13/94.php. Retrieval date: May 1, 2011.

19. Ramsey, W., & Owen, C. (2006). Is there a role for peer review in performance appraisal of medical students? *Medical Education, 40*(2), 95–96.

20. Dierdoff, E. C., & Surface, E. A. (2007). Placing peer ratings in context: Systematic influences beyond rate performance. *Personnel Psychology, 60*, 93–126.

21. Antonioni, D. (1994). The effects of feedback accountability on upward appraisal ratings. *Personnel Psychology, 47*, 349–356.

22. Jelley, R. B., & Goffin, R. D. (2001). Can performance-feedback accuracy be improved? Effects of rater priming and rating-scale format on rating accuracy. *Journal of Applied Psychology, 86*, 134–145.

23. Useem, J. (2005). America's most admired companies. *Fortune, 151*(5), 66–70.

24. Serwer, A. (2005). The education of Michael Dell. *Fortune, 151*(5), 76.

25. Greguras, G. J., Robie, C., Schleicher, D. J., & Goff, M. (2003). A field study of the effects of rating purpose on the quality of multisource ratings. *Personnel Psychology, 56*, 1–21.

26. Atkins, P. W. B., & Wood, R. E. (2002). Self-versus others' ratings as predictors of assessment center ratings: Validation evidence for 360-degree feedback programs. *Personnel Psychology, 55*, 871–904.

27. van Hooft, E. A. J., van der Flier, H., & Minne, M. R. (2006). Construct validity of multi-source performance ratings: An examination of the relationship of self-, supervisor-, and peer-ratings with cognitive and personality measures. *International Journal of Selection & Assessment, 14*, 67–81.

28. Wells, B., & Spinks, N. (1990). How companies are using employee self-evaluation forms. *Journal of Compensation & Benefits, 6*, 42–47.

29. Simmons, J., & Lovegrove, I. (2005). Bridging the conceptual divide: Lessons from stakeholder analysis. *Journal of Organizational Change Management, 18*, 495–513.

30. Milliman, J. F., Zawacki, R. A., Schulz, B., Wiggins, S., & Norman, C. A. (1995). Customer service drives 360-degree goal setting. *Personnel Journal, 74*, 136–142.

31. Franke, G. R., Murphy, J. H., & Nadler, S. S. (2003). Appraising account executive performance appraisals: Current practices and managerial implications. *Journal of Current Issues & Research in Advertising, 25*, 1–11.

32. Facteau, J. D., & Craig, S. B. (2001). Are performance appraisal ratings from different rating sources comparable? *Journal of Applied Psychology, 86*, 215–227.

33. Brutus, S., Petosa, S., & Aucoin, E. (2005). Who will evaluate me? Rater selection in multi-source assessment contexts. *International Journal of Selection and Assessment, 13*, 129–138.

34. Viswesvaran, C., Schmidt, F. L., & Ones, D. S. (2002). The moderating influence of job performance dimensions on convergence of supervisory and peer ratings of job performance: Unconfounding construct-level convergence and rating difficulty. *Journal of Applied Psychology, 87*, 345–354.

35. Jaramillo, F., Carrillat, F. A., & Locander, W. B. (2005). A meta-analytic comparison of managerial ratings and self-evaluations. *Journal of Personal Selling & Sales Management, 25*, 315–328.

36. Murphy, K. R., & Cleveland, J. N. (2005). *Understanding performance appraisal: Social, organizational, and goal-based perspectives.* Thousand Oaks, CA: Sage.

37. Longenecker, C. O., Sims, H. P., & Gioia, D. A. (1987). Behind the mask: The politics of employee appraisal. *Academy of Management Executive, 1*, 183–193.

38. Murphy, K. R. (2008). Perspectives on the relationship between job performance and ratings of job performance. *Industrial and Organizational Psychology, 1*, 197–205.

39. Spence, J. R., & Keeping, L. M. (2010). The impact of non-performance information on ratings of job performance: A policy-capturing approach. *Journal of Organizational Behavior, 31*, 587–608.

40. Fletcher, C. (2001). Performance appraisal and management: The developing research agenda. *Journal of Occupational and Organizational Psychology, 74*, 473–487.

41. Murphy, K. R., Cleveland, J. N., Skattebo, A. L., & Kinney, T. B. (2004). Raters who pursue different goals give different ratings. *Journal of Applied Psychology, 89*, 158–164.

42. Murphy, K. R. (2008). Explaining the weak relationship between job performance and ratings of job performance. *Industrial and Organizational Psychology, 1*, 148–160.

43. Curtis, A. B., Harvey, R. D., & Ravden, D. (2005). Sources of political distortions in performance appraisals: Appraisal purpose and rater accountability. *Group & Organization Management, 30*, 42–60.

44. Mero, N. P., Guidice, R. M., & Brownlee, A. L. (2007). Accountability in a performance appraisal context: The effect of audience and form of accounting on rater response and behavior. *Journal of Management, 33*, 223–252.

45. Wang, X. M., Wong, K. F. E., & Kwong, J. Y. Y. (2010). The roles of rater goals and ratee performance levels in the distortion of performance ratings. *Journal of Applied Psychology, 95*, 546–561.

Implementing a Performance Management System

Implementing a Performance Management System

Training is everything.

—Mark Twain

LEARNING OBJECTIVES

By the end of this chapter, you will be able to do the following:

- Understand that there are crucial steps that must be taken before the performance management system is launched, including implementing a communication plan, an appeals process, training programs for raters, and pilot testing the system to fix any glitches.

- Design a communication plan that answers the key questions: What is performance management? How does performance management fit in the organization's strategy? How does everyone benefit from the system? How does the performance management system work? What are employees' and supervisors' key roles and responsibilities in implementing the system? How is performance management related to other key organizational initiatives?

- Design a communication plan that will include features aimed at reducing the effect of cognitive biases on how the performance management system is perceived and help minimize the impact of intentional rating errors.

- Be aware of cognitive biases that affect how people take in, use, and recall information, including selective exposure, selective perception, and selective retention.

- Understand that setting up an appeals process helps gain support for the performance management system.

- Design an appeals process including two levels: Level 1, which involves the human resources (HR) department in the role of mediator, and Level 2, which involves a panel of managers and peers and, possibly, a senior-level manager in the role of arbitrator and final decision maker.

- Describe unintentional and intentional types of errors that raters are likely to make in evaluating performance.

- Implement training programs such as rater error, frame of reference, and behavior observation that will minimize the impact of unintentional rating errors.

- Implement a self-leadership training program that will allow supervisors to increase confidence in their skills to manage the performance management process and, consequently, allow them to minimize rating errors.

- Understand the importance of conducting a pilot test before the performance system is implemented organization-wide.

- Conduct a pilot test of the performance management system using a selected group of employees and managers from the organization.

- As soon as the performance management system is in place, collect various measurements that will provide information regarding the system's effectiveness, the extent to which it is working the way it should, and whether it is producing the expected results.

- Understand issues involved in implementing a performance management system online.

This chapter addresses operational issues in implementing a performance management system. Specifically, it addresses the steps needed before the system is put in place, such as setting up good communication and appeals procedures that will gain system acceptance, implementing training programs to minimize rating errors, and pilot testing the system. Finally, the chapter describes how to monitor the system once it is in place to make sure it is working properly as well as the possibility of implementing the system online.

1 PREPARATION: COMMUNICATION, APPEALS PROCESS, TRAINING PROGRAMS, AND PILOT TESTING

As should be evident by now, the implementation of a performance management system requires the involvement of many players. Specifically, the successful implementation of the system requires a clear understanding of how the system works and a clear understanding of its benefits from the different perspectives of all involved. In other words, successful implementation requires wide organizational support and acceptance. Initially, it may be that each organizational layer and unit will include only one or just a handful of individuals who are knowledgeable and supportive of the system. These "champions" are likely to serve as advocates and resources for the system. Eventually, however, the system cannot be implemented successfully if only a handful of organizational members are on board.

Before the system is launched, a successful communication plan must be implemented that will gain system acceptance. Part of the communication plan includes a description of the appeals process. Then, as part of the preparation phase before the system is actually launched, raters are trained to observe and evaluate performance as well as to give feedback. The system should then be tested, and the results of a pilot test should be used to fix any glitches. Only after these presystem implementation steps are taken can the system be launched with confidence. Finally, after the system has been tested and launched, there is a need to monitor and evaluate the system on an ongoing basis to determine whether it is working properly and what adjustments may be needed to make it work. The ongoing monitoring of the system is crucial because the system may eventually lose support if no data are provided to show the system's benefits.

Next, let's discuss what needs to be done before the system is actually implemented, including formulating a communication plan, establishing an appeals process, training raters, and pilot testing the system.

2 COMMUNICATION PLAN

In general, having more and better knowledge of the performance management system leads to greater employee acceptance and satisfaction.[1] Organizations often design a communication plan to ensure that information regarding the performance management system is widely disseminated in the organization. A good communication plan answers the following questions:[2]

- *What is performance management?* Answering this question involves providing general information about performance management, how performance management systems are implemented in other organizations, and the general goals of performance management systems.
- *How does performance management fit into our strategy?* To answer this question, we should provide information on the relationship between performance management and strategic planning. Specifically, information is provided on how the performance management system will help accomplish strategic goals.
- *What's in it for me?* A good communication plan describes the benefits of implementing performance management for all those involved.
- *How does it work?* Answering this question entails giving a detailed description of the performance management process and time line: for example, when meetings will take place, what the purposes of each meeting are, and when decisions about rewards will be made.
- *What are my responsibilities?* The communication plan should include information on the role and responsibilities of each person involved at each stage of the process. For example, it includes a description of the employees' and supervisors' main responsibilities in the performance management process.
- *How is performance management related to other initiatives?* The communication plan should include information on the relationship between performance management and other initiatives and systems such as training, promotion, and succession planning.

Consider the performance management system for the position of Senior Executive Service (SES) in the U.S. Department of Justice.[3] SES members serve in key leadership positions directly below the top presidential appointees. SES members link the appointees to the rest of the federal government, and they are charged with overseeing various governmental activities in 75 federal agencies.

The communication plan that the Department of Justice implemented for this performance management system is described in a document divided into three chapters: Chapter 1, "General Information," Chapter 2, "Performance Appraisal for the Senior Executive Service," and Chapter 3, "Actions Based on Less Than Fully Successful Performance." This is how their plan answered each of the questions discussed in the previous list:

- *What is performance management?* Chapter 1 states the reasons for the department's implementing a performance management system and discusses what it is expected to accomplish. For example, the chapter notes that performance management aims at promoting efficient and effective attainment of the department's mission, program objectives, and strategic planning initiatives, and it also aims at motivating high levels of achievement and accountability. This chapter also includes definitions of several key terms, including *performance management system, performance, progress review, rating levels,* and *annual summary rating.*
- *How does performance management fit into our strategy?* Chapter 2 begins with a list of principles that guide the system, including, "The Department of Justice federal leaders and managers create a climate for excellence by communicating their vision, values and expectations clearly." It goes on to detail all of the ways in which leaders in the agency do this. In addition, in a memorandum that was sent with the chapters, the director of the Office of Personnel Management (OPM) included this quote from President George W. Bush: "We are not here to mark time, but to make progress, to achieve results, and to leave a record of excellence." The director then describes how the system would be used to implement the key principles of the president's administration.
- *What's in it for me?* Throughout the memo, there is clear information on how the performance management system will help the SES members be more effective leaders so that the president's mission can be achieved.
- *How does it work?* Chapter 2 outlines the steps in a performance management process, detailing the managers' responsibilities at each step. For example, it outlines the performance dimensions, the rating categories, and how to assign an overall rating.
- *What are my responsibilities?* The communication plan outlines the responsibilities of the SES members as well as their rating official, or the person in charge of rating their performance. The plan emphasizes that leaders must create a culture performing at a high level by continually communicating expectations and rewarding high-achieving performers.
- *How is performance management related to other initiatives?* The communication plan touches briefly on the importance of linking system outcomes to performance-based pay. The importance of training to maximize performance is also considered.

In summary, the communication plan implemented by the Department of Justice is extremely detailed and provides answers to most, if not all, of the key questions that should be addressed by a good plan. However, even if a communication plan answers all or most of the important questions, the fact that the information has been made available does not necessarily mean the communication plan will be successful in gaining acceptance. This is because people have cognitive biases that affect what information is taken in and how it is processed. Specifically, there are three types of biases that affect the effectiveness of a communication plan, regardless of how well it has been implemented. These are *selective exposure*, *selective perception*, and *selective retention*.

First, selection exposure is a tendency to expose our minds only to ideas with which we already agree. Those employees who already agree that performance management is a good idea may become involved in the communication plan activities, including reading about the system and attending meetings describing how the system works. On the other hand, those who do not see much value in performance management may choose not to read information about it and not to attend meetings related to performance management. Second, selective perception is a tendency to perceive a piece of information as meaning what we would like it to mean even though the information, as intended by the communicator, may mean the exact opposite. Someone who believes performance management is about only rewards and punishments may incorrectly interpret that receiving formal performance feedback at the end of each quarter translates into receiving a pay increase or a bonus. Third, selective retention is a tendency to remember only those pieces of information with which we already agree. If an employee perceives his employer as vindictive, that employee is not likely to remember information about how the appeals process works or about other fair and equitable aspects of the system.

Selective exposure, selective perception, and selective retention biases are pervasive and could easily render the communication plan ineffective. Fortunately, there are several ways to minimize the negative impact of these biases and, therefore, help gain support for the system. Consider the following:[4]

- *Involve employees.*   Involve employees in the design of the system. People support what they help create. The higher the level of participation is in designing the system, the greater the support for the system will be.[5]
- *Understand employee needs.*   Understand the needs of the employees, and identify ways in which these needs can be met through performance management. Basically, provide a personal, clear, and convincing answer to the "What's in it for me?" question.
- *Strike first.*   Create a positive attitude toward the new performance system before any negative attitudes and rumors are created. Make communications realistic, and do not set up expectations you cannot deliver. Discuss some of the arguments that might be used against the system, and provide evidence to counter them.
- *Provide facts and consequences.*   Because of the employee biases, facts do not necessarily speak for themselves. Clearly explain facts about the system, and explain what they mean or what the consequences are. Don't let users draw their own conclusions because they may differ from yours.
- *Put it in writing.*   In Western cultures, written communications are usually more powerful and credible than spoken communications because they can be carefully examined and challenged for accuracy. Create documentation, which can be made available online, describing the system.
- *Use multiple channels of communication.*   Use multiple methods of communication, including meetings, e-mail, and paper communication. In other words, allow

employees to be exposed repeatedly to the same message delivered using different communication channels. Of course, make sure the channels all convey consistent information.

- *Use credible communicators.* Use credible sources to communicate the performance management system. In companies where HR department members are perceived as "HR cops" because they continually emphasize what cannot be done as opposed to how one's job can be done better, it may be better to use a different department or group. Instead, in such situations, communication should be delivered by people who are trusted and admired within the organization. It also helps if those delivering the communication and endorsing the system are regarded as key and powerful organizational players.
- *Say it, and then say it again.* Repeat the information frequently. Since people can absorb only a small amount of information at a time, the information must be repeated frequently.

Table 1 summarizes what can be done to minimize cognitive biases, including selective exposure, selective perception, and selective retention. Consider the Department of Justice communication process, described earlier in this chapter. That plan attempts to minimize negative biases and gain support for the performance management system. For example, although it is a government agency, and the performance management system is a federal mandate, the OPM offered to help managers tailor the systems to their specific agencies. This is likely to help employees become more involved and is also helpful in addressing the specific needs of the employees in the various agencies. The memorandum from the director of the OPM, who is also a credible source of information on both the performance management system and the president's policies, sets an extremely positive tone and appeals to employees' patriotism by including a message from the president reminding them of the importance of serving the "American people." The communication plan also provides facts and conclusions about the system. For example, it explains the reasoning for realigning the performance management system with the fiscal year, how to carry out this time line, and the importance of doing so. The communication plan is also posted on the department's Web site. There are also links to other Web sites with information about performance management. It is not clear whether the Department of Justice distributed this memorandum and accompanying system information using other media. Finally, the information presented in the memorandum and in the

TABLE 1	Considerations to Minimize the Effects of Communication Barriers

Involve employees

Understand employee needs

Strike first

Provide facts and consequences

Put it in writing

Use multiple channels of communication

Use credible communicators

Say it, and then say it again

chapter is repeated and clarified. The memorandum gives an overview of the importance of the performance management system; the first chapter in the document gives an overview of performance management systems, and the second chapter provides details of the system. All in all, the plan implemented by the Department of Justice is a good example of a communication plan that attempts to minimize the impact of the various communication barriers.

In addition to implementing a communication process, support for the performance management system can be gained by implementing an appeals process. This topic is discussed next.

3 APPEALS PROCESS

The inclusion of an appeals process is important in gaining employee acceptance for the performance management system because it allows employees to understand that if there is a disagreement regarding performance ratings or any resulting decisions, then such disagreements can be resolved in an amicable and nonretaliatory way. In addition, the inclusion of an appeals process increases perceptions of the system as fair.[6]

When an appeals process is in place, employees have the ability to question two types of issues: judgmental and administrative.[7] Judgmental issues center on the validity of the performance evaluation. For example, an employee may believe that a manager's performance ratings for that employee do not reflect his actual performance. Administrative issues involve whether the policies and procedures were followed. For example, an employee may argue that her supervisor did not meet with her as frequently as he had with her coworkers and that the feedback she is receiving about her performance is not as thorough as that received by her coworkers.

Typically, when an appeal is first filed, the HR department serves as a mediator between the employee and the supervisor. An appeal sent to the HR department is usually called a Level 1 or Level A appeal. The HR department is in a good position to judge whether policies and procedures have been implemented correctly and has good information about the various jobs, levels of performance expected, and levels of performance of other employees within the unit and organization. The HR department gathers the necessary facts and brings them to the attention of either the rater to encourage reconsideration of the decision that caused the appeal or to the complainant to explain why there have been no biases or violations. In other words, the HR department either suggests corrective action to the supervisor or informs the employee that the decision or procedures were correct.

If the supervisor does not believe corrective action should be taken, or if the employee does not accept the HR decision, and the appeal continues, then an outside and unbiased arbitrator makes a final and binding resolution. This is usually called a Level 2 or Level B appeal. This arbitrator can consist of a panel of peers and managers. The panel reviews the case, asks questions, interviews witnesses, researches precedents, and reviews policy. Then, they simply take a vote to make the decision. In some cases, the vote represents the final decision. In other cases, the vote is forwarded to a high-level manager (vice president or higher level) who takes the panel's vote into consideration in making the final decision.

The box "Selected Excerpts from the University of North Carolina Performance Management Appeals Process" shows some of the key sections of the performance management appeals process for employees at the University of North Carolina.[8] The appeals process is intended to air concerns and to resolve disagreements. The purpose of this specific policy is to provide employees and management with a means for resolving disagreements involving performance evaluations and performance pay issues.

The information shown in the box describing the appeals process at the University of North Carolina spells out the steps involved, the time line that should be followed, and the various outcomes that could be expected. Given that such a policy is in place, employees are given assurances that, if there is an appeal, the case will be treated fairly and as objectively as possible. Once again, this should help gain support for the performance management system.

BOX 1

Selected Excerpts from the University of North Carolina Performance Management Appeals Process

General Provisions

Under State policy neither party in the Appeals Process may be represented by an attorney. State law and policy provide that the Chancellor's decision on an appeal is final and cannot be appealed further.
The Appeals Process has jurisdiction over the following issues only:

- the overall evaluation received as part of the Annual Review
- the rating on one or more principal functions
- the explanatory remarks included in the evaluation

Depending on the actions taken by the General Assembly regarding salary increases related to the performance evaluation process, the following issues also may be appealed:

- failure to receive a performance increase and/or performance bonus when eligible
- the amount of the increase or bonus received

An employee is limited to one appeal for any work cycle, regardless of the number of issues involved. The employee should describe the complete remedy desired should the appeal be decided in his/her favor. For example, an employee who appeals the overall evaluation should specify the overall evaluation requested. If such an overall evaluation would result in eligibility for a performance increase, an increase percentage should be stated as part of the remedy requested in the appeal.
By request (and with management approval) an employee may be granted a maximum of 12 hours off from regular duties for processing an appeal under this Appeals Process without any loss of pay and without charge to leave.

Performance Management Review Board

The Chancellor appoints the Chair of the Performance Management Review Board (Board Chair) and the other members of the Review Board. When a Level B appeal is received, the Board Chair selects a three-member Panel and appoints a Panel Leader. The Board Chair notifies the employee of the name, job title, and department of each proposed Panel member. The employee has the right to disqualify up to two proposed members by notifying the Board Chair before the date stated in the letter of notification.
Each panel will have one member with supervisory responsibility and two members with no supervisory responsibility. No member of the Panel will be from the employee's own department.

(continued)

Box 1 *(Continued)*

Any member may be designated as Panel Leader. The Panel determines what information is needed. The involved parties must provide the information requested by the Panel.

The Panel Leader notifies the employee and the department head in writing of the hearing date and location. Every effort must be made to arrange for a timely hearing. The Level B hearing is confidential. It is not open to the media or other persons whose attendance is not approved in advance by the Panel Leader. The employee, the department head, and supervisors involved in the performance review are allowed to appear in person at the hearing. However, any party may elect not to appear and to have the Panel's Level B recommendation based only on documentation presented to the Panel. The chair must receive advance notification if anyone other than the employee and department head is to provide information to the Review Board. The employee and management must request approval in advance for witnesses to address the Panel. Only witnesses approved in advance may appear at the hearing.

After the hearing, the Panel decides whether additional information is needed. Any information requested and received after the hearing is shared with the employee and the department head. After considering all of the information presented, the Panel makes its recommendation by majority vote and submits its written recommendation through the Board Chair to the Chancellor. The Chancellor either accepts, modifies, or rejects the Panel's recommendation and issues the University decision within 15 calendar days of receiving the Panel recommendation. If the Chancellor rejects the Panel recommendation, the written decision will state the reason(s) for rejection. The Chancellor sends the written decision to the employee.

Source: Performance management appeals process. Available online at http://hr.unc.edu/Data/SPA/perfmgt/perf-appeal. Retrieval date: March 12, 2007.

4 TRAINING PROGRAMS FOR THE ACQUISITION OF REQUIRED SKILLS

Training the raters is another step necessary in preparing for the launching of the performance management system. Training not only provides participants in the performance management system with needed skills and tools to do a good job implementing it but also helps increase satisfaction with the system.[9]

The content areas that can be included in rater training programs are listed in Table 2.

TABLE 2	Content Areas That Can Be Included in Rater Training Programs
	1. Reasons for implementing the performance management system
	2. Information on the appraisal form and system mechanics
	3. How to identify and rank job activities
	4. How to observe, record, and measure performance
	5. How to minimize rating errors
	6. How to conduct an appraisal interview
	7. How to train, counsel, and coach

Consider the list of content areas included in Table 2. The first two content areas are not unique to rater training programs. In fact, these are common components of the communication plan in which all organizational members participate, not just the raters. Given the suggestion that the same information should be presented many times and through different communication channels, however, it does not hurt to include this content area as part of a rater training program. Content areas 3–5 involve the general issue of identifying, observing, recording, and evaluating performance. Content areas 6 and 7 involve the general issue of how to interact with the employee receiving performance information. Next, we address various choices in terms of implementing training programs specific to content areas 3–5.

4.1 Rater Error Training

Many performance management systems are plagued with rater errors. For example, about 1,700 years ago, the Wei dynasty in China implemented a performance management system for its household members. The philosopher Sin Yu has been quoted as saying that "an Imperial Rater of Nine Grades seldom rates men according to their merits, but always according to his likes and dislikes."[10] Accordingly, the goal of rater error training (RET) is to make raters aware of what rating errors they are likely to make and to help them develop strategies to minimize those errors. The goal of RET is to increase rating accuracy by making raters aware of the unintentional errors they are likely to make.

RET programs typically include definitions of the most typical errors and a description of possible causes for those errors. Such programs also allow trainees to view examples of common errors and to review suggestions on how to avoid making errors. This can be done by showing videotaped vignettes designed to elicit rating errors and asking trainees to fill out appraisal forms regarding the situations that they observed on the videotapes. Finally, a comparison is made between the ratings provided by the trainees and the correct ratings. The trainer then explains why the errors took place, which specific errors were made, and ways to overcome the errors in the future.

RET does not guarantee increased accuracy. Raters do become aware of the possible errors they can make but, because many of the errors are unintentional, simple awareness of the errors does not mean that errors will not be made. Nevertheless, it may be useful to expose raters to the range of possible errors. These errors include the following:

- *Similar-to-me error.* Similarity leads to attraction so that we tend to favor those who are similar to us. Consequently, in some cases, supervisors are more likely to give higher performance ratings to those employees who are perceived to be more similar to them in terms of attitudes, preferences, personality, and demographic variables including race and gender.
- *Contrast error.* Contrast error occurs when, even if an absolute measurement system is in place, supervisors compare individuals with one another instead of against predetermined standards. For example, when a supervisor rates an individual of only average performance, the rating may actually be higher than deserved if the other individuals rated by the same supervisor display substandard performance levels: the average performer may seem to be better in comparison to the others. This error is most likely to occur when supervisors complete multiple

appraisal forms at the same time because, in such situations, it is difficult to ignore the ratings given to other employees.

- *Leniency error.* Leniency error occurs when raters assign high (lenient) ratings to most or all employees. In other words, leniency involves artificial rating inflation. Leniency is mostly an intentional error caused by a desire to maximize the merit raise/rewards, to encourage employees, to avoid creating a written record of poor performance, to avoid a confrontation with employees, to promote undesired employees out of unit, or to make the manager look good to his supervisor. Also, recent research indicates that individuals with certain personality traits are more likely to be more lenient: those low on conscientiousness (i.e., individuals who do not always strive for excellence) and high on agreeableness (i.e., individuals who are more trustful, cooperative, and polite).[11] Leniency is a very common problem in performance management systems. In fact, survey results suggest that leniency bias is believed to compromise the validity of the obtained performance ratings in more than three-fourths of all organizations implementing performance management systems.[12]

- *Severity error.* Severity error occurs when raters assign low (severe) ratings to most or all employees. That is, severity involves artificial rating deflation. Severity is mostly an intentional type of error caused by the supervisor's desire to shock employees, to teach employees a lesson, to send a message that the employee should consider leaving, or to build a record of poor performance.

- *Central tendency error.* Central tendency error occurs when raters use only the middle points on the rating scales and avoid using the extremes. The result is that most or all employees are rated as "average." This is also an intentional type of error and is mainly caused by a supervisor's desire to play it safe. One negative consequence of this error is that it is hard to make performance-based distinctions among employees rated by the same rater.

- *Halo error.* Halo error occurs when raters fail to distinguish among the different aspects of performance being rated. If an employee receives a high score on one dimension, she also receives a high score on all other dimensions, even though performance may not be even across all dimensions. For example, if an employee has a perfect attendance record, then the rater may give her a high mark on dedication and productivity. The perfect attendance record, however, may be caused by the fact that the employee has large loan payments to make and cannot afford to miss work, not because the employee is actually an excellent overall performer. In other words, being present at work is not the same as being a productive employee. This error is typically caused by the supervisor's assigning performance ratings based on an overall impression about the employee instead of evaluating each performance dimension independently.

- *Primacy error.* Primacy error occurs when performance evaluation is influenced mainly by information collected during the initial phases of the review period. For example, in rating communication skills, the supervisor gives more weight to incidents involving communication that took place toward the beginning of the review period as opposed to incidents taking place at all other times.

- *Recency error.* Recency error occurs when performance evaluation is influenced mainly by information gathered during the last portion of the review period. This is the opposite of the primacy error: raters are more heavily influenced by behaviors taking place toward the end of the review period instead of giving equal importance and paying attention to incidents occurring throughout the entire review period.

- *Negativity error.* Negativity error occurs when raters place more weight on negative information than on positive and neutral information. For example, a rater may have observed one negative interaction between the employee and a customer and several positive interactions in which customers' expectations were surpassed. The rater may focus on the one negative incident in rating the "customer service" dimension. The negativity error explains why most people have a tendency to remember negative rather than positive news that they read in the newspaper or watch on television.

- *First impression error.* First impression error occurs when raters make an initial favorable or unfavorable judgment about an employee and then ignore subsequent information that does not support the initial impression. This type of error can be confounded with the "similar-to-me error" because first impressions are likely to be based on the degree of similarity: the more similar the person is to the supervisor, the more positive the first impression will be.

- *Spillover error.* Spillover error occurs when scores from previous review periods unjustly influence current ratings. For example, a supervisor makes the assumption that an employee who was an excellent performer in the previous period ought to be an excellent performer also during the current period and provides performance ratings consistent with this belief.

- *Stereotype error.* Stereotype error occurs when a supervisor has an oversimplified view of individuals based on group membership. That is, a supervisor may have a belief that certain groups of employees (e.g., women) are unassertive in their communication style. In rating women, therefore, he may automatically describe communication as being "unassertive" without actually having any behavioral evidence to support the rating.[13] This type of error can also lead to biased evaluations of performance when an individual (e.g., woman) violates stereotypical norms by working in an occupation that does not fit the stereotype (e.g., assembly of airplane parts).[14] This type of error can also result in consistently lower performance ratings for members of certain groups. For example, a study including an identical sample of black and white workers found that white supervisors gave higher ratings to white workers relative to black workers than did black supervisors. In other words, if a white worker is rated, then it does not really matter whether the supervisor is black or white; however, if a black worker is rated, the supervisor's ethnicity matters because this worker is likely to receive a higher rating from a black supervisor than from a white supervisor.[15]

- *Attribution error.* The attribution error takes place when a supervisor attributes poor performance to an employee's dispositional tendencies (e.g., personality, abilities) instead of features of the situation (e.g., malfunctioning equipment). In other words, different supervisors may place different relative importance on the environment in which the employee works in making performance evaluations. If supervisors make incorrect inferences about the employees' dispositions and ignore situational characteristics, actions taken to improve performance may fail because the same situational constraints may still be present (e.g., obsolete equipment).[16]

Table 3 includes a summary list of possible errors that raters may make in assigning performance ratings. These errors can be classified as intentional or unintentional.

TABLE 3	Errors Likely to Be Made in Providing Performance Ratings
Unintentional	**Intentional**
Similar to me	Leniency
Contrast	Severity
Halo	Central tendency
Primacy	
Recency	
Negativity	
First impression	
Spillover	
Stereotype	
Attribution	

To minimize the intentional errors shown in Table 3, we must focus on the rater's motivation. In other words, we must demonstrate to the raters that the benefits of providing accurate ratings outweigh the benefits of intentionally distorting ratings by inflation, deflation, or central tendency. Once again, this goes back to the "What's in it for me?" question. For example, the communication program should include a clear description of the benefits that supervisors can expect to receive if their performance ratings lack intentional distortion.

RET exposes raters to the different errors and their causes; however, being aware of unintentional errors does not mean that supervisors will no longer make these errors.[17] Awareness is certainly a good first step, but we need to go further if we want to minimize unintentional errors. One fruitful possibility is the implementation of frame of reference training.

4.2 Frame of Reference Training

Frame of reference (FOR) training helps improve rater accuracy by thoroughly familiarizing raters with the various performance dimensions to be assessed. The overall goal is to give raters skills so that they can provide accurate ratings of each employee on each dimension by developing a common FOR.

A typical FOR training program includes a discussion of the job description for the individuals being rated and the duties involved. Raters are then familiarized with the performance dimensions to be rated by reviewing the definitions for each dimension and discussing examples of good, average, and poor performance. Raters are then asked to use the appraisal forms to be used in the actual performance management system to rate fictitious employees usually shown in written or videotaped practice vignettes. The trainees are also asked to write a justification for the ratings. Finally, the trainer informs trainees of the correct ratings for each dimension and the reasons for such ratings and discusses differences between the correct ratings and those provided by the trainees. Typically, FOR training programs include the following formal steps:[18]

1. Raters are told that they will evaluate the performance of three employees on three separate performance dimensions.

2. Raters are given an appraisal form and instructed to read it as the trainer reads aloud the definition for each of the dimensions and the scale anchors.

3. The trainer discusses various employee behaviors that illustrate various performance levels for each rating scale included in the form. The goal is to create a common performance theory (frame of reference) among raters so that they will agree on the appropriate performance dimension and effectiveness level for different behaviors.

4. Participants are shown a videotape of a practice vignette, including behaviors related to the performance dimensions being rated, and are asked to evaluate the employee's performance using the scales provided.

5. Ratings provided by each participant are shared with the rest of the group and discussed. The trainer seeks to identify which behaviors participants used to decide on their assigned ratings and to clarify any discrepancies among the ratings.

6. The trainer provides feedback to participants, explaining why the employee should receive a certain rating (target score) on each dimension, and shows discrepancies between the target score and the score given by each trainee.

Consider how the Canadian military uses FOR training.[19] First, the training program includes a session regarding the importance of performance management systems in the military. In the next session, raters are told that they will be evaluating the performance of four subordinates. They are given the appraisal form to be used and information on each of the scales included in the form. As the trainer reads through each of the scales, participants are encouraged to ask questions. At the same time, the trainer gives examples of behaviors associated with each level of performance. The trainer thus makes sure that the trainees come to a common FOR concerning what behaviors constitute the different levels of performance. Participants are shown a videotape of a soldier, and they are asked to evaluate the performance using the appraisal form explained earlier. Next, the ratings are discussed as a group, focusing on the behaviors exhibited in the videotape and the ratings that would be most appropriate in each case. This process is repeated several times. Finally, the participants are given three more samples of behavior to rate, as displayed by three hypothetical soldiers, and they receive feedback on how well they evaluated each soldier.

It should be evident by now that FOR training can take quite a bit of time and effort to develop and administer, but it is well worth it. Specifically, as a consequence of implementing this type of training, raters not only are more likely to provide consistent and more accurate ratings, but they are also more likely to help employees design effective development plans. This is because sharing a common view of what constitutes good performance allows supervisors to provide employees with better guidelines to employ to reach such performance levels.[20]

4.3 Behavioral Observation Training

Behavioral observation (BO) training is another type of program implemented to minimize unintentional rating errors. BO training focuses on how raters observe, store, recall, and use information about performance. Fundamentally, this type of training improves raters' skills at observing performance.

For example, one type of BO training involves showing raters how to use observational aids such as notes or diaries. These observational aids help raters record a preestablished number of behaviors on each performance dimension. Using these aids helps raters increase the sample of incidents observed and recorded during a specific time period. In addition, an aid such as a diary is an effective way to standardize the observation of behavior and record of critical incidents throughout the review period. In addition, it serves as a memory aid when filling out evaluation forms. Memory aids are beneficial because ratings based on memory alone, without notes or diaries, are likely to be distorted due to factors of social context (e.g., friendship bias) and time (i.e., duration of supervisor–subordinate relationship).[21]

Consider how BO training is implemented by the Canadian military. The Canadian military has found that a combination of FOR and BO training works best. Earlier, we described how the Canadian military uses FOR training. BO training is added to the FOR training program. In addition to FOR training, there are sessions on the importance of BO and common BO errors, including first impression, stereotypes, and halo effects. Finally, the participants are trained in the importance of keeping diaries and taking notes on their subordinates throughout the year. Furthermore, the trainer explains the criteria for each performance dimension and provides written descriptions of the different levels of performance. The participants are given a chance to practice keeping a diary while watching the vignettes used in the FOR training section of the training program. After watching each vignette, participants are given tips on note taking and recording behaviors as well as the outcomes.

4.4 Self-Leadership Training

The goal of self-leadership (SL) training is to improve a rater's confidence in her ability to manage performance. SL training techniques include positive self-talk, mental imagery, and positive beliefs and thought patterns.[22] The assumption is that if there is increased self-direction, self-motivation, and confidence, there will be increased accuracy. Overall, SL emphasizes intrinsic (i.e., internal) sources of behavioral standards and emphasizes doing things for their intrinsic value.

SL training has become a popular tool in the context of performance management systems and as a type of training program beneficial for supervisors even when they are not necessarily involved in a performance management system. Several studies have shown that SL training can be effective in enhancing mental processes and increasing self-efficacy (i.e., the belief that one can do something if one tries). Designing an SL training program involves the following steps:[23]

1. Observe and record existing beliefs and assumptions, self-talk, and mental imagery patterns. For example, what are the beliefs about the performance management system? How do managers visualize their role in the performance management system? Do they believe they have the capacity to observe and record performance accurately?
2. Analyze the functionality and constructiveness of the beliefs, self-talk, and imagery patterns uncovered in step 1. For example, are the beliefs about the system detrimental to the system's expected success?
3. Identify or develop more functional and constructive beliefs and assumptions, self-verbalizations, and mental images to substitute for dysfunctional ones; for example, develop images of employees being satisfied, as opposed to defensive and confrontational, after receiving performance feedback from their supervisors.

4. Substitute the more functional thinking for the dysfunctional thoughts experienced in actual situations. For example, more constructive assumptions, ways of talking to oneself, and mental images of the likely outcome of a performance discussion with an employee can be worked out and written down on paper.

5. Continue monitoring and maintaining beliefs, self-verbalizations, and mental images over time.

A related type of training program is labeled self-efficacy training for raters (SET-R).[24] The goal of this type of training is to decrease a rater's discomfort with the interpersonal demands of performance management and to enhance a manager's belief that he has the necessary skills to manage employees' performance. This type of training includes the following steps:

1. Raters watch a videotape of a vicarious success experience including a manager conducting a successful performance review meeting with a subordinate.

2. Raters engage in a follow-up discussion of the specific behaviors observed in the videotape that contributed to the meeting's success. This follow-up discussion has the dual goals of (1) focusing the raters' attention on the techniques used by the videotaped manager to convey negative feedback and (2) allowing for an opportunity to persuade raters that they too would be able to conduct such a successful meeting.

3. Raters participate in a role-play exercise that requires providing feedback to an employee. This role-play exercise is repeated until raters demonstrate an appropriate level of mastery.

In summary, raters are likely to make both intentional and unintentional errors when providing performance information. Intentional errors are largely due to motivational issues; in some cases, raters see more benefit in distorting ratings than in providing accurate information. Unintentional errors are largely due to cognitive biases that are the product of the complex tasks of observing, encoding, storing, and retrieving performance information. Through the combined use of a good communication plan and various training programs, ratings errors can be substantially minimized. Regarding the communication plan, it is important that it include convincing reasons that it is more advantageous to provide accurate than inaccurate performance information. Regarding training programs, these often focus on describing the errors that raters usually make (i.e., RET programs). In addition, they should allow raters to generate a common FOR to be used in evaluating performance as well as offer raters tools to improve observation and memory skills and help mitigate the discomfort generated by the interpersonal demands of the performance management process. FOR training is particularly beneficial when performance measurement emphasizes behaviors. On the other hand, BO training is particularly beneficial when performance measurement emphasizes results because raters learn not only how to observe behaviors but also how these behaviors are linked to results.

Thus far, this chapter has described how to prepare for the implementation of a performance management system by designing a communication plan and an appeals process and by delivering training programs. Next, we turn to the final set of activities required before the performance management system is put into practice: pilot testing.

5 PILOT TESTING

Before the performance management system is implemented formally, it is a good idea to test a version of the entire system so that adjustments and revisions can be made as needed.[25] In the pilot test of the system, evaluations are not recorded in employee files; however, the system is implemented in its entirety from beginning to end, including all the steps that would be included if the system had actually been implemented. In other words, meetings take place between supervisor and employee, performance data are gathered, developmental plans are designed, and feedback is provided. The most important aspect of the pilot test is that all participants maintain records noting any difficulties they encountered, ranging from problems with the appraisal form and how performance is measured to the feedback received. The pilot test allows for the identification and early correction of any flaws before the system is implemented throughout the organization.

We should not assume that the performance management system will necessarily be executed or that it will produce the anticipated results. The pilot test allows us to gain information from the perspective of the system's users on how well the system works, to learn about any difficulties and unforeseen obstacles, to collect recommendations on how to improve all aspects of the system, and to understand personal reactions to it. In addition, conducting a pilot test is yet another way to achieve early acceptance from a small group who can then act as champions for the performance management system, rather than putting the burden on the HR department to sell the idea. A final reason for conducting a pilot test is that end users are likely to have a higher system acceptance rate knowing that stakeholders in the company had a say in its design, rather than feeling that the system was created by the HR department alone.

An important decision to be made is the selection of the group of employees with whom the system will be tested. In choosing this group, we need to understand that the managers who will be participating should be willing to invest the resources required to do the pilot test. In addition, this group should be made up of managers who are flexible and willing to try new things. Thus, managers should know what the system will look like and receive a realistic preview before they decide to participate in the pilot test.

In selecting the group, we must also consider that the group should be sufficiently large and representative of the entire organization so that reactions from the group will be generalizable to the rest of the organization. Thus, in selecting the group, we should select jobs that are similar to those throughout the company, and the group selected should not be an exception in either a positive or a negative way. Specifically, the group should not be regarded as particularly productive, loose, hardworking, lazy, and so forth.

Pilot tests provide crucial information to be used in improving the system before it is actually put in place. Pilot testing the system can provide huge savings and identify potential problems before they become irreversible and the credibility of the system is ruined permanently. For example, consider the case of the Washington State Patrol.[26] In 1997, the organization realized that several changes were occurring in its department as well as in patrol departments in other states, thereby prompting the revision of its performance management system. It established a committee to develop the new appraisals. Before implementing the system, the state patrol pilot tested it in two districts. First, the committee prepared a training chapter that included a preappraisal work group meeting. In this meeting, employees discussed their roles and expectations surrounding the performance management system and applied those discussions to a common goal.

BOX 2

Performance Management System Rollout at BT Global Services

BT Global Services (http://www.btglobalservices.com) utilized several steps to effectively roll out a new performance management system called "Maximizing Performance," designed to bring new consistency to managing and developing employees and to create a high-performance culture. BT Global Services, a global communication services company, employs more than 20,000 people. After obtaining support from senior management, the first steps included a series of communications, including a workshop for executives so that all employees would receive a clear message about why a new system was being developed, what roles employees would play, and how those roles would contribute to the success of the company. The next step included training line managers, to ensure involvement and commitment, including the important role these managers play in ensuring success. Among other areas covered, training included how to set effective goals with employees, providing coaching and feedback to facilitate development. Roles were reviewed and clarified to ensure employees understood expectations and how their work contributes to the success of their team, business unit, and the company as a whole. For ongoing monitoring of the program, data were collected through employee surveys, face-to-face meetings with line managers, and team meetings. In summary, BT Global Services illustrates an example of an effective rollout of a new performance management system including communication plan, training, and ongoing commitment to monitoring and improvement.[27]

The training also focused on how new developments in the patrol led to the new elements in the performance management system. During the training, the trainers encouraged the participants to ask questions regarding the shift to the new approach. The trainers then used the feedback received in these sessions to fix specific operational issues before introducing the training to the entire agency. After the appraisal process was fine-tuned, it was submitted for the approval of the troopers' and sergeants' associations. A select number of individuals across the districts received "train the trainer" training. Finally, the system was instituted agency wide. Each of these steps allowed for the identification of potential barriers that could have prevented the system from being successful.

6 ONGOING MONITORING AND EVALUATION

When the testing period is over and the performance management system has been implemented organization-wide, it is important to use clear measurements to monitor and evaluate the system.[28] In a nutshell, a decision needs to be made about how to evaluate the system's effectiveness, how to evaluate the extent to which the system is being implemented as planned, and how to evaluate the extent to which it is producing the intended results. The U.S. federal government takes the evaluation of performance management systems very seriously. Since the early 1990s, several laws have been passed that mandate federal agencies to develop a strategic plan, a performance plan, and a performance report.[29] Although these initiatives concern agencies and not individuals, ultimately the performance of any agency depends on the performance of the individuals working in that agency. The net result of such laws as the Government Performance and Results Act is an increase in accountability and funding allocation based on performance. Thus, federal agencies are required to evaluate the relative efficiency of their various management techniques including performance management systems.

Evaluation data should include reactions to the system and assessments of the system's operational and technical requirements. For example, a confidential survey could be administered to all employees asking about perceptions and attitudes regarding the system. This survey can be administered during the initial stages of implementation and then at the end of the first review cycle to find out if there have been any changes. In addition, regarding the system's results, one can assess performance ratings over time to see what positive effects the implementation of the system is having. Finally, interviews can be conducted with key stakeholders including managers and employees who have been involved in developing and implementing the performance management system.[30]

Several additional measures can be used on a regular basis to monitor and evaluate the system:

- *Number of individuals evaluated.* One of the most basic measures is to assess the number of employees who are actually participating in the system. If performance evaluations have not been completed for some employees, we need to find out who they are and why a performance review has not been completed.
- *Distribution of performance ratings.* An indicator of quality of the performance assessments is whether all or most scores are too high, too low, or clumped around the center of the distribution. This may indicate intentional errors such as leniency, severity, and central tendency. Distributions of performance ratings can be broken down by unit and supervisor to determine whether any trends exist regarding rating distortion and whether these distortions are localized in particular units. Note that there may be exceptional units in which most employees are outstanding performers and units in which most employees are poor performers. This is the exception to the rule, however, and such distributions usually indicate intentional errors on the part of raters.
- *Quality of information.* Another indicator of quality of the performance assessments is the quality of the information provided in the open-ended sections of the forms. For example, how much did the rater write? What is the relevance of the examples provided?
- *Quality of follow-up actions.* A good indicator of the quality of the system is whether it leads to important follow-up actions in terms of development activities or improved processes. For example, to what extent do follow-up actions involve exclusively the supervisor as opposed to the employee? If this is the case, then the system may not be working as intended because it may be an indicator that employees are not sufficiently involved.[31]
- *Quality of performance discussion meeting.* A confidential survey can be distributed to all employees on a regular basis to gather information about how the supervisor is managing the performance discussion meetings. For example, is the feedback useful? Has the supervisor made resources available so that the employee can accomplish the developmental plan objectives? How relevant was the performance review discussion to one's job? To what degree have developmental objectives and plans been discussed?[32]
- *System satisfaction.* A confidential survey could also be distributed to assess the perceptions of the system's users, both raters and ratees. This survey can include questions about satisfaction with equity, usefulness, and accuracy.

- *Overall cost/benefit ratio or return on investment (ROI).* A fairly simple way to address the overall impact of the system is to ask participants to rate the overall cost/benefit ratio for the performance management system. This is a type of bottom-line question that can provide convincing evidence for the overall worth of the system. The cost/benefit ratio question can be asked in reference to an individual (employee or manager), her job, and her organizational unit.
- *Unit-level and organization-level performance.* Another indicator that the system is working well is provided by the measurement of unit- and organization-level performance. Such performance indicators might be customer satisfaction with specific units and indicators of the financial performance of the various units or the organization as a whole. We need to be aware that it may take some time for changes in individual and group performance level to be translated into unit- and organization-level results. We should not expect results as soon as the system is implemented; however, we should start to see some tangible results at the unit level a few months after the system is in place.

Consider the case of Caterpillar, which was founded in 1925, manufactures more than 300 products in 23 countries, and serves customers in 200 countries worldwide (http://www.cat.com). In their own words, Caterpillar's "value advantage" is to "have the people, processes, tools and investments to deliver the quality, reliability and durability customers expect from Caterpillar in each new product introduction." Given this value proposition, Caterpillar has a strategic view of how managers should manage and improve the performance of their people. As a result, the organization has had a performance management system in place for many years. More recently, Caterpillar embarked on an impressive initiative to evaluate its performance management system. Specifically, the goal of this evaluation was to assess the cost/benefit ratio—return on investment (ROI)—of the training portions of the system that targeted managers and included modules about goal setting and coaching, among others. This evaluation included three steps. First, there was an estimated ROI based on how much performance management training would cost and its expected benefits. This information was used prior to implementing the program to establish the program's business case. Second, there was an ROI forecast, which enabled the program's leaders to better understand how to make full deployment of the initiative successful. Participants in this study completed a questionnaire in which they described the potential financial and nonfinancial effects of the program. Third, an ROI study was conducted three months after the performance management training intervention to learn about financial as well as non-tangible returns. This was done via focus groups that documented both how training participants had used the knowledge they had acquired and how much the business impact and financial benefits that the performance management training seemed to generate. Finally, a follow-up study was conducted two months later to confirm the results of the third step. This final study included an online questionnaire completed by the subordinates of the managers who had participated in the program. This final step provided cross-validation data from the perspective of subordinates.

Results were quite impressive. For example, results of the ROI study indicated that 88% of respondents believed the program had a positive impact on the organization, 53% reported that their personal productivity increased, 28% reported that product quality improved, and 33% reported that costs were reduced. The overall ROI was calculated as follows: (Benefits − Costs) / Costs) × 100. Benefits were annualized, treated as sustainable benefits to the business, and one-time benefits were excluded, and were not treated at face value—rather, they included weighting factors. For example, assume a respondent who reported that his productivity increased 5 hours per week, his estimate of percentage of these hours saved due to the performance management training program was 60%, and his confidence in this estimate is 75%. If the hourly rate is estimated at $65 and we consider 48 weeks per year, then 5 hours × $65 × 48 = $15,600. This estimate was revised taking into account the answers to the follow-up questions (i.e., hours due to performance management and confidence in the estimate). In other words, $15,600 × 60% × 75% = $7,020. This resulting dollar figure was added to the total benefits pool. Finally, costs included all those associated with the program including administration, communication, training design and delivery, evaluation, vendor fees, and so forth. What was the bottom line? The final calculation indicated an impressive ROI of 194%.[33]

Now, let's return to the performance management system at the Washington State Patrol to examine how it evaluates effectiveness now that the system is implemented.[34] The patrol has several measures in place for continual evaluation of the effectiveness of the program. First, before all employees are reviewed using the system, they are surveyed regarding their satisfaction with the new system. This input is then used to further improve the appraisal process. In addition, the patrol uses the results of a biyearly citizen's survey conducted by Washington State University. The results of this survey are used to determine whether the state patrol's customers are satisfied with its performance, and the data are also used to adjust and reprioritize performance objectives. In addition, the data are used to measure division-level performance, which is one indicator of the success of the performance management process. The Washington State Patrol collects other types of data as well. For example, every six months, division managers give presentations regarding performance management to their peers and to several executives. Initially, the meetings focused on efforts to implement the new performance management system and increase quality, but this will change as new issues arise. The presentation is 30–40 minutes long, followed by 20–30 minutes of questions from peers and executives. The feedback from these presentations is used to measure how well the system is being implemented, and feedback on the success of the meetings will be used to make any necessary changes to the system.

The Washington State Patrol may also want to consider measuring how many people are participating in the system. The patrol would also benefit from assessing whether the new system is distinguishing high- from low-level performers and benefit from ascertaining the overall cost/benefit ratio of implementing the system.

7 ONLINE IMPLEMENTATION

The implementation of much of the interventions described in this chapter can be facilitated by doing so online. For example, the communication plan can include e-mails as well as electronic newsletters. There can also be a Web site dedicated to the performance management system that includes updates regarding the system. The appeals process can also include an online component, and there can be a dedicated Web site for employees to file appeals, if needed. Training raters can also be accomplished with the help of online tools. For example, there are FOR training programs that can be implemented fully online.[35] Also, performance ratings can be gathered using online tools.

An important advantage of implementing performance management online is that the system can be linked to other HR functions such as training and selection. For example, if an employee receives a low rating on the performance dimension "communication," then there may be an automatic trigger so that the system suggests resources that the employee can use to address this performance dimension. For example, one such resource can be a learning module available online that teaches employees how to improve their communication skills. Another advantage of an online system is that it is easier to monitor unit-level and organization-level trends over time. Another advantage is automation. For example, a pop-up screen may appear on a supervisor's screen upon logging on, and she may not be allowed to open any files until the performance evaluation is completed.

How effective are online performance management systems in practice? In spite of the above mentioned benefits, it is important to evaluate whether the quality of evaluations improves and whether users are satisfied with the system. A recent study included 631 staff employees at a large U.S. university and provided a unique opportunity to evaluate the evaluation portion of the system in two modalities: (a) paper and pencil and (b) online. Results indicated that the online system had overall positive effects or, in some cases, null effects on employees perceptions of rater accountability, employee participation in the system, security and utility of the performance ratings, and satisfaction with the evaluation.[36]

One important issue to keep in mind is that online tools are simply a type of medium. Although they may add efficiency and bells and whistles to the system, ultimately the system's success will depend on following best-practice recommendations offered throughout this book. Taking advantage of online applications can help speed up processes, lower cost, and gather and disseminate information faster and more effectively. Thus, such tools can make a good system even better. On the other hand, systems that are not implemented following best practices will not necessarily improve by using online components. In fact, online implementation may lead to highly undesirable outcomes: a more complicated system that is simply a big waste of time and resources for all those involved.

Summary Points

- Some important steps need to be taken before the performance management system is implemented. These include implementing a communication plan and an appeals process, which will help gain system acceptance; training programs for raters, which will help minimize errors in performance ratings; and pilot testing the system, which will allow revisions and changes to be made before the system is actually implemented. Careful attention to these presystem implementation steps will help improve the success of the system.
- The main goal of the communication plan is to gain support for the system.

A good communication plan addresses the following questions:

- What is performance management? What are its general goals? How have performance management systems been implemented in other organizations?
- How does performance management fit with the organizational strategy?
- What are the tangible benefits of the performance management system for all parties involved?
- How does the system work? What are the various steps in the process?
- What are the roles and responsibilities of each organizational member?

- How does performance management relate to other initiatives and programs such as training, promotion, and compensation?

Including detailed, convincing, and clear answers for each of these questions is likely to help increase support for the system.

- People have biases in how they take in and process information. Even though a good communication plan may be in place, these biases may distort the information presented. Biases to take into account are selective exposure, selective perception, and selective retention. Selective exposure is a tendency to expose our minds only to ideas with which we already agree. Selective perception is a tendency to perceive a piece of information as meaning what we would like it to mean even though the information, as intended by the communicator, may mean the exact opposite. Finally, selective retention is a tendency to remember only those pieces of information with which we already agree.
- The negative effects of cognitive biases can be minimized by involving employees in system design, considering employees' needs in designing and implementing the system, delivering the communication plan before negative attitudes are established and rumors start circulating, putting information concerning the system in writing, providing facts and consequences and not just facts, using multiple channels of communication to present information about the system, using credible and powerful communicators, and repeating the information frequently. A good communication plan includes as many of these features as possible.
- In addition to a communication plan, the establishment of an appeals process helps gain system acceptance. An appeals process allows employees to

understand that, if there is a disagreement regarding performance ratings or any resulting decisions, such disagreements can be resolved in an amicable and nonretaliatory way.
- The appeals process begins with an employee filing an appeal with the HR department, which serves as a mediator between the employee and her supervisor. This is a Level 1 appeal. If the appeal is not resolved, then an outside and unbiased arbitrator makes a final and binding resolution. This is a Level 2 appeal. The arbitrator for a Level 2 appeal is usually a panel that includes peers and managers.
- In rating performance, raters may make intentional or unintentional errors. Intentional errors take place when raters believe it will be more beneficial to them to provide distorted instead of accurate ratings. For example, a supervisor may not want to give a low rating to avoid a possible confrontation with an employee. Intentional errors include leniency (giving better scores than warranted), severity (giving worse scores than warranted), and central tendency (giving scores only around the midpoint of the scales). Motivation is the key to minimize intentional errors. In other words, we must demonstrate to the raters that the benefits of providing accurate ratings outweigh the benefits of intentionally distorting ratings by inflation, deflation, or central tendency. The communication plan takes care of this by addressing the "What's in it for me?" question, including the "What's in for me if I provide accurate ratings?" question.
- Unintentional errors occur because observing, encoding, storing, and retrieving performance information is a complex cognitive task. Unintentional errors include the following: (1) similar to me, (2) contrast, (3) halo, (4) primacy, (5) recency, (6) negativity, (7) first

impression, (8) spillover, (9) stereotype, and (10) attribution. Unintentional errors can be minimized by implementing rater training programs.

- Rater error training (RET) exposes raters to the different errors and their causes. RET does not guarantee rating accuracy, but becoming aware of what types of errors are likely to occur and the reasons for these errors is a very good first step in minimizing them.
- Frame of reference (FOR) training familiarizes raters with the various performance dimensions to be assessed. The goal is that raters will develop a common FOR in observing and evaluating performance. This type of training is most appropriate when performance measurement focuses on behaviors.
- Behavioral observation (BO) training focuses on how raters observe, store, recall, and use information about performance. For example, this program teaches raters how to use aids such as diaries to standardize performance observation. This type of training is most appropriate when performance measurement focuses on counting and recording how frequently certain behaviors and results take place.
- Self-leadership (SL) training aims at improving raters' confidence in their ability to manage performance. SL training includes positive self-talk, mental imagery, and positive beliefs and thought patterns.
- Pilot testing the system before it is instituted fully is useful because it allows potential problems and glitches to be discovered and corrective action to be taken before the system is put in place. Pilot testing consists of implementing the entire system, including all of its components, but only with a select group of people. Results are not recorded in employees' records. Instead, the goal is that the people

participating in the pilot test provide feedback on any possible problems and on how to improve the system.

- The group participating in the pilot test needs to understand that the test will take time and resources. A representative group should be selected so that conclusions drawn from the group can be generalized to the organization as a whole. The group should not be regarded as an exception in either a positive or negative way.
- After the system has been implemented, there should be a measurement system to evaluate the extent to which it is working the way it should and producing the results that were expected. Such measures include confidential employee surveys assessing perceptions and attitudes about the system and whether there is an upward trend in performance scores over time. Other measures include number of individuals evaluated, distribution of performance ratings, quality of performance information gathered, quality of performance discussion meetings, user satisfaction with the system, overall cost/benefit ratio, and unit- and organization-level performance indicators. Taken together, these indicators are a powerful tool that can be used to demonstrate the value of the performance management system.
- Taking advantage of online applications can help speed up processes, lower cost, and gather and disseminate information faster and more effectively. Thus, online implementation of performance management can make a good system even better. On the other hand, systems that are not implemented following best practices will not necessarily improve by using online components. In fact, online implementation may lead to highly undesirable outcomes: a more complicated system that is simply a big waste of time and resources for all those involved.

CASE STUDY 1

Implementing a Performance Management Communication Plan at Accounting, Inc.

Accounting, Inc. is a consulting and accounting firm headquartered in Amsterdam, the Netherlands. Recently, Accounting, Inc. implemented a performance management system. The first step in the implementation of the new system was the development of a set of core competencies that would be used to evaluate most employees regardless of function or level. In addition, each employee was evaluated using more job-specific performance dimensions.

As the first step in the communication plan, the employees received individual e-mail messages asking them to define what the core competencies meant to them and to give descriptions and examples of how each of the core competencies played out in their specific positions. Next, the company held meetings, handed out frequently asked questions (FAQs) sheets, and placed posters around the company detailing how the core competencies were related to the organization's

strategic priorities and how performance scores would be related to monetary rewards. In these communications, Accounting, Inc. detailed how the performance system worked, how the raters were chosen, how performance feedback was used, and other details about the system. The information also outlined the benefits employees could expect from the new system as well as employees' responsibilities regarding the system.

Please evaluate Accounting, Inc.'s communication plan. Specifically, does it answer all of the questions that a good communication plan should answer? Which questions are left unanswered? How would you provide answers to the unanswered questions (if any)?

Source: Adapted from P. Brotherton, "Meyners Pays for Performance: Changing a Compensation System Is a Sensitive Undertaking; Here's How One Firm Handled It," *Journal of Accountancy,* *196*(2003): 41–46. ■

CASE STUDY 2

Implementing an Appeals Process at Accounting, Inc.

Following up on Case Study 1, when the system was implemented many employees were not happy with the scores and the type of performance feedback information they received from their supervisors. If you were to design an appeals process to

handle these complaints well, what would the appeals process be like? (Hint: Use the appeals process shown in Box 1, *Selected Excerpts from the University of North Carolina Performance Management Appeals Process,* as a model.) ■

CASE STUDY 3

Evaluation of Performance Management System at Accounting, Inc.

This is a follow-up to Case Study 1 and Case Study 2. After the performance system had been put in place, Accounting, Inc. implemented several measures to evaluate the system. First, the company distributed an employee survey to assess employee satisfaction with the new system. In addition, the HR department examined the distribution of ratings to determine whether scores were being influenced by leniency, central

tendency, or severity biases. Finally, the HR department kept track of the allocation of rewards in the various departments to ascertain whether any departments stood out. From your perspective, what other types of data can be collected to assess the effectiveness of the system? What kind of information would each measure provide? What is the rationale for implementing each type of measure? ■

CASE STUDY 4

Training the Raters at Big Quality Care

Founded near the city of Caesarea, Israel, Big Quality Care Center is a big nursing home facility for the elderly. Because of the sheer size and diverse range of occupants served, the Center predominantly relies on very highly skilled nursing professionals. Because Caesarea has had a long-term shortage of quality nursing professionals, the Center has some of the state-of-the-art HR practices to both retain and maximize the performance of the Center's nurses.

Recently, however, you have received several anonymous complaints from the nursing staff that many ratings seemed inaccurate and inconsistent. Concerned that the Center may lose many of its quality nurses to competitors if the complaints are left unaddressed, the head of HR at the Center has decided to implement an organization-wide rater training program to appease the nurses and to correct for any

true rater inaccuracies and inconsistencies. Luckily for you, the head of HR has gathered enough trust with you that she has decided to let you design the rater-training program. But before letting you do so, she wants you to organize and deliver a presentation about the overview and details of your recommended training program during a meeting where the CEO and all the department heads will attend. Although you are somewhat nervous and scared, you soon regain your confidence and comfort level when you find out that you had kept a copy of a textbook called "Performance Management."

Using the information in Section 4, Training Programs for the Acquisition of Required Skills, create a presentation with 15–25 slides that communicate (i) a brief explanation of the nature of your suggested rater training program; (ii) its advantages; and (iii) its requirements. ■

End Notes

1. Williams, J. R., & Levy, P. (2000). Investigating some neglected criteria: The influence of organizational level and perceived system knowledge on appraisal reactions. *Journal of Business and Psychology, 14*, 501–513.

2. Grote, D. (1996). *The complete guide to performance appraisal.* New York. AMACOM.

3. U.S. Department of Justice, Human Resources, Senior Executive Service, Performance Management System for SES Employees. Available online at http://www.usdoj.gov/jmd/ps/sespmsplan.htm. Retrieval date: September 7, 2011.

4. Morhman, A. M., Resnick-West, S. M., & Lawler, E. E. (1989). *Designing performance appraisal systems* (p. 133). San Francisco, CA: Jossey-Bass.

5. Kleingfeld, A., van Tuijl, H., & Algera, J. A. (2004). Participation in the design of performance management systems: A quasi-experimental field study. *Journal of Organizational Behavior, 25*, 831–851.

6. Greenberg, J. (1986). Determinants of perceived fairness of performance evaluations. *Journal of Applied Psychology, 71*, 340–342.

7. Grote, D. (1996). *The complete guide to performance appraisal* (pp. 263–269). New York: AMACOM.

8. University of North Carolina at Chapel Hill, Office of Human Resources. *Performance management policy (SPA).* Available online at http://hr.unc.edu/policies-procedures-guidelines/spa-employee-policies/performance-management/PM-SPA. Retrieval date: September 7, 2011.

9. Spears, M. C., & Parker, D. F. (2002). A probit analysis of the impact of training on performance appraisal satisfaction. *American Business Review, 20*, 12–16.

10. Holland, K. (2006, September 10). Performance reviews: Many need improvement. *The New York Times, Section 3-Money and Business/Financial Desk*, 3.

11. Bernardin, H. J., Cooke, D. K., & Villanova, P. (2000). Conscientiousness and aggreableness as predictors of rating leniency. *Journal of Applied Psychology, 85*, 232–234.

12. Bretz, R. D., Milkovich, G. T., & Read, W. (1992). The current state of performance appraisal research and practice: Concerns,

directions, and implications. *Journal of Management, 18,* 321–352.

13. Aguinis, H., & Adams, S. K. R. (1998). Social-role versus structural models of gender and influence use in organizations: A strong inference approach. *Group and Organization Management, 23,* 414–446.

14. Heilman, M. E., Wallen, A. S., Fuchs, D., & Tamkins, M. M. (2004). Penalties for success: Reactions to women who succeed at male gender-typed tasks. *Journal of Applied Psychology, 89,* 416–427.

15. Stauffer, J. M., & Buckley, M. R. (2005). The existence and nature of racial bias in supervisory ratings. *Journal of Applied Psychology, 90,* 586–591.

16. Jawahar, I. M. (2005). Do raters consider the influence of situational factors on observed performance when evaluating performance? Evidence from three experiments. *Group & Organization Management, 30,* 6–41.

17. London, M., Mone, E. M., & Scott, J. C. (2004). Performance management and assessement: Methods for improved rater accuracy and employee goal setting. *Human Resource Management, 43,* 319–336.

18. Pulakos, E. D. (1986). The development of training programs to increase accuracy with different rating tasks. *Organizational Behavior and Human Decision Processes, 38,* 76–91.

19. Noonan, L. E., & Sulsky, L. M. (2001). Impact of frame-of-reference and behavioral observation training on alternative training effectiveness criteria in a Canadian Military Sample. *Human Performance, 14,* 3–26.

20. Stamoulis, D. T., & Hauenstein, N. M. A. (1993). Rater training and rating accuracy: Training for dimensional accuracy versus training for rate differentiation. *Journal of Applied Psychology, 78,* 994–1003.

21. Duarte, N. T., Goodson, J. R., & Klich, N. R. (2004). Effects of dyadic quality and duration on performance appraisal. *Academy of Management Journal, 37,* 499–521.

22. Neck, C. P., Stewart, G. L., & Manz, C. C. (1995). Thought self-leadership as a framework for enhancing the performance of performance appraisers. *Journal of Applied Behavioral Science, 31,* 278–302.

23. Neck, C. P., Smith, W. J., & Godwin, J. L. (1997). Thought self-leadership: A self-regulatory approach to diversity management. *Journal of Managerial Psychology, 12,* 190–203.

24. Bernardin, H. J., & Villanova, P. (2005). Research streams in rater self-efficacy. *Group & Organization Management, 30,* 61–88.

25. Grote, D. (1996). *The complete guide to performance appraisal* (pp. 254–256). New York: AMACOM.

26. Cederblom, D., & Pemerl, D. E. (2002). From performance appraisal to performance management: One agency's experience. *Public Personnel Management, 31,* 131–140.

27. Kelly, S. (2004). Maximizing performance at BT Global Services. *Strategic HR Review, 3,* 32–35.

28. Grote, D. (1996). *The complete guide to performance appraisal* (pp. 260–263). New York: AMACOM.

29. Mulvaney, R. R. H., Zwahr, M., & Baranowski, L. (2006). The trend toward accountability: What does it mean for HR managers? *Human Resource Management Review, 16,* 431–442.

30. Harper, S., & Vilkinas, T. (2005). Determining the impact of an organisation's performance management system. *Asia Pacific Journal of Human Resources, 43,* 76–97.

31. Fletcher, C. (2008). *Appraisal, feedback, and development: Making performance review work.* New York: Routledge.

32. Dipboye, R. L., & de Pontbriand, R. (1981). Correlates of employee reactions to performance appraisal and appraisal systems. *Journal of Applied Psychology, 66,* 248–251.

33. Goh, F. A., & Anderson, M. C. (2007). Driving business value from performance management at Caterpillar. *Organization Development Journal, 25,* 219–226.

34. Cederblom, D., & Pemerl, D. E. (2002). From performance appraisal to performance management: One agency's experience. *Public Personnel Management, 31,* 131–140.

35. Aguinis, H., Mazurkiewicz, M. D., & Heggestad, E. D. (2009). Using web-based frame-of-reference training to decrease biases in personality-based job analysis: An experimental field study. *Personnel Psychology, 62,* 405–438.

36. Payne, S. C., Horner, M. T., Boswell, W. R., Schroeder, A. N., & Stine-Cheyne, K. J. (2009). Comparison of online and traditional performance appraisal systems. *Journal of Managerial Psychology, 24,* 526–544.

Performance Management and Employee Development

*One of the tests of leadership is the ability to recognize a
problem before it becomes an emergency.*

—Arnold H. Glasow

LEARNING OBJECTIVES

By the end of this chapter, you will be able to do the following:

- Describe the importance and benefits of including a developmental plan as part of
  the performance management system.
- Describe the various short-term and long-term objectives of a developmental plan.
- Design a high-quality developmental plan.
- Learn about the key activities that will help the successful implementation of a
  developmental plan.
- Understand the role that the direct supervisor plays in the design and
  implementation of a developmental plan.
- Implement a 360-degree feedback system with the goal of providing feedback on
  and improving performance.
- Implement an online 360-degree feedback system.
- Understand the advantages as well as the risks of implementing a 360-degree
  feedback system.
- Evaluate the quality of a 360-degree feedback system.

There are two key stakeholders in the developmental process: (1) the employees who are improving their own performance, and (2) the managers who help guide the process of employee development for their staff and support it so that it can successfully occur. Developmental planning is a joint activity entered into by both the employee and the manager. This chapter addresses how to use a performance management system to help employees develop and improve their performance. Let's begin this chapter by discussing personal developmental plans.

1 PERSONAL DEVELOPMENTAL PLANS

Personal developmental plans specify courses of action to be taken to improve performance. Achieving the goals stated in the developmental plan allows employees to keep abreast of changes in their fields or professions. Such plans highlight an employee's strengths and the areas in need of development, and they provide an action plan to improve in areas of weaknesses and further develop areas of strength.[1] In a nutshell, personal developmental plans allow employees to answer the following questions:

- How can I continually learn and grow in the next year?
- How can I do better in the future?
- How can I avoid performance problems faced in the past?

Developmental plans can be created for every job, ranging from entry level to the executive suite. No matter how high up the position within the organization and how simple or complex the nature of the job in question, there is always room for improvement. Information to be used in designing developmental plans comes from the appraisal form. Specifically, a developmental plan can be designed based on each of the performance dimensions evaluated. For example, if the performance dimension "communication" is rated as substandard, this area would be targeted by the developmental plan. In addition, however, developmental plans focus on the knowledge and skills needed for more long-term career aspirations.

In addition to improved performance, the inclusion of development plans and, in more general terms, the identification of employee strengths and weaknesses as part of the performance management system have another important benefit: employees are more likely to be satisfied with the system.[2] For example, a study including 137 employees at a production equipment facility in the southern United States showed that the greater the extent to which employees believed that the system was being used for developmental purposes, the more satisfied they were with the system. On the other hand, perceptions of the extent to which the system was used for evaluative purposes did not relate to employee satisfaction with the system. In other words, using the system for evaluative purposes did not relate to employee satisfaction with the system, but using the system for developmental purposes had a positive relationship with satisfaction.

BOX 1

Individual Developmental Plans at General Mills

At General Mills (http://www.generalmills.com), individual developmental plans (IDPs) are promoted strongly throughout the company. The Minneapolis, Minnesota-based General Mills is an international foods company. Some of the best-known brands include Pillsbury, Cheerios, Green Giant, and Yoplait. The formally written IDPs are completed annually, but the expectation is for ongoing conversations between managers and employees, focusing not only on competencies that are well developed and those that are in need of improvement but also on the employee's career aspirations. The company's IDP sessions promote the process for employees by hosting speakers, offering Web-based learning tools, and holding workshops for employees and managers to get the most out of the process. Some of these sessions are specifically tailored to different kinds of positions within the company with different needs in the development process. Also, the IDP is kept separate from the annual performance appraisal, as the belief is that development planning cannot be sufficiently addressed in the context of appraisal. In summary, General Mills provides an example of a company that has made a strong commitment to the growth and learning of all employees.[3]

1.1 Developmental Plan Objectives

The overall objective of a developmental plan is to encourage continuous learning, performance improvement, and personal growth. In addition, developmental plans have other more specific objectives:

- *Improve performance in current job.* A good developmental plan helps employees meet performance standards. Thus, a developmental plan includes suggested courses of action to address each of the performance dimensions that are deficient. This is an important point given that recent surveys have shown that about 25% of federal employees and between 11 and 16% of private sector employees in the United States are not performing up to standards.[4]
- *Sustain performance in current job.* A good developmental plan provides tools so that employees can continue to meet and exceed expectations regarding the current job. Thus, the plan includes suggestions about how to continue to meet and exceed expectations for each of the performance dimensions included in the appraisal form.
- *Prepare employees for advancement.* A good developmental plan includes advice and courses of action that should be taken so that employees will be able to take advantage of future opportunities and career advancement. Specifically, a good plan indicates which new competencies and behaviors should be learned to help with career advancement.
- *Enrich the employee's work experience.* Even if career opportunities within the organization are not readily available, a good plan provides employees with growth opportunities and opportunities to learn new skills. These opportunities provide employees with intrinsic rewards and a more challenging work experience, even if the new skills learned are not a formal part of their jobs. Such opportunities can make jobs more attractive and serve as a powerful employee retention tool. In addition, the new skills can be useful in case of lateral transfers within the organization.

Consider the employee developmental plan used by Texas A&M University in College Station, Texas (http://employees.tamu.edu/employees/training/online/pd/pdForms.aspx). Since the developmental plan is a formal component of the university's performance management system, the developmental plan is included within the appraisal form. The appraisal form used by Texas A&M first lists the six objectives of the performance management system:

1. Provide employees with feedback to improve or maintain job performance
2. Outline areas for employee development
3. Set standards for the next review period
4. Recognize job-related accomplishments
5. Enhance communication and working relationships
6. Identify job performance deficiencies (any factor "Does Not Meet Expectations"), and report to the next level of supervisory responsibility

Based on objective 2, the employee developmental plan is an important component of the performance management system. The inclusion of this objective up front sets the tone for the developmental process by helping managers understand that this is an important issue.

After the sections in the form in which the manager rates employee performance, the following material is included:

SECTION B: PROFESSIONAL DEVELOPMENT PLAN

Please list professional development activities to be completed and resources needed to support these activities, if applicable (link to examples of suggested employee development: http://hr.tamu.edu/ed/suggest.pdf)

Professional Development Needs	Resources/Support Needed	Time Frame
_____	_____	_____
_____	_____	_____
_____	_____	_____
_____	_____	_____

The inclusion of this information after performance ratings allows the manager and employee to focus on developmental areas identified as weaknesses in the performance review process. In this way, the developmental plans created for employees at Texas A&M are directly related to performance dimensions important for the unit and the overall organization. In addition, including the developmental plan at the end of the review and after setting annual performance goals allows the employee to determine whether there are areas he or she needs to develop in order to attain the specified goals.

Why does goal setting work? In other words, based on studies of more than 40,000 people in eight countries, why have "stretch" goals led to better performance than "do your best" or easy goals?[5] There are four basic reasons. First, when an employee commits to a goal, he or she diverts attention away from activities that are not relevant to the goal and toward activities that are relevant. Second, challenging goals are energizing and lead to higher levels of effort. Third, stretch goals lead to persistence (e.g., tight deadlines lead to a faster pace than do loose deadlines). Finally, stretch goals motivate employees to use the knowledge they have to reach the goal or to search for new knowledge that they may need.[6]

1.2 Content of Developmental Plan

What does a developmental plan look like? Plans should include a description of specific steps to be taken and specific objectives to reach. In other words, what is the new skill or knowledge that will be acquired and how will this occur? This includes information on the resources and strategies that will be used to achieve the objectives. For example, will the employee learn the skill from a coworker through on-the-job training? Will the company reimburse the employee for expenses associated with taking an online course?

The plan's objectives should include not only the end product, such as the new skill to be learned, but also the completion date and how the supervisor will know whether the new skill has indeed been acquired. For example, in the case of the online course, the objective could state that the course will be completed by July 23, 2012, and the employee is expected to receive a grade of B+ or better. Overall, objectives included in the developmental plans should be practical, specific, time oriented, linked to a standard, and developed jointly by the supervisor and the employee.

An additional important feature of developmental plans is that they should keep the needs of both the organization and the employee in mind. The choice of what specific skills or performance areas will be improved is dictated by the needs of the organization, especially when the organization is investing in the plan. In addition, the plan created is dictated by the needs of the individual. The supervisor and the employee need to agree on what development or new skills will help enrich the employee's work experience as well as help accomplish organizational goals now or in the near future.

As an example, consider the content of the developmental plan at Texas A&M. First, employees are directed to a Web site that includes examples of possible developmental activities (http://hr.tamu.edu/ed/suggest.pdf). This list includes workshops; certifications; local, state, and national conferences; on-the-job training; and other activities. This information presents employees and managers with various options they can use to achieve the developmental objectives. Second, the form includes space so that each professional developmental need is paired with a description of resources or support needed and a time frame for completion. For example, the developmental plan for an administrative assistant in the business school may look like this:

Overall, the Texas A&M plan includes all of the required components. There is a description of developmental objectives, activities that will be conducted to reach these objectives, and dates of completion. One important piece is missing, however. The plan does not include specifics of how the accomplishment of each objective will be measured. Specifically, how will the supervisor know if the administrative assistant has

SECTION B: PROFESSIONAL DEVELOPMENT PLAN

Please list professional development activities to be completed and resources needed to support these activities, if applicable (link to examples of suggested employee development: http://hr.tamu.edu/ed/suggest.pdf)

Professional Development Needs	Resources/Support Needed	Time Frame
1. Knowledge of Excel (spreadsheet program)	Reimbursement for online course	Course to be completed by August 1, 2012
2. Customer service skills in dealing with students and faculty	Reimbursement for 1-day workshop. Time to receive on-the-job training from administrative assistant in psychology department.	Workshop to be completed by October 15, 2012. On-the-job training completed by November 8, 2012.

a good working knowledge of Excel after she has completed the online course? How will the supervisor know if the administrative assistant's customer service skills have improved after she has attended the workshop and has undergone on-the-job training? The Excel training could be measured by the administrative assistant's performance in the course or by examining answers to questions about knowledge of Excel that faculty and others giving Excel assignments to the administrative assistant answer in filling out appraisal forms. Regarding customer service skills, the accomplishment of the objective might be measured by questioning those customers served by the administrative assistant (i.e., faculty and students).

1.3 Developmental Activities

There are several ways through which employees can reach the objectives stated in their developmental plans, including

- *On-the-job training.* Each employee is paired with a coworker or supervisor who designs a formal on-the-job training course. The design of these mini-training programs includes how many hours a day or week training will take place and specific learning objectives.
- *Courses.* Some large organizations such as McDonald's, Motorola, Capgemini and Ernst & Young offer in-house courses given at their own corporate universities. Other organizations may provide tuition reimbursement. Given the proliferation of online courses, employees have a wide variety of options from which to choose.
- *Self-guided reading.* Employees can read books and study other resources on their own. Once again, it is important that an objective be set regarding what will be read and within what time frame as well as what measure(s) will be used to assess whether learning has taken place.
- *Mentoring.* Many organizations have mentoring programs. In general terms, mentoring is a developmental process that consists of a one-on-one relationship

between a senior (mentor) and junior (protégé) employee. For such programs to be successful, it is best to allow the mentor and protégé to choose each other rather than arbitrarily assigning who will be mentoring whom. In general, mentors serve as role models and teach protégés what it takes to succeed in the organization. In more specific terms, mentors can help protégés gain targeted skills.

- *Attending a conference.* Another way to acquire required knowledge and skills is to sponsor an employee's attendance at a conference or trade show. It is useful to require that the employee provide a written report or even deliver a presentation upon returning from the conference. In this way, it is easier to assess what has been learned and, in addition, the knowledge gained can be shared with other organizational members.

- *Getting a degree.* Some organizations provide tuition reimbursement benefits for their employees to obtain additional degrees or certifications. For example, the organization can sponsor an employee's MBA program or an employee's taking a course with the goal of earning a certification designation (e.g., Certified Novell Administrator, Professional in Human Resources). In most cases, employees commit to continuing the relationship with their employer for a prespecified amount of time after completing the degree. If the employee leaves the organization before this time frame, he may have to reimburse the organization for the cost of his education.

- *Job rotation.* Another way to gain necessary skills is to be assigned to a different job on a temporary basis. This is the model followed in the medical profession in which residents have to rotate across specialty areas for several months (e.g., OB-GYN, psychiatry, pediatrics). For example, residents may be required to rotate across the various emergency medicine services for a 19-month period.

- *Temporary assignments.* A less systematic rotation system includes the opportunity to work on a challenging temporary assignment. This allows employees to gain specific skills within a limited time frame.

- *Membership or leadership role in professional or trade organizations.* Some employers sponsor membership in professional or trade organizations. Such an organization distributes publications to its members and holds informal and formal meetings in which employees have an opportunity to learn about best practices and other useful information for their jobs. For example, this could include the Society for Human Resource Management (www.shrm.org) or the Chartered Institute of Personnel and Development (http://www.cipd.co.uk/) for human resources (HR) professionals. Also, presentation, communication, planning, and other skills can be learned while serving in a leadership role in a volunteer organization outside of work.

Table 1 includes a summarized list of developmental activities that may be available to achieve goals included in a developmental plan. Based on your own preferences and learning style, which of these activities do you believe would be most beneficial to you? Please rank these activities in terms of your preference.

An example of a developmental plan is included in Figure 1. The developmental plan can be part of the appraisal form, or it can be included in a separate form. The form included in Figure 1 shows that employees have several choices in terms of developmental activities. Note that the form includes space so that information can be inserted regarding what activities will take place when, what the objectives are, and whether the objective has been met or not.

Performance Management and Employee Development

TABLE 1	Summary List of Developmental Activities

On-the-job training
Courses
Self-guided reading
Mentoring
Attending a conference
Getting a degree
Job rotation
Temporary assignments
Membership or leadership role in professional or trade organizations

Update Date:
Name:
Job Title/Job Code:
Department:
Primary Reviewer:
Education:
Prior Training:
Job History:
Career Goals:
     Next 1 year
     Next 2 years
     Next 3 years
     Next 5 years

Dev. Options OJT (on the job) training Classes Conferences On-line Self-study Job rotation Videos Books Temp. assignment Mentorship Other (specify)	Description Current Qtr. ___ Next. Qtr. ___ Current +2 ___ Current +3	Type of Development	When	How Long	Completed Hours (this Qtr.)	Comments— Approx. Cost —Other	Objectives/ Evaluation

FIGURE 1 **Example of a Developmental Plan Form** *Source:* Based on Information Systems and Technology Development Plan. Available online at http://web.mit.edu/is/competency/devplan.html. Retrieval date: May 1, 2011.

208

Consider your future career expectations and developmental needs. Then fill out the form included in Figure 1, assuming your current or future employer will be willing to provide any developmental opportunities of your choosing. What does your plan look like? What did you discover about what you would like to learn in the future? What does this information tell you about your level of aspirations and future prospects for your career advancement?

2 DIRECT SUPERVISOR'S ROLE

The direct supervisor or line manager has an important role in the creation and completion of the employee's developmental plan. Because of the pivotal role of the direct supervisor in the employee development process, it is a good idea for the supervisor to have her own development plan. This will help the supervisor understand the process from the employee's perspective, anticipate potential roadblocks and defensive attitudes, and create a plan in a collaborative fashion.[7]

First, the supervisor needs to explain what would be required for the employee to achieve the desired performance level, including the steps that an employee must take to improve her performance. This information needs to be provided together with information on the probability of success if the employee completes the suggested steps. A good tool that supervisors can use to accomplish this goal is to use the *feedforward interview* (FFI). The goal of the FFI is to understand the types of behaviors and skills that individuals have that allow them to perform well and to think about ways to use these same behaviors and skills in other contexts to make further improvements in the future. The FFI includes a meeting between the supervisor and employee and involves the following three steps:[8]

1. *Eliciting a success story.* The supervisor sets the stage as follows: "All of us have both negative and positive experiences at work. I would like to meet with you to discuss some positives aspects only and see how we can learn from those experiences about things that work well." Then, the supervisor can ask, "Could you please tell me about a story about an event or experience at work during which you felt at your best, full of life and in flow, and you were content even before the results of your actions were known?" It is important that the story be very specific about an actual incident and not a general statement about "In general, these are the things I do at work . . ." So, the story must be situated within a specific context. After the supervisor hears the story, he or she can summarize it for the employee to hear it, and then the supervisor can ask whether any information is missing or anything else should be added to the story. A follow-up question is, "Would you be happy to experience a similar process again?" If the answer is in the affirmative, then the subsequent questions attempt to go deeper into the details of the story. If the story is associated with mixed feelings and is not completely positive, then a different story must be elicited.

2. *Uncover the underlying success factors.* The second step involves understanding the factors that led to the successful story. For example, the supervisor can ask, "What were some of the things you did or did not do, such as your specific personal strengths and capabilities, that made this success story

possible?" and "What were the conditions that made this success story possible?" It is important to uncover both the personal and contextual factors that led to the success story. This step is similar to conducting detective work to try to understand the various factors that led to success, including the role that the work environment (e.g., technology) and others (e.g., customers, peers) played in the story.

3. *Extrapolating the past into the future.* The third step involves asking questions that will lead to an employee's ability to replicate the conditions that led to success in the past into the future. So, the supervisor can first note that "The conditions you have just described seem to be your personal code for reaching [insert the key achievement in the story such as happiness at work, optimal performance, and outstanding leadership]." Then, follow up with questions such as, "Think about your current actions, priorities, and plans for the near future (e.g., next week, month, or quarter), and tell me how you think you may be able to replicate these conditions to be able to achieve the same level of [insert satisfaction, achievement, performance, etc.] as you did before."

Results of the FFI may suggest that there may be resources that the employee needs to achieve his or her developmental goals. Thus, as a second step in terms of a supervisor's role, he or she has a primary role in referring the employee to appropriate developmental activities that can assist the employee in achieving her goals. This includes helping the employee select a mentor, appropriate reading resources, courses, and so forth. Third, the supervisor reviews and makes suggestions about the developmental objectives. Specifically, the supervisor helps assure the goals are achievable, specific, and doable. Fourth, the supervisor has primary responsibility for checking on the employee's progress toward achieving the developmental goals. For example, the supervisor can remind the employee of due dates and revise goals if needed. Finally, the supervisor needs to provide reinforcements so the employee will be motivated to achieve the developmental goals. Reinforcements can be extrinsic and include rewards such as bonuses and additional benefits, but reinforcements can also include the assignment of more challenging and interesting work that takes advantage of the new skills learned.

Supervisors themselves need to be motivated to perform functions that will support the employees' completion of their developmental objectives, including conducting FFIs. For this to happen, supervisors must be rewarded for doing a good job in helping their employees develop. Consider how this is done at KLA-Tencor Corporation (www.kla-tencor.com), one of the world's top 10 manufacturers of semiconductor equipment. At KLA-Tencor, between 10 and 30% of supervisors' bonus pay is directly tied to employee development. Employee development is measured in terms of employee training and certification levels. Managers are given at least quarterly updates on the status of their staff development. In addition, employees themselves are rewarded for engaging in developmental activities. In fact, only employees with up-to-date training and certification levels are eligible for bonuses. Thus, employee development is successful at KLA-Tencor because both employees and managers are directly rewarded for employee development. After several years of implementing

TABLE 2	Factors Promoting Successful Implementation of Personal Developmental Plans

All employees have a plan (including managers from all levels in the organization).

All employees are entitled to developmental opportunities on an ongoing basis.

Managers are involved in the assessment of objective accomplishment and monitor progress toward accomplishing developmental objectives.

Managers are committed to the development of their employees and to helping their employees fulfill their career aspirations.

The developmental plan becomes an integral part of the performance management system.

The performance of managers is evaluated, in part, based on how well they manage the developmental process for their employees.

Source: Hgigson, M., & Wilson, J. P. (1995). Implementing personal development plans: A model for trainers, managers and supervisors. *Industrial & Commercial Training, 27,* 25–29.

these practices, employee development has become the norm and is part of the KLA-Tencor's culture.[9]

In short, the direct supervisor plays a key role in the success of the developmental plan. Table 2 summarizes many of the points we have discussed thus far that will promote successful implementation of personal developmental plans.

BOX 2

Role of Direct Supervisor in Development at Diageo

Diageo (http://www.diageo.com) has recognized the value of employee development and expects supervisors to play an important role in the process with their direct reports. Diageo, headquartered in London, England, employs 22,000 people and was formed in 1997 with the merger of Guinness and GrandMet. The company produces premium alcoholic beverages, including such brands as Smirnoff, Baileys, Guinness, and Sterling Vineyard. The company's career development program includes a formal review and goal-setting, along with regular meetings to keep development fresh in the minds of employees. The supervisor facilitates the process in several ways. The supervisor helps identify specific development goals that are aligned with the employee's career aspirations. Monthly meetings, referred to as "call overs," are held to review progress toward goals and adjust goals as necessary. Also, the supervisor helps provide a means for development and reaching goals by ensuring that employees receive training, course work, or reading material on relevant topics. Another strategy includes giving assignments outside of one's current job responsibilities, such as leading a project to test one's skills and practice what he or she has learned in the development process. In summary, Diageo has recognized that emphasizing development with active management responsibilities not only benefits the individual employee's growth but also aids in aligning employee skills and actions with the strategic goals of the organization as a whole.[10]

---

3 360-DEGREE FEEDBACK SYSTEMS

The 360-degree feedback system has become a preferred tool for helping employees, particularly those in supervisory roles, improve performance by gathering information on their performance from different groups.[11] These systems are called 360-degree systems because information is gathered from individuals all around the employee. Specifically, information on what performance dimensions could be improved is gathered from superiors, peers, customers, and subordinates. This information is usually collected anonymously to minimize rating inflation. Employees also rate themselves on the various performance dimensions and compare self-perceptions with the information provided by others. A gap analysis is conducted to examine the areas for which there are large discrepancies between self-perceptions and the perceptions of others. A 360-degree feedback system report usually includes information on dimensions for which there is agreement that further development is needed. This information is used to create a developmental plan as described earlier in the chapter. For example, a study including over 2,000 managers demonstrated that the objectives included in personal developmental plans were driven by performance dimensions that received low scores in 360-degree feedback systems.[12]

The 360-degree feedback system is most helpful when it is used for developmental purposes only and not for administrative purposes.[13] This is because people are more likely to be honest if they know the information will be used to help the individual improve and not to punish or to reward him or her. However, it is possible to implement such systems successfully for administrative purposes after they have been in place for some time—usually two years or so.[14] The 360-degree feedback system is usually implemented for individuals who have supervisory roles, but these systems can be used for all positions within the organization.

Many organizations take advantage of technology to minimize the amount of paperwork and time involved in collecting such data. The Internet is becoming a pervasive medium by which to administer 360-degree feedback systems. The service provider, usually an outside consulting firm, sends an e-mail message with instructions and time frames for assessment to each employee to be rated. Then, employees can access a secure Web site and, after entering their personal IDs and passwords, create individual lists of raters who will be asked to provide feedback about their performance. To make things easier, the employee can even select names from a drop-down menu that includes company managers and employees. Allowing employees to select the raters who will provide information on their performance is likely to increase acceptance of the results.[15] The raters selected are asked to visit the Web site and to provide performance feedback within a certain time period. After the data have been collected electronically, it is fairly easy to compile the results and e-mail a report to the employee who has been evaluated.

Some Internet-based systems also provide online training for raters on how to complete the feedback forms in helpful and constructive ways. Some systems even include features that allow for the detection of rating errors. For example, a window may pop up if a rater gives the maximum score to an employee on all dimensions. Raters may even see a graph on the screen that shows the extent to which the ratings they have provided agree with the ratings provided by other people rating the same employee. Some systems even include an online virtual feedback coach to help create developmental plans. The final plan, however, must be consensually decided upon in a meeting between the employee and his supervisor. Unless the developmental plan has an employee's complete acceptance, it is likely to become another inconsequential HR-mandated task.[16]

Feedback reports can include graphs showing the areas in which employees' perceptions differ the most from the perceptions of other raters. They can also show average scores across sources of information so that the areas that need improvement are readily identified. The resulting report can be e-mailed automatically to the employee and his supervisor so that both have an opportunity to review the results before meeting to create a developmental plan.

A trend adopted by software companies that offer Internet-based 360-degree systems is to offer a bundle of systems including 360-degree feedback together with learning management, compensation, and even recruiting and succession planning. These integrative applications, usually called "talent management" systems, allow organizations to manage data about employees in a systematic and coordinated way.[17] Such integrative software applications allow organizations to create an inventory of their human capital and better understand their strengths and weaknesses at the organizational level. For example, an organization that uses such applications is quickly able to deploy project teams with the appropriate mix of skills and experience after doing a quick search in the database. Another important advantage of these integrative applications is that performance management can be more easily linked to recruiting, compensation, training, and succession planning. In other words, the system can keep track of an employee's developmental needs and how these needs have been addressed (e.g., via training) over time.

Table 3 includes a nonexhaustive list of vendors that offer Internet-based 360-degree feedback systems and a brief description of their products. This table also includes information on whether a demonstration of it is available online. As can be seen by the information included in this table, many such systems are available.

TABLE 3 Examples of Vendors Offering 360-Degree Feedback Systems

Vendor	Verbatim Description Provided on Vendor's Web site
Panoramic Feedback http://www.panoramicfeedback.com (demo available online)	Pure browser-based application: ask anyone, anything, anytime, anywhere. English, European, American Languages, Chinese, Japanese, Korean, and Cyrillic. Extensive knowledge base, strong track record, HRIS integration, aggregate reporting to guide strategy.
Halogen Software http://www.halogensoftware.com/products/e360open.php (demo available online)	Halogen e360 is a sophisticated Web-based software solution that streamlines the multirater process. It provides a simple, proven approach to employee 360 assessments that significantly reduces the time and effort required to get useful insight. Creating an evaluation, monitoring the process, and generating reports can all be done with point-and-click ease.
The Booth Company http://www.boothco.com/home.html (demo available online)	The Booth Company provides the only 360-degree feedback tools statistically validated on more than 150 million responses and a validated theory of management and leadership. Its comprehensive battery of surveys measures key skills in the most significant organizational roles, such as executive, change leader, middle management, team membership and leadership, and project leadership.

(continued)

TABLE 3 (Continued)

Vendor	Verbatim Description Provided on Vendor's Web site
Personnel Decisions International http://www.personneldecisions.com/offerings/multitrater.asp	PDI is not only one of the founders of 360-degree feedback but also experts on what it takes to change behavior. Nearly half of the Fortune 100 companies rely on PDI PROFILOR® instruments. They're the most tested, most widely used, and most accurate feedback tools in the world.
Development Dimensions International http://www.ddiworld.com/default.asp	Seven standard survey options—available in English, French, German, and Spanish—and a listing of 72 competencies enable you to assess different skill sets and job levels, or we can customize a system that is specifically aligned with the key factors your organization views as critical to job success. Comprehensive reports can be used to monitor the developmental process, prioritize learning and developmental approaches, evaluate training effectiveness, identify trends, and measure organizational performance or success over time.
IRI Consultants to Management http://www.irisolutions.com/default.asp	IRI's 360-degree feedback includes a standard set of questions, or we can use a set of questions developed by the client. This provides the client with the flexibility of linking items to organizational efforts already begun, or to organizational efforts planned for future deployment.
Center for Creative Leadership http://www.ccl.org/leadership/assessments/design360Overview.aspx?pageId=47	360 BY DESIGN is a 360-degree feedback and development process that can be tailored to reflect the competencies important to your organization. It provides online assessment and feedback as well as developmental planning, featuring 360 best practices pioneered by the Center for Creative Leadership (CCL®).
MindSolve http://www.sumtotalsystems.com/products/stperf.html (demo available online)	Multi-Rater/360 Feedback: Assesses competencies through feedback from multiple angles, and delivers results that will make an impact on participants' performance.
2020 Insight Gold www.2020insight.net (demo available online)	20/20 Insight GOLD is extremely user-friendly software that lets you create and use practically any kind of multisource feedback survey you can imagine—including 360-degree feedback projects, pre- and post-training competency surveys, team and organization climate surveys, customer satisfaction surveys, and many more.

As an illustration, consider the system offered by CheckPoint (http://ourworld.compuserve.com/homepages/gately/chkpoint.htm). This system, designed for employees in supervisory roles, includes information on the following competencies:

- Communication (listens to others, processes information, communicates effectively)
- Leadership (instills trust, provides direction, delegates responsibility)
- Adaptability (adjusts to circumstances, thinks creatively)

- Relationships (builds personal relationships, facilitates team success)
- Task management (works efficiently, works competently)
- Production (takes action, achieves results)
- Development of others (cultivates individual talent, motivates successfully)
- Personal development (displays commitment, seeks improvement)

The CheckPoint system includes self-evaluations as well as evaluations provided by the direct supervisor, direct subordinates, and peers. After performance information has been collected from all these sources, the evaluated manager receives feedback in the form of the graph shown in Figure 2. This graph illustrates the discrepancies between self- and others' ratings as well as the scores obtained for each competency. For example, this graph shows that this particular manager has the greatest gap for the

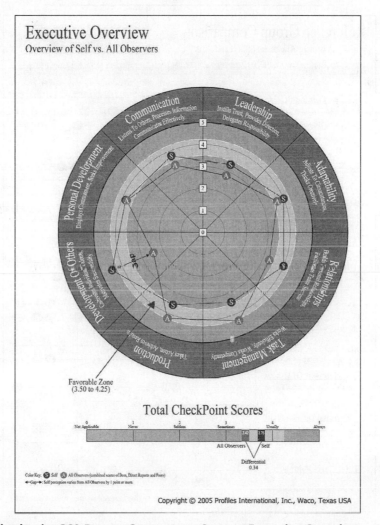

FIGURE 2 Checkpoint 360-Degree Competency System: Executive Overview *Source:* Bob Gately, Strategic Business Partner of Profiles International, Inc. 508-634-7748, bob@gatelyconsulting.com, http://www.gatelyconsulting.com/chkpoint.htm. Courtesy of Profiles International, Inc.

competency "development of others." Specifically, the manager assigned a score of about 4.5 to herself, whereas the average score provided by her direct supervisor, direct subordinates, and peers is only 2.55. The CheckPoint system uses the following scale to rate competencies:

0	**Not applicable** (not averaged into scores)
1	**Never** demonstrates this
2	**Seldom** demonstrates this
3	**Sometimes** demonstrates this
4	**Usually** demonstrates this
5	**Always** demonstrates this

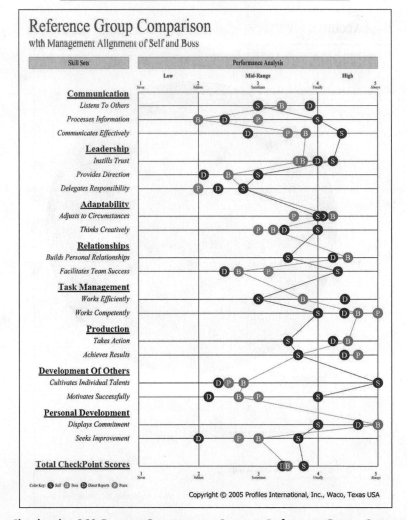

FIGURE 3   **Checkpoint 360-Degree Competency System: Reference Group Comparison**

Source: Bob Gately, Strategic Business Partner of Profiles International, Inc. 508-634-7748, bob@gately consulting.com, http://www.gatelyconsulting.com/chkpoint.htm. Courtesy of Profiles International, Inc.

In this particular illustration, the manager believes that she displays behaviors indicating the competency "development of others" somewhere between "usually" and "always." By contrast, her boss, employees, and peers believe that she demonstrates these behaviors somewhere between "seldom" and "sometimes." In other words, the self-rating falls within the favorable zone whereas the ratings provided by others do not.

To explore this gap further, the report provided to the manager also includes more detailed information on the scores provided by each source of information. The Reference Group Comparison chart included in Figure 3 shows this information. An examination of the scores provided for the competency "development of others" indicates that all sources, except for the manager herself, agree that work is needed regarding this competency because all scores are between the "seldom" and "sometimes" categories. By contrast, the manager believes she is doing an exceptional job of cultivating individual talent (score of 5) and motivating successfully (score of 4).

It is not sufficient, however, just to provide scores regarding each of the competencies. Becoming aware that there is a problem with a competency is a very good first step, but a good 360-degree feedback system also provides concrete suggestions about what to do to improve competencies.[18] The CheckPoint system does this by providing what is called a *development summary*. The development summary describes strengths and areas that should be developed further. An example of this is shown in Figure 4. According to the graph, this particular manager has several strengths but also some areas that deserve further development. For example, there is a need to work on the "facilitates team success" dimension of the competency "relationships." The report also includes specific suggestions on how to improve this competency that are shown in Figure 5. Specifically, the manager is given tips and advice regarding concrete steps to be taken to improve performance. For example, in terms of learning to collaborate on team decisions, the manager is given advice about how to compromise and reach win-win decisions and how to gain support for decisions.

360-degree feedback systems are not necessarily beneficial for all individuals and organizations. For example, individuals who are high on self-efficacy (i.e., they believe they can perform any task) are more likely to improve their performance based on feedback received from peers compared to individuals low on self-efficacy.[19] Also, the effect of receiving feedback from multiple sources is most beneficial for individuals who perceive there is a need to change their behavior, react positively to feedback, believe change is feasible, set appropriate goals to improve their performance, and take concrete actions that lead to performance improvement.[20] On the other hand, individuals who score lower on self-efficacy pay more attention to the feedback received from their line managers. In other words, an employee's confidence in her own performance influences which sources of feedback are most useful to her.

In terms of organizational characteristics, 360-degree systems work best in organizations that have cultures that support open and honest feedback. Also, these systems work best in organizations that have a participatory, as opposed to authoritarian, leadership style in which giving and receiving feedback is the norm and is regarded as valuable. For example, consider the case of the Patent Office of the United Kingdom. This organization is characterized by a hierarchical structure typical of many civil service organizations as opposed to a flat structure where employees are involved and teamwork is the norm. The implementation of a 360-degree feedback system did not lead to the anticipated positive results, and there was a mismatch of expectations between what the board members wanted (i.e., better working relations and a culture

Development Summary
for Darcy Walker

Skill Set	All Observers Rating

Strengths

A consensus of your reference group ratings shows these competencies are clear strengths, as they fall in or above the Favorable Zone.

	Rating
S Displays Commitment	4.73
Works Competently	4.60
SE Achieves Results	4.33
Takes Action	4.15
Builds Personal Relationships	4.15
Works Efficiently	4.12
S Adjusts to Circumstances	4.00
Instills Trust	3.88
Listens To Others	3.79

Development Areas

A consensus of your reference group ratings shows these competencies (which fall below the Favorable Zone) as in need of improvement and should be considered a top priority for your career development.

		Rating
Thinks Creatively		3.31
B Communicates Effectively		3.24
SE Facilitates Team Success	Critical Development Area!	2.65
S Processes Information		2.53
B Seeks Improvement	Critical Development Area!	2.45
Motivates Successfully		2.45
Cultivates Individual Talents		2.45
B Provides Direction	Critical Development Area!	2.40
SE Delegates Responsibility	Critical Development Area!	2.35

The critical development areas are determined by input from Boss and Self and the relationship of the Favorable Zone.

Color Key: S or B Chosen by Self or Boss as a Critical Skill Set   SE Chosen by both Self and Boss as a Critical Skill Set

Copyright © 2005 Profiles International, Inc., Waco, Texas USA

FIGURE 4   Checkpoint 360-Degree Competency System: Development Summary
Source: Bob Gately, Strategic Business Partner of Profiles International, Inc. 508-634-7748, bob@gately consulting.com, http://www.gatelyconsulting.com/chkpoint.htm. Courtesy of Profiles International, Inc.

change) and what the employees wanted (i.e., individual improvement). Moreover, managers did not show a good understanding of the behaviors they were expected to display, and their performance did not show improvement. Overall, the 360-degree feedback system was not sufficiently linked to other HR systems and policies.[21]

Answering the following questions can give a good indication as to whether implementing a 360-degree system would be beneficial in a specific organization:

1. Are decisions that are made about rewards and promotion fairly free of favoritism?
2. Are decisions made that take into account the input of people affected by such decisions?
3. Do people from across departments usually cooperate with each other and help each other?

Development Summary

for Darcy Walker

The following suggestions will help direct your development efforts:

Facilitates Team Success

Handle Conflict in a Direct and Effective Manner.

- Don't ignore conflict, thinking it will disappear. It won't. And don't expect a conflict-free workplace. Some discord is inevitable and constructively dealing with it will create a more productive work environment.
- Listen carefully to all viewpoints in a disagreement. Define the problem. Then begin the process of resolution.
- Explore multiple options. Then resolve differences with solutions that are acceptable to all involved parties.

Encourage Cooperation in Order to Reap the Benefits of a Strongly Unified Group Effort.

- When recognizing outstanding performance, go beyond the acknowledgment of individual successes. Give equal emphasis to team achievements and effective cooperation among teams.
- Validate the importance of each and every team member's contribution.

Learn to Collaborate on Team Decisions.

- Practice the art of compromise when making decisions, creating win/win situations.
- To gain support for decisions, involve the team in considering alternative approaches. Strive for consensus in order to increase commitment to the final decision.

Establish Team Objectives.

- As much as possible involve the team in formulating goals consistent with, and supportive of, the overall mission of your business. Also solicit input when planning the implementation of the goals.
- Make sure everyone understands the team's goals, as well as their role in attaining the goals.
- Keep everyone apprised of team progress.

Develop Group Dynamics That Bring Out the Best in Everyone.

- Recruit individuals with talents that will complement the skills of other team members.
- Capitalize on each person's strengths and experiences to create a potent team effort.

FIGURE 5 Checkpoint 360-Degree Competency System: Suggestions for Improvement
Source: Bob Gately, Strategic Business Partner of Profiles International, Inc. 508-634-7748, bob@gatelyconsulting.com, http://www.gatelyconsulting.com/chkpoint.htm. Courtesy of Profiles International, Inc.

4. Is there little or no fear of speaking up?
5. Do people believe that their peers and subordinates can provide valuable information about their performance?
6. Are employees trusted to get the job done?
7. Do people want to improve their performance?

In sum, the successful implementation of a 360-degree feedback system is heavily dependent on the culture of the organization and the work context.[22] If the answer to most of these questions is "yes," the implementation of a 360-degree feedback system is likely to be successful and lead to performance improvement.

3.1 Advantages of 360-Degree Feedback Systems

Organizations and individuals can gain several advantages as a consequence of implementing a 360-degree feedback system. These include the following:

- *Decreased possibility of biases.* Because these systems include information from more than one source, there is a decreased possibility of biases in the identification of employees' weaknesses.

- *Increased awareness of expectations.* Employees become very aware of others' expectations about their performance. This includes not only the supervisor's expectations but also the expectations of other managers, coworkers, subordinates, and customers.
- *Increased commitment to improve.* Employees become aware of what others think about their performance, which increases their commitment to improve because information about performance is no longer a private matter.
- *Improved self-perceptions of performance.* Employees' distorted views of their own performance are likely to change as a result of the feedback received from other sources. In other words, it is difficult to continue to have distorted views of one's own performance in the presence of overwhelming evidence that these perceptions may not be correct.
- *Improved performance.* Although receiving information about one's performance is not sufficient cause to improve, it is certainly a very important step. Thus, having information on one's performance, if paired with a good developmental plan, is likely to lead to performance improvement.
- *Reduced "undiscussables."* 360-degree feedback systems provide an excellent opportunity to coworkers, superiors, and subordinates to give information about performance in an anonymous and nonthreatening way. Many supervisors may feel uncomfortable about providing negative feedback, but a 360-degree system makes providing such feedback easier.
- *Employees enabled to take control of their careers.* By receiving detailed and constructive feedback on weaknesses and strengths in various areas, employees can gain a realistic assessment of where they should go with their careers.

Table 4 includes a summarized list of benefits that organizations can obtain from implementing a 360-degree feedback system. Consider how some of these benefits were realized when a system was implemented at Sonoco Products, a supplier of industrial and consumer packaging.[23] First, two-thirds of the respondents to a survey indicated that their expectations about performance were clearer and that they were able to understand more clearly the link between individual performance and organizational goals. Second, respondents to this same survey also felt more responsible for managing their performance, which the company took as an indication that individuals also had a better understanding of their jobs and self-perceptions of performance. Overall, while we do not have evidence

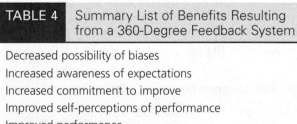

TABLE 4	Summary List of Benefits Resulting from a 360-Degree Feedback System

Decreased possibility of biases

Increased awareness of expectations

Increased commitment to improve

Improved self-perceptions of performance

Improved performance

Reduced "undiscussables"

Employees enabled to take control of their careers

that all of the benefits listed in Table 4 were realized with this system, there is sufficient documentation to show that several important benefits resulted from implementing it.

3.2 Risks of Implementing 360-Degree Feedback Systems

We have discussed the many advantages of 360-degree feedback systems, but we should also consider that there are some risks involved.[24] For example, negative feedback can hurt an employee's feelings, particularly if those giving the feedback do not offer their comments in a constructive way. Second, the system is likely to lead to positive results only if individuals feel comfortable with the system and believe they will be rated honestly and treated fairly. User acceptance is an important determinant of the system's success. Third, when very few raters are providing the information, say, two or three, it may be easy for the employee being rated to identify who the raters are. When anonymity is compromised, raters are more likely to distort the information they provide. Fourth, raters may become overloaded with forms to fill out because they need to provide information on so many individuals (peers, superiors, and subordinates). Finally, implementing a 360-degree feedback system should not be a one-time-only event. The system should be in place and data collected over time on an ongoing basis. The implementation of ongoing 360-degree feedback systems is sometimes labeled a 720-degree feedback system, referring to the fact that the collection of 360-degree data takes place at least twice. In short, administering the system only once will not be as beneficial as administering the system repeatedly.

The risks associated with implementing a 360-degree system can be illustrated by Watson Wyatt's 2001 Human Capital Index (HCI).[25] This is an ongoing study of the effects of HR practices on the stock value of more than 700 publicly traded companies. One particular result was especially alarming. Of the companies surveyed, those that had implemented 360-degree feedback had lower stock value! Specifically, the companies that used peer reviews had 4.9% lower market value than did similar companies that did not implement peer reviews. Furthermore, companies that implemented upward feedback, where employees rated managers, had a 5.7% lower stock value than did similar companies that did not implement upward feedback. Does this necessarily mean that implementing 360-degree feedback systems causes the stock price to decrease? Based on the data collected, there is no definitive answer to this question. It could be that organizations that are not performing well financially decide to implement 360-degree feedback systems precisely to help improve their performance. Nevertheless, these results highlight the importance of following best practices in implementing 360-degree feedback systems in order to avoid any negative consequences of implementing such a system.

3.3 Characteristics of a Good System

Fortunately, there are several things that can be done to maximize the chance that the system will work properly. First, in general terms, consider the following advice:

> 360-degree feedback systems...are always work in progress—subject to vulnerabilities, requiring sensitivity to hidden conflicts as much as to tangible results,

but nevertheless responsive to thoughtful design and purposeful change. Companies that have success with these programs tend to be open to learning and willing to experiment. They are led by executives who are direct about the expected benefits as well as the challenges. . . . By laying themselves open to praise and criticism from all directions and inviting others to do the same, they guide their organizations to new capacities for continuous improvement.[26]

Second, in more specific terms, when systems have the following characteristics, they are most likely to be successful:[27]

- *Anonymity.* In good systems, feedback is anonymous and confidential. When such is the case, raters are more likely to provide honest information regarding performance, particularly when subordinates are providing information about superiors.
- *Observation of employee performance.* Only those with good knowledge and first-hand experience with the person being rated should participate in the process. There is no point in asking for performance feedback from people who are not able to observe performance.
- *Feedback interpretation.* Good systems allow the person being rated to discuss the feedback received with a person interested in the employee's development. In most cases, feedback is discussed with the direct supervisor. In other cases, the discussion can involve a representative of the HR department or a superior to whom the person does not report directly.
- *Follow-up.* The information gathered has little value if there is no follow-up action. Once feedback is received, it is essential that a developmental plan is created right away.
- *Used for developmental purposes only (at least initially).* When 360-degree feedback systems are used for administrative purposes such as promotions and compensation, raters are likely to distort the information provided. Make it clear that the purpose of the system is developmental and developmental only. Initially, the information collected should not be used for making reward allocations or any other administrative decisions. However, the system may be used for administrative purposes after it has been in place for some time—approximately two years or so.
- *Avoidance of survey fatigue.* Survey fatigue can be avoided if individuals are not asked to rate too many employees at the same time. For example, data collection can be staggered so that not all surveys are distributed at the same time.
- *Emphasis on behaviors.* Although systems can include feedback on both behaviors (competencies) and results, it is better to emphasize behaviors. Focusing on behaviors can lead to the identification of concrete actions that the person being rated can take to improve performance.
- *Raters go beyond ratings.* In addition to providing scores on the various dimensions, raters should provide written descriptive feedback that gives detailed and constructive comments on how to improve performance. It is helpful if this information also includes specific examples that help support the ratings and recommendations provided.
- *Raters are trained.* As in the case of providing evaluations for administrative purposes, raters should be trained. Mainly, this includes skills to discriminate good from poor performance and how to provide feedback in a constructive manner.

BOX 3

360-degree Feedback at AAH Pharmaceuticals

AAH Pharmaceuticals (AAH) (http://www.aah.com) utilizes a 360-degree feedback system that includes several characteristics of a good system. The company, which employs 3,800 people, is a wholesaler of pharmaceuticals, providing medical products and services in the United Kingdom. AAH, with the help of professional consultants, found the process helpful in providing feedback and useful information for development planning. To help ease employee concern, the company clearly outlined for employees that development planning and feedback were the only purposes of the instrument, and information would not be used for any other purpose. Employees were also given the option of sharing information with supervisors. The system included gathering performance ratings from several sources through an automated online system of questionnaires and ensuring that information was anonymous and confidential. After the results were obtained, participants attended a one-day meeting about the results away from the office that included one-on-one interpretation and discussion with the consultant to initiate a development plan. Six-month follow-up meetings were held to review progress toward developmental objectives. AAH found the process to be successful with a first group of managers who went through the process and made plans for a broad rollout of the program for more employees to take advantage of developmental opportunities. In summary, the system utilized by AAH provides an example of several of the components of a successful 360-degree feedback instrument.[28]

Table 5 includes a summarized list of characteristics of good 360-degree feedback systems. Consider the Compass system, which is offered by Right Management Consultants (www.right.com). This 360-degree feedback tool has many of the ideal characteristics found in Table 5. Compass is a tool based on leadership competencies. It allows raters to assess how well the leader executes each of the behaviors associated with various competencies such as "communication." The survey raters are anonymous. Right Management Consultants offers tailored feedback programs in which coaching is given in individual or group sessions to help interpret the information collected. Right can also certify internal organizational employees to give the feedback.

TABLE 5	Characteristics of a Good 360-Degree Feedback System

Anonymity
Observation of employee performance
Feedback interpretation
Follow-up
Used for developmental purposes only (at least initially)
Avoidance of survey fatigue
Emphasis on behaviors
Raters go beyond ratings
Raters are trained

After the assessment, a developmental plan is constructed, based on each individual's strengths and weaknesses. Furthermore, an online leadership developmental suite is available that includes a self-initiated online 6-month and 12-month follow-up. Given the availability of Compass and other systems such as those described in Table 3, there is little excuse to implement a system that does not include most of the characteristics listed in Table 5.

Summary Points

- Personal developmental plans are a key component of a performance management system because they specify courses of action to be taken to improve performance. A performance management system that lacks information about how to improve performance will not help employees learn skills beyond what they know and use already. In a nutshell, a good developmental plan allows employees to answer the following three questions: How can I continually learn and grow in the next year? How can I do better in the future? How can I avoid performance problems faced in the past?

- Developmental plans focus on both the short term and the long term. Specifically, developmental plans address how to improve performance in the current job, how to sustain good levels of performance in the current job, and how to prepare employees for future advancement. In addition, developmental plans provide employees with growth opportunities so that, even if advancement within the organization is not clear, employees are able to enrich their daily work experiences.

- Good developmental plans include a description of the specific steps to be taken and specific developmental objectives. A good plan includes information about (1) developmental objectives, (2) how the new skills or knowledge will be acquired, (3) a time line regarding the acquisition of the new skills or knowledge, and (4) standards and measures that will be used to assess whether the objectives have been achieved. Learning objectives should be designed to take into account both the needs of the individual and those of the organization.

- Developmental objectives can be achieved by one or more of the following activities: (1) on-the-job training, (2) courses, (3) self-guided reading, (4) mentoring, (5) attending a conference, (6) getting a degree, (7) job rotation, (8) temporary assignments, and (9) membership or leadership role in professional or trade organizations. Developmental activities for specific objectives are chosen by the employee and his or her direct supervisor. This choice is guided by taking into account the employee's learning preferences, the developmental objective in question, and the organization's available resources.

- The direct supervisor has a key role in helping the employee define the scope of the developmental plan and in explaining the relationship between the developmental objectives and strategic priorities for the unit and the organization. The direct supervisor also has direct responsibility for checking on the employee's progress toward achieving the developmental objectives and providing resources so that the employee will be able to engage in the appropriate activities (e.g., courses, mentoring).

Also, supervisors can help the employee uncover the factors that lead to achievement and job satisfaction by conducting feedforward interviews. Supervisors must reinforce an employee's accomplishments toward completing a developmental plan so that the employee remains motivated. Finally, supervisors themselves must be motivated to perform all these functions in support of their employees' developmental plans. To do so, supervisors' performance regarding how well they help their employees develop should be measured and rewarded appropriately.

- 360-degree feedback systems are tools that help employees build new skills and improve their performance in general by gathering and analyzing performance information from several sources, including peers, superiors, subordinates, and oneself. Performance information gathered from oneself is compared to information gathered by other sources to perform a gap analysis showing discrepancies between how one sees one's own performance in relation to how others see one's performance. These types of systems are also used to identify performance dimensions for which all, or most, performance information sources agree there is little or substantial room for improvement. Accordingly, this information can be used in creating a developmental plan.

- Many organizations implement 360-degree feedback systems electronically because doing so facilitates data collection and analysis. Many vendors offer systems that can be implemented online. Some systems are comprehensive and include rater training, data analysis, and detailed feedback reports for those evaluated.

- The implementation of 360-degree feedback systems can produce many benefits including (1) decreased possibility of biases, (2) increased awareness of performance expectations, (3) increased commitment to improve, (4) improved self-perceptions of performance, (5) improved performance, (6) reduction of undiscussables, and (7) increased career control on the part of employees.

- In spite of the many advantages associated with implementing 360-degree feedback systems, there are some risks involved. For example, negative feedback can hurt an employee's feelings; individuals may not be ready to receive such feedback and may therefore not participate willingly; anonymity may be compromised and therefore information may be distorted; and raters may be overloaded with forms to fill out. These risks, and the associated failure of the system, are particularly high when the organization does not value participation in decision making; there is little cooperation among employees; there is favoritism; employees do not value the opinion of others (i.e., peers, subordinates); decisions are based on hearsay; and/or employees are not trusted to get the job done.

- There are some features that will enhance the success rate of a 360-degree feedback system. These features include the following: there is anonymity; raters have firsthand knowledge of the performance of the person being evaluated; feedback is interpreted by a person interested in the development of the person evaluated; there is follow-up after receiving feedback; the system is used for development purposes only; raters do not become fatigued; there is an emphasis on behaviors instead of results; raters provide information beyond performance ratings only; and raters are trained. The presence of these characteristics is likely to lead to the successful design and implementation of the system.

CASE STUDY 1

Developmental Plan Form at Old Dominion University

Consider the following developmental plan form used for employees at Old Dominion University in Norfolk, Virginia.[29]

What are some positive features of this form? What are some features that could be improved? ■

CONFIDENTIAL

OLD DOMINION UNIVERSITY/221

EMPLOYEE WORK PROFILE

PERFORMANCE PLANNING & EVALUATION

> Parts V, VI, VII, VIII, and X are written or reviewed by the supervisor and discussed with the employee at the end of the evaluation cycle.

The following pages are printed separate remainder of the EWP because they contain confidential employee information.

Part III – Employee DevelopmentPosition Identification Information

26. Position Number:	27. Department:
28. Employee Name:	29. Social Security or Employee ID Number.

Part IV – Employee Development Plan

30. Professional development goals:

31. Steps to be taken by the supervisor to assist employee to enhance job performance and in furthering professional development:

32. Steps to be taken by the employee toward enhancing job performance and in furthering professional development:

CASE STUDY 2

Evaluation of a 360-degree Feedback System Demo

Visit Hr-survey.com and click on the following link to see the demo: http://hr-survey.com/360Feedback.htm. Please view the demo questionnaire and results. Then, answer the following questions:

1. What are the good features of this system?
2. What are the features that could be improved? ■

CASE STUDY 3

Implementation of 360-degree Feedback System at Ridge Intellectual

When Ridge Intellectual, a graphics design firm, implemented 360-degree feedback in its organization two years ago, it was met with resistance and was eventually discontinued. Ron Bartlett, the president of Ridge Intellectual, had seen a demonstration by a 360-degree vendor at a trade conference and decided to use the system at Ridge. Subsequently, Bartlett worked with the consultant to implement the system. Specifically, he sent out a company-wide e-mail stating the reasons for changing to the new system, how the ratings collected using the new system would be linked to bonuses, and the importance of completing the online training course on the system. The consultants provided online rater training for those who were interested as well as links to documents describing how to observe, assess, and record performance behaviors. After the surveys were made available, individuals were encouraged to contact HR if they had any problems.

Based on the information here what could Ridge have done to implement the 360-degree feedback system more successfully? Please refer to the characteristics of a good system listed in Table 5 in answering this question. ■

CASE STUDY 4

Personal Developmental Plan at Brainstorm, Inc.—Part I

Cathy is a sales manager at Branstorm, Inc., a computer software training company that sells Microsoft, Novell, Corel, and Open Office training, located in Lehi, Utah. Some of Cathy's responsibilities are to complete annual performance evaluations with all of her subordinates and create individual developmental plans for these employees based on their performance evaluations. Recently, Jay, an inside sales representative and Cathy's subordinate, finished his first year's performance evaluation with Cathy. Cathy's performance evaluation of Jay's key competencies and key results is as follows:

Performance Appraisal Form

Key Competencies	Supervisor Comments	Score
Sales and Marketing: Demonstrate knowledge of principles and methods for showing, promoting, and selling products or services.	Could be more proficient with greater product knowledge. Needs greater understanding of the benefits of each of the products.	B–
Customer and Personal Service: Knowledge of principles and processes for providing high-quality customer and personal services.	Good verbal and sales skills most of the time. Had a couple occasions when customers felt like they weren't getting enough personal assistance with recently purchased product.	B+
Interpersonal Communication: Talking to others to convey information effectively as well as giving full attention to what other people are saying, taking time to understand the points being made, and asking questions as appropriate.	Very good. Always enthusiastic with customers and quickly develops a good rapport with new customers.	A–

(Continued)

(Continued)

Persuasion and Negotiation: Persuading others to change their minds or behavior. Bringing others together and trying to reconcile differences.	Adequate, but could be more direct and persuasive with customers.	B
Problem Sensitivity and Ethics: The ability to tell when something is wrong or is likely to go wrong, ethically or otherwise. It does not involve solving the problem, only recognizing there is a problem.	Excellent. Shown great ability to anticipate if contract negotiations are taking an unethical or unprofitable turn for the worse.	A
Key Results	**Supervisor Comments**	**Score**
Degree to which employee met monthly sales goals ($50,000 in sales revenue a month):	Adequate. Met sales goals 66% of the time in the last six months.	B
Degree to which employee met referral goals (10 referrals a month):	Needs improvement. Met referral goals 50% of the time in the last six months.	B-
Number of cold calls made monthly (250):	Excellent. Tirelessly exhibits persistence and hard work in reaching out to businesses.	A

Source: Adapted from an appraisal form developed by Boston College.

Place yourself in Cathy's shoes, and use the above performance evaluation to develop an individual developmental plan for Jay. Use the information provided in the chapter to build up the content of the developmental plan. ■

CASE STUDY 5

Personal Developmental Plan at Brainstorm, Inc.—Part II

Cathy, one of the Partners of Brainstorm, Inc., has been looking into developmental plans as a possible way of increasing the productivity and morale of the company's sales force. To help her in this project, Cathy has adapted a developmental plan form from a business magazine she has recently seen and asks you for feedback. Since Cathy is unfamiliar with the characteristics of good developmental plans, she is particularly interested in your critique of a developmental plan that she developed for a sales representative, Jay. Note: Brainstorm, Inc., may not be able to finance much in the way of outside learning; however, the company could provide some paid time off and may be able to negotiate some better rates for attending classes or conferences, based on various industry memberships.

1. How would you improve and/or change the following form and its contents?
2. Since there are only six employees in the company, how would you adapt the form to meet the needs of this small business? Provide an example. ■

Brainstorm, Inc., Developmental Plan

Updated: June 28, 2011

Name: Jay

Job Title/Job Code: Sales Representative

Department: Sales

Developmental Options

OJT (On-the-job Training)

Classes

Conferences

Online

Self-study

Job Rotation

Videos

Books

Temporary Assignment

Mentorship

Other (specify)

Description

Type of Development

When

How Long

Completed Hours (this Quarter)

Comments—Approximate Cost—Other

Objectives/

Evaluation

Current Quarter

Next Quarter

Current +2

Current +3

Primary Reviewer: Cathy

Education: High school graduate

Prior Training: Bachelor's degree in Sales and Marketing

Job History: 10 years of experience in sales. Two years of experience in software training sales.

Career Goals:

Next 1 year

Next 2 years

Next 3 years

Next 5 years—Become head of sales and lead sales trainer.

Source: Based on MIT Human Resources. (2011). Strategic Planning of Talent. Available online at http://hrweb.mit.edu/ctm/managers/ retaining-developing-workforce/development-planning. Retrieval date: September 7, 2011.

End Notes

1. Reyna, M., & Sims, R. R. (1995). A framework for individual management development in the public sector. *Public Personnel Management, 24*, 53–65.

2. Boswell, W. R., & Boudreau, J. W. (2000). Employee satisfaction with performance appraisals and appraisers: The role of perceived appraisal use. *Human Resource Development Quarterly, 11*, 283–299.

3. Ellis, K. (2004, December). Individual development plans: The building blocks of development. *Training, 41* , 20–25.

4. Tyler, K. (2004). One bad apple: Before the whole bunch spoils, train managers to deal with poor performance. *HR Magazine, 49*, 77–86.

5. Locke, E. A. (2004). Goal-setting theory and its applications to the world of business. *Academy of Management Executive, 18*, 124–125.

6. Latham, G. (2004). The motivational benefits of goal-setting. *Academy of Management Executive, 18*, 126–129.

7. Dunning, D. (2004). *TLC at work: Training, leading, coaching all types for star performance.* Palo Alto, CA: Davies-Black.

8. Kluger, A. N., & Nir, D. (2010). The feedforward interview. *Human Resource Management Review, 20*, 235–246.

9. Ellis, K. (2003). Developing for dollars. *Training, 40*, 34–38.

10. Garretson, C. (2005, January). Diageo distills IS Leaders. *Network World*, 42.

11. Morgeson, F. P., Mumford, T. V., & Campion, M. A. (2005). Coming full circle: Using research and practice to address 27 questions about 360-degree feedback programs. *Consulting Psychology Journal: Practice and Research, 57*, 196–209.

12. Brutus, S., London, M., & Martineau, J. (1999). The impact of 360-degree feedback on planning for career development. *Journal of Management Development, 18*, 676–693.

13. Toegel, G., & Conger, J. A. (2003). 360-degree assessment: Time for reinvention. *Academy of Management Learning & Education, 2*, 297–311.

14. Mone, E. M., & London, M. (2010). *Employee engagement through effective performance management.* New York: Routledge.

15. Becton, J. B., & Schraeder, M. (2004). Participant input into rater selection: Potential effects on the quality and acceptance of ratings in the context of 360-degree feedback. *Public Personnel Management, 33*, 23–32.

16. Stringer, R., & Cheloha, R. (2003). The power of a development plan. *Human Resource Planning, 26*, 10–17.

17. Frauenheim, E. (2006). Talent management software is bundling up. *Workforce Management, 85*, 35–35.

18. Luthans, F., & Peterson, S. J. (2003). 360-degree feedback with systematic coaching: Empirical analysis suggests a winning combination. *Human Resource Management, 42*, 243–256.

19. Bailey, C., & Austin, M. (2006). 360 degree feedback and developmental outcomes: The role of feedback characteristics, self-efficacy and importance of feedback dimensions to focal managers' current role. *International Journal of Selection and Assessment 14*, 51–66.

20. Smither, J. W., London, M., & Reilly, R. R. (2005). Does performance improve following multisource feedback? A theoretical model, meta-analysis, and review of empirical findings. *Personnel Psychology, 58*, 33–66.

21. Morgan, A., Cannan, K., & Cullinane, J. (2005). 360° feedback: A critical enquiry. *Personnel Review, 34*, 663–680.

22. Maurer, T. J., Barbeite, F. G., & Mitchell, D. R. (2002). Predictors of attitudes toward a 360-degree feedback system and involvement in post-feedback management development activity. *Journal of Occupational & Organizational Psychology, 75*, 87–107.

23. Maloney, R. Competency-based integrated HR systems Sonoco Products. DDI client successes. Available online at www.ddiworld.com. Retrieval date: May 1, 2011.

24. Frisch, M. H. (2001). Going around in circles with "360" tools: Have they grown too popular for their own good? *Human Resource Planning, 24*, 7–8.

25. Pfau, B., & Kay, I. (2002). Does 360-degree feedback negatively affect company performance? *HR Magazine, 47*, 54–59.

26. Peiperl, M. A. (2001, January). Getting 360 degree feedback right. *Harvard Business Review, 79,* 147.

27. Some of these recommendations are adapted from A. S. DeNisi and A. N. Kluger, "Feedback Effectiveness: Can 360-degree Appraisals Be Improved?" *Academy of Management Executive, 14*(2000): 129–139; and A. M. McCarthy and T. N. Garavan, "360° Feedback Process: Performance, Improvement and Employee Career Development," *Journal of European Industrial Training, 25*(2001): 5–32.

28. Towner, N. (2004, February). Turning appraisals 360 degrees. *Personnel Today,* 18. Available online at http://www.personeltoday.com/Articles/2004/02/17/22398/turning-appraisals-360-degrees.html. Retrieval date: May 1, 2011.

29. The EWP—Employee Development Plan. Available online at http://www.odu.edu/af/humanresources/performance/Performance%20Planning%20-%20Dream/EWP%-20-%20Part%203–4%20-%20Employee%20-Development%20Plan.htm. Retrieval date: May 1, 2011.

Performance Management Skills

From Chapter 9 of *Performance Management*, Third Edition. Herman Aguinis. Copyright © 2013 by Pearson Education, Inc. All rights reserved.

Performance Management Skills

A leader becomes complete only after giving something back.

—LAURENCE S. LYONS

LEARNING OBJECTIVES

By the end of this chapter, you will be able to do the following:

- Understand that managers need several key skills to manage the performance of their employees effectively, including skills regarding coaching, giving feedback, and conducting performance review meetings.

- Understand four guidelines that provide a framework for successful coaching including the importance of a good coaching relationship, the central role of the employee as the source and director of change, understanding employees as unique and whole, and realizing that the coach is the facilitator of the employee's growth.

- Define coaching, and describe its major functions, including giving advice, providing guidance and support, and enhancing employee confidence and competence.

- Identify behaviors that managers need to display to perform the various coaching functions.

- Understand that a manager's personality and behavioral preferences determine his or her coaching style.

- Understand your own coaching style and the need to adapt your coaching style to the situation and your subordinates' preferences.

- Describe the coaching process and its components including setting developmental goals, identifying developmental resources and strategies, implementing strategies, observing and documenting developmental behavior, and giving feedback.

- Understand the time, situational, and activity constraints involved in observing and documenting an employee's progress toward the achievement of developmental goals and good performance in general.

- Implement a communication plan and training programs that will minimize the impact of constraints present when observing and documenting performance.

- Describe the benefits of accurate documentation of an employee's developmental activities and performance.

- Implement several recommendations that will lead to documenting performance in a useful and constructive manner.

- Understand the purposes served by feedback on performance regarding the achievement of developmental goals and performance in general.

- Implement several recommendations that will lead to creating useful and constructive feedback systems.

- Understand why people do not feel comfortable giving negative feedback, and recognize what happens when managers refuse to give negative feedback.

- Implement a disciplinary or termination process if an employee does not overcome performance problems over time.

- Understand the various purposes served by performance review meetings and the various types of meetings that can be conducted.

- Understand the signs of employee defensiveness, implement suggestions to minimize employee defensiveness before a performance review meeting takes place, and deal with defensiveness during the performance review meeting.

A performance management system can be used to help employees develop and improve their performance and to address more long-term career goals and aspirations. Performance management systems are not likely to help employees develop and improve their performance if managers do not have the necessary skills to help employees accomplish these goals. Such skills include being able to serve as coaches, to observe and document performance accurately, to give both positive and negative feedback, and to conduct useful and constructive performance review discussions. Unfortunately, these skills seem to be in short supply; hence, this chapter addresses each of these topics. For example, a survey conducted by the consulting firm Watson Wyatt found that, in about 50% of the organizations included in the study, managers are only slightly effective in helping underperforming employees improve their performance.[1] This lack of supervisory skills is not unique to the United States. For example, a study including more than 100 organizations in Barbados found that, overall, employees are not satisfied with their performance management system and some of the culprits are "poor management of the process" and "low levels of supervisory motivation."[2] Let's begin with the first of these issues: coaching.

1 COACHING

Coaching is a collaborative, ongoing process in which the manager interacts with his or her employees and takes an active role and interest in their performance.[3] In general, coaching involves directing, motivating, and rewarding employee behavior. Coaching is a day-to-day function that involves observing performance, complimenting good work, and helping to correct and improve any performance that does not meet expectations and standards. Coaching is also concerned with long-term performance and involves ensuring that the developmental plan is being achieved. Being a coach thus is similar to serving as a consultant and, for coaching to be successful, a coach must establish a helping relationship.[4] Establishing this helping and trusting relationship is particularly important when the supervisor and subordinate do not share similar cultural backgrounds, as is often the case with expatriates or when implementing global performance management systems.[5] In such situations, a helping and trusting relationship allows for what is labeled *cultural transvergence* in performance management, which means that cultural differences are discussed openly, and alternate practices, which enhance individual and team performance, are implemented.

Coaching is a pervasive organizational activity and, since the mid-1990s, there has been an explosion of interest in coaching. Specifically, the first scholarly article on coaching was published in 1955, and between then and December 2005, 393 articles have been published on the topic.[6] Increased interest in recent years is evidenced by the fact that, of the total of 393 articles, 318 have been published since 1996. Although many theories on coaching exist, there are four guiding principles that provide a good framework for understanding successful coaching:[7]

1. *A good coaching relationship is essential.* For coaching to work, it is imperative that the relationship between the coach and the employee be trusting and collaborative. As noted by Farr and Jacobs, the "collective trust" of all stakeholders in the process is necessary.[8] To achieve this type of relationship, first the coach must listen in order to understand. In other words, the coach needs to try to walk in the employee's shoes and view the job and organization from his or her perspective. Second, the coach needs to search for positive aspects of the employee because this is likely to lead to a better understanding and acceptance of the employee. Third, the coach needs to understand that coaching is not something done *to* the employee but done *with* the employee. Overall, the manager needs to coach with empathy and compassion. Such compassionate coaching will help develop a good relationship with the employee. In addition, there is an important personal benefit for the coach. This type of compassionate coaching has the potential to serve as an antidote to the chronic stress experienced by many managers.[9] It has been argued that this type of coaching can ameliorate stress because the experience of compassion elicits responses within the human body that arouse the parasympathetic nervous system (PSNS), which can help mitigate stress.

2. *The employee is the source and director of change.* The coach must understand that the employee is the source of change and self-growth. After all, the purpose of coaching is to change employee behavior and set a direction for what the employee will do differently in the future.[10] This type of change will not happen if the employee is not in the driver's seat. Accordingly, the coach needs to facilitate the employee's setting the agenda, goals, and direction.

3. *The employee is whole and unique.* The coach must understand that each employee is a unique individual with several job-related and job-unrelated identities (e.g., computer network specialist, father, skier) and a unique personal history. The coach must try to create a whole, complete, and rich picture of the

employee. It will be beneficial if the coach has knowledge of the employee's life and can help the employee connect his life and work experiences in meaningful ways.

4. *The coach is the facilitator of the employee's growth.* The coach's main role is one of facilitation. A coach must direct the process and help with the content (e.g., of a developmental plan) but not take control of these issues. The coach needs to maintain an attitude of exploration; help expand the employee's awareness of strengths, resources, and challenges; and facilitate goal setting.

In more specific terms, coaching involves the following functions:[11]

- Giving *advice* to help employees improve their performance. In other words, coaching involves not only describing what needs to be done but also how things need to be done. Coaching is concerned with both results and behaviors.

- Providing employees with *guidance* so that employees can develop their skills and knowledge appropriately. Coaching involves providing information both about the skills and knowledge that are required to do the work correctly and information about how the employee can acquire these skills and knowledge.

- Providing employees *support* and being there only when the manager is needed. Coaching involves being there when the employee needs help, but it also involves not monitoring and controlling an employee's every move. In the end, coaching is

---

BOX 1

Taking Coaching Seriously at Becton, Dickinson, and Company

A coaching culture and leadership development are viewed as competitive strengths at Becton, Dickinson, and Company (BD, http://www.bd.com). The U.S.-based company manufactures and sells medical supplies, devices, laboratory instruments, antibodies, reagents, and diagnostic products to health-care organizations, clinical laboratories, private industry, and the public. The coaching culture at BD includes the following points, as noted by Joseph Toto, the company's director of leadership development and learning:

1. We place high expectations on corporate leaders to model coaching as a productive and effective way to improve performance.
2. We expect leaders at all management levels to be coached as well as to coach the development of others.
3. We establish coaching as a norm. Leaders must view coaching and development as some of the key responsibilities and deliverables in their roles.

Part of the company's training program includes developing skills through peer coaching and building management skills through peer interaction, support, and guidance. The training sessions emphasize several skills, including listening, asking facilitating and open-ended questions, sharing experiences, and challenging assumptions or discussing actions that might not be productive in the view of the coach. Training also involves self-assessment of strengths and weaknesses and identifying behaviors that would assist leaders in any given circumstance in which they might find themselves as managers in the company. In summary, BD has utilized training programs to develop and reinforce a coaching culture. This culture is credited with developing leaders to provide direction to others in a constantly changing business environment.[12]

about facilitation. The responsibility for improving performance ultimately rests on the shoulders of the employee.

- Giving employees *confidence* that will enable them to enhance their performance continuously and to increase their sense of responsibility for managing their own performance. Coaching involves giving positive feedback that allows employees to feel confident about what they do, but it also involves giving feedback on things that can be improved.
- Helping employees gain greater *competence* by guiding them toward acquiring more knowledge and sharpening the skills that can prepare them for more complex tasks and higher-level positions. Coaching involves a consideration of both short-term and long-term objectives, including how the employee can benefit from acquiring new skills and knowledge that could be useful in future positions and in novel tasks.

Based on this list of the various functions of coaching, it is evident that coaching requires a lot of effort from the managers. For example, consider the case of NCCI Holdings, Inc., a company based in Boca Raton, Florida, that manages the largest database of workers' compensation insurance information in the United States (www.ncci.com). NCCI analyzes industry trends, prepares workers' compensation insurance rate recommendations, assists in pricing proposed legislation, and provides a variety of data products to maintain a healthy workers' compensation system and reduce the frequency of employee injuries. At NCCI Holdings, supervisors undergo extensive coaching training, including learning how to listen and how to be empathic. Managers also attend monthly roundtables where they can learn from one other's coaching experiences. At these roundtables, managers can solicit feedback from other managers regarding their own coaching performance.[13]

Coaching helps turn feedback into results. For this to happen, coaches need to engage in the following:

- *Establish development objectives.* The manager works jointly with the employees in creating the developmental plan and its objectives.
- *Communicate effectively.* The manager maintains regular and clear communication with employees about their performance, including both behaviors and results.
- *Motivate employees.* Managers must reward positive performance. When positive performance is rewarded, employees are motivated to repeat the same level of positive performance in the future.
- *Document performance.* Managers observe employee behaviors and results. Evidence must be gathered regarding instances of good and poor performance.
- *Give feedback.* Managers measure employee performance and progress toward goals. They praise good performance and point out instances of substandard performance. Managers also help employees avoid poor performance in the future.
- *Diagnose performance problems.* Managers must listen to employees and gather information to determine whether performance deficiencies are the result of a lack of knowledge and skills, abilities, or motivation or whether they stem from situational factors beyond the control of the employee. Diagnosing performance problems is important because such a diagnosis dictates whether the course of action should be, for example, providing the employee with resources so that she can

acquire more knowledge and skills or addressing contextual issues that may be beyond the control of the employee (e.g., the employee is usually late in delivering the product because he receives the parts too late).

- *Develop employees.* Managers provide financial support and resources for employee development (e.g., funding training, allowing time away from the job for developmental activities) by helping employees plan for the future and by giving challenging assignments that force employees to learn new things.

Not all coaches perform all the coaching functions by engaging in all of the behaviors described here. Managers who do so, of course, are highly effective. In fact, some have become legendary leaders. Consider Table 1, which summarizes the critical functions served by coaching and the behaviors coaches used to perform these functions. For example, take the case of Jack Welch who was extremely dedicated to developing his employees by engaging in several of the coaching behaviors described here when he was CEO of General Electric (GE).[14] To get involved with his employees, Welch spoke during a class held at a three-week developmental course for GE's high-potential managers. Over the course of his career, he attended more than 750 of these classes, engaging over 15,000 GE managers and executives. During these presentations, he expected to answer hard questions, and he communicated honestly and candidly with his employees. After the class, he invited all the participants to talk with him after the course. In addition to attending these sessions, he held meetings with his top 500 executives every January. Although Welch did not engage in formal coaching, he used the opportunities to communicate his expectations and receive feedback from the various business groups at GE.

Welch also conducted formal performance reviews in which he engaged in several of the behaviors included in Table 1, including establishing developmental objectives, motivating employees, documenting performance, giving feedback, and diagnosing performance problems. He set performance targets and monitored them throughout the year. Each year the operating heads of GE's 12 businesses received individual two-page, handwritten notes about their performance. Welch attached the previous year's comments to the new reviews with comments in the margin about the progress made by the individual managers toward his goal or the work that he still needed to do to reach the goal. Then, he distributed bonuses and reiterated the goals for the upcoming year. This process cascaded throughout the

TABLE 1 Coaching	
Major Functions	**Key Behaviors**
Give advice	Establish developmental objectives
Provide guidance	Communicate effectively
Give support	Motivate employees
Give confidence	Document performance
Promote greater competence	Give feedback
	Diagnose performance problems
	Develop employees

organization, as other operating heads engaged in the same performance review discussions with their subordinates.

Another example of Welch's coaching behaviors occurred after he had heard customer complaints about a specific product. Welch charged the manager of the division with improving the productivity of that product fourfold. The manager sent Welch detailed weekly reports over the course of the next four years. Welch would send the reports back every three or four weeks with comments congratulating successes or pointing out areas in which the manager needed to improve. The manager stated that the fact that the CEO took the time to read his reports each week and send back comments motivated him to reach the lofty goal that Welch had set for him.

In addition to this, Jack Welch took the time to recognize hourly workers and managers who impressed him. For example, after one high-ranking leader turned down a promotion and transfer because he did not want his daughter to change schools, Welch sent him a personal note stating that he admired the man for many reasons and that he appreciated his decision to put his family first. The employee explained later that this incident proved that Welch cared about him both as a person and as an employee.

In short, Jack Welch was a legendary leader who developed his employees by setting expectations, communicating clearly, documenting and diagnosing performance, motivating and rewarding his employees, and taking an interest in their personal development. In fact, he engaged in virtually all the behaviors and performed most of the coaching functions listed in Table 1. How does Jack Welch compare to the CEO of your current company or to a CEO you have known or heard about?

We can see that Welch was an extremely effective coach. In general, however, how do we know whether a manager is doing a good job of coaching her employees? From a results point of view, we could simply measure how many of a manager's employees go on to become successful on their own. But, as in the case of evaluating performance in general, we should also consider behaviors in evaluating coaching performance. Consider the good coach questionnaire included in Table 2. If you are or have been in a management position, answer the questions about yourself; otherwise, think about your current or latest supervisor or someone you know. To how many of these questions can you answer "yes"? To how many would you answer "no"? Overall, given your responses, what is the evaluation of this person (yourself or someone else) as a coach from a behavioral point of view?

TABLE 2 The Good Coach Questionnaire

1. Do you listen to your employees?
2. Do you understand the individual needs of your employees?
3. Do you encourage employees to express their feelings openly?
4. Do you provide your employees with tangible and intangible support for development?
5. Do your employees know your expectations about their performance?
6. Do you encourage open and honest discussions and problem solving?
7. Do you help your employees create action plans that will solve problems and create changes when needed?
8. Do you help your employees explore potential areas of growth and development?

---

2 COACHING STYLES

A manager's personality and behavioral preferences are more likely to influence his or her coaching style. There are four main coaching styles: driver, persuader, amiable, and analyzer. First, coaches can adopt a driving style in which they tell the employee being coached what to do. Assume that the coach wants to provide guidance regarding how to deal with a customer. In this situation, the preference for a *driver* is to say to the employee, "You must talk to the customer in *this* way." Such coaches are assertive, speak quickly and often firmly, usually talk about tasks and facts, are not very expressive, and expose a narrow range of personal feelings to others. Second, coaches can use a persuading style in which they try to sell what they want the employee to do. Someone who is a *persuader* would try to explain to the employee why it is beneficial for the organization as well as for the employee himself to talk to a customer in a specific way. Like drivers, persuaders are assertive, but they tend to use expansive body gestures, talk more about people and relationships, and expose others to a broad range of personal feelings. Third, other coaches may adopt an *amiable* style and want everyone to be happy. Such coaches are likely to be more subjective than objective and direct employees to talk to customers in a certain way because it "feels" like the right thing to do or because the employee feels it is the right way to do it. Such coaches tend not to be very assertive and to speak deliberately and pause often, seldom interrupt others, and make many conditional statements. Finally, coaches may have a preference for analyzing performance in a logical and systematic way and then follow rules and procedures when providing a recommendation. To use the same example, such *analyzer* coaches may tell employees to talk to a customer in a specific way "because this is what the manual says." Analyzers, then, are not very assertive but, like drivers, are likely to talk about tasks and facts rather than personal feelings.

Which of these four styles is best? Are drivers, persuaders, amiable coaches, or analyzers most effective? The answer is that no style is necessarily superior to the others. Good coaching should be seen as a learning opportunity and as an opportunity to set clear goals and delegate action. Coaching involves sometimes providing direction, sometimes persuading employees how to do things a certain way, sometimes showing empathy and creating positive effects, and sometimes paying close attention to established rules and procedures. One thing is for sure, however: an exclusive emphasis on one of these four styles is not likely to help employees develop and grow. Ineffective coaches stick to one style only and cannot adapt to use any of the other styles. On the other hand, adaptive coaches who are able to adjust their style according to an employee's needs are most effective. In fact, 56% of participants in a survey of employees who had a coach at work reported that coaching was not helping them because there was a mismatch between coaching style and employee need.[15] In sum, a combination of styles is needed.

3 COACHING PROCESS

The coaching process is shown in Figure 1. We have already discussed many of the components of this process in previous chapters. The first step involves setting developmental goals. These developmental goals are a key component of the developmental plan. These goals must be reasonable, attainable, and derived from a

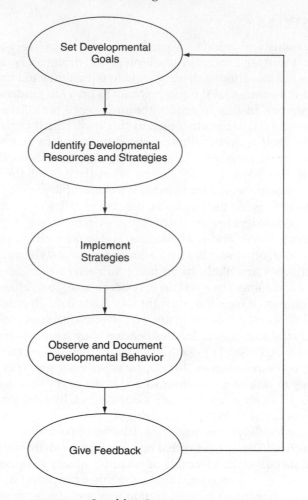

FIGURE 1 Coaching Process

careful analysis of the areas in which an employee needs to improve. In addition, goals should take into account both short- and long-term career objectives.

The second step in the coaching process is to identify resources and strategies that will help the employee achieve the developmental goals. These can include on-the-job training, attending courses, self-guided reading, mentoring, attending a conference, getting a degree, job rotation, a temporary assignment, and membership or a leadership role in a professional or trade organization.

The third step involves implementing the strategies that will allow the employee to achieve the developmental goals. For example, the employee may begin her job rotation plan or take a course online.

The next step in the process is to collect and evaluate data to assess the extent to which each of the developmental goals has been achieved. Finally, the coach provides feedback to the employee, and, based on the extent to which each of the goals has been achieved, the developmental goals are revised, and the entire process begins again.

BOX 2

Training Coaches at Hallmark

Hallmark (http://www.hallmark.com) sought to improve management communications with employees and initiated a training program that has been well received and viewed as a strategic benefit to the company. U.S.-based Hallmark is a retailer and wholesaler of greeting cards, stationery, flowers, and gifts with operations in the United States and Great Britain. The company initiated training to help managers become more effective in communications, enhancing their ability to provide leadership and coaching to employees. The training program sought to provide skill development in increasing two-way communication, with a greater frequency of communication and increased interaction of managers with employees. Training sessions included self-assessment, small group role-playing, and viewing video clips to enhance understanding of the role of communication. Engagement training focused on gaining the trust of employees as well as their involvement and ownership in business outcomes. Follow-up resources were also made available for managers to continue to improve their leadership competency. Following the training in this area, managers gave positive feedback, and employee surveys have shown that employee engagement has increased at all levels of the organization. In summary, Hallmark provides an example of a company that made a commitment to leadership and coaching through training managers and focusing on communication skills that has translated into a more engaged workforce and enhanced strategic business results.[16]

The coaching model includes developmental goals and developmental resources and strategies. Let's discuss two remaining components of the coaching model: observing and documenting developmental behavior data and giving feedback.

3.1 Observation and Documentation of Developmental Behavior and Outcomes

People may make intentional and unintentional errors Performance. Managers may make similar errors in observing and evaluating behaviors related to developmental goals. For example, a manager might make a halo error by assuming that if an employee does a good job at working toward one developmental goal (e.g., improving her typing skills), she is also doing a good job at working toward a different developmental goal (e.g., improving customer service). As is the case for performance in general, it is important to observe and document behaviors specifically related to developmental activities. Documentation can include memos, letters, e-mail messages, handwritten notes, comments, observations, descriptions, and evaluations provided by colleagues.[17] Although the discussion presented in this section is specifically related to behaviors regarding developmental activities, it can be easily generalized to behaviors related to performance in general. In other words, the following discussion applies to the observation of all performance behaviors, not just those displayed while working toward achieving developmental goals.

Observing an employee's progress in achieving developmental goals is not as easy as it may seem. Consider the following constraints that managers might experience in attempting to observe an employee's performance regarding developmental activities:

- *Time constraints.* Managers may be too busy to gather and document information about an employee's progress toward his developmental goals. Consequently, too much time may elapse between the assignment of the activity and the manager's checking on the employee's progress.

- *Situational constraints.*   Managers are often unable to observe employees as they engage in developmental activities and therefore may not have firsthand knowledge about their performance. For example, managers do not observe the extent to which an employee enrolled in an online course is an active participant and contributor or is a passive learner.
- *Activity constraints.*   When the developmental activity is highly unstructured, such as an employee's reading a book, the manager may have to wait until the activity is completed to assess whether the activity has been beneficial.

How can we address these constraints and make sure that a manager will be able to observe and evaluate an employee's performance regarding developmental activities? One recommendation is a good communication plan to explain the benefits of implementing a developmental plan effectively. This helps managers accept the plan. Also, managers should be trained so that they minimize errors (i.e., rater error training), share notions of what it means to complete developmental activities successfully (i.e., frame-of-reference training), observe performance accurately (i.e., behavioral observation training), and are confident and comfortable in managing employees' developmental activities (i.e., self-leadership training). Finally, we need to understand the forces that motivate managers to invest time and effort or not in the development of their employees. In other words, what does the manager gain if her employee's developmental activities are supervised appropriately?

The importance of documenting an employee's progress toward the achievement of developmental goals cannot be overemphasized. Similarly, it is critical to document employee performance in general. Why is this so important? Consider the following reasons:

- *Minimize cognitive load.*   Observing and evaluating developmental activities, and performance in general, is a complex cognitive task. Thus, documentation helps prevent memory-related errors.
- *Create trust.*   When documentation exists to support evaluations, there is no mystery regarding the outcomes. This, in turn, promotes trust and acceptance of decisions based on the evaluation provided.
- *Plan for the future.*   Documenting developmental activities and their outcomes enables discussion about specific facts instead of assumptions and hearsay. A careful examination of these facts permits better planning of developmental activities for the future.
- *Provide legal protection.*   Specific laws prohibit discrimination against members of various classes (e.g., sex or religion) in how developmental activities are allocated. For example, it is prohibited to provide male employees with better developmental opportunities than female employees. In addition, some court rulings have determined that employees working under contract may challenge a dismissal. Thus, keeping accurate records of what developmental activities employees have completed and with what degree of success as well as performance in general provides a good line of defense in case of litigation based on discrimination or wrongful termination.

The importance of keeping thorough performance documentation and taking actions consistent with this documentation is illustrated by the outcome of several cases. In one such case, John E. Cleverly, an employee at Western Electric Co., was discharged after 14 years of good service.[18] Western Electric was found guilty of age discrimination, and Cleverly was awarded back pay because the documentation indicated that Cleverly had been given adequate performance ratings and increases to his salary over a course of 14 years. Upon his discharge, six months before his pension vested, Cleverly was informed that one reason for his discharge was to make room for younger employees. As illustrated by this case, documentation of performance should be taken seriously. In this case, the documentation available indicated the employee had a valid claim. In other cases, documentation could be used to discount charges of discrimination. If Cleverly had alleged age discrimination, but the company could show that his performance was deteriorating over time, then the company would have won the case.

What can managers do to document performance regarding developmental activities and performance in general in a useful and constructive way? Consider the following recommendations:[19]

- *Be specific.* Document specific events and outcomes. Avoid making general statements such as "He's lazy." Provide specific examples to illustrate your point, for example, "He turns in memos after deadlines at least once a month."
- *Use adjectives and adverbs sparingly.* The use of evaluative adjectives (e.g., good, poor) and adverbs (e.g., speedily, sometimes) may lead to ambiguous interpretations. In addition, it may not be clear whether the level of achievement has been average or outstanding.
- *Balance positives with negatives.* Document instances of both good and poor performance. Do not focus only on the positives or only on the negatives.
- *Focus on job-related information.* Focus on information that is job related and specifically related to the developmental activities and goals at hand.
- *Be comprehensive.* Include information on performance regarding all developmental goals and activities, and cover the entire review period as opposed to a shorter time period. Also, document the performance of all employees, not just those who are not achieving their developmental goals.
- *Standardize procedures.* Use the same method and format to document information for all employees.
- *Describe observable behavior.* Phrase your notes in behavioral terms and avoid statements that would imply subjective judgment or prejudice.

Obviously, not all managers do a good job of documenting performance about the accomplishment of developmental goals or performance in general. Table 3 includes a summarized list of recommendations to follow in the documentation process.

Now, consider the recommendations listed in Table 3 in evaluating the set of quotes appearing in Table 4 reportedly taken from actual employee performance evaluations in a large corporation in the United States.[20]

We can be sure that the employees at the receiving end of these quotes would not be very happy with them. It also goes without saying that this type of documentation

TABLE 3	Documentation of Performance and Performance in Developmental Activities: Some Recommendations

Be specific.

Use adjectives and adverbs sparingly.

Balance positives with negatives.

Focus on job-related information.

Be comprehensive.

Standardize procedures.

Describe observable behavior.

would be extremely detrimental to the performance management system. In fact, this organization would have serious problems beyond the scope of its performance evaluation system.

Now, let's turn to the final important component of the coaching process: giving feedback.

TABLE 4	Individual Quotes Taken from Actual Employee Performance Evaluations

Since my last report, this employee has reached rock bottom . . . and has started to dig.

I would not allow this employee to breed.

This employee is really not so much of a has-been, but more of a definitely won't be.

Works well when under constant supervision and cornered like a rat in a trap.

He would be out of his depth in a parking lot puddle.

He sets low personal standards and then consistently fails to achieve them.

This employee is depriving a village somewhere of an idiot.

This employee should go far, . . . and the sooner he starts, the better.

He's been working with glue too much.

He would argue with a signpost.

He has a knack for making strangers immediately detest him.

He brings a lot of joy whenever he leaves the room.

If you see two people talking and one looks bored . . . he's the other one.

Donated his brain to science before he was done using it.

Gates are down, the lights are flashing, but the train isn't coming.

If he were any more stupid, he'd have to be watered twice a week.

If you gave him a penny for his thoughts, you'd get change.

If you stand close enough to him, you can hear the ocean.

One neuron short of a synapse.

Some drink from the fountain of knowledge . . . he only gargled.

Takes him 2 hours to watch *60 Minutes*.

The wheel is turning, but the hamster is dead.

3.2 Giving Feedback

Giving feedback to an employee regarding her progress toward achieving her goals is a key component of the coaching process.[21] Feedback is information about past behavior that is given with the goal of improving future performance. Although "back" is part of feed*back*, giving feedback has both a past and a future component. This is why, when done properly, feedback can be relabeled feed *forward*.[22]

Feedback includes information about both positive and negative aspects of job performance and lets employees know how well they are doing with respect to meeting the established standards.[23] For example, the so-called 2+2 performance appraisal model for teachers includes peer teachers who observe each other perform in the classroom and then offer two compliments and two suggestions for improvement.[24] Feedback is important in the context of performance regarding development activities and goals. Our discussion of feedback, however, goes beyond that and includes feedback about performance in general. Feedback is not a magic bullet for performance improvement;[25] however, it serves several important purposes:

- *Helps build confidence.* Praising good performance builds employee confidence regarding future performance. It also lets employees know that their manager cares about them.
- *Develops competence.* Communicating clearly about what has been done right and how to do the work correctly is valuable information that helps employees become more competent and improve their performance. In addition, communicating clearly about what has not been done right and explaining what to do next time provide useful information so that past mistakes are not repeated.
- *Enhances involvement.* Receiving feedback and discussing performance issues allow employees to understand their roles in the unit and organization as a whole. This, in turn, helps employees become more involved in the unit and the organization.

Unfortunately, however, the mere presence of feedback, even if it is delivered correctly, does not necessarily mean that all of these purposes will be fulfilled. For example, a review of 131 studies that examined the effects of feedback on performance concluded that 38% of the feedback programs reviewed had a *negative* effect on performance.[26] In other words, in many cases, the implementation of feedback led to *lower* performance levels. This can happen when, for example, feedback does not include useful information or is not delivered in the right way. For example, feedback can have detrimental effects if it focuses on the employee as a whole as opposed to specific behaviors at work. This is precisely the case of a very successful woman who made many personal sacrifices such as not starting a family to reach the top echelons of the organizational hierarchy.[27] She received feedback that included information that she had failed to retain a valued client. The feedback was accurate and delivered in the correct manner; however, after receiving the feedback, she began to question her life choices in general instead of focusing on how to retain valued clients in the future. In this example, feedback was not instrumental in improving performance; instead, the feedback created self-doubt and questions about identity.

Although some feedback systems do not work well, the advantages of providing feedback generally outweigh any disadvantages. Also, consider the possible cost of *not* providing feedback. First, organizations would be depriving employees of a chance to improve their performance. Second, organizations might be stuck with chronic poor performance because employees did not recognize any performance problems and felt justified in continuing to perform at substandard levels. Finally, employees might develop inaccurate perceptions of how their performance is regarded by others.

Given that, overall, feedback systems are beneficial, what can we do to make the most of them? Consider the following suggestions to enhance feedback:[28]

- *Timeliness.*   Feedback should be delivered as close to the performance event as possible. For feedback to be most meaningful, it must be given immediately after the event.
- *Frequency.*   Feedback should be provided on an ongoing basis, daily if possible. If performance improvement is an ongoing activity, then feedback about performance should also be provided on an ongoing basis.
- *Specificity.*   Feedback should include specific work behaviors, results, and the situation in which these behaviors and results were observed.[29] Feedback is not about the employee and how the employee "is," but about behaviors and results and situations in which these behaviors and results occurred.
- *Verifiability.*   Feedback should include information that is verifiable and accurate. It should not be based on inferences or rumors. Using information that is verifiable leads to more accurate feedback and subsequent acceptance.
- *Consistency.*   Feedback should be consistent. In other words, information about specific aspects of performance should not vary unpredictably between overwhelming praise and harsh criticism.
- *Privacy.*   Feedback should be given in a place and at a time that prevent any potential embarrassment. This applies to both criticism and praise, because some employees, owing to personality or cultural background, may not wish to be rewarded in public.
- *Consequences.*   Feedback should include contextual information that allows the employee to understand the importance and consequences of the behaviors and results in question. For example, if an employee became frustrated and behaved inappropriately with an angry customer and the customer's complaint was not addressed satisfactorily, feedback should explain the impact of these behaviors (e.g., behaving inappropriately) and results for the organization (e.g., the customer's problem was not resolved, the customer was upset, the customer was not likely to give repeat business to the organization).
- *Description first, evaluation second.*   Feedback should first focus on describing behaviors and results rather than on evaluating and judging behaviors and results. It is better first to report what has been observed and, once there is agreement about what happened, to evaluate what has been observed. If evaluation takes place first, employees may become defensive and reject the feedback.
- *Performance continuum.*   Feedback should describe performance as a continuum, going from less to more in the case of good performance and from more to less in the case of poor performance. In other words, feedback should include information on how to display good performance behaviors more often and poor performance behaviors less often. Thus, performance is a matter of degree, and even the worst performer is likely to show nuggets of good performance that can be described as a starting point for a discussion on how to improve performance.

- *Pattern identification.* Feedback is most useful if it is about a pattern of poor performance rather than isolated events or mistakes. Identifying a pattern of poor performance also allows for a better understanding of the causes leading to poor performance.
- *Confidence in the employee.* Good feedback includes a statement that the manager has confidence that the employee will be able to improve her performance. It is important for the employee to hear this from the manager. This reinforces the idea that feedback is about performance and not the performer. Note, however, that this should be done only if the manager indeed believes the employee can improve her performance. In the case of a chronic poor performance, this type of information could be used out of context later if the employee is fired.
- *Advice and idea generation.* Feedback can include advice given by the supervisor about how to improve performance. In addition, however, the employee should play an active role in generating ideas about how to improve performance in the future.

Many of the above-mentioned recommendations are particularly useful when feedback is given to employees who score low on a personality trait labeled *core self-evaluation*, which is a combination of four traits: self-esteem (i.e., the degree to which an individual holds a favorable attitude toward himself), self-efficacy (i.e., the degree to which an individual believes he is capable of taking action and taking control over events), emotional stability (i.e., the degree to which an individual is *not* insecure, guilty, or timid), and locus of control (i.e., the degree to which an individual believes he can control events and outcomes in his live). Individuals with low core self-evaluations feel they are less able to deal with the world and, consequently, are overall less satisfied with their jobs and lives. Thus, supervisors need to be aware that feedback is likely to be received by individuals with low versus high core self-evaluations.[30] For example, low core self-evaluation employees may feel hurt and helpless after receiving negative feedback. Thus, the recommendations about "confidence in the employee" are particularly relevant. Similarly, the recommendations about "advice and idea generation" are also particularly helpful so that there is a clear course of action—rather than feelings of helplessness and lack of direction.

Consider the following vignette in which Andrea, a supervisor, has observed a specific performance event and provides feedback to her subordinate. Andrea is the manager of a small retail store with approximately five employees. With a small staff, Andrea looks for coaching opportunities on a weekly basis. Andrea is working with Matt today, and she has just witnessed him complete a customer sale. Matt did not follow several steps, however, that should be included at each sale and, because the store is now empty, Andrea decides it is a perfect opportunity for a coaching session.

ANDREA: Hey, Matt, that was great the way that you just assisted that customer in finding her correct size in the jeans. Thanks for taking the extra time to help her.

MATT: Thanks, Andrea, not a problem.

ANDREA: I would like to go over the sales transaction with you.

MATT: Sure.

ANDREA: After you helped the woman find her jeans, you promptly brought her over and rang her up. That was a good sale because those jeans were a full-priced item; however, you didn't complete all of the tasks associated with closing a sale. In the training last week, we discussed the importance of adding on additional sales, entering the customer's personal contact information in our computer, and letting them know about upcoming sales.

MATT: Yes, I just remembered us talking about that. When customers seem in a hurry, I feel bad about asking them additional questions.

ANDREA That's a very valid concern. Can we think of ways to increase the efficiency of adding these few steps into the sales transaction process so that you feel comfortable performing them in the future? I would like to help you do that because increasing the number of items you sell during each transaction could help you win the upcoming sales contests.

MATT: That would be great. I would really like some new ideas about talking to customers.

ANDREA: No problem; I know that you are a very capable salesperson. You have great customer service skills, and I think that you can improve your sales and possibly win one of the upcoming contests.

Andrea and Matt then generate ideas about how to improve Matt's performance.

In this vignette, Andrea demonstrated several of the feedback behaviors listed in Table 5. She was specific about the behaviors and results, the information was verifiable, and it was timely because the behavior had just occurred. In addition, since Andrea communicates her expectations on a weekly basis, the information she provides is consistent. Finally, she described the behavior first and then evaluated its effectiveness; she communicated confidence in Matt, and she offered to help him generate ideas about how to improve his effectiveness. On the other hand, Andrea left out several important things while coaching Matt. First, she did not communicate the consequences of his behavior (e.g., his failure to follow the procedures could hurt sales for the entire store). Although the vignette does not describe the idea generation portion of the feedback session, Andrea did not describe small behaviors that Matt could use to improve his

TABLE 5	Most Effective Feedback Should Be
Timely	
Frequent	
Specific	
Verifiable	
Consistent	
Private	
Consequential	
Descriptive first and evaluative second	
Related to a performance continuum	
Based on identifiable patterns of performance	
A confidence builder for employees	
A tool for generating advice and ideas	

performance. Finally, Andrea did not communicate to Matt whether this behavior was a one-time incident or whether it was a pattern that was affecting his overall work performance.

Overall, if Andrea continues to look for coaching opportunities with her employees, her relationship with her employees and their performance in the store will continue to improve. To be more effective, however, she may need to work on communicating the patterns of behavior that lead to poor performance and the consequences of continued poor performance.

3.2.1 PRAISE Good feedback includes information about both good and poor performance. Although most people are a lot more comfortable giving feedback on good performance than they are on poor performance, some guidelines must be followed when giving praise so that the feedback is useful in terms of future performance. First, praise should be sincere and given only when it is deserved. If praise is given repeatedly and when it is not deserved, employees are not able to see when a change in direction may be needed.[31] Second, praise should be about specific behaviors or results and be given within context so that employees know what they need to repeat in the future. For example, a manager can say the following:[32] "John, thanks for providing such excellent service to our client. Your efforts helped us renew our contract with them for another two years. It's these types of behaviors and results that our group needs to achieve our goal for this year. And, this is exactly what our company is all about: providing outstanding customer service." Third, in giving praise, managers should take their time and act pleased, rather than rush through the information looking embarrassed. Finally, avoid giving praise by referring to the absence of the negative, for example, "not bad" or "better than last time." Instead, praise should emphasize the positives and be phrased, for example, as "I like the way you did that" or "I admire how you did that."[33]

Consider the following vignette which illustrates how a manager might give praise to his employee.

After the successful completion of a three-month project at a large telecommunications company, Ken, the manager, wants to congratulate Mike on a job well done. Ken calls Mike into his office one day after the project is completed.

KEN: Thanks for stopping by Mike, and thank you for all of your hard work over the past three months. I know that I might not have congratulated you on every milestone you reached along the way, but I wanted to take the time to congratulate you now. Your organizational skills and ability to interact successfully with multiple departments led to the successful completion of the project on time and within budget.

MIKE: Thanks, Ken. I have really been putting extra effort into completing this project on time.

KEN: It shows, Mike, and I appreciate all of your hard work and dedication to this team and our department. Thanks again and congratulations on a great end to a long three months.

In this vignette, Ken delivered praise to Mike successfully and followed the recommendations provided earlier. He was sincere and made sure not to praise Mike too often so that when he did praise him, it was meaningful. He described how Mike's organizational and project management skills led to the successful completion of the project. Finally, Ken took his time in delivering the praise and made sure that Mike took the praise seriously.

3.2.2 NEGATIVE FEEDBACK   Negative feedback includes information that performance has fallen short of accepted standards. The goal of providing negative feedback is to help employees improve their performance in the future; it is not to punish, embarrass, or chastise them. It is important to give negative feedback when it is warranted because the consequences of not doing so can be detrimental for the organization as a whole. For example, Francie Dalton, president of Dalton Alliances, Inc., noted, "In organizations where management imposes no consequences for poor performance, high achievers will leave because they don't want to be where mediocrity is tolerated. But mediocre performers will remain because they know they're safe. The entire organizational culture, along with its reputation in the marketplace, can be affected by poor performers."[34]

In spite of the need to address poor performance, managers are usually not very comfortable providing negative feedback. Why is this so? Consider the following reasons:

- *Negative reactions and consequences.*   Managers may fear that employees will react negatively. Negative reactions can include being defensive and even becoming angry at the information received. In addition, managers may fear that the working relationship, or even friendship, with their subordinates may be affected adversely and that giving negative feedback can introduce elements of mistrust and annoyance.
- *Negative experiences in the past.*   Managers themselves may have received negative feedback at some point in their careers and have experienced firsthand how feelings can be hurt. Receiving negative feedback can be painful and upsetting, and managers may not want to put their subordinates in such a situation.
- *Playing "god."*   Managers may be reluctant to play the role of an all-knowing, judgmental god. They may feel that giving negative feedback puts them in that position.
- *Need for irrefutable and conclusive evidence.* Managers may not want to provide negative feedback until after they have been able to gather irrefutable and conclusive evidence about a performance problem. Because this task may be perceived as too onerous, managers may choose to skip giving negative feedback altogether.

What happens when managers avoid giving negative feedback and employees avoid seeking it? A *feedback gap* results, in which managers and employees mutually instigate and reinforce lack of communication which creates a vacuum of meaningful exchanges about poor performance.[35] A typical consequence of a feedback gap is that, in the absence of information to the contrary, the manager gives the employee the message that performance is adequate. When performance problems exist, they are likely to become more intense over time. For example, clients may be so dissatisfied with the service they are receiving that they may eventually choose to close their accounts and work instead with the competition. At that time, it becomes impossible for the manager to overlook the performance problem, and she has no choice but to deliver the negative feedback. At this stage of the process, however, feedback is delivered too late and often in a punitive fashion. Of course, feedback delivered so late in the process and in a punitive fashion is not likely to be helpful.

Alternatively, negative feedback is most useful when early coaching has been instrumental in identifying warning signs and the performance problem is still manageable. Negative feedback is also useful when it clarifies unwanted behaviors and consequences and focuses on behaviors that can be changed. There is no point in providing feedback on issues that are beyond the employee's control because there is not much she can do to improve the situation. In addition, employees are more likely to respond constructively to negative feedback when the manager is perceived as being trustworthy and making a genuine attempt to improve the employee's performance. In other words, the manager needs to be perceived as credible and as instrumental in improving the employee's performance in the future.[36] Finally, negative feedback is most likely to be accepted when it is given by a source who uses straight talk and not subtle pressure and when it is supported by hard data. The supervisor must control her emotions and stay calm. If managers follow these suggestions, it is more likely that employees will benefit from negative feedback, even if employees are not particularly open to receiving it.[37] Following these suggestions leads to what has been labeled "actionable feedback," meaning that such feedback will allow employees to respond in constructive ways and will lead to learning and performance improvement.[38]

Overall, regardless of whether the feedback session includes praise or a discussion of needed areas of improvement, it should provide answers to the following questions:[39,40]

1. How is your job going? Do you have what you need to do your job?
2. Are you adequately trained? Do you have the skills and tools you need to do your job?
3. What can be done to improve your and your unit's/organization's job/products/services?
4. How can you better serve your internal and external customers?

3.3 Disciplinary Process and Termination

In some cases, an employee may not respond to the feedback provided and may not make any improvements in terms of performance. In such cases, there is one intermediate step that can be taken before the employee enters a *formal disciplinary process* which involves a verbal warning, a written warning, and may lead to *termination*. The employee can be given a once-in-a-career *decision-making leave*.[41] This is a "day of contemplation" that is paid and allows the employee to stay home and decide whether working in this organization is what he or she really wants to do. This practice is based on adult learning theory, which holds individuals responsible for their actions. Unlike a formal disciplinary action, the decision-making leave does not affect employee pay. As noted by Tim Field, principal of a consulting firm in Los Angeles, California, "This element of holding people accountable without negatively impacting their personnel file or payroll tends to catch people off guard, because problem employees, like problem children, are often expecting negative attention for their bad behavior." How can the decision to grant an employee a decision-making leave be communicated?

Assuming this is a company policy and there is senior management support, you can communicate the leave as follows:[42]

> Lucy, as you know, you and I have met on several occasions to talk about your performance. In spite of these feedback sessions, I see that you are still having some difficulties with important tasks and projects. Consistent with my observations, I have received comments from some of your peers related to some performance deficiencies they have also noticed. I think that issuing a written warning would be counterproductive—I am concerned that it may decrease your motivation and do more harm than good. Instead, what I am going to do is to put you on what we call a "decision-making leave" for a day. This is a type of intervention that has worked very well with other individuals in your same position in the past. I want you to know that this is a once-in-a-career benefit that you should use to your advantage and I decided to do this because I truly believe that you are capable of improving your performance. It works like this. I am going to ask you to not come to the office tomorrow but you will be paid for that day, so you don't have to worry about your paycheck being affected. While you are away from the office tomorrow, I want you to give serious thought about whether you really want to work in this company. You and I will meet when you return to the office the day after tomorrow and I will ask you to tell me whether you'd rather resign and look for work elsewhere. I will understand and will be fully supportive if that is your decision. On the other hand, if when we meet you tell me you want to keep your job here, then I will give you an additional assignment on which I want you to work while you are away from the office tomorrow. Recall that you are being paid for the day, so here is what I want you to do. Please prepare a one-page letter addressed to me convincing me that you assume full and total responsibility for the performance issues we discussed during our feedback sessions. You will have to provide clear and specific arguments as well as describe a specific set of actions you will take to convince me that you will address the problems. I will keep the letter in a safe place but I am not planning on including it in your personnel file for now. To be clear, however, this letter is a personal commitment from you to me and our agreement is that if you don't stick to the terms of your letter, you will essentially fire yourself. This is a very important moment for you and for me, and it could be a turning point in your career development. Now that I have explained the process, I would like to hear any questions or comments you may have about this "decision-making leave day" that you will be taking tomorrow.

Using a decision-making leave as part of the performance management system can be a powerful tool to give problem employees an opportunity to improve their performance. However, this tool may not lead to the desired outcomes, and the employee may have to enter into a disciplinary process. Note that a demotion or transfer may be a more appropriate action when there is evidence that the employee is actually trying to overcome the performance deficiencies but is not able to do so. However, termination is the appropriate action when performance does not improve and the employee continues to make the same mistakes or fails to meet standards. Also, termination is the appropriate course of action when an employee engages in serious violations of policies, laws, or regulations such as theft, fraud, falsifying documents, and related serious offences.

The disciplinary process should not come as a surprise to the employee or supervisor if there is a good performance management system in place because there are plenty of opportunities for the employee to overcome performance problems and for the supervisor to offer support and feedback so that willing and able employees will be able to do so. However, when a disciplinary process seems to be the only recourse, it is important to follow a set of steps so as not to fall into legal problems. Also, all employees, even those who are terminated, deserve to be treated with respect and dignity. Nevertheless, even if there is a top-notch performance management system in place, there are several pitfalls that must be avoided and specific actions supervisors can take to do so, which are the following:[43]

1. *Pitfall 1: Acceptance of poor performance.* Many supervisors may just want to ignore poor performance hoping that the problem will go away. Unfortunately, in most cases, the performance problems escalate and become worse over time.
   Suggested course of action: Do not ignore the problem. Addressing it as soon as possible can not only avoid negative consequences for the employee in question, coworkers, and customers but also help put the employee back in track in terms of his career objectives.
2. *Pitfall 2: Failure to get the message through.* The poor performing employee may argue that she did not know the problem was serious or that it existed at all.
   Suggested course of action: In the decision-making leave described earlier, make sure to be very specific about the performance problem and the consequences of not addressing it effectively. Make sure you document the action plan and that you have secured the employee's agreement regarding the plan.
3. *Pitfall 3: Performance standards are "unrealistic" or "unfair."* The employee may argue that performance standards and expectations are unrealistic or unfair.
   Suggested course of action: Remind the employee that his performance standards are similar to others holding the same position. Also, remind the employee that performance standards have been developed over time with the participation of the employee in question, and share with him documentation regarding past review meetings, including past appraisal forms with the employee signature on them.
4. *Pitfall 4: Negative affective reactions.* The employee may respond emotionally ranging from tears to shouts and even threats of violence. This, in turn, may create an emotional response on the part of the supervisor.
   Suggested course of action: Do not let emotional reactions derail you from your mission, which is to describe the nature of the problem, what needs to be done, and consequences of not doing so. If the employee is crying, do offer compassion, and give him some space to compose himself. You can give the employee some time and resume the meeting a few minutes later or a rescheduling of the meeting at a later time may be a good alternative. If the employee reaction involves a threat or suggest possible violence, call security immediately. If such threats do take place, report them to the human resources (HR) department.
5. *Pitfall 5: Failure to consult HR.* There are hundreds of wrongful termination cases that have cost millions of dollars to organizations that have not followed the appropriate termination procedures.
   Suggested course of action: If you are planning on implementing a disciplinary or termination process, consult with your HR department regarding legal requirements. For the most part, if you have a good performance management

system in place, you have all necessary steps in place. However, consulting with HR is a good idea to ensure you are following all appropriate steps.

Avoiding the above pitfalls will minimize the possibility of problems during the formal disciplinary process. If the goals are not reached, there will be a need for a termination meeting. This meeting is of course extremely unpleasant for all involved, to say the least. However, it is the right and fair thing to do at this stage. Suggestions for the termination meeting are as follows:[44]

1. *Be respectful.* It is important to treat the terminated employee with respect and dignity. Keep the information about the termination confidential, although it is likely others will learn about it in subsequent days.

2. *Get right to the point.* At this stage, the less said, the better. Summarize the performance problems, actions taken to try to overcome these problems, outcomes of these actions, and the decision about termination that you have reached.

3. *Wish the employee well.* The purpose of the meeting is not to rehash every single reason why you are letting the employee go and every single instance of poor performance. Instead, use the meeting to wish the person well in her next job and endeavors, and tell her that she will be missed.

4. *Send the employee to HR.* Let the employee know that he needs to go to HR to receive information on benefits, including vacation pay, and to receive information on legal rights. If you are working in a small business, seek outside legal counsel regarding the information to give to the terminated employee.

5. *Have the employee leave immediately.* Keeping the terminated employee on-site can lead to gossip and conflict, and disgruntled employees may engage in sabotage.

6. *Have the termination meeting at the end of the day.* It is better to conduct the termination meeting at the end of the day so that the employee can leave the office as everyone else when there are fewer people around.

The aforementioned information regarding the disciplinary process and termination may be used as a follow-up to a formal performance review meeting held because of a lack of remedial action on the part of the employee. So, let's discuss performance review meetings next, which may or may not lead to the disciplinary process and termination we just discussed.

4 PERFORMANCE REVIEW MEETINGS

Supervisors who manage employee performance often feel uncomfortable in this role because managing performance requires that they judge and coach at the same time.[45] In other words, supervisors serve as judges by evaluating performance and allocating rewards. In addition, supervisors serve as coaches by helping employees solve performance problems, identify performance weaknesses, and design developmental plans that will be instrumental in future career development. In addition, supervisors feel uncomfortable because they feel they need to convey bad news and employees may react negatively. In other words, there is a concern that managing performance unavoidably leads to negative surprises.

Not surprisingly, employees are usually not satisfied with their performance reviews. For example, a survey of Australian employees conducted by the Gallup organization found that less than 20% of employees reported that their performance reviews helped them improve their performance. Overall, the majority of respondents reported being dissatisfied with the level of feedback and frequency of performance reviews from managers.[46]

Because supervisors play these paradoxical roles, it is usually helpful to separate the various meetings related to performance. Separating the meetings also minimizes the possibility of negative surprises.[47] Moreover, when meetings are separated, it is easier to separate the discussion of rewards from the discussion about future career development. This allows employees to give their full attention to each issue, one at a time.

Performance management systems can involve as many as six formal meetings. Each of these sessions should be seen as a work meeting with specific goal, including the following:

- *System inauguration.* The purpose of this meeting is to discuss how the performance management system works, which requirements and responsibilities rest primarily on the employee, and which rest primarily on the supervisor.
- *Self-appraisal.* The purpose of this meeting is to discuss the self-appraisal prepared by the employee.
- *Classical performance review.* The purpose of this meeting is to discuss employee performance, including the perspectives of both the supervisor and the employee.
- *Merit/salary review.* The purpose of this meeting is to discuss what, if any, compensation changes will result from the employee's performance during this period.
- *Developmental plan.* The purpose of this meeting is to discuss the employee's developmental needs and what steps will be taken so that performance will be improved during the following period.
- *Objective setting.* The purpose of this meeting is to set performance goals that are both behavior and results oriented for the following review period.

Although six types of meetings are possible, not all six take place as separate meetings. For example, the self-appraisal, classical performance review, merit/salary review, developmental plan, and objective setting meetings may all take place during one umbrella meeting labeled "performance review meeting." As noted above, however, it is better to separate the various types of information discussed so that the employee and supervisor focus on each of the components separately. Note, however, that the conversation about compensation should be related to performance (i.e., employees must understand the direct link between performance and compensation decisions).

Regardless of the specific type of meeting, there are several steps that must be taken before the meeting takes place. Specifically, it is useful to give at least a two-week advance notice to the employee to inform her of the purpose of the meeting and enable her to prepare for it. Also, it is useful to block out sufficient time for the meeting and arrange to meet in a private location without interruptions. Taking these steps sends a clear message that the meeting is important and that, consequently, performance management is important.

As noted above, most organizations merge several meetings into one labeled "performance review meeting." The typical sequence of events for such a meeting is the following:[48]

- *Explain the purpose of the meeting.* The first step includes a description of the purpose of the meeting and the topics to be discussed.

- *Conduct self-appraisal.* The second step includes asking the employee to summarize her accomplishments during the review period. This is more easily accomplished when the employee is given the appraisal form to be used by the supervisor before the meeting. This portion of the meeting allows the employee to provide her perspective regarding performance. The role of the supervisor is to listen to what the employee has to say and to summarize what he hears. This is not an appropriate time for the supervisor to disagree with what the employee says.

- *Share ratings and explain rationale.* Next, the supervisor explains the rating he provided for each performance dimension and explains the reasons that led to each score. It is more effective to start with a discussion of the performance dimensions for which there is agreement between the employee's self-appraisal and the supervisor's appraisal. This is likely to reduce tension and to demonstrate to the employee that there is common ground and that the meeting is not confrontational. Also, it is better to start with a discussion of the performance dimensions for which the scores are highest and then move on to the dimensions for which the scores are lower. For areas for which there is disagreement between self- and supervisor ratings, the supervisor must take great care in discussing the reason for his rating and provide specific examples and evidence to support the score given. At this point, there should be an effort to resolve discrepancies, and the supervisor should take extra care with sensitive areas. The employee should be provided with the opportunity to explain her viewpoint thoroughly. This is a very useful discussion because it leads to clarifying performance expectations. For dimensions for which the score is low, there should be a discussion of the possible causes for poor performance. For example, are the reasons related to lack of knowledge, lack of motivation, or contextual factors beyond the control of the employee?

- *Discuss development.* After the supervisor and employee have agreed on the scores given to each performance dimension, there should be a discussion about the developmental plan. At this point, the supervisor and the employee should discuss and agree on the developmental steps that will be taken to improve performance in the future.

- *Ask employee to summarize.* Next, the employee should summarize, in her own words, the main conclusions of the meeting: what performance dimensions are satisfactory, which ones need improvement, and how improvement will be achieved. This is an important component of the meeting because it gives the supervisor an opportunity to determine whether he and the employee are in accord.

- *Discuss rewards.* The next step during the meeting includes discussing the relationship between performance and any reward allocation. The supervisor should explain the rules used to allocate rewards and how the employee would be able to reach higher reward levels as a consequence of future performance improvement.

- *Hold follow-up meeting.* Before the meeting is over, it is important to schedule the next performance-related formal meeting. It is important that the employee understand that there will be a formal follow-up and that performance management is not just about meeting with the supervisor once a year. Usually, the next meeting will take place just a few weeks later to review whether the developmental plan is being implemented effectively.

- *Discuss approval and appeals process.* Finally, the supervisor asks the employee to sign the form to attest that the evaluation has been discussed with him. This is also an opportunity for the employee to add any comments or additional information he would like to see included on the form. In addition, if disagreements about ratings have not been resolved, the supervisor should remind the employee of the appeals process.
- *Conduct final recap.* Finally, the supervisor should use the "past-present-future model." In other words, the supervisor summarizes what happened during the review period in terms of performance levels in the various dimensions, reviews how rewards will change based on this level of performance, and sums up what the employee will need to do in the next year to maintain and enhance performance.

Performance review discussions serve very important purposes. First, these discussions allow employees to improve their performance by identifying performance problems and solutions for overcoming them. Second, they help build a good relationship between the supervisor and the employee because the supervisor shows that she cares about the employee's ongoing growth and development and that she is willing to invest resources, including time, in helping the employee improve.

Unfortunately, these purposes are not always realized because employees may be defensive, and many supervisors do not know how to deal with this attitude because they lack the necessary skills to conduct an effective performance review. How can we tell when an employee is being defensive? Typically, there are two patterns of behavior that indicate defensiveness.[49] First, employees may engage in a *fight response*. This includes blaming others for performance deficiencies, staring mutely at the supervisor, and other, more aggressive responses such as raising her voice or even pounding the desk. Second, employees may engage in a *flight response*. This includes looking away, turning away, speaking softly, continually changing the subject, or quickly agreeing with what the supervisor is saying without basing the agreement on a thoughtful and thorough discussion about the issues at stake. When employees have a fight-or-flight response during the performance review discussion, it is unlikely that the meeting will lead to improved performance in the future. What can supervisors do to prevent defensive responses? Consider the following suggestions:

- *Establish and maintain rapport.* It is important that the meeting take place in a good climate. As noted earlier, this can be achieved by choosing a meeting place that is private and by preventing interruptions from taking place. Also, the supervisor should emphasize two-way communication and put the employee at ease as quickly as possible. This can be done by sitting next to the employee as opposed to across a desk, by saying his name, by thanking him for coming, and by beginning with small talk to reduce the initial tension. When good rapport is established, both the supervisor and the employee are at ease, relaxed, and comfortable. They can have a friendly conversation, and neither is afraid to speak freely. Both are open-minded and can express disagreement without offending one another. On the other hand, when there is no good rapport, both participants may be nervous and anxious. The conversation is cold and formal and both may fear to speak openly. The supervisor and employee are likely to interrupt each other frequently and challenge what the other is saying.

- *Be empathetic.* It is important for the supervisor to put herself in the shoes of the employee. The supervisor needs to make an effort to understand why the employee has performed at a certain level during the review period. This includes not making attributions that any employee success was caused by outside forces (e.g., a good economy) or that employee failures were caused by inside forces (e.g., employee incompetence).
- *Be open-minded.* If the employee presents an alternative and different point of view, be open-minded, and discuss them directly and openly. There is a possibility that the employee may provide information that is relevant and of which you are not aware. If this is the case, ask for specific evidence.[50]
- *Observe verbal and nonverbal cues.* The supervisor should be able to read verbal and nonverbal signals from the employee to determine whether further clarification is necessary. The supervisor should be attentive to the employee's emotions and react accordingly. For example, if the employee becomes defensive, the supervisor should stop talking and allow the employee to express her point of view regarding the issue being discussed.
- *Minimize threats.* The performance review meeting should be framed as a meeting that will benefit the employee, not punish him.
- *Encourage participation.* The employee needs to have her own conversational space to speak and express her views. The supervisor should not dominate the meeting; rather, she should listen without interrupting and avoid confrontation and argument.

In spite of these suggestions, defensiveness may be unavoidable in some situations. In such situations, supervisors need to recognize that employee defensiveness is inevitable, and they need to allow it. Rather than ignoring the defensive attitude, supervisors need to deal with the situation head on. First, it is important to let the employee vent and to acknowledge the employee's feelings. To do this, the supervisor may want to pause to accept the employee's feelings. Then, the supervisor may want to ask the employee for additional information and clarification. If the situation is reaching a point where communication becomes impossible, the supervisor may want to suggest suspending the meeting until a later time.[51] For example, the supervisor may say, "I understand that you are angry and that you believe you have been treated unfairly. It's important that I understand your perspective, but it's difficult for me to absorb the information when you are so upset. This is an important matter. Let's take a break, and get back together at 3:00 P.M. to continue our discussion." To be sure, if the relationship between the supervisor and the employee is not good, the performance review meeting is likely to expose these issues in a blatant and often painful way.

Consider the following vignette. Jason is the manager at a large accounting firm, and Susan is one of the employees on his team. He chooses a conference room with privacy away from the other offices.

JASON: Hi, Susan. I wanted to meet with you today to discuss your performance appraisal for this quarter. At any time, please offer your input and ask questions if you have any.

SUSAN: OK.

JASON: You did meet two important objectives that we set this quarter: sales and customer service. Thanks for your hard work.

SUSAN:	No problem.
JASON:	You did miss three of the other objectives.
SUSAN:	What? I worked as hard as I could! It wasn't *my* fault that the other people on the team did not carry their weight.
JASON:	Susan, I am not here to blame anyone or to attack you. I want to generate some ideas on what we can do to ensure that you meet your objectives and receive your bonus next quarter.
SUSAN:	*SITTING BACK WITH CROSSED ARMS:* I told you I worked as hard as I could.
JASON:	I know that you worked hard, Susan, and I know how hard it is to balance all of the objectives that we have in our department. When I first started, I had a hard time meeting all of the objectives as well.
SUSAN:	It is hard and I try my best.
JASON:	Susan, can you think of anything that we can work on together that would help you meet the last three objectives? Is there any additional training or resources that you need?
SUSAN:	I am having a hard time prioritizing all of my daily tasks. There is a class offered online on prioritizing, but I feel I am too busy to take it.
JASON:	That is good that you think the class will help. Take the class online, which will not disrupt your work schedule, and I will go to all of your meetings and follow up with clients as needed.
SUSAN:	Thanks, Jason. I really appreciate your help.

How did Jason do in dealing with Susan's defensiveness? Overall, he did a good job. Jason was empathetic, he picked up on Susan's nonverbal behavior, he had her offer her input, he held the meeting in a comfortable, private location, and he emphasized that the meeting was to work on future performance and not to punish her. In the end, he was able to address Susan's defensiveness and turned a meeting that could have gone very poorly into a productive exchange of information and ideas.

Summary Points

- Managers must possess several important skills to manage the performance of their employees effectively. Managers need to serve as coaches, to observe and document performance accurately, to give both positive and negative feedback, and to conduct performance review meetings.
- Coaching is an ongoing process in which the manager directs, motivates, and rewards employee behavior. Coaching includes several key functions such as giving advice about what is expected about performance and how to perform well, giving employees guidance so employees know how to improve their performance, providing employees with support without being controlling, and enhancing employees' confidence and competence. Coaching must be based on a helping and trusting relationship. This is particularly important when the

supervisor and the subordinate do not share similar cultural backgrounds.

- Managers need to engage in a complex set of behaviors to perform the various coaching functions. These include the following: establish developmental objectives, communicate effectively, motivate employees, document performance, give feedback, diagnose performance problems, and develop employees.

- Managers' personalities and behavioral preferences determine their coaching style. Some managers prefer to be drivers and just tell employees what to do. Others prefer to be persuaders and try to sell what they want the employees to do. Yet others adopt an amiable style in which feelings take precedence and urge the employee to do what feels right or what the employee feels is the right way to do things. Finally, others prefer to be analyzers and have a tendency to follow rules and procedures in recommending how to perform. None of these four styles is necessarily better than the others. The best coaches are able to change their styles and adapt to the needs of the employees.

- The coaching process is ongoing and cyclical, and it includes the following five components: (1) setting developmental goals, (2) identifying the resources and strategies needed to achieve the developmental goals (e.g., securing resources that will allow employees to engage in activities to achieve their developmental goals), (3) implementing strategies (e.g., enrolling the employee in an online course), (4) observing and documenting developmental behaviors (e.g., checking on the progress of the employee toward the attainment of his developmental goals), and (5) giving feedback (e.g., providing information to the employee that will help him adjust his current developmental goals and guide his future goals).

- Observing and documenting performance in general and performance regarding developmental goals in particular are not as easy as it may seem. Time constraints can play a role when managers are too busy to gather performance information. Situational constraints may prevent managers from observing the employee directly. Finally, activity constraints may be a factor; when developmental activities are unstructured, such as reading a book, the manager may have to wait until the activity is completed to assess whether any new skills and knowledge have been acquired.

- Observation and documentation of performance can be improved in several ways. These issues include implementing a good communication plan that managers accept and establishing training programs that help managers minimize rater errors (i.e., rater error training); share notions of what it means to complete developmental activities successfully (i.e., frame-of-reference training); observe performance more accurately (i.e., behavioral observation training); and become more confident about managing employee performance (i.e., self-leadership training).

- Documenting an employee's progress toward achieving developmental goals and improving performance in general has several important benefits. These include the reduction of the manager's cognitive load, the enhancement of trust between the employee and the manager, the collection of important input to be used in planning developmental activities in the future, and the development of a good line of defense in case of litigation.

- For documentation to be most useful, it must be specific, use adjectives and adverbs sparingly, balance positives with negatives, focus on job-related information, be comprehensive, be standardized across employees, and be stated in behavioral terms.

- Feedback about performance in general and about developmental activities in particular serves several important purposes. These include building employee confidence, developing employee competence, and enhancing employee involvement with the unit and the organization as a whole.

- The mere presence of feedback does not mean that there will be positive effects on future performance. For feedback to be most useful, it must be timely, frequent, specific, verifiable, consistent over time and across employees, given in private, and tied closely to consequences (e.g., rewards); address description first and evaluation second; discuss performance in terms of a continuum and not in terms of dichotomies (i.e., more and less and not all or nothing); address patterns of behavior and not isolated events; include a statement that the manager has confidence in the employee; and include the active participation of the employee in generating ideas about how to improve performance in the future.

- In general, managers do not feel comfortable about giving negative feedback. They may fear that employees will react negatively because they themselves have been given negative feedback in the past in a way that was not helpful and do not want to put their employees in the same situation, because they don't like playing god, or because they think they need to collect an onerous amount of information and evidence before giving negative feedback. When negative feedback is warranted, however, and managers refuse to give it, poor performers may get the message that their performance is not that bad. Eventually, the situation may escalate to the point that the manager has no choice but to give negative feedback; the situation then becomes punitive, and feedback is not likely to be useful. For negative feedback to be useful, it must be given early when the performance problem is still manageable.

- Supervisors play the paradoxical roles of judge and coach at the same time. These roles are assumed during the performance review meetings, which can include as many as six separate formal meetings: system inauguration, self-appraisal, classical performance review, merit/salary review, developmental plan, and objective setting. In most organizations, these meetings are merged into one or two meetings. It is most effective to separate the meetings so that employees can focus on one issue at a time (e.g., supervisor's view on the employee's performance, rewards allocation, developmental plan).

- In some cases, an employee may be unwilling or unable to overcome performance problems. When that happens, there is a need to implement a formal disciplinary process including a verbal warning, followed by a written warning, and eventually, if needed, termination. When implementing a disciplinary process, supervisors must be aware of several pitfalls including the acceptance of poor performance, failing to get the message through, arguments that performance standards are unfair or unrealistic, employee and supervisor emotional reactions, and the failure to consult with HR.

- The termination meeting creates important challenges and is extremely unpleasant for both the employee and supervisor. For termination meetings to be more effective and less painful, supervisors must (1) be respectful, (2) get right to the point, (3) wish the employee well, (4) send the employee to HR (or offer information based on the advice of outside counsel), (5) have the employee leave immediately, and (6) conduct the termination meeting at the end of the day. Overall, all employees deserve to be treated with dignity and respect, even those who are being terminated.

- When all the performance review meetings are merged into one, the components of such a meeting include the following: (1) explanation of the purpose of the meeting, (2) self-appraisal, (3) discussion of the supervisor's performance ratings and rationale and resolution of discrepancies with self-appraisal, (4) developmental discussion, (5) employee summary, (6) rewards discussion, (7) setting up follow-up meeting,

(8) approval and appeals process discussion, and (9) final recap.

- In meeting with the supervisor to discuss performance issues, employees may become defensive. Defensiveness is indicated by a fight-or-flight response. The supervisor can minimize defensiveness by (1) establishing and maintaining rapport, (2) being empathetic, (3) observing verbal and nonverbal cues, (4) minimizing threats, and (5) encouraging employee participation.

- When defensiveness becomes unavoidable, the employee's attitude must be recognized and allowed expression. If the situation becomes intolerable, the meeting may be interrupted and rescheduled for a later time.

CASE STUDY 1

Was Robert Eaton a Good Coach?

Robert Eaton was CEO and chairman of Chrysler from 1993 to 1998, replacing Lee Iacocca who retired after serving in this capacity since 1978. Eaton then served as cochairman of the newly merged DaimlerChrysler organization from 1998 to 2000. With 362,100 employees, DaimlerChrysler achieved revenues of EUR 136.4 billion in 2003. DaimlerChrysler's passenger car brands include Maybach, Mercedes-Benz, Chrysler, Jeep, Dodge, and Smart. Commercial vehicle brands include Mercedes-Benz, Freightliner, Sterling, Western Star, and Setra.

From the beginning of his tenure as CEO, Eaton communicated with the people under him. He immediately shared his plans for the future with his top four executives and then took the advice of his colleague, Bob Lutz, to look around the company before making any hasty decisions concerning the state of affairs at Chrysler. Eaton and Lutz ascertained that Chrysler was employing the right staff and that they did not need to hire new people; they just had to lead them in a different manner, that is, in a more participative style.

Eaton listened to everyone in the organization, including executives, suppliers, and assembly-line workers, to determine how to help the company succeed. Eaton also encouraged the employees at Chrysler to talk with one another. The atmosphere of collaboration and open-door communication between Eaton and Lutz (the two men sat across the hall from one another and never closed their doors) permeated the entire organization. Eaton and Lutz's walk-around management style indicated to employees that they were committed to and engaged in the organization. Furthermore, Eaton and Lutz held meetings with their executive team on a regular basis to exchange ideas and information from all areas of the organization.

Eaton even reorganized the manner in which Chrysler designed cars based on a study, previously disregarded by Iacocca, that indicated that Chrysler needed to be more flexible and its executives needed to be in constant communication with the product design team. One employee was quoted as saying, "Bob Eaton does not shoot the messenger when he hears something he doesn't like or understand. He knows that not every idea is right. But Bob is off-the-wall himself. . . . He'll say something, and we'll tell him that it's a crazy idea. . . . He may not change his mind in the end, but he'll spend the time explaining to you what is behind his thought processes. Do you know what kind of confidence that inspires?" This type of open communication at the top proved extremely successful, as summed up by one designer: "It's a system that recognizes talent early and rewards it, and that creates a sense of enthusiasm for your work, and a sense of mission."

Another program that Eaton describes as empowering employees at Chrysler includes requiring all employees, including executives, to participate in the process of building a new vehicle. Eaton explains that this shows all of the employees in the plant that executives are concerned about the proper functioning of new cars, and it gives executives the opportunity to understand and solve problems at the factory level. Eaton states, "When we're done with our discussions, these guys know where we want to go and how we want to get there, and they go back and put the action plans together to do that. This goes for every single thing we do." He concludes, "Clearly at a company there has to be a shared vision, but we try to teach people to be a leader in their own area, to know where the company wants to go, to know how that affects their area, to benchmark the best in the world, and then set goals and programs to go after it. We also encourage people not only to go after the business plan objectives but to have stretch goals. And a stretch goal by definition is a fifty-percent increase . . . . If we go after fifty percent, something dramatic has to happen. You have to go outside of the box."

Based on the above description, please evaluate Bob Eaton's coaching skills using the accompanying table. If a certain coaching behavior or function is missing, please provide recommendations about what he could have done more effectively. ■

Major Functions	Present? (Y/N)	Comments/Recommendations
Give advice		
Provide guidance		
Give support		
Give confidence		
Promote greater competence		

Key Behaviors	Present? (Y/N)	Comments/Recommendations
Establish development objectives		
Communicate effectively		
Motivate employees		
Document performance		
Give feedback		
Diagnose performance problems		
Develop employees		

Source: Based on information provided by M. Puris, *Comeback: How Seven Straight-Shooting CEOs Turned Around Troubled Companies* (New York: Times Books, 1999), 80–118, specifically Chap. 4, "Robert Eaton and Robert Lutz; The Copilots."

CASE STUDY 2

What Is Your Coaching Style?

Below are 15 rows of four words each. From each row, select and circle two words out of the four that best describe the way you see yourself. If all four words sound like you, select the two that are most like you. If none of the four sounds like you, select the two that are closest to the way you are. Then, total the number of words selected under each respective column.

After you have totaled the number of words circled under each respective column, plot those numbers on their

	A	B	C	D
1	All-business	Bold	Personable	Deliberate
2	Organized listening	Telling	Courteous	Listening
3	Industrious	Independent	Companionable	Cooperative
4	No-nonsense	Decisive	Talkative	Reflective
5	Serious	Determined	Warm	Careful
6	To-the-point	Risk-taker	Amiable	Moderate
7	Practical	Aggressive	Empathetic	Nonassertive
8	Self-controlled	Authoritative	Shows emotions	Thorough
9	Goal-directed	Assertive	Friendly	Patient
10	Methodical	Unhesitating	Sincere	Prudent
11	Businesslike	Definite	Sociable	Precise
12	Diligent	Firm	Demonstrative	Particular
13	Systematic	Strong-minded	Sense of humor	Thinking
14	Formal	Confident	Expressive	Hesitative
15	Persevering	Forceful	Trusting	Restrained
Total				

respective axes of the grid here. For example, if you circled six words in column A, mark the A axis next to the 6. Complete the same procedures for columns B, C, and D. Then extend the marks into each respective quadrant to create a rectangle. For example, consider the example of circling nine words from the A list, eight from the B list, seven from the C list, and eight from the D list. The rectangle would be the following:

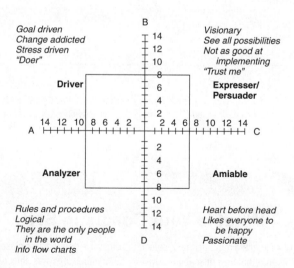

266

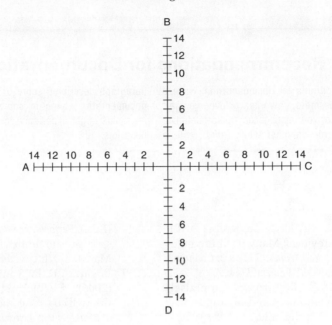

In this particular example, the area covered by the rectangle shows that this person is predominantly a driver and an analyzer but can also be a persuader and amiable. Now, create your own rectangle using your scores:

What is your coaching style? Is there a dominance of one style over the other three as indicated by an area predominantly covering one of the quadrants and not the others? If there is, what can you do to start using the other styles as well? ■

Source: Coaching Guides. Available online at http://www.specialolympics.org. Used with the kind permission of Special Olympics, Inc. Retrieval date: July 27, 2011.

Source: Coaching Guides. Available online at http://www.specialolympics.org. Used with the kind permission of Special Olympics, Inc. Retrieval date: July 27, 2011.

CASE STUDY 3

Preventing Defensiveness

Spencer, Jeff's manager, needs to talk to Jeff about his poor performance over the previous quarter. Jeff enters the room and sits across the desk from Spencer.

JEFF: Spencer, you wanted to talk to me?

SPENCER: Yes, Jeff, thanks for coming by. I wanted to talk about your performance last quarter. (*Spencer's phone rings and he answers it. Five minutes later Jeff is still waiting for Spencer. Jeff finally gets frustrated and Spencer notices Jeff looks at his watch several times.*) Sorry for the interruption Jeff, I know it is frustrating to be kept waiting.

JEFF: I am very busy. Can we get on with this?

SPENCER: Yes, absolutely. As you know you had some problems meeting all of your goals last quarter.

JEFF: Now wait a second. I met the most important goal.

SPENCER: Yes, you did, but you missed the other four.

JEFF: Just by a little, and it wasn't my fault.

SPENCER: Jeff, you need to accept responsibility for your own performance and not push blame onto others. You need to meet your goals this coming quarter or I will have to take more serious action.

JEFF: One bad quarter, and you threaten to fire me? I can't believe this!

SPENCER: Just meet all of your goals, and I won't have to take that action.

Given this vignette, what could Spencer have done to combat Jeff's defensiveness more effectively? ■

CASE STUDY 4

Recommendations for Documentation

Using the recommendations for documentation, write a journal entry of a classmate, coworker, or even yourself (from the perspective of your manager/instructor) detailing his/her performance for the past week. Also, write a paragraph describing some of the challenges with your documentation, tying in some of the constraints that managers might experience in documenting performance behaviors. ■

End Notes

1. Holland, K. (2006, September 10). Performance reviews: Many need improvement. *The New York Times, Section 3, Column 1 Money and Business/Financial Desk*, 3.
2. Nurse, L. (2005). Performance appraisal, employee development and organizational justice: Exploring the linkages. *International Journal of Human Resource Management, 16*, 1176–1194.
3. Allenbaugh, G. E. (1983). Coaching . . . A management tool for a more effective work performance. *Management Review, 72*, 21–26.
4. Schein, E. H. (2006). Coaching and consultation revisited: Are they the same? In M. Goldsmith & L. S. Lyons (Eds.), *Coaching for leadership: The practice of leadership coaching from the world's greatest coaches*. 2nd ed. (pp. 17–25). San Francisco, CA: John Wiley.
5. Vance, C. M. (2006). Strategic upstream and downstream considerations for effective global performance management. *International Journal of Cross Cultural Management, 6*, 37–56.
6. Grant, A. M. (2006). Workplace and executive coaching: A bibliography from the scholarly business literature. In D. R. Stober & A. M. Grant (Eds.), *Evidence based coaching handbook: Putting best practices to work for your clients* (pp. 367–388). Hoboken, NJ: John Wiley.
7. Stober, D. R. (2006). Coaching from the humanistic perspective. In D. R. Stober & A. M. Grant (Eds.), *Evidence based coaching handbook: Putting best practices to work for your clients* (pp. 17–50). Hoboken, NJ: John Wiley.
8. Farr, J. L., & Jacobs, R. (2006). Trust us: New perspectives on performance appraisal. In W. Bennett, C. E. Lance, & D. J. Woehr

(Eds.), *Performance measurement: Current perspectives and future challenges* (pp. 321–337). Mahwah, NJ: Lawrence Erlbaum.
9. Boyatzis, R. E., Smith, M. L., & Blaize, N. (2006). Developing sustainable leaders through coaching and compassion. *Academy of Management Learning & Education, 5*, 8–24.
10. Peterson, D. B. (2006). People are complex and the world is messy: A behavior-based approach to executive coaching. In D. R. Stober & A. M. Grant (Eds.), *Evidence based coaching handbook: Putting best practices to work for your clients* (pp. 51–76). Hoboken, NJ: John Wiley.
11. Hunt, J. M., & Weintraub, J. R. (2002). *The coaching manager: Developing top talent in business*. Thousand Oaks, CA: Sage.
12. Toto, J. (2006, April). Untapped world of peer coaching. *T+D, 60*, 69–70.
13. Kiger, P. J. (2002, May). How performance management reversed NCCI's fortunes. *Workforce, 81*, 48–51.
14. Byne, J. A. (1998, June 8). How Jack Welch runs GE. *Business Week*. Available online at http://www.businessweek.com/1998/23/b3581001.htm. Retrieval date: September 8, 2011.
15. Bacon, T. R., & Spear, K. I. (2003). *Adaptive coaching: The art and practice of a client-centered approach to performance improvement*. Palo Alto, CA: Davies-Black.
16. Fletcher, N., & Rodenbough, D. (2006, June/July). Coaching Hallmark's managers to value communication. *Strategic Communication Management, 10*, 26–29.
17. Foster, P. (2002). Performance documentation. *Business Communication Quarterly, 65*, 108–114.

18. *Cleverly v. Western Electric Co.*, 594 F.2d 638 (8th Cir. 1979).

19. Walther, F., & Taylor, S. (1988). An active feedback program can spark performance. In A. D. Timpe (Ed.), *Performance: The art & science of business management* (pp. 293–299). New York: Facts on File Publications.

20. These quotes have circulated worldwide on the Internet. See, for example, http://www.cnenigeria.com/jokes/joke101.htm, and http://www.avolites.org.uk/jokes/apprai-sals.htm. Retrieval date: September 8, 2011.

21. Blake Jelley, R., & Goffin, R. D. (2001). Can performance-feedback accuracy be improved? Effects of rater priming and rating-scale format on rating accuracy. *Journal of Applied Psychology, 86*, 134–144.

22. Goldmith, M. (2006). Try feed *forward* instead of feedback. In M. Goldsmith & L. S. Lyons (Eds.), *Coaching for leadership: The practice of leadership coaching from the world's greatest coaches.* 2nd ed. (pp. 45–49). San Francisco, CA: John Wiley.

23. Becker, T. E., & Klimoski, R. J. (1989). A field study of the relationship between the organizational feedback environment and performance. *Personnel Psychology, 42*, 343–358.

24. Allen, D. W., & LeBlanc, A. C. (2005). *Collaborative peer coaching that improves instruction: The 2 + 2 performance appraisal model.* Thousand Oaks, CA: Corwin.

25. Silverman, S. B., Pogson, C. E., & Cober, A. B. (2005). When employees at work don't get it: A model for enhancing individual employee change in response to performance feedback. *Academy of Management Executive, 19*, 135–147.

26. Kluger, A. N., & DeNisi, A. S. (1996). The effects of feedback interventions on performance: Historical review, a meta-analysis, and a preliminary feedback intervention theory. *Psychological Bulletin, 119*, 254–284.

27. DeNisi, A. S., & Kluger, A. N. (2000). Feedback effectiveness: Can 360-degree appraisals be improved? *Academy of Management Executive, 14*, 129–139.

28. London, M. (2003). *Job feedback: Giving, seeking, and using feedback for performance improvement.* 2nd ed. Mahwah, NJ: Lawrence Erlbaum.

29. Goodman, J. S., Wood, R. E., & Hendrickx, M. (2004). Feedback specificity, exploration, and learning. *Journal of Applied Psychology, 89*, 248–262.

30. Kamer, B., & Annen, H. (2010). The role of core self-evaluations in predicting performance appraisal reactions. *Swiss Journal of Psychology/Schweizerische Zeitschrift für Psychologie/Revue Suisse de Psychologie, 69*, 95–104.

31. Audia, P. G., Locke, E. A., & Smith, K. G. (2000). The paradox of success: An archival and a laboratory study of strategic persistence following a radical environmental change. *Academy of Management Journal, 43*, 837–853.

32. Nelson, B. (1996). Providing a context for recognition. *Executive Edge Newsletter, 27*(11), 6.

33. Watkins, T. (2004). Have a heart. *New Zealand Management, 51*, 46–48.

34. Tyler, K. (2004). One bad apple: Before the whole bunch spoils, train managers to deal with poor performance. *HR Magazine, 49*, 79.

35. Moss, S. E., & Sanchez, J. I. (2004). Are your employees avoiding you? Managerial strategies for closing the feedback gap. *Academy of Management Executive, 18*, 32–44.

36. Kinicki, A. J., Prussia, G. E., Wu, B. J., & McKee-Ryan, F. M. (2004). A covariance structure analysis of employees' response to performance feedback. *Journal of Applied Psychology, 89*, 1057–1069.

37. Audia, P. G., & Locke, E. A. (2003). Benefiting from negative feedback. *Human Resource Management Review, 13*, 631–646.

38. Cannon, M. D., & Witherspoon, R. (2005). Actionable feedback: Unlocking the power of learning and performance improvement. *Academy of Management Executive, 19*, 120–134.

39. Laumeyer, J. A. (2002). *Performance management systems: What do we want to accomplish?* Alexandria, VA: Society for Human Resource Management.

40. Gill, J. (2007, March). How to help an underachiever. *Inc. Magazine*, 44.

41. Falcone, P. (2007). Days of contemplation. *HR Magazine, 52*, 107–111.

42. Based on P. Falcone. (2007). Days of contemplation. *HR Magazine, 52,* 107–111.

43. Stone, F. M. (2007). *Coaching, counseling, & mentoring.* 2nd ed. New York: American Management Association.

44. Stone, F. M. (2007). *Coaching, counseling, & mentoring.* 2nd ed. New York: American Management Association.

45. McGregor, D. (1957). An uneasy look at performance appraisal. *Harvard Business Review, 35,* 89–94.

46. Moullakis, J. (2005, March 30). One in five workers "actively disengaged." *The Australian Financial Review,* 10.

47. Falcone, P. (2007). *Productive performance appraisals.* 2nd ed. New York: American Management Association.

48. Adapted from D. L. Kirkpatrick. *How to Improve Performance Through Appraisal and Coaching* (New York: AMACOM, 1982), 55–57.

49. Grote, D. (2002). *The performance appraisal question and answer book* (pp. 131–132). New York: AMACOM.

50. Mone, E. M., & London, M. (2010). *Employee engagement through effective performance management.* New York: Routledge.

51. Daniel, T. A. (2010). Managing difficult employees and disruptive behaviors. SHRH White Paper. *SHRM Online.* Available online at http://www.shrm.org/Research/Articles/Articles/Pages/ManagingDifficult Employees.aspx. Retrieval date: September 8, 2011.

Reward Systems and Legal Issues

You have to get rewarded in the soul and the wallet.
The money isn't enough, but a plaque isn't enough
either . . . you have to give both.

—Jack Welch

LEARNING OBJECTIVES

By the end of this chapter, you will be able to do the following:

- Distinguish between traditional and contingent pay plans, and know how each of these reward systems relates to the performance management system.
- Understand the reasons for the popularity of contingent pay plans.
- Describe how contingent pay plans can help improve employee motivation and performance.
- Be aware of the reasons contingent pay plans fail.
- Design a contingent pay plan, taking into account key variables such as the organization's culture and strategic business objectives.
- Understand that pay is only one of many tools that can be used to motivate employees.
- Use rewards effectively so that they produce the effects intended.
- Know the principles of how to design an organization's pay structure, including how to conduct a job evaluation.
- Understand the advantages of the broad-banding approach to designing a pay structure.

From Chapter 10 of *Performance Management*, Third Edition. Herman Aguinis. Copyright © 2013 by Pearson Education, Inc. All rights reserved.

- Understand the role played by six legal principles in the implementation of performance management systems: employment at will, negligence, defamation, misrepresentation, adverse impact, and illegal discrimination.

- Identify the point at which a performance management system allows illegal discrimination.

- Know what type of evidence employees need so that they can prove illegal discrimination and what type of evidence employers need to prove lack of illegal discrimination.

- Know the impact of the key laws that prohibit discrimination based on race, sex, religion, age, disability status, and sexual orientation on the design and implementation of performance management systems.

- Design a performance management system that is legally sound.

1 TRADITIONAL AND CONTINGENT PAY PLANS

A traditional approach in implementing reward systems is to reward employees for the positions they fill as indicated by their job descriptions and not necessarily by how they do their work. In other words, employees are rewarded for filling a specific slot in the organizational hierarchy. In such traditional pay systems, one's job directly determines pay and indirectly determines benefits and incentives received. Typically, there is a pay range that determines minimum, midpoint, and maximum rates for each job. For example, a university may have five ranks for professors who have just been hired:

1. Instructor (pay range: $30,000–$45,000)
2. Senior instructor (pay range: $40,000–$55,000)
3. Assistant professor (pay range: $60,000–$90,000)
4. Associate professor (pay range: $85,000–$105,000)
5. Professor (pay range: $100,000–$140,000)

As noted above, in a traditional reward system, each of these positions would have a minimum, midpoint, and the maximum salary. For assistant professors, the minimum is $60,000 per year, the midpoint is $75,000, and the maximum is $90,000. Salary increases at the end of the year would be determined by seniority or by a percentage of one's base salary (and the same percentage would be used for all workers). Rewards would not be based on teaching quality, as indicated by student teaching ratings, or research productivity, as indicated by the number and quality of publications. If an assistant professor's base salary is $90,000, she cannot realize an increase in her salary unless she is promoted to associate professor because $90,000 is the maximum possible salary for this job title. In short, in traditional reward systems, the type of position and seniority are the determinants of salary and salary increases, not performance. In such reward systems, there is no relationship between performance management and rewards. This type of system is quite pervasive in numerous organizations, particularly outside of North America. Korea is one country where systems based on seniority are still quite pervasive.[1] In Korea, as is the case in other collectivistic cultures (e.g., China), employees tend to avoid confrontation for fear of losing face.[2] Thus, supervisors may be reluctant to give employees unsatisfactory performance ratings or ratings based on individual performance because this would single out individuals. Instead, systems that measure and reward team performance may be more appropriate in collectivistic cultures. It is possible, however, to move away from more traditional systems based mainly on seniority by establishing clear links between performance management and other functions such as training. When such links have been clearly established, employees are more likely to see the benefits of the performance management system and believe that the system is fair.

Contingent pay (CP), also called *pay for performance*, means that individuals are rewarded based on how well they perform on the job. Thus, employees receive increases in pay based wholly or partly on job performance. These increases can either be added to an employee's base salary or be a one-time bonus. When increases are not added to an employee's base salary, as in the case of one-time bonuses, they are called *variable pay*.

Originally, CP plans were used only for top management. Gradually, the use of CP plans extended to sales jobs. Currently, CP plans are more pervasive. For example, in 2001, 70% of workers in the United States were employed by organizations implementing some type of variable pay plan, and many of these organizations tie variable pay (e.g., bonus, commission, cash award, lump sum) directly to performance. Similarly, a study of human resources (HR) practices worldwide found that organizations in Canada, Latin America, Taiwan, and the United States generally emphasize the link between performance and pay.[3] Finally, even universities, which typically have traditional organizational cultures for which pay for performance can be quite a foreign concept, are adopting CP plans for their staff. For example, results of a survey of 129 higher education institutions in the United Kingdom revealed that 77% of universities are using some type of CP plan and only 6% of universities have decided not to implement such plans.[4]

Let's return to the example of salaries for university professors. When a CP plan is implemented, pay raises are determined in part or wholly based on performance. For example, two assistant professors may be hired at the same time at the same salary level (e.g., $75,000). If one of them outperforms the other year after year for several years, then eventually the better performing assistant professor may make $110,000, which may be a higher level of pay than most associate professors make. This is because every year this assistant professor receives a substantial salary increase, part of which may be added to the base salary, based on her outstanding teaching and research performance. On the other hand, the other assistant professor may still be making the same amount, or close to the same amount, he was making when he was first hired. Under a traditional pay plan, an assistant professor would not receive a higher salary than most associate professors. Under such a plan, the assistant professor would have to be promoted to associate professor before she could receive a salary of $110,000, which is outside the traditional range for assistant professors.

2 REASONS FOR INTRODUCING CONTINGENT PAY PLANS

Why are organizations embracing CP plans? The results of a recent survey of Fortune 500 companies indicated that performance management systems are more effective when results are directly tied to the reward system.[5] When the performance management system has a direct relationship with the reward system, performance measurement and performance improvement are taken more seriously. In other words, CP plans force organizations to define effective performance clearly and to determine what factors are likely to lead to effective performance. When a CP plan is implemented, organizations need to make clear what is expected of employees, what specific behaviors or results will be rewarded, and how employees can achieve these behaviors or results. This, in and of itself, serves an important communication goal because supervisors and employees are better able to understand what really matters. Also, high-achieving performers are attracted to organizations that reward high-level performance, and high-level performers are typically in favor of CP plans.[6] This tendency is called the *sorting effect*: top performers are likely to be attracted to and remain within organizations that have implemented CP plans.[7] An organization's ability to retain its top performers is obviously crucial if an organization wants to win the talent war and have a people-based competitive advantage.[8] For example, a study conducted at a glass installation company found that productivity improved by 44% when the compensation system was changed from salaries to individual incentives.[9] A closer look at the data indicated that about 50% of the productivity improvement was due to the current employees being more productive, whereas the other 50% improvement was due to less productive employees quitting and the organization's ability to attract and recruit more productive workers. Consequently, CP plans can serve as a good tool to recruit and retain top performers as a result of the sorting effect, which, in turn, can lead to greater productivity. Finally, CP plans can project a good corporate image because the organization has implemented a system of rewards that is fair and based on clearly communicated expectations and standards.

Hicks Waldron, former CEO of cosmetics giant Avon, in an eloquent statement, explained why CP plans are becoming so popular: "It took me 30 years to figure out that people don't do what you ask them to do; they do what you pay them to do." How about organizations that are struggling financially? Can they still implement CP plans? Can they afford to give performance-based rewards to their employees? The answer is yes to both questions. Making sure that top performers are rewarded appropriately can help keep them motivated and prevent them from leaving the organization in difficult times. It is these top performers who are the organization's hope for recovery in the future. In fact, giving rewards to poor performers means that these rewards are taken away from high-level performers.[10] Consider the case of Corning, Inc., a fiber-optic cable manufacturer (http://www.corning.com/). In 2002, sales were at an unprecedented low level, and the stock price was just over $1, which was about 1% of its value in 2000. Corning had slashed more than 16,000 jobs in two years and had not been profitable since early 2001; nevertheless, they gave bonuses to employees who met performance goals during the year.[11]

Overall, CP plans enhance employee motivation to accomplish goals that match organizational needs. More specifically, CP plans have the potential to help people change behavior and improve performance. For example, assume an organization is trying hard to improve customer satisfaction. Some units in this organization decide to implement a CP plan that awards cash to employees who improve their customer satisfaction ratings. By contrast, other units continue with a traditional pay plan in which there is no clear tie between performance levels and rewards. Who do you think will perform better—employees under the CP plan or those under the traditional plan? Well, if all other things are equal, it is likely that employees under the CP plan will improve the service they offer to customers.[12] In fact, a review of several studies concluded that using individual pay incentives increased productivity by an average of 30%.[13] Similarly, a study of 21 fast-food franchises showed a 30% increase in average profits and a 19% decrease in the drive-through times as a result of the implementation of a CP plan.[14] These figures, of course, are averages, and productivity and profits do not necessarily improve by 30% in every case. An employee's performance is determined by the joint effects of declarative knowledge, procedural knowledge, and motivation. CP plans address the motivational component. In other words, employees are likely to choose to expend effort, choose to expend a high level of effort, and choose to persist in this high level of expenditure of effort in the presence of financial incentives. The fact that employees are trying hard to provide good customer service does not mean, however, that they will necessarily succeed. They still need the declarative and procedural knowledge to do so. If they do not know how to please customers, then they won't be able to satisfy them no matter how hard they try.

CP plans can help improve the motivation of employees when each of the following conditions is present:

1. Employees see a clear link between their efforts and the resulting performance (expectancy).
2. Employees see a clear link between their performance level and the rewards received (instrumentality).
3. Employees value the rewards available (valence).

There is a multiplicative relationship among these three determinants of motivation so that

$$\text{Motivation} = \text{Expectancy} \times \text{Instrumentality} \times \text{Valence}$$

If the expectancy, instrumentality, or valence conditions are not met, the CP plan is not likely to improve performance. For example, consider the situation in which the instrumentality condition is not present. Employees may value the rewards available and may want to get them (valence). They may also see that if they exert sufficient effort, they will be able to achieve the desired performance level (expectancy). They believe, however, that the rewards received are not necessarily related to their performance level (i.e., no instrumentality). In this situation, employees are not likely to choose to exert effort because this will not get them the desired rewards.

CP plans and pay in general should not be regarded as the Holy Grail of employee performance. First, pay can affect only the motivation aspect of performance. If an employee is not performing well, pay may not solve the problem if poor performance results from a lack of declarative or procedural knowledge as opposed to a lack of motivation. All of the three conditions must be present for CP plans to have an impact on employee motivation. We should be aware that pay is not necessarily the perfect solution and that giving people more money will not automatically solve performance problems.

3 POSSIBLE PROBLEMS ASSOCIATED WITH CONTINGENT PAY PLANS

In spite of the potential positive impact of CP plans, we should be aware that not all CP plans work as intended. For example, in the 1990s, Hewlett Packard implemented CP plans in 13 separate sites; however, the plans were eventually abandoned in all but one. Hewlett Packard decided to abandon CP because the benefits did not outweigh the costs.[15] Why is it that CP plans may not succeed? Consider the following reasons:[16]

- *A poor performance management system is in place.* What happens when a CP plan is paired with a poorly designed, poorly implemented performance management system, one that includes biased ratings and the measurement of unrelated performance dimensions? This situation may lead some employees to challenge the CP plan legally. Also, rewarding behaviors and results that are not job related is likely to cause good performers to leave the organization. Finally, those who stay are not likely to be motivated to perform well.

- *There is the folly of rewarding A while hoping for B.*[17] What happens when the system rewards results and behaviors that are not those that will help the organization succeed? Employees are likely to engage in these often counterproductive behaviors when this behavior is what will earn them the desired rewards. One such example is the hope that executives will focus on long-term growth and environmental responsibility when, in fact, they are rewarded based on quarterly earnings. Given this situation, what are these executives likely to do? Will they think in the long term or quarter by quarter? A second example is an organization that would like its employees to be more entrepreneurial and innovative, but it does not reward employees who think creatively. What are employees likely to do? Will they be innovative and risk not getting rewards, or will they continue to do things the old way? A third example is an organization that would like employees to focus on teamwork and a one-for-all spirit, but it rewards employees based on individual results. This happens in many professional sports teams. What are professional athletes likely to do? Will they pass the ball, or will they try to score themselves to improve their own individual statistics?

- *Rewards are not considered significant.* What happens when a CP plan includes pay increases and other rewards that are so small that they don't differentiate between outstanding and poor performers? For example, what happens when the top performers receive a 5% pay increase and an average performer receives a 3% or 4% pay increase? In this context, rewards are not viewed as performance-based rewards, and they do not make an impact. The message sent to employees is that performance is not something worth being rewarded. For rewards to be meaningful, they need to be significant in the eyes of the employees. Usually, an increase of approximately 12%–15% of one's salary is regarded as a meaningful reward and would motivate people to do things they would not do otherwise.

- *Managers are not accountable.* What happens when managers are not accountable regarding how they handle the performance and the performance evaluation of their employees? They are likely to inflate ratings so that employees receive what the manager thinks are appropriate rewards. Similarly, employees may set goals that are easily attainable so that performance ratings will lead to the highest possible level of reward. In other words, when managers are not held accountable, rewards may become the driver for the performance evaluation instead of the performance evaluation being the driver for the rewards.

- *There exists extrinsic motivation at the expense of intrinsic motivation.* What happens when there is so much, almost exclusive, emphasis on rewards? Employees may start to lose interest in their jobs, which, in turn, can decrease motivation. In some cases, the extrinsic value of doing one's job (i.e., rewards) can supersede the intrinsic value (i.e., doing the work because it is interesting and challenging). Sole emphasis on rewards can lead to ignoring the fact that employee motivation can be achieved not only by providing rewards but also by creating a more challenging, more interesting work environment in which employees have control over what they do and how they do it.

- *Rewards for executives are disproportionately large compared to rewards for everyone else.* In many organizations, executive rewards are disproportionately large compared to the rewards received by everyone else in the organization. A study conducted by Pearl Meyer & Partners in 2004 revealed that the average compensation received by CEOs in major U.S. corporations was US $9.84 million, compared to an average compensation for employees in nonsupervisory roles of $27,485. The compensation for these CEOs was more than 360 times that of their employees! Such a large difference, particularly when the performance of the organization is not stellar, can lead to serious morale problems. CEOs should be compensated according to their performance, and an important indicator of CEO performance is overall firm performance (e.g., stock price in the case of publicly traded organizations).

Table 1 summarizes reasons for the failure of CP plans. Consider two examples of situations in which CP plans failed because of one or more of the reasons listed in this table. First, consider what happened at Green Giant, which is part of the General Mills global food conglomerate which includes such brands as Betty Crocker, Wheaties, and Bisquick. Green Giant implemented a bonus plan that rewarded employees for removing insects from vegetables. What was the result regarding performance? Initially, managers were pleased because employees were finding and removing a substantially higher number of insects. The initial enthusiasm disappeared, however, when managers found out that employees were bringing insects from home, putting them into vegetables, and removing them to get the bonus! A second example comes

TABLE 1 Reasons Why Contingent Pay Plans Fail

A poor performance management system is in place.

There is the folly of rewarding A while hoping for B.

Rewards are not significant.

Managers are not accountable.

There exists an extrinsic motivation at the expense of intrinsic motivation.

Rewards for executives are disproportionately large compared to rewards for everyone else.

from the automotive division of Sears, a leading retailer of apparel, home, and automotive products and services, with annual revenues of more than US $40 billion. Its CP plan rewarded employees on the basis of parts and services sold to customers who brought cars in for repair. In California, a disproportionate number of Sears auto centers were making repairs. The California Consumer Affairs Commission conducted an 18-month investigation, during which it sent some of its members to the auto centers posing as customers. What did they find? Sears employees were "finding" a lot of problems and making a lot of unnecessary repairs. Half of Sears' 72 auto-service centers in California were routinely overcharging customers for repairs, and Sears mechanics billed the undercover agents for work that was never done on 34 of the 38 undercover operations.[18]

4 SELECTING A CONTINGENT PAY PLAN

Assuming an organization wishes to implement a CP plan, what should the plan look like? Recall the discussion of various forms of compensation provided in Chapter 1. What considerations should be taken into account in choosing, for example, among offering employees group incentives, profit sharing, or individual sales commissions? A critical issue to consider is that of organizational culture. An organization's culture is defined by its unwritten rules and procedures. For example, is the organization fundamentally built around individual performance, or is teamwork the norm? Is the organization one in which high-level performers are regarded as role models who should be emulated, or are they viewed as a threat to upper management?[19] Are we happy with the current culture, or do we wish to change it? CP plans are powerful tools that help solidify the current culture, and that can be used to create a new type of culture. There should be a careful consideration of the culture of the organization before a specific type of CP plan is selected.

Consider the types of systems that can be implemented in cultures that we can label traditional or involvement cultures. Traditional cultures are characterized by top-down decision making, vertical communication, and clearly defined jobs. What type of plan should be implemented in organizations with this type of culture? An effective choice would be a plan that rewards specific and observable measures of performance, where that performance is clearly defined and directly linked to pay. Examples of such CP systems are the following:

- *Piece rate.* Employees are paid based on the number of units produced or repaired. This system is usually implemented in manufacturing environments. In service organizations, this could involve the number of calls made or the number of clients, or potential clients, contacted. This system is usually implemented in call centers.
- *Sales commissions.* Employees are paid based on a percentage of sales. This system is usually implemented in car dealerships.
- *Group incentives.* Employees are paid based on extra group production based on result-oriented measures (e.g., sales volume for the group). This system is implemented frequently in the retail industry.

Involvement culture is different from traditional culture. Organizations with involvement cultures are characterized by shared decision making, lateral communications, and loosely defined roles. Examples of systems that work well in organizations with involvement cultures are the following:

- *Profit sharing.* Employees are paid based on the performance of a group (e.g., team or unit) and on whether the group has exceeded a specific financial goal. This type of system is implemented in many large law firms.
- *Skill-based pay.* Employees are paid based on whether they acquire new knowledge and skills that are beneficial to the organization. This type of system is usually implemented in knowledge-based organizations such as software development companies.

In addition to the organization's culture, an important consideration in selecting a CP plan is the organization's strategic direction. Strategy is not only a key element in designing the performance management system, but it is also a key element in designing a CP plan. Table 2 includes a selected list of strategic objectives and CP plans that are most conducive to achieving the objective.

According to Table 2, if employee development is a key strategic priority, rewards should emphasize new skills acquired. If customer service is a priority, then rewards should emphasize competencies related to customer service and gain sharing. Gain sharing links individual and group pay to an organization's overall profitability: The greater the organization's overall profit, the greater the rewards given to individuals and teams in the organization. In this case, gain sharing would be based on whether customer service ratings improve during the review period. If the major goal of the CP plan is to increase the organization's overall profit, choices include executive pay and profit or stock sharing. Executive pay includes cash bonuses that are given in response to successful organizational performance. Usually, however, executive pay includes company stock to ensure that executives' activities are consistent with the shareholders' interests and to encourage executives to tend to the long-term performance of the organization. This is also called profit sharing, although profit sharing is usually short term and focused on organizational goals while stock sharing and executive pay are more long term.

TABLE 2 Plans Recommended for Various Strategic Business Objectives

Strategic Business Objective	CP Plan
Employee development	Skill-based pay
Customer service	Competency-based pay Gain sharing
Productivity: Individual	Piece rate Sales commissions
Productivity: Group	Gain sharing Group incentives
Teamwork	Team sales commissions Gain sharing Competency-based pay
Overall profit	Executive pay Profit or stock sharing

BOX 1

Contingent Pay at Nucor Corporation

At Nucor Corporation (http://www.nucor.com), contingent pay has for many years been a part of the company's approach to compensation. Nucor, based in Charlotte, North Carolina, is the largest producer of steel in the United States. The company employs 11,500 people. The pay practice at Nucor includes putting a considerable amount of pay at risk, and the size of paychecks depends upon results achieved. For comparison, competitors often pay an experienced steelworker between $16 and $21 per hour. The similarly qualified employee at Nucor would have a guarantee of $10 per hour; however, the bonus system at Nucor allows employees to make three times the average pay under certain circumstances, such as producing steel without any defects. Bonuses are based on performance and paid on a weekly basis. The system also means that substandard performance is penalized by a loss in pay. For example, errors may result in a lost bonus opportunity. Managers in the company are also paid a lower than average base pay, generally 75%–90% of industry average rates, but bonus payments could reach 75%–90% of base salary, depending on the performance outcomes established for the plant as a whole. In summary, Nucor Corporation has utilized contingent pay plans to motivate employee performance and reward positive outcomes.[20]

Stock sharing has caught media attention in recent years. In this type of plan, stock is distributed as a reward, or executives are given the option to buy company stock at a reduced rate per share. Unfortunately, this type of CP plan has led many executives to attempt to maximize their personal wealth by inflating the price of their personal stock, often through fraudulent means, and selling their stock before the public is aware of the situation. This happened at Enron and WorldCom, where thousands of investors lost their retirement funds. This is an example of the folly of rewarding A while hoping for B, described in the previous section.

5 PUTTING PAY IN CONTEXT

Is pay the main motivating factor driving people? For most of the twentieth century, the belief was that people go to work to collect a paycheck and money was the main, or even the sole, motivator. In the twenty-first century, however, we now recognize that pay is not everything. For most people, money is an important motivator because it supplies many things from fulfilling basic needs (e.g., food and shelter) to providing higher education for one's children and a means for retirement.[21] People seek more than just a paycheck, however, when they go to work. People want to work in an environment of trust and respect, where they can have fun, develop relationships with others, and do meaningful and interesting work. People also want to balance their work and home lives. For example, a 2004 survey by the online job-searching site CareerBuilder.com showed that 42% of working fathers say they are willing to see a reduction in their pay if this means having a better balance between work and home.[22] In addition, people look for learning and developmental opportunities that may lead to better career opportunities in the future. Thus, managers must realize that pay is just one element in a set of management practices that can either improve or reduce employee commitment and satisfaction, teamwork, and performance. It is true that people do work for money and an organization's pay level and pay structure affect productivity.[23] On the other hand, people also seek meaning in their lives and need leisure time to pursue nonwork interests. Organizations that believe that money is all that motivates people are basically bribing their employees and will eventually pay a high price in a lack of employee loyalty and commitment.[24]

When we think about rewards, then, we should think in broader terms than just pay. We can define a reward as something that increases the frequency of an employee action. In other words, when an employee is given a reward, we expect to increase the chances that specific results and behaviors will be repeated or that the employee will engage in new behaviors and produce better results. If pay raises are not producing this result, because they are not meaningful or are given arbitrarily, then they should not be viewed as rewards. Praise and recognition for a job well done, without a monetary value attached, can be a powerful reward *if* such praise and recognition enhance the chances that specific results and behaviors will be repeated. Similarly, praise and recognition should not be considered rewards if they do not motivate employees to perform well in the future.

What can organizations do to ensure that actions intended to be rewards are actually regarded as rewards? What can we do to make rewards work? Consider the following recommendations:[25]

- *Define and measure performance first, then allocate rewards.* Before rewards are allocated, there must be a good performance management system in place that (1) defines performance and performance expectations, and (2) measures performance well. In many cases, organizations believe that they have a rewards problem when in fact the problem is with the definition and measurement of performance.
- *Use only rewards that are available.* If the organization does not have financial rewards available, then employee expectations should be adjusted accordingly, and the focus should be on nonfinancial rewards. It makes no sense to discuss pay raises as an important component of a CP plan if existing budget constraints mean meager raises.
- *Make sure that all employees are eligible.* In many organizations, top executives receive benefits such as profit sharing, stock options, executive life and liability insurance, invitations to meetings in attractive locations, and permission to fly first-class. Are these benefits truly rewards as we have defined them here? Do these incentives enhance motivation? In general, they seem to do so because they motivate lower-level employees to strive to become executives; however, what would happen if these types of incentives were extended to the lower ranks of an organization? What if nonexecutive members of organizations were also eligible for such rewards based on their performance level? By making more employees eligible for the potential reward, there is a greater chance that more employees will strive to become top performers.
- *Make rewards visible.* Rewards should be visible to those who receive them. Rewards should also be visible to others, together with information about what needs to happen for an employee to receive the reward in the future. This recommendation applies to both financial and nonfinancial rewards. Nonfinancial rewards in particular are usually more effective if they are made public.

An exception to the visibility recommendation is that some individuals may prefer a nonvisible reward allocation to avoid being singled out for attention or to prevent the disruption of group harmony.

- *Make rewards contingent.* Rewards should be tied to performance directly and exclusively. Imagine that an outsider is asked to guess the salary levels for various employees in an organization. Assume that she can ask the following questions: *What* do people do (e.g., administrative assistant, mailroom clerk, VP for HR)? *How long* have they done it? *How well* have they done it? If information based on the "How well?" question is not the most useful one in guessing what salaries are, then the organization is not making rewards contingent on performance. Unfortunately, this is the case in many organizations in which what people do and how long they have done it are far better predictors of their salaries than how well they perform. As an illustration, in many countries around the world, including Eritrea in Africa, all employees receive one month's extra salary as a noncontingent reward each year.[26] In other words, employees receive pay for a "13th month." When rewards are not contingent on performance, organizations can alienate their best workers, precisely those who make the greatest contributions and can easily find employment elsewhere.
- *Make rewards timely.* Rewards should be given soon after the occurrence of the result or behavior being rewarded. Experimental psychologists know that if a mouse in a cage pulls a lever and a lump of sugar appears 10 months later (on the mouse's anniversary date), no learning will take place. This is why many organizations implement on-the-spot rewards.[27] For example, at Lake Federal Bank in Hamburg, Indiana, the president has an annual budget that he can use to give relatively small, spur-of-the-moment gifts to employees who are performing well. These spot bonuses do not have to be cash awards. They can be theater tickets, a prime parking space, or anything else that targets an employee's specific needs. How does he know what type of reward to give? The answer is simple: He gets to know his employees and watches what they do and how they spend their time when they have a chance to choose. If this does not work, he can simply ask them.
- *Make rewards reversible.* Increasing an employee's base pay creates an annuity for the employee's tenure with the organization. If mistakes are made in the allocation of increases in base salary (especially upward), they are usually irreversible and can be very costly over time. This is why variable pay, which is not added to an employee's base salary, has become an attractive option for many organizations. Variable pay is consistent with the recommendations that rewards be contingent and reversible. If high-quality performance occurs again, then the employee receives the additional compensation again. If high-quality performance does not occur, then the additional compensation is not given.
- *Use nonfinancial rewards.* Unfortunately, many organizations underestimate the impact of nonfinancial rewards, including the following:

  - Formal commendations and awards
  - Favorable mention in company publications
  - Private, informal recognition for jobs well done
  - Public recognition, including praise, certificate of accomplishment, and letters of appreciation

- Status indicators, such as a new and enhanced job title, larger work area, improved office decoration (e.g., prints, flowers), promotion, ability to supervise more people, and newer or more equipment
- Time, such as taking a longer break, leaving work earlier, and getting time off with or without pay
- A more challenging work environment, responsibility, and freedom
- Sabbaticals (i.e., paid time off work to devote to job-related growth and development activities such as learning new skills or traveling abroad)

Because so many organizations underestimate the value and impact of nonfinancial rewards, they use the phrase "rewards *and* recognition" to mean that rewards are financial and meaningful, whereas recognition is nonfinancial and not as meaningful. As noted above, we must put pay in context, and understand that pay is important, but people go to work for other reasons as well. One advantage of nonfinancial rewards is that they are typically allocated following the recommendations provided here for making rewards work in general. That is, nonfinancial rewards are usually available (there is an unlimited supply of praise); all employees are usually eligible; and nonfinancial rewards are visible and contingent, usually timely, and certainly reversible. But do they work? Fortunately, the answer is yes. For example, think about the following professions and what they have in common: teachers, soldiers, sailors, police officers, nurses, and volunteer workers in not-for-profit organizations. They all involve nonfinancial rewards including challenge, responsibility, and interesting and meaningful work. The financial rewards for doing these jobs are not very high or nonexistent. In spite of this, people in these professions tend to be highly motivated to do their jobs well.

In sum, the concept of a reward is broader than just pay. Of course, money allows people to do great many things, and people do incredible things to get more and more out of it. For rewards to be effective, however, they must motivate employees to become, or continue to be, excellent performers. Pay can do this if it is allocated based on the recommendations listed in Table 3. We should not forget that people go to work for reasons other than money. If an organization is trying to solve performance problems by focusing on money only, one result is expected for sure: The organization will spend a lot of money. It is not always clear that anything will change unless rewards are given taking into account the recommendations listed in Table 3.

TABLE 3 Recommendations for Making Rewards Work

Define and measure performance first, and then allocate rewards.
Use only rewards that are available.
Make sure all employees are eligible.
Make rewards visible.
Make rewards contingent.
Make rewards timely.
Make rewards reversible.
Use nonfinancial rewards.

BOX 2

Financial and Nonfinancial Rewards at Graniterock

Graniterock (http://www.graniterock.com) utilizes a number of strategies to recognize and reward performance. Graniterock provides materials to the construction industry, including products such as asphalt, concrete, and building materials. The U.S.-based company employs 750 people. The company utilizes both financial and nonfinancial incentives. Employees earn bonus pay of as much as $1,000 for specific performance achievements that require an effort that go "above and beyond" normal job expectations. Several nonfinancial incentives are also utilized, such as a letter from the president along with cash rewards. The company holds regular events called "recognition days" where employees give presentations before the CEO, executives, and coworkers about improvements they have made on the job. This gives employees the chance to receive credit in a highly visible manner, directly from others in the company. As part of an emphasis on improvement, employees continually seek better ways of handling processes, and about one-third of all company processes are changed each year as a result. The company publishes stories about special efforts in a weekly newsletter. Supervisors also utilize rewards on a day-to-day and less formal basis, such as providing lunch to a group of employees who are putting forth a strong effort on a large job pouring concrete. In summary, Graniterock utilizes both financial and nonfinancial rewards to motivate employees and to reinforce a culture that values constant improvement and innovation in the workplace.[28]

We should also understand that providing nonfinancial rewards in meaningful ways can be a powerful motivator. Consider the example of the SAS Institute, the world's leader in business analytics software (www.sas.com). This company is legendary for having one of the lowest turnover rates in the software industry. Does SAS pay higher salaries than its competitors? Not really. What do SAS employees say about their organization? They say that they do not leave for other, perhaps more lucrative, jobs because SAS offers opportunities to work with the most up-to-date equipment, jobs have variety, other employees are congenial and smart, and the organization cares about its employees and appreciates their work.[29]

Think about your current job or the last job you had. How were rewards allocated? Which of the eight recommendations listed in Table 3 were followed in the process of allocating rewards? Based on this, how effective were the rewards that were given? Did they help improve employee motivation and performance?

6 PAY STRUCTURES

Regardless of whether organizations implement a reward system based on performance, they face the question of what salaries to assign to *new* employees. An organization's pay structure classifies jobs into categories based on their relative worth. To return to the university example at the beginning of this chapter, how does this particular university assign salaries to new professors? Specifically, how does a university decide to create salary bands for each of five categories (i.e., instructor, senior instructor, assistant professor, associate professor, full professor)? How wide should these bands be? How many bands should be included in the system? Information to answer each of these questions is provided by what is called a *job evaluation*.

6.1 Job Evaluation

Job evaluation is a process of data collection through which an organization can understand the worth of various jobs and, as a result, create a pay structure. Job evaluation includes a consideration of the skills, knowledge, and abilities that are required for each job, how valuable the job is for the organization, and how much pay other organizations allocate to these jobs. Several job evaluation methods are available, but the most popular are ranking, classification, and point.[30]

Of the three, the *ranking method* is the fastest and simplest to implement. It consists of two steps. First, a job description is created for each job. A job description, which results from a job analysis, summarizes the job duties; needed knowledge, skills, and abilities (KSAs); and working conditions for each job. Second, job descriptions are compared to each other in terms of how valuable each job is for the organization. As a result of these comparisons, jobs are ranked from most to least valuable. The most valuable job will be given the highest pay, followed by the second most valuable job, and so forth. The ranking method requires little time, and minimal effort is needed to administer it. On the other hand, it has some drawbacks. First, the criteria for ranking may not be understood clearly. That is, evaluators may not share the same views regarding which criteria should be used to rank the various positions in terms of relative worth to the organization. Second, the distance between each rank is not necessarily equal. That is, the distance between the job ranked number 1 and the job ranked number 2 may not be the same as the distance between the number 2 job and the number 3 job. These unequal distances may not be reflected in the resulting differences in pay between the jobs.

The *classification method* also consists of two steps. First, a series of classes or job families are created. Each job class, sometimes referred to as a "grade," has a unique label and includes a sufficiently detailed description of the work performed so that it will be easy to classify all individual jobs within one class. Second, each individual job is placed within a job class. The end result is a set of classes, each including several jobs. For example, the pay structure of the U.S. federal government includes 18 classes. Each class includes several jobs. For example, class 1 includes all jobs that are performed under immediate supervision, such as routine work in office, business, and fiscal operations, and the elementary work of a technical character in a professional, scientific, or technical field. This class, in turn, includes a number of jobs considered equal in terms of the contribution they make to the organization and, therefore, should be paid equally. Jobs falling in different classes are considered differently and are compensated differently. The classification method has several advantages, including the fact that jobs can be quickly slotted into the structure. In addition, classification levels are readily accepted by employees because they seem to be valid. On the other hand, the classification method requires extensive time and effort to administer, and, similar to the ranking method, differences between classification levels may not be equal.

The *point method* is the most time-consuming of the three, but it is the one that provides the most accurate results in terms of the pay scale for each job compared to all other jobs in the organization. The first step includes identifying *compensable factors*, or those characteristics of jobs that add value to the organization and for which the organization is willing to pay. For example, an organization may decide that four factors are important: skills required, experience required, responsibility, and working conditions. Specifically, the more the skills, experience, and responsibility required and the worse the working conditions, the more the job is worth to the organization. Second, factors are scaled. For example, a five-point scale may be used for each factor ranging from 1 (i.e., very little is needed for this position) to 5 (i.e., a great deal is needed for this position). For example, for the factor "responsibility," an entry-level job would receive a score of 1 and a managerial job a score of 4. It is important that each score be associated with a narrative description of what each number means; otherwise, evaluators may not understand the meaning and differences between the various scores. For "responsibility," a score of 1 could be "is mainly responsible for one's own job performance," whereas a score of 3 could be "is responsible for the performance of a work unit of at least 20 individuals." Third, each factor is assigned a weight so that the sum of weights for all factors should be 100%. For example, "skills" may receive a weight of 35%, "experience" 15%, "responsibility" 40%, and "working conditions" 10%. Returning to our university example, the job evaluation form for the job of instructor may be as follows.[31]

Job Evaluation Form

Position: Instructor

Compensable Factors	Degree	×	Weight	=	Points
Skills	1		35		35
Experience	2		15		30
Responsibility	1		40		40
Working conditions	2		10		20
				Total	125

The evaluation for the position of associate professor may be as follows:

Job Evaluation Form

Position: Associate Professor

Compensable Factors	Degree	×	Weight	=	Points
Skills	3		35		105
Experience	4		15		60
Responsibility	4		40		160
Working conditions	2		10		20
				Total	345

Using the point system, each job is assigned a specific number of points that can then be translated into specific monetary figures. For example, each point may be worth $300 so that the median salary for instructors would be $125 \times \$300 = \$37,500$, and the median salary for associate professors would be $325 \times \$300 = \$97,500$. How does the organization determine the amount of money to be allocated to each point? This is usually done through the collection of market compensation data. In other words, the university gathers information on how much other universities pay to instructors, senior instructors, and so forth. In the case of business schools, this is done annually by the Association to Advance Collegiate Schools of Business (AACSB). Other organizations can design their own surveys or rely on organizations that do this on a regular basis (e.g., http://www.salary.com, http://www.haypaynet.com). Then, this information is used to adjust the monetary value given to each point so that the resulting pay ranges for the various types of jobs are comparable to those of the organization's competitors.

When compensation surveys are conducted, they include not only information on base pay but also information on all types of compensation (e.g., bonuses) and on benefits (e.g., allowances, income protection). Ultimately, the consideration of what salaries are assigned to the various jobs or types of jobs is dependent on the information obtained through compensation surveys. The important issue to recognize is that the relative difference in pay between the various positions has been established through an internally consistent method, regardless of the monetary value assigned to each point. The point system helps establish the worth of each job *relative to all other jobs* within the organization.

The point method has two notable advantages. First, it involves a comprehensive measurement of the relative worth of each job for the organization. Second, ranking jobs is easy to do once the total points for each job are known. On the other hand, it requires extensive time and effort to administer.

A study of different job evaluation systems that considered more than 16,000 jobs found that the resulting ranking of jobs was similar, regardless of the job evaluation method used.[32] This suggests that, given that different methods produced the same end result, the ranking method should be used because it is the most advantageous from a practical standpoint (i.e., it requires less time and effort to administer). However, this same study found that pay grade classification was very much affected by the type of system used. That is, small changes in total job worth scores had a profound impact on the resulting pay structure. Thus, this result argues in support of using the point method because it is more precise and accurate regarding the computation of total job worth scores. Regardless of the job evaluation method used, fairness is an important issue to consider. Evaluators should be regarded as impartial and objective. In most cases, evaluators include supervisors and job evaluation analysts who are hired from outside of the organization (i.e., from a consulting firm).

6.2 Broad Banding

In recent years, many organizations have chosen to collapse job classes into fewer categories, usually about five. Each of these broader pay categories is called a *band*. In the case of our university example, one band may include the two instructor positions (which do not require a research component as part of the job), and a second band may include the three professor jobs (which require research as well as administrative duties as part of the job). Alternatively, one band may include all five teaching categories. Other bands within the university pay structure could include administrators and staff, for a total of not more than five bands that would include all jobs, from security guards to professors to university president.

Broad banding has become increasingly popular worldwide. For example, a survey distributed to 193 organizations by the Institute of Personnel and Development (IPD) showed that broad banding is the most commonly used pay structure.[33] This same survey indicated that the foremost reason for implementing broad banding is that it provides more flexibility in rewarding people. Other reasons include the need to reflect changes in organizational structure, to provide a better base for rewarding growth in competence, to devolve more responsibility for pay decisions to managers, and to provide a better basis for rewarding career progression.

The fact that so many organizations are embracing broad banding to design their pay structures is reflective of changes in the nature of work. Because of the democratization of information produced by the Internet, workers can gather data about what other organizations are paying employees with similar skills and experience. Those workers who believe that they are underpaid can try to find work elsewhere. Organizations cannot afford to lose their most competent workers, and having a pay structure based on broad banding allows salary increases for individuals based on merit that do not require a change in job classification or even job title. In addition, organizations are becoming flatter and less hierarchical, and broad banding reflects these organizational changes. Because of this, the IPD report concluded that "whatever the many forms broad banding takes, it seems to be here to stay."

So far, this chapter has discussed the relationship between performance management and reward systems. Next, we turn to a different topic: the relationship between performance management and the law.

7 PERFORMANCE MANAGEMENT AND THE LAW[34]

Although we have not discussed legal issues in depth, several chapters have touched upon how to design and implement performance management systems to be fair and acceptable. Usually performance management systems that are fair and acceptable to employees are also legally sound. A basic principle that guides the design of a fair system is the application of standardized procedures to all employees. In other words, when the rules and procedures are known by everyone, and they are applied in the same way to everyone, the system is likely to be regarded as a fair one. This is also the basic principle that underlies the implementation of performance management systems that are legally sound. Legislation and court cases in the United States, the United Kingdom, and many other countries around the world indicate that discriminatory effects of a performance management system can be minimized by applying this basic principle: Treat everyone in exactly the same way. Unfortunately, this does not happen very often. As a consequence, there has been a 100% increase in the number of employment discrimination cases filed in the United States from 1995 to 2005, and many of these cases have involved issues around the design and implementation of the performance management system.[35]

BOX 3

Evolution of Legislation and Performance Management Practices in China

Given its increasing global importance and economic power, it is interesting to consider how recent legislation is affecting performance management and reward systems in firms in China. The Chinese government has recognized that performance management systems can contribute to firm productivity and to the competitiveness of China in the global arena. Thus, the Chinese government is accelerating economic reforms related to performance management such as giving employers more rights to terminate employees. These changes have led to what can be considered very innovative performance management practices in many Chinese companies. For example, software developers Ufida, Shanda, and Natease are adopting practices that are quite consistent with those used by U.S. firms. Ufida uses performance information to determine as much as 25% of annual salaries, and Shanda has a company-wide performance management system with clearly specified standards: Employees are evaluated twice a year, there is a 360-degree feedback system, and bonuses are awarded based on performance ratings.[36]

8 SOME LEGAL PRINCIPLES AFFECTING PERFORMANCE MANAGEMENT

There are six important concepts that often come into play in the case of litigation related to the implementation of a performance management system: employment at will, negligence, defamation, misrepresentation, adverse impact, and illegal discrimination.

- *Employment at will.* In employment at will, the employer or employee can end the employment relationship at any time. This type of employment relationship gives employers considerable latitude in determining whether, when, and how to measure and reward performance. Thus, an employer could potentially end the employment relationship without documenting any performance problems. There are two exceptions regarding an organization's ability to terminate an employee under these circumstances. First, there may be an implied contract derived from conversations with others in the organization or from information found in the company's documentation (e.g., employee handbook) indicating that employees would be terminated for just cause only. Second, decisions about terminating an employee should consider a potential violation of public policy. A 1995 case decided by the Supreme Court of Hawaii illustrates the implied contract exception to the employment at will doctrine.[37] Harry Michael Mathewson, a pilot for Aloha Airlines, was fired just two weeks before a one-year at-will probationary period would have expired. The termination was based on supposed poor peer performance ratings. It turned out, however, that Mathewson had been blacklisted by the pilots' union for having worked as a scab for another airline during a strike, and he received negative reviews based on that fact and not on his performance at Aloha. The airline violated an implied contract to provide fair and unbiased evaluations, which was based in part on the company's employee handbook. This case illustrates the benefits of basing termination decisions on information from a good performance management system, even under employment at will.

- *Negligence.*   Many organizations outline a performance management system in their employee manual, employment contract, or other materials. When the system is described in such documents and not implemented as described, legal problems can arise. For example, there may be a description of how frequently appraisals take place, or how frequently supervisors and employees are to meet formally to discuss performance issues. If an employee receives what she believes is an unfair performance evaluation and the system has not been implemented as was expected, she may be able to challenge the system based on negligence on the part of the organization.
- *Defamation.*   Defamation is the disclosure of untrue, unfavorable performance information that damages an employee's reputation. An employee can argue that the organization defamed her if the employer states false and libelous information during the course of the performance evaluation. Defamation can also occur if the organization negligently or intentionally communicates these statements to a third party such as a potential future employer, thus subjecting the employee to harm or loss of reputation. Note that the definition of *defamation* includes the disclosure of *untrue* information. Defamation can take place when an employee is evaluated based on behaviors that are irrelevant and not job related, when an evaluator does not include information that would explain or justify poor performance, or when an evaluator revises a prior evaluation in an attempt to justify subsequent adverse action taken against the employee. Defamation does not exist when information regarding poor performance is clearly documented.
- *Misrepresentation.*   Whereas defamation is about disclosing untrue unfavorable information, misrepresentation is about disclosing untrue *favorable* performance, and this information causes risk or harm to others. When a past employer provides a glowing recommendation for a former employee who was actually terminated because of poor performance, that employer is guilty of misrepresentation. As an example, consider a case decided by the Supreme Court of California.[38] Randi W., a 13-year-old female student enrolled in a middle school, accused her school vice-principal, Robert Gadams, of sexual molestation. Gadams had received glowing letters of recommendation from other school districts (i.e., his former employers), who had recommended him without reservation. For example, one letter of recommendation stated, "I wouldn't hesitate to recommend [the vice-principal] for any position!" However, the former employers knew that Gadams had performance problems that included hugging female students and making sexual overtures to them. In fact, he had been pressured to resign because of such behavior. The Supreme Court of California ruled that employers can be held liable for negligent misrepresentation or fraud when an employer fails to use reasonable care in recommending former employees without disclosing material information that has a bearing on their performance.
- *Adverse impact.*   Adverse impact, also called *unintentional discrimination*, occurs when the performance management system has an unintentional impact on a protected class.[39] This can happen when women receive consistently lower performance ratings than men. For example, adverse impact can take place for the position of firefighter if a performance dimension deals with physical strength. If members of a protected class receive consistently lower performance ratings, then the employer must be able to demonstrate that the performance dimension measured is

an important part of the job. In this case, the fire department should demonstrate that physical strength is a key KSA for the job of firefighter and, based on the argument of business necessity, an appropriate measure should be included as part of the perform- ance evaluation and every employee should be evaluated in the same fashion. As a precautionary measure, data should be gathered on an ongoing basis regarding performance scores obtained by members of various groups, broken down by the categories indicated by the law (e.g., sex, ethnicity). A periodic review of these data can help detect the presence of adverse impact, and the organization can take corrective action if necessary.

- *Illegal discrimination.* Illegal discrimination, also called disparate treatment, means that raters assign scores differentially to various employees based on factors that are not performance related, such as race, nationality, color, or ethnic and national origin. As a consequence of such ratings, some employees receive more training, feedback, or rewards, than others. This definition of illegal discrim- ination is given, for example, in the Race Relations Act of 1976 in the United Kingdom and in Title VII of the Civil Rights Act of 1964 in the United States. Illegal discrimination is usually referred to as *disparate treatment* because employees claim they were intentionally treated differently because of their sex, race, ethnicity, national origin, age, disability status, or other status protected under the law.

The majority of legal cases involving performance management systems involve a claim of disparate treatment. What can an employee do if, for example, she feels she was given unfairly low performance scores and skipped over for promotion because she is a woman? To make such a claim, an employee can present direct evidence of discrimination, such as a supervisor making sexist comments that may have influenced the performance management process. Alternatively, she needs to provide evidence regarding the following issues:

- She is a member of a protected class.
- She suffered an adverse employment decision as a result of a performance evalua- tion (i.e., was skipped over for promotion).
- She should not have been skipped over for promotion because her performance level deserved the promotion.
- The promotion was not given to anyone, or it was given to an employee who is not a member of the same protected class (i.e., another woman).

If an employee provides this kind of evidence, the employer must articulate a legit- imate and nondiscriminatory reason for not having given the promotion to this female employee. Usually this involves a reason that is clearly performance related. This is the point at which employers benefit from having designed and implemented a system that is used consistently with all employees. Such a system is legally defensible, and any decisions that resulted from the system, such as promotion decisions, are also defensible.

We must distinguish *illegal* discrimination from *legal* discrimination. A good performance management system is able to discriminate among employees based on their levels of performance, and this is legal discrimination. A system that does not do this is not very useful. A good performance management system does not discriminate illegally. Illegal discrimination is based on variables that should not usually be related to performance such as sex, national origin, and ethnicity.

9 LAWS AFFECTING PERFORMANCE MANAGEMENT

In the past few decades, several countries have passed laws prohibiting discrimination based on race, ethnicity, national origin, sex, religion, age, disability status, and sexual orientation. For example, the following laws have been passed in the United Kingdom:

- *Equal Pay Act of 1970.* Aims to give individuals the right to the same contractual pay and benefits as a person of the opposite sex in the same employment.
- *Race Relations Act of 1976.* Makes it illegal to discriminate against someone on the grounds of color, race, nationality or ethnic or national origins.
- *Sex Discrimination Act of 1975.* Makes it illegal to discriminate on the grounds of sex, marital status, and gender reassignment in a limited manner.
- *Disability Discrimination Act of 1995.* Makes it illegal to discriminate on the grounds of disability status.
- *Employment Equality (Sexual Orientation) Regulations 2003.* Makes it illegal to discriminate on the grounds of sexual orientation.
- *Employment Equality (Religion or Belief) Regulations 2003.* Makes it illegal to discriminate on the grounds of religion and belief.

Similarly, the following laws have been passed in the United States:

- *Equal Pay Act of 1963.* Prohibits sex discrimination in the payment of wages.
- *Civil Rights Act of 1964 (as amended by the Equal Employment Opportunity Act of 1972).* Prohibits discrimination on the basis of race, color, religion, sex, or national origin.
- *Age Discrimination in Employment Act of 1967 (as amended in 1986).* Prohibits discrimination on the basis of age.
- *Americans with Disabilities Act of 1990.* Makes it illegal to discriminate against people with disabilities.

Taken together, these laws, which have similar counterparts in other countries, aim at forcing organizations to implement performance management systems that are applied consistently to all employees, regardless of demographic characteristics. Although these laws are not enforced to the same degree throughout the world, their collective goal is that performance management systems focus on measuring performance by assessing job-related factors and not personal, individual characteristics.

Designing a system that is legally defensible is not a difficult goal to achieve, and it is a natural consequence of implementing a system following our recommendations. Table 4 lists key recommendations on how to implement a legally sound performance management system.

Two researchers from the United States reviewed 295 different U.S. circuit court decisions regarding litigation involving performance management systems.[40] The goal of their study was to understand the factors carrying the most weight in the decisions reached by the court. They investigated various features of the performance management systems that were challenged in court, including many of the characteristics listed

TABLE 4	Characteristics of Legally Sound Performance Management Systems

Performance dimensions and standards are clearly defined and explained to the employee, are job related, and are within the control of the employee.

Procedures are standardized and uniform for all employees within a job group.

The system is formally explained and communicated to all employees.

Employees are given timely information on performance deficiencies and opportunities to correct them.

Employees are given a voice in the review process and are treated with courtesy and civility throughout the process.

The system includes a formal appeals process.

Performance information is gathered from multiple, diverse, and unbiased raters.

Supervisors are provided with formal training and information on how to manage the performance of their employees.

The system includes thorough and consistent documentation, including specific examples of performance based on firsthand knowledge.

The system includes procedures to detect potentially discriminatory effects or biases and abuses in the system.

Source: Adapted from Exhibits 2.2 and 2.3 in S. B. Malos, "Current legal issues in performance appraisal." In J. W. Smither (Ed.), *Performance appraisal: State of the art in practice* (pp. 49–94). San Francisco: Jossey-Bass; 1998.

in Table 4. What was their conclusion? They found that systems that emphasized the measurement of job-related performance dimensions, provided written instructions to raters, and allowed employees to review appraisal results were more likely to withstand legal challenge. Overall, these researchers concluded that the employees' perceptions of whether the system was fair and whether they were given due process were the most salient issues considered by the courts. This conclusion reinforces the recommendation offered throughout this course: to allow employees to participate in the design and implementation of the system because employee participation leads to the design of systems viewed as fair.

Summary Points

- Traditional pay plans do not have a link with the performance management system. Instead, pay and other rewards are allocated based on position and seniority. By contrast, contingent pay plans, also called pay for performance plans, allocate rewards wholly or partly based on job performance. When rewards given in the context of contingent pay plans are not added to an employee's base pay, they are called variable pay.

- Contingent pay plans are increasingly popular because, when they are in place, performance measurement and performance improvement are taken more seriously. Specifically, these plans force organizations to define effective performance and to determine what factors are likely to lead to effective performance. In addition, these plans can serve as a good tool to recruit and retain top performers because they are attracted to organizations that reward high-level performance.

- Contingent pay plans also enhance employee motivation to accomplish goals that match organizational needs. For contingent pay plans to affect motivation positively, however, there needs to be a clear link between employee effort and employee performance (expectancy) and between employee performance and the rewards received (instrumentality), and employees need to value the rewards available (valence).

- Contingent pay plans often fail for several reasons. First, they may be tied to a poor performance management system in which the performance dimensions measured are not relevant to organizational success. Second, the system may be rewarding behaviors and results that are counter to the needs of the organization, such as rewarding executives for short-term results as opposed to long-term growth and environmental responsibility. Third, employees may not view the rewards as valuable, for example, when the difference between the rewards received by the best and the worst performers is not really meaningful. Fourth, managers may not be accountable for the system and implement it ineffectively. Fifth, the focus may be only on extrinsic rewards, such as pay and other tangible compensation, instead of also on intrinsic rewards, such as a challenging and interesting work environment in which employees have control over what they do and how they do it. Finally, rewards for executives are disproportionately large compared to the rewards for everyone else.

- There are many choices in the design of a contingent pay plan. It is important that the plan be congruent with the culture of the organization. People in organizations that have a traditional or an involvement culture are likely to feel more comfortable with different types of plans. For example, organizations with a traditional culture involving top-down decision making and clearly defined jobs are likely to find that a system including piece rate, sales commissions, and group incentives works well. On the other hand, organizations with an involvement culture, including shared decision making and loosely defined jobs, would benefit most from a system that includes profit sharing and skill-based pay. In addition to an organization's culture, the strategic business objectives may determine which type of system would work best. For example, if an organization prioritizes customer service, then competency-based pay would work well, whereas an organization prioritizing teamwork would benefit most from a plan including team sales commissions and gain sharing. In sum, decisions about how rewards are allocated and what types of rewards are given must be made based on the organization's culture and strategic business objectives.

- Pay is not the only factor that motivates people. People want more out of a job than a paycheck. People seek an environment based on trust and respect, where they can have fun and develop relationships with others, and engage in meaningful and interesting work. Reward systems that focus exclusively on pay and other monetary rewards at the expense of nonfinancial rewards are basically bribing employees and eventually will pay a high price in a lack of employee loyalty and commitment. Rewards systems must go beyond pay and consider rewards as anything that increases the chances that specific behaviors and results will be repeated, or that employees will engage in desirable behaviors and produce desirable results in the future. Defined this way, rewards can include the following:

- Formal commendations and awards
- Favorable mention in company publications
- Private, informal recognition for jobs well done
- Public recognition, including praise, certificates of accomplishment, and letters of appreciation
- Status indicators, such as a new job title, larger work area, promotion, ability to supervise more people, and newer or more equipment
- Time, such as taking a longer break, leaving work earlier, and getting time off with or without pay
- A more challenging work environment, responsibility, and freedom

- Several recommendations must be followed for rewards to work as intended. First, performance must be defined clearly and measured well before rewards are allocated. Second, if financial rewards are not available, employee expectations should be adjusted accordingly and the focus should be on nonfinancial rewards only. Third, all employees must be potentially eligible to receive the rewards. Fourth, rewards must be visible. Fifth, rewards must be contingent on performance and received only if the desired behaviors are displayed and the desired results are produced. Sixth, rewards must be timely and given soon after the result or behavior being rewarded has taken place. Seventh, rewards must be reversible so that employees do not feel a sense of entitlement and continue to be motivated by the desire to obtain the reward again in the future. Finally, rewards should be both financial and nonfinancial.

- An organization's pay structure classifies jobs into categories based on their relative worth. There are three popular job evaluation methods that allow organizations to design a pay structure: ranking, classification, and point. The ranking method consists of comparing job descriptions and ranking jobs based on overall relative worth. The classification method consists of first creating classes or categories of jobs (based on relative worth), and then placing all jobs into an appropriate category. The point method consists of identifying compensable factors and assigning scores to all jobs based on their standing regarding each compensable factor. The point method is the most accurate of the three, but it is also the most time consuming and difficult to administer. Ultimately, salaries are assigned to the various jobs or types of jobs is dependent on information obtained through compensation surveys.
- Broad banding is a type of pay structure that collapses all job classes into a few categories, usually about five. Broad banding has become very popular because it gives organizations flexibility in rewarding people. In addition, broad banding reflects changes in organizational structure, provides a better base for rewarding growth in competence, gives more responsibility for pay decisions to managers, and provides a better basis for rewarding career progression.
- One or more of six legal principles are usually involved in cases of litigation regarding performance management systems. First, employment at will implies that the employer can end the relationship at any time and gives employers latitude in determining whether, when, and how to measure and reward performance. Even in employment at will relationships,

however, organizations benefit from having a well-designed, well-implemented performance management system to guide decisions because other principles, such as implied contract and violation of public policy, may take precedence over employment at will. Second, employers can be accused of negligence if they do not follow the performance management practices outlined in training manuals, employee handbooks, or other official documents. Third, employers can be accused of defamation if they make false statements during the course of the performance evaluation, or if they negligently or intentionally communicate these statements to a third party such as a potential future employer, thereby subjecting employees to harm or loss of reputation. Employers can be accused of misrepresentation if they disclose untrue, favorable performance information that causes risk or harm to others. Fourth, employers can be accused of adverse impact, also called unintentional discrimination, if the performance management system has an unintentional impact on members of a protected class (e.g., women) and if they receive consistently lower performance evaluations than members of other classes (e.g., men). Finally, employers can be accused of illegal discrimination, also called disparate treatment, when evaluators assign scores differentially to various employees based on factors that are not performance related, such as race, nationality, color, or ethnic and national origin.

In the context of performance management, an employee alleging illegal discrimination needs to show that he or she is a member of a protected class, suffered an adverse employment decision as a result of a performance evaluation, should not have suffered this adverse impact because he or she performed adequately, and any rewards he or she deserved (e.g., promotion) were not given to anyone or were not given to an employee who is not a member of the same protected class (e.g., religious minority, ethnic minority, women). On the other hand, if an organization receives a legal challenge, it needs to provide evidence that the decision made was based on a legitimate and nondiscriminatory reason that was clearly performance related. In contrast to *illegal* discrimination, *legal* discrimination, an essential characteristic of a good performance management system, differentiates among employees based on performance-related factors.

- Several countries, such as the United Kingdom and the United States, have passed laws prohibiting discrimination based on race, sex, religion, age, disability status, and sexual orientation. Although the enforcement of these laws is uneven across countries, these laws have as their goal that organizations implement performance management systems that are applied consistently to all employees, regardless of demographic or other personal characteristics that are not job related.
- Designing and implementing a performance management system that is legally sound is not a difficult task. This simply involves creating a system following the best-practice recommendations described throughout this text. Specifically, performance dimensions and standards should be clearly defined and explained, job related, and within the control of the employee. Procedures should be standardized, used uniformly, and communicated to all employees. Employees should be given timely information on performance deficiencies and opportunities to correct them. Employees should be given a voice in the review process and treated with courtesy and civility throughout the process. The system should include a formal appeals process,

and performance information should be gathered from multiple, diverse, and unbiased raters. Supervisors should be provided with formal training, and the system should include consistent and thorough documentation as well as procedures to detect potentially discriminatory effects or biases and abuses.

CASE STUDY 1

Making the Case for a CP Plan at Architects, Inc.

Architects, Inc. is a large commercial architectural firm that specializes in the design of small- to medium-sized structures such as churches, private schools, and business offices. The company employs commercial architects and engineers with various levels of education, credentials, and experience. The current performance management system utilizes a traditional pay system that uses seniority for the basis of pay ranges and increases. The company currently has three ranks for architects and engineers. Each of these pay ranges determines minimum, midpoint, and maximum rates. The following outlines the three ranks:

1. Entry-level architect/engineer (pay range: $35,000–$50,000)

2. Junior architect/engineer (pay range: $45,000–$75,000)

3. Senior architect/engineer (pay range: $55,000–$100,000)

Seniority and a percentage of the base salary determine salary increases at the end of the year, and the same percentage is used for all employees. Rewards are not based on the quality of work performed, new design innovations, productivity, or customer satisfaction. Therefore, if a junior architect/engineer reaches a base salary of $75,000, the employee cannot realize a salary increase unless he or she is promoted to a senior architect/engineer position because the maximum salary for a junior architect/engineer is $75,000.

You believe implementing a CP plan is a good idea. Please write a one-page memo to the president of the company describing the potential benefits of doing so to gain approval for implementing the new CP plan. ■

CASE STUDY 2

Selecting a CP Plan at Dow AgroSciences

Dow AgroSciences LLC, based in Indianapolis, Indiana, is a global leader in providing pest management and biotechnology products that improve the quality and quantity of the earth's food supply and contribute to the health and quality of life of the world's growing population. Dow AgroSciences employs approximately 6,000 people in more than 50 countries and has worldwide sales of approximately US$ 3 billion. Dow AgroSciences is a wholly owned subsidiary of the Dow Chemical Company.

Consider the following information about Dow AgroSciences:

Mission. Dow AgroSciences delivers innovative technology that exceeds market needs and improves the quality of life of the world's growing population. We do this through responsible pest control, aiding the production of an abundant, nutritious food supply, and the use of plants as a renewable agricultural resource to produce new and improved agricultural outputs.

Vision. We are a premier company applying chemical, biochemical, and genetic solutions to agricultural and specialty market needs.

Core Values. To ensure the prosperity and well-being of Dow AgroSciences employees, customers, and shareholders, cumulative long-term profit growth is essential. How we achieve this objective is as important as the objective itself. Fundamental to our success are our core values we believe in and practice:

- Employees are the source of Dow AgroSciences' success. We communicate openly, treat each other with respect, promote teamwork, and encourage personal initiative and growth. Excellence in performance is sought and rewarded.

- Customers receive our strongest commitment to meet their needs with high-quality products and superior service.

Reward Systems and Legal Issues

- Products are based on innovative technology, continuous improvement, and added value for our customers and end users.

- Our conduct demonstrates a deep concern for human safety and environmental stewardship, while embracing the highest standards of ethics and citizenship.

In light of the Dow AgroSciences' mission, vision, and core values, what type of CP plan is likely to be successful? Explain the rationale behind your choice. ◼

Source: This case study is based, in part, on information available online at http://www.dowagro.com/about. Retrieval date: March 15, 2007.

CASE STUDY 3

Contingency Pay Plan at Altenergy LLC

Jack, Tom, and Ed are all former employees of Accenture and have just started their own energy consulting company called Altenergy. For the past six months, Jack, Tom, and Ed have been the only consultants in the company. They have now picked up enough business that they want to add five new consultants in order to have three different consulting teams. Because Altenergy LLC has such a unique niche in the consulting market and is a recent start-up, Jack, Tom, and Ed feel that it is necessary that they hire consultants with (a) experience with dealing with alternative energy sources, (b) connections to a variety of alternative energy companies, and (c) sales experience since these new consultants will be responsible for finding and obtaining new clients. Based upon past experience with Accenture, Jack, Tom, and Ed know that it will be very difficult not only to attract consultants with this kind of experience but also to retain them. In order to combat these concerns, Jack, Tom, and Ed feel that, if they can implement a proper contingency pay plan, they will be able to recruit and retain consultants with the necessary experience.

Based upon this information and your knowledge of various contingency pay systems, how would you recommend that Altenergy LLC structure a contingency pay plan for these new consultants? Please explain why you gave the recommendation that you did and why you didn't recommend the other contingency pay systems possible. As a way to get started on this case exercise, consider the table below (based on Table 2 from Section 4 of the text), and imagine that you have 100 "weight" points that you can assign to different strategic business objectives. For example, if you think that Altenergy should place a pretty heavy emphasis on the strategic business objective of providing excellent customer service, then you might assign 35 weight points to competency-based pay and 15 weight points to gain sharing. Then, 35% of the total compensation will come from competency-based pay, and 15% of the total compensation will come from gain sharing for each employee. ◼

Plans Recommended for Various Strategic Business Objectives

Strategic Business Objective	CP Plan
Employee development	Skill-based pay
Customer service	Competency-based pay Gain sharing
Productivity: Individual	Piece rate Sales commissions
Productivity: Group	Gain sharing Group incentives
Teamwork	Team sales commissions Gain sharing Competency-based pay
Overall profit	Executive pay Profit or stock sharing

CASE STUDY 4

Possible Illegal Discrimination at Tractors, Inc.

Tractors, Inc., is a family-owned heavy equipment (e.g., excavators, tractors, paving equipment) company that has been in business for more than 25 years. Over the past several years, the company has experienced rapid growth, increasing from 100 employees to 500 employees. Tractors, Inc., is beginning to realize that it needs to change or enhance its current performance management system. The company still uses the performance management system it implemented more than 10 years ago.

The current performance management system consists of the following documented process:

- Performance reviews are to be conducted on a yearly basis (at the time of the employee's anniversary date with the company). One month prior to the employee's anniversary date, the supervisor/manager is to complete the standard performance appraisal form and pay increase form (if applicable), which should then be reviewed by the supervisor's manager prior to the supervisor's meeting with the employee. There are no set guidelines about how to complete the form or rate the employee's actual job performance—this is left to the reviewing supervisor's discretion.
- Once approvals have been secured, the supervisor schedules a formal meeting with the employee to discuss the appraisal.
- During the meeting, the manager reviews the ratings with the employee, including any comments that the manager may have made, discusses opportunities for improvement and development, and informs the employee about his or her change in pay (if applicable). At that time, the employee is given the opportunity to add any comments and sign the form for official submittal to the human resources department. The company's unwritten policy is that employees are not permitted to keep copies of their performance reviews; however, they can go to the human resources department at any time to request permission to review their past performance

appraisals. Employee performance reviews are kept on file in the human resources department during the employee's tenure at the organization.

In recent months, the company has received several com-plaints from female employees regarding the performance management system. Examples include the following:

- The employee does not have the opportunity to provide input into her performance evaluation prior to the actual meeting.
- Managers do not complete performance reviews in a timely manner. For instance, several employees have complained that they received their reviews three to six months after their actual anniversary dates.
- Two female employees have complained that they were passed up for promotions for reasons other than performance issues. One employee cited the example of her rating in the "attendance" category as follows: "Overall Sue's attendance is acceptable and she works the hours necessary to complete her job; however, if she were to make better arrangements for handling her children's after-school activities, she would be available to work longer hours." Sue felt that, because she is a single mother, men in her department with less experience and job knowledge are promoted because they either do not have families or have stay-at-home wives to take care of their children.

Consider Tractors, Inc.'s performance management system in light of what we have discussed as an ideal system and how a company can ensure that its system is legally sound. As the new human resources manager, you have been asked to identify those areas of the current performance management system that could face a legal challenge. Please develop a one-page summation, identifying the potentially illegal aspects of the current system and your suggestions for making the current system more legally sound. ■

End Notes

1. Chang, E., & Hahn, J. (2006). Does pay-for-performance enhance perceived distributive justice for collectivistic employees? *Personnel Review, 35,* 397–412.

2. Aguinis, H., & Roth, H. A. (2005). Teaching in China: Culture-based challenges. In I. Alon & J. R. McIntyre (Eds.), *Business and management education in China: Transition, pedagogy,*

and training (pp. 141–164). Hackensack, NJ: World Scientific Publishing.

3. Milliman, J., Nason, S., Zhu, C., & De Cieri, H. (2002). An exploratory assessment of the purposes of performance appraisals in North and Central America and the Pacific Rim. *Human Resource Management, 41*, 87–102.

4. Baty, P. (2006, October 13). Bonus culture sweeps sector. *Times Higher Education Supplement.* Available on-line at http://www.timeshighereducation.co.uk/story.asp?storyCode=205956&sectioncode=26. Retrieval date: September 8, 2011.

5. Lawler III, E. E. (2003). Reward practices and performance management system effectiveness. *Organizational Dynamics, 32*, 396–404.

6. Trevor, C. O., Gerhart, S. L., & Boudreau, J. W. (1997). Voluntary turnover and job performance: Curvilinearity and the moderating influences of salary growth and promotions. *Journal of Applied Psychology, 82*, 44–61.

7. Rynes, S. L., Gerhart, B., & Parks, L. (2005). Personnel psychology: Performance evaluation and pay for performance. *Annual Review of Psychology, 56*, 571–600.

8. Sturman, M. C., Trevor, C. O., Boudreau, J. W., & Gerhart, B. (2003). Is it worth it to win the talent war? Evaluating the utility of performance-based pay. *Personnel Psychology, 56*, 997–1035.

9. Lazear, E. P. (1986). Salaries and piece rates. *Journal of Business, 59*, 405–431.

10. Wells, S. J. (2005). No results, no raise. *HR Magazine, 50*, 76–80.

11. Bates, S. (2003). Top pay for best performance. *HR Magazine, 48*, 30–38.

12. Heneman, R. L. (2002). *Strategic reward management: Design, implementation, and evaluation.* Greenwich, CT: Information Age.

13. Locke, E. A., Feren, D. B., McCaleb, V. M., Shaw, K. N., & Denny, A. T. (1980). The relative effectiveness of four methods of motivating employee performance. In K. D. Duncan, M. M. Gruenberg, & D. Wallis (Eds.), *Changes in working life* (pp. 363–388). New York: Wiley.

14. Peterson, S. J., & Luthans, F. (2006). The impact of financial and nonfinancial incentives on business-unit outcomes over time. *Journal of Applied Psychology, 91*, 156–165.

15. Beer, M., & Cannon, M. D. (2004). Promise and peril in implementing pay-for-performance. *Human Resource Management, 43*, 3–48.

16. Adapted from D. Grote, *The complete guide to performance appraisal.* New York: AMACOM, 1996, chap. 14.

17. Kerr, S. (1975). On the folly of rewarding A while hoping for B. *Academy of Management Journal, 18*, 769–783.

18. "Systematic Looting:" In an undercover sting, Sears' auto-repair service gets nailed. (1992, June 22) *Time.* Available online at http://www.time.com/time/magazine/article/0,9171,975793,00.html. Retrieval date: September 8, 2011.

19. Risher, H. (2002). Pay-for performance: The keys to making it work. *Public Personnel Management, 31*, 317–332.

20. Byrnes, N., & Arndt, M. (2006, May). The art of motivation. *Business Week.* Available online at http://www.businessweek.com/magazine/content/06_18/b3982075.htm. Retrieval date: September 8, 2011.

21. Rynes, S. L., Gerhart, B., & Minette, K. A. (2004). The importance of pay in employee motivation: Discrepancies between what people say and what they do. *Human Resource Management, 43*, 381–394.

22. Singletary, M. (2004, June 20). Divorced fathers need to be more than cash machines. *The Denver Post*, 1. K13.

23. Brown, M. P., Sturman, M. C., & Simmering, M. J. (2003). Compensation policy and organizational performance: The efficiency, operational, and financial implications of pay levels and pay structure. *Academy of Management Journal, 46*, 752–762.

24. Pfeffer, J. (1998). Six dangerous myths about pay. *Harvard Business Review, 76*(3), 109–111.

25. These recommendations are adapted from Kerr, S. (1999). Organizational rewards: Practical, cost neutral alternatives that you may know, but don't practice. *Organizational Dynamics 28*: 61–70.

26. Ghebregiorgis, F., & Karsten, L. (2006). Human resource management practices in Eritrea: Challenges and prospects. *Employee Relations, 28*, 144–163.

27. Taylor, C. (2004). On-the-spot incentives. *HR Magazine, 49*, 80–84.

28. Henneman, T. (2005). Graniterock reinforces innovation. *Workforce Management, 84*, 46–48.

29. Pfeffer, J. (1998). Six dangerous myths about pay. *Harvard Business Review, 76*, 109–111.

30. The description of job evaluation methods is drawn from Milkovich, G. T., Newman, J. M., and Gerhart, B. (2011). *Compensation.* (10th ed.). New York: McGraw-Hill Irwin and Heneman, R. L. (2003). Job and work evaluation: A literature review. *Public Personnel Management, 32*, 47–71.

31. These job evaluation forms are based on material from Milkovich, G. T., Newman, J. M., and Gerhart., B (2011). *Compensation* (10th ed.) (p. 147). New York: McGraw-Hill Irwin.

32. Van Sliedregt, T., Voskuijl, O. F., & Thierry, H. (2001). Job evaluation systems and pay grade structures: Do they match? *International Journal of Human Resource Management, 12*, 1313–1324.

33. IPD Survey Report 11. (2000). *Study of broadbanded and job family pay structures.* Institute of Personnel and Development. London, UK: Author.

34. This section draws heavily from S. B. Malos, "Current legal issues in performance appraisal." In J. W. Smither (Ed.). *Performance appraisal: State of the art in practice* (pp. 49–94). San Francisco: Jossey-Bass, 1998.

35. Latham, G. P., Almost, J., Mann, S., & Moore, C. (2005). New developments in performance management. *Organizational Dynamics, 34*, 77–87.

36. Tsang, D. (2007). Leadership, national cultural and performance management in the Chinese software industry. *International Journal of Productivity and Performance Management, 56*, 270–284.

37. *Mathewson v. Aloha Airlines, Inc.*, 82 Haw. 57, 919 P.2d 969 (1996).

38. *Randi W. v. Muroc Joint Unified School District*, 14 Cal. 4th 1066, 60 Cal.Rptr.2d 263 (1997).

39. Aguinis, H., & Smith, M. A. (2007). Understanding the impact of test validity and bias on selection errors and adverse impact in human resource selection. *Personnel Psychology, 60*, 165–199.

40. Werner, J. M., & Bolino, M. C. (1997). Explaining U.S. courts of appeals decisions involving performance appraisal: Accuracy, fairness, and validation. *Personnel Psychology, 50*, 1–24.

Index

307